ALLEGORICAL BODIES: POWER AND GENDER IN LATE MEDIEVAL FRANCE

Allegorical Bodies: Power and Gender in Late Medieval France

DAISY DELOGU

UNIVERSITY OF TORONTO PRESS
Toronto Buffalo London

Toronto Buffalo London
www.utppublishing.com

ISBN 978-1-4426-4187-7

Library and Archives Canada Cataloguing in Publication

Delogu, Daisy, author
Allegorical bodies : power and gender in late medieval France / Daisy Delogu.

Includes bibliographical references and index.
ISBN 978-1-4426-4187-7 (bound)

1. French literature – To 1500 – History and criticism. 2. France – Symbolic representation. 3. Women in literature. 4. Symbolism in literature. 5. Group identity in literature. 6. French literature – Political aspects. 7. France – Politics and government – 1328–1589. 8. Women – France – Social conditions. 9. Université de Paris – History. 10. Allegory. I. Title.

PQ155.A44D45 2015 840.9'15 C2014-906035-1

University of Toronto Press acknowledges the financial assistance to its publishing program of the Canada Council for the Arts and the Ontario Arts Council, an agency of the Government of Ontario.

Canada Council for the Arts Conseil des Arts du Canada

University of Toronto Press acknowledges the financial support of the Government of Canada through the Canada Book Fund for its publishing activities.

Contents

Acknowledgments vii

Introduction 3

1 Allegory Is a Woman 19

2 From *douce France* to the *dame renommée*: Figuring the French Body Politic 45

3 Jean Gerson and the University of Paris 85

4 Envisioning the Body Politic before and after the Treaty of Troyes 125

Coda: What to Say about Joan of Arc? 167

Notes 179

Bibliography 235

Index 265

Acknowledgments

Having arrived at the end of this project, it is truly a joy to recognize and thank the many people who have helped me to produce my best work. Over the past several years I have presented work at the University of Chicago Divinity School, the University of Tennessee's annual Marco Symposium, Johns Hopkins University, the Chicago Area Renaissance Seminar, the Conference on Medieval Studies, the University of Chicago Society of Fellows, the Western Mediterranean Workshop, the Medieval Studies Workshop, the Medieval Academy, and the Modern Language Association. I am very grateful to the audiences at these venues for providing comments and suggestions that helped me to refine my thinking. Some material from chapters 3 and 4 was published in an article entitled "The King's Two Daughters: Isabelle of France, and the University of Paris, *fille du roy*" in the journal *Republics of Letters: A Journal for the Study of Knowledge, Politics, and the Arts*. I thank the journal editors for their permission to reprint the material, in revised form, here. I gratefully acknowledge that the publication of this book has been made possible by generous donations from Harve A. Ferrill and other members of the Humanities Visiting Committee at the University of Chicago.

Many individuals have read parts of my manuscript in progress and offered valuable comments and suggestions: Renate Blumenfeld-Kosinski has been one of my most important interlocutors, as well as Niall Atkinson, Kevin Brownlee, Shanna Carlson, Ryan Giles, Cecily Hilsdale, Alison James, Nicole Lassahn, Jonathan Lyon, Françoise Meltzer, David Nirenberg, Christine Reno, Justin Steinberg, Andrea Tarnowski, Craig Taylor, and my colleagues in the French section of RLL. I am very grateful to the thorough and thoughtful readers at the University of Toronto Press, whose suggestions helped me to transform a bunch of chapters into a book, to my editor Suzanne Rancourt, who always believed in this project, and to Alexandra Peters, for her help with my bibliography and other technical matters.

In 2012 I had the privilege of teaching the graduate seminar "'Other-speech' and 'Visible words': Allegory, the allegorical, and allegoresis before modernity" with my friend and colleague Aden Kumler. The work we did collectively allowed me to clarify many of my own beliefs and understandings of allegory, and provided the energy and direction I needed to complete my manuscript. To her, and to the diligent, open-minded, and exuberant students in our seminar, my special thanks are due. I also owe particular thanks to Lucy Pick, who has been acquainted with this project since its early days as a myth, and who, with infinite patience, generosity, and enthusiasm, has read this manuscript almost as many times as I have. This wonderful community of scholars, found both near and far, has enabled me to produce my best work; its inevitable shortcomings are mine alone.

I could not complete these acknowledgments without recognizing my parents, who have been steadfast in their love and their support of my work. Finally, I would like to express my deepest and most abiding thanks to the beloved trio on the home front, whose quirky wonderful selves remind me daily of what is most important in my life. I dedicate this book, with thanks and love, to them.

ALLEGORICAL BODIES: POWER AND GENDER IN LATE MEDIEVAL FRANCE

Introduction

Woe to you, O land, when your king is a child.

Ecclesiastes 10:16

The over-forty-year (1380–1422) rule of Charles VI of France, *le fou* – known also rather poignantly as the *bien aimé* – was marked by turmoil.[1] The kingdom suffered the madness of its ruler, the riotousness of its princes, and the depredations of a rival monarch claiming to be the legitimate king of France. With the fate of France at stake, the writers and intellectuals of Charles's reign imagined figurative, institutional, and legal solutions to the profound destabilization of French political legitimacy and identity wrought by the absence of their king. By means of poems and treatises, dream visions and sermons, the authors in this study constructed a foundation for collective political identity and action that functioned independently of the person of the king, sought to ensure the stability of the monarchy, and struggled to tame the centrifugal forces that threatened to tear the kingdom apart. Throughout their works their reading publics were invited to imagine the kingdom of France through gendered categories that could be employed to ensure masculine rule, to conceptualize and celebrate the French body politic, or to provide for just, royal governance.

In this book I will examine the sudden emergence in literary works of the late fourteenth century of the allegorical figures of France, represented as a queen and the mother of the French people, and of the University of Paris, the *fille du roy*, as well as the ways in which both kingdom and University were imagined in metaphorical terms, as bodies. In addition I will look at how, during the same period, the principle of female exclusion from royal rule that was implemented and consolidated over the course of the fourteenth century was formalized and broadcast in the early fifteenth century as the famous Salic Law of the French. Salic Law declared that women could neither occupy the throne, nor serve as "pont et planche" [bridge and plank] for their male offspring,[2] while the allegory of France gave a defined (female) form and a sense of coherence to the kingdom at a time when, in geo-political terms, it lacked both. Thus, just as real women were being excluded from royal succession in the name of what might be considered a proto-nationalistic policing of boundaries, the kingdom itself was being imagined as a woman. This simultaneous exile of women from the official exercise of power, and forceful inscription of female allegorical figures into the political imaginary, may seem paradoxical. As we shall see, however, both employed gender as a means to conceptualize, define, and shape political communities and structures, to imagine the French body politic, and to generate a population of masculine political subjects.

The troubles that beset Charles VI began long before his succession to the throne in 1380, at the age of twelve. One might say that they began with the crises of succession that marked the final decades of Capetian rule.[3] In 1314 King Philippe IV le Bel (r. 1285–1314) died and his eldest son ascended the throne as Louis X. However, Louis X died only two years later, leaving a young daughter and a pregnant wife. During the queen's pregnancy Louis's younger brother Philippe served as regent, and when her infant son died after a few days Philippe succeeded in excluding Louis's daughter from the throne on the basis that the "customs" of France did not allow women to rule.[4] These supposed customs were founded more on the serendipitous fact that for over three hundred years the Capetian kings had consistently produced sons capable of succeeding their fathers, rather than on the existence of any established laws related to succession.[5] As Paul Viollet demonstrated, Philippe V's victory was the product of political cunning, bribery, and intimidation, and was not at all a foregone conclusion, nor certainly one based upon any clear-cut legal foundation.[6]

Over a century later Jean Juvénal des Ursins affirmed that at the time of Louis X's death "il fut dit, jugié, sentencié et prononcié par maniere d'arrest que fille ne devoit point succeder ne ne succederoit ou royaulme" [it was said, judged, concluded, and proclaimed in the form of a decree that a maiden ought not succeed nor would succeed to the kingdom].[7] If only this had been true the events of the fourteenth century might have unfolded quite differently than they did. Unfortunately for the Valois, the various assemblies of notables and of University masters who approved Philippe's regency, and later his succession to the throne, did not produce any proclamation or ordinance governing royal succession. Indeed, it is precisely this documentary void that the Valois supporters found themselves still seeking to overcome a century later, and in the context of which Salic Law (see chapter 4) would prove so useful.[8]

When Philippe V died in 1322 leaving only daughters, it was a foregone conclusion that his brother Charles de la Marche would succeed him.[9] Charles IV, the last son of Philippe IV, died in 1328 leaving daughters and a pregnant queen, but no more brothers. The regency was entrusted to his cousin, Philippe de Valois.[10] When Charles IV's wife gave birth to a daughter, there was no question of her inheriting, for by this time the custom of female exclusion from rule had been firmly established.[11] Philippe de Valois was a clear candidate for the throne, but there was another claimant, Edward III of England (r. 1327–77), the son of Philippe IV's daughter Isabelle and nephew of the last three Capetian kings. Edward was the closest male heir to Charles IV, but his claim passed through a cognate line. Could a woman transmit a right that she could not herself exercise or possess? In the end, an assembly of barons decided in favour of Philippe de Valois on the basis that just as women could not rule in France, neither could they transmit the right to rule to their male issue.[12] Though initially he accepted the kingship of Philippe VI, in 1337 Edward III asserted his rights to the French throne, resulting in the protracted series of conflicts that would come to be known as the Hundred Years' War (1337–1453).[13]

Philippe VI's great grandson, Charles VI, was crowned in 1380, just shy of his twelfth birthday. The boy-king's father, Charles V (r. 1364–80), had stipulated that in the event of his own premature death his brother Louis d'Anjou was to assume the regency of the kingdom, and his other brother Philippe de Bourgogne the tutelage of the royal children.[14] Louis d'Anjou soon departed Paris to pursue an Italian throne, leaving France and Charles VI to the direction of the remaining royal uncles, Philippe de Bourgogne and Jean de Berri, and his maternal uncle, Louis de Bourbon. In 1389, prompted by his younger brother Louis d'Orléans, Charles embarked upon his personal rule.

Just three years later, in August 1392, Charles suffered the first of what would prove to be countless attacks of insanity.[15] As the years wore on it became clear that the king's "absences," as his contemporaries called them, were a permanent feature of his person and his reign. These absences varied in severity, duration, and frequency, but all effectively precluded his ability to govern. Unlike his ancestor Louis IX (r. 1226–70), whose mother Blanche of Castile officially governed as regent of the realm both during the king's minority and while he was on crusade, Charles VI did not entrust the kingdom to his queen, Isabeau de Bavière. Instead, Charles VI stipulated that during his absences a council, comprised of those "closest to the king's blood" would rule.[16] However like Charles V's brothers, the members of the king's council did not govern harmoniously. In March and July 1402 the king gave Isabeau the authority to mediate, with the help of the council, between Louis d'Orléans and Philippe de Bourgogne.[17] In subsequent years, additional ordinances further modified the composition of the council and the duties of its members. The constant reordering of this governing body points to its inadequacy as a mechanism for coping with the absences of the king. The tensions and rivalries between members of the council, and the alternation between the rule of the council and periods of personal rule by the king, meant that royal directives were constantly subject to change, and the government of Charles VI was woefully ineffective, at best.[18]

The death of Philippe de Bourgogne, Charles's most powerful uncle, in 1404, destabilized the fragile balance of power between king and council members in a manner from which it never really recovered. Philippe's son Jean sans peur, the new duke of Burgundy, sought to dominate the royal council and the kingdom. The tension between Jean and the king's brother, Louis d'Orléans, mounted steadily, culminating in the assassination of the latter in November 1407. The unrepentant Jean sans peur defended his action on the basis that he had rid the kingdom of a tyrant. This stance created an impossible situation. The king could not forgive someone who refused to acknowledge his crime, and yet the widow and children of Louis d'Orléans, as well as their allies, demanded justice. The kingdom broke into two factions, one of which, the Burgundians, made common cause with the English. For the remainder of Charles VI's reign and for many years afterwards, civil war compounded the troubles already engendered by the war with England. Charles VI's turbulent rule concluded with the "tel desraisonnable, tres deshonneste et desnaturel traictié" [so unreasonable, dishonest, and unnatural treaty] of Troyes (1420),[19] discussed in chapter 4, by means of which Charles VI named the English king Henry V (r. 1413–22) heir to the throne. This repudiation of the biological son fundamentally transformed the ideological issues to which those loyal to the Valois were forced to respond, as we shall see.

As is clear from the events of his reign, Charles VI's absences were far more damaging to the kingdom than his death would have been, for they effectively deprived France of its head, while preventing the possibility of obtaining a new one. The organological or corporeal metaphor, in which the body politic is compared to a human body, was one of the mainstays of medieval political philosophy.[20] Passages such as those from Romans 12:5–6 and 1 Corinthians 12 were applied to the polity to illustrate both the unity of the whole, and the diversity of functions or social roles within that whole, while texts from classical antiquity, like Cicero's fable of the stomach and the members (see *De Officiis* 3.22) also suggested that human society might be envisioned organically. The corporeal metaphor highlighted relationality, as well as the unity and interdependence of the body's constitutive parts. At the same time, the comparison of the body politic to the human form projected a fantasy of wholeness and clearly demarcated boundaries onto polities that often lacked these very qualities. The human body thus provided an imaginary space onto which might be mapped an ideal social order.

During the reign of Charles VI organological metaphors for the kingdom did not cease to be meaningful, but they sometimes proved troublesome, since the head of the French body politic was compromised, while the bitter struggles between the princes of the blood showed that the body of the kingdom was a fragmented and traumatized one. The theologian Jean Gerson (see chapter 3) used the metaphor of autophagia to communicate his horror at witnessing the violence perpetrated by the French upon one another. I contend that the inadequacy of the metaphor of the body politic made it necessary to supplement (though not to supersede) metaphorical representations of the kingdom with allegorical ones.

Like the metaphor of the body politic, the late medieval allegory of France took a geo-politically unstable category – France – and transformed it into a bounded, coherent, and autonomous whole, one that provided the basis for an emergent and distinctive French identity founded upon birth or (figurative) kinship, political allegiance, law, and a shared history and set of beliefs. The allegorical figure of France (see chapters 2 and 4), depicted as a noble woman and the mother of the French people, marks a significant departure from previous modes of imagining the realm in figurative terms, not least with respect to gender. Inasmuch as the metaphorical body is unmarked, it functions as a masculine one.[21] From its male king or head to its masculine constitutive parts, including clerics, knights, royal advisers, and judges, the metaphorical representation of the kingdom implicitly envisions the political realm as one comprised of men. Thus, metaphors of the body politic privilege the male body as a vehicle for the expression of conceptions about political unity and integrity, and occlude the space that real women occupied within the body politic as well as the power that they exercised.

In striking contrast to metaphors of the body politic, the allegory of France codes political coherence and unity as specifically and overtly female. Hailed as a "dame renommée" [celebrated lady] by the *Grandes chroniques de France*,[22] and depicted with vivid realism in the works of Eustache Deschamps, Christine de Pizan, Alain Chartier, and Jean Juvénal des Ursins, the figure of France gave presence and voice to the kingdom, allowing for the conceptualization of the kingdom as an entity distinct from the king.[23]

The various representations of France that I shall examine conform to normative expectations of femininity for medieval women, themselves developed and promulgated in literary works. Eustache Deschamps, for instance, exploits the conventions associated with lyric poetry in order to represent the kingdom as a courtly beloved, the object of the poet's affection and desire. In many texts France is depicted as a victimized woman, one who is wounded or ill, mistreated or bereft. In these instances she contrasts her glorious past with her deplorable present condition. By portraying France as a damsel in distress, the authors of such allegorical fictions invite a masculine, and in particular chivalric, public to come to the aid of the kingdom, in accordance with medieval expectations of masculinity.[24] Finally, the notion of France as a mother – whether of the princes of the blood, the three orders of French society, or the French subjects – suggests a fictive or imaginary kinship upon which to construct a sense of collective identity. The cherished conviction that since the founding of the kingdom the kings of France had succeeded to one another without interruption, the belief in a "seamless web of legitimate rule"[25] upon which the legitimacy of French kingship had long been predicated, is supplemented, even displaced, by an imaginary kinship in which every subject is the child of the kingdom. In this formulation, political allegiance is naturalized because founded upon one's birth within (to?) the kingdom of France. France's maternity binds the inhabitants of the kingdom to their mother country, and to one another. Thus, the allegorical figure of France, one who performs (though not simultaneously) all the positive roles available to medieval women – from fair beloved to cherished mother – supplants the problematic figure of the real king by becoming, herself, the focal point for the obedience, loyalty, and love of the French people.

The figure of France was joined by another – less common but no less fascinating – allegorical figure, also a royal woman, the University of Paris, daughter of the king. In addition to the forces and influences that contributed to the development of the allegorical figure of France, the allegory of the University was also informed by notions of corporation theory and legal personhood emerging from Roman law. From the opening years of the thirteenth century, the masters of the University of Paris came to conceive of their organization as a corporate body.[26] Over the course of the thirteenth and fourteenth centuries, the University masters fought to define and defend what they perceived to be the rights, privileges, and authority of the University in ever clearer and more forceful terms.[27] At the time of Philippe IV's struggles with Pope Boniface VIII the University, wary on its own account of papal incursions into its authority, was a staunch ally of the king and proponent of royal power.[28] In turn Philippe IV and later kings of France routinely confirmed the fiscal and legal privileges enjoyed by the University masters and students. In 1358 the future king Charles V formalized and broadcast the privileged relationship that united University and crown by referring to the institution, in a royal charter, as the "eldest daughter of the king."[29]

The epithet *fille du roy*, used to designate the University, is employed by a range of authors, including Philippe de Mézières in the *Songe du vieil pelerin*, Christine de Pizan in her biography of Charles V, and the Religieux of Saint Denis in his chronicle of the reign of Charles VI, but the allegorical representation of the University is most extensively developed in the sermons of Jean Gerson, which I will discuss in chapter 3. As Gerson would have it, the University is the king's good daughter, both an ideal subject and royal counsellor, one able to support and protect Charles VI during periods of crisis, without challenging his royal authority. The University's imagined relationship of filial descent from the king makes her a potential repository of his political authority, yet without threatening in any way the literal, biological lines of succession that governed the transmission of the crown from one generation to the next. Staging the voice and presence of the humble and obedient *fille du roy* allows Gerson to suppress the heterogeneity and internal dissent that characterized the University and to present his views as those of a coherent and unified body, that of the king's good daughter.[30]

Gerson's recourse to the vocabulary of kinship is particularly significant given the political prominence of the princes of the blood in early-fifteenth-century France as a distinct and privileged group. The political authority conferred by blood is visible, as we have seen, in the councils created to rule during the absences of Charles VI. Yet, despite the ideals associated with natural kinship, which was supposed to ensure loyalty and harmony, during the reign of Charles VI consanguinity manifestly failed to maintain peace. The bitter struggles, hatreds, and assassinations (of Louis d'Orléans in 1407 and Jean sans peur in 1419) that kept the kingdom in a protracted state of disorder took place between male kinsmen – brothers and cousins, nephews and uncles. The allegories of kingdom and University exploit the power derived from blood, while substituting imaginary genealogical bonds and lines of descent for natural ones, and kinswomen for kinsmen.

In what follows I will argue that in response to the weakness and inadequacy – the *absence* – of the king, as well as the challenges to French identity that arose from the English claims to the French throne (including the military victories and demoralizing scorched-earth campaigns of the English, as well as the contest to Valois legitimacy), the writers in this volume used gendered figures, language, and thinking to imagine a bounded and autonomous space – one understood in cultural, political, legal, and affective terms – to forge a concept of France and the French with the force to withstand attacks from without, and fragmentation from within.

To affirm that this idea of France functioned on a conceptual rather than a material level is not to assert its unreality, nor its inefficacy.[31] Indeed, one of the points that I will develop in this study is that social and political identity is not constructed exclusively of tangibles – of sex, birthplace, legal status, social class, native language – but also, and perhaps more effectively, of intangibles – of beliefs, memories, affections, loyalties, priorities, perceptions of likeness or difference, of belonging or exclusion.[32] It is within the realm of the imaginary that the works in my study operate, and it is by shaping the individual and collective consciousnesses of their readers that these works seek to exert influence over the material realm of social and political practice.

The authors in this study may be said to participate in something similar to what Lauren Berlant has called – with reference to a quite different time and place – the "fantasy-work of national identity,"[33] an expression that captures well the importance of imagination to identity formation.[34] Berlant defines this "work" as the construction of "images, narratives, monuments, and sites" that circulate within a given culture and that mediate between and connect individual and collective identity.[35] Long before the reign of Charles VI, a set of accepted beliefs, stories, and attributes about France and the French had slowly accreted. Myths of origin,[36] of divine election,[37] and of cultural and intellectual supremacy[38] provided a common history and a set of beliefs about what it meant to be French.[39]

The fantasy elements introduced and promulgated by the works in this study – the maternal figure of France, the University of Paris as *fille du roy*, and the Salic Law of the French – constitute powerful additions and refinements to existing notions of France and Frenchness, and ones with enduring significance. The figure of France reappears in works by Martin

Le Franc, Jean Bodin, Ronsard, and others,[40] and is arguably transformed and reborn as Marianne, the symbol of the French republic whose proud likeness adorns many a French public space. Law, like metaphorical and allegorical representations of the kingdom, traces the contours of an ideal social order, one that is coherent and stable. In addition, the notion of legal fictions or fictive persons allowed for the adjudication of legal problems. Indeed, little separates the idea that the University of Paris constitutes a person in legal terms – one capable of entering into agreements with other persons, or representing the interests of the University before Parlement –from the allegory of the *fille du roy* (who does precisely that).[41] In turn, Salic Law demonstrates the processes by which collective fantasies grounded in a mythologized and authorizing past, and projected into a future defined as exceptional and superior, can be translated into legal action with very material social and political effects.

In addition to their significance within a collective French imaginary, the allegorical figures of kingdom and University are expressly and persistently connected to the individual readers of the works in this study.[42] Mediation, as Isabeau de Bavière shows us and as we shall see in chapter 1, is a role often assigned to women (especially noble ones), and the mediation between individual readers and collective social bodies is effected precisely by means of female allegorical figures. The authors in this study invite their readers to interpret their allegorical texts on multiple levels, as pertaining to the individual subject or soul, to the temporal kingdom, and also to the spiritual realm. These various levels of allegorical interpretation allow for a dynamic dialectic between text, reader, social and political setting, and the eventual salvation of individual readers and of God's new chosen people. The fantasy elements proposed by these authors may thus be actualized in the lives of individual readers/subjects who, it is to be hoped, will be shaped as an effect of reading and of discourse, and in turn will reinflect the social bodies of which they are a part.

These contributions to the political imaginary help to forge and to convey a very distinct sense of *France* and of *Frenchness* during the reign of Charles VI, and beyond. While I sometimes employ the terms "nation" or "national" to refer to a perception of French singularity or identity, I do not seek to join the critical fray with respect to nations, nationalism, or nation states.[43] I am in agreement with Ardis Butterfield, who has persuasively argued that efforts to define "nation," and consequently to assign the emergence of "the nation" to a point in time or a historical moment, obscure the complex and ongoing processes by which collective identity is (re)formed.[44] In this project I remain sensitive to the contingent and multiple ways in which one may conceive of the self as such and in relation to others, as I attempt to interrogate the ongoing, "under construction" processes of individual and collective identity formation during the reign of Charles VI as they are shaped by allegorical and metaphorical figures, and by gendered language, law, and thought.

In this volume I employ gender as a critical lens through which to examine the allegorical and metaphorical bodies of kingdom and University in order to illuminate the political philosophy and practice of late medieval France. Among these elements – gender, allegory, and political thought and practice – previous scholarship has examined two out of three, but this particular configuration of critical elements has not, to my knowledge, received sustained scholarly treatment. As I shall show, critical awareness of the interactions among these three domains reveals how gender, embodied here in the figural language of allegory and metaphor, is used to articulate and to define individual, social, and political consciousness and identity in late medieval France.

The history of scholarship on allegorical composition and interpretation, in both Christian and classical settings, is a long and robust one, and if recent publications may be taken as any indication, allegory is enjoying an upsurge of critical enthusiasm. A number of edited volumes have provided a prismatic perspective of the varying manifestations and potentialities of allegory,[45] while numerous monographs have sought to explore the presence and effects of allegory in more closely defined and limited terms.[46] Among these, several important works deal, in whole or in part, with political allegory during the later Middle Ages,[47] and yet none of these incorporates gender into their consideration of allegory in a sustained or comprehensive manner.

The ubiquity of female allegorical figures, when considered alongside the paucity of scholarship that reflects on the connection of gender to allegory, has cause to surprise us. The classic works of Edwin Honig (1959), Angus Fletcher (1964), Rosamund Tuve (1966), Paul Piehler (1971), Stephen Barney (1979), Maureen Quilligan (1979), Paul de Man (1979), and Jon Whitman (1987) and, on the French side, Hans-Robert Jauss (1964), Paul Zumthor (1972), Marc-René Jung (1971), and Armand Strubel (1989 and 2002),[48] evince little interest in gender as a feature of allegory. I contend that the gender of allegory has been naturalized in some sense, and consequently has largely remained beneath critical notice. In the first century AD Demetrius asserted that the gendering of allegorical figures as female was constitutive of the form,[49] and most subsequent attempts to explain the fact that for centuries allegories were consistently female simply cited grammar as the reason.[50] (This of course fails to explain why, for centuries, no one seemed to allegorize masculine nouns.)

This critical blind spot has been addressed in more recent scholarship that interrogates the connections between gender and allegory. In *Fortune Is a Woman*, for instance, Hanna Fenichel Pitkin explores the role that Fortune plays in Renaissance notions of autonomy and masculinity.[51] Barbara Newman has considered how allegories like Nature, Philosophy, and Wisdom provided a discursive space in which to conceptualize and debate theological questions without seeming to put male prerogative into doubt.[52] The allegorical figure of Nature, for instance, was able to suggest ideas that might have been denounced or repressed as heretical, but because Nature was "only" a poetic figure, and "only" a woman, the speech attributed to her was less threatening. In *Wisdom and Her Lovers* Emily Francomano explores the dissonance between female personifications of wisdom and the cultural belief that wisdom and women do not go together.[53] Often, Wisdom is personified as a sexually desirable woman whose possession permits the male protagonist's acquisition and mastery of a body of knowledge. In a recent article Maureen Quilligan has suggested that "allegory would thus appear to be a genre most conducive to investigations into the problematic exercise of female agency" (166).[54] Indeed, as I will discuss in chapter 1, the structure of allegory has affinities with medieval perceptions of women that render it particularly well suited to a discussion of how gendered language and thinking shape and inform structures of power, community, and identity.

The works cited above have been essential to my own work of the past several years, inasmuch as they have informed my approach to my own allegorical texts by showing how female allegorical figures, or the relationships between such figures and their often male interlocutors, can be leveraged to conceptualize, construct, preserve, or impose medieval structures of power such as those that govern access to knowledge, political authority, or the divine. Since, as Joan Scott has shown, "gender is a primary field within which or by means of which power is articulated," by examining the issues raised and explored by the allegory of France, as well as the other allegories, metaphors, and myths I shall consider in this study, we can better understand the ways in which France as a kingdom, and the concept of French identity, are being constituted over the later Middle Ages.[55]

Gender has not been absent from scholarship on political power and action in the Middle Ages. On the contrary, many recent studies have sought to re-evaluate medieval women's access to power and authority.[56]

Not surprisingly, a large number of these have focused on queens or other influential noble women such as Blanche of Castile, Ermengarde of Narbonne, or Charles VI's queen, Isabeau of Bavaria, as these were among the most visible female political agents in the Middle Ages, and those whose rank permitted them the greatest latitude to engage directly in political affairs. Other studies have sought to recalibrate our understanding of political power so that we might recognize the degree to which the exercise of power functions as a distributed and fluid network or system, one which includes multiple and changing actors, including women.[57] By relinquishing our notion of power as a *thing*, one which is wielded (by men), we are able to perceive how women participated in structures of authority in ways that might not previously have been recognized. In other scholarship, power has been reimagined in social, cultural, artistic, and literary terms that focus on women's roles in patronage, religious and spiritual practices, shared artisanal work, or knowledge production.[58] Such studies have effectively recuperated the contributions of women to medieval domestic, economic, spiritual, intellectual, and political life, and in so doing have shifted how we think about power and authority themselves so as not to automatically discount or exclude women.

My study differs from this body of scholarship inasmuch as I seek to illuminate the leverage that women had not as people, but as a conceptual category, over the entire structure of late medieval French culture and thought. The gender binary that has pervaded thought and culture from the Middle Ages to our own times provides a ready-made and almost universally accepted hierarchy which can be deployed in a range of other contexts to express ideas about the respective situations of persons or groups. The allegorical figures of France and the University of Paris conform to normative paradigms of femininity and of sexuality that provide a model of natural and appropriate political conduct for their readers/public. These female figures shape and bear a range of meanings about who is French, what it means to be a subject of the kingdom, by whom power can legitimately be wielded, and the connection of political conduct to salvation. They structure relationships of inclusion and exclusion, establish hierarchies, and help to define both self and other.[59] Emerging as a supplement to the absence of the king, and refined in the crucible of Charles VI's madness, the allegories of kingdom and University nevertheless interact with their readers with an efficacy and consequences that surpass the limits of his reign, privileging and naturalizing the love of the French for their "mother," France.[60]

My opening chapter, "Allegory Is a Woman," lays out what I see as the specificity and the utility of late medieval figural representations of kingdom and University in the context of Charles VI's "absences." Both allegory and metaphor serve to conceptualize collectives such as the kingdom or the University, but two important factors distinguish how metaphor and allegory function in the works I examine here. First, metaphor supposes a reading public that is incorporated into the body politic, while allegory posits a reader who is distinct from the kingdom or University; and second, the move from metaphor to allegory requires a gender shift from universal/masculine to feminine. The structure of allegory, which I suggest is predicated upon a sustained and productive tension between form and meaning, as well as upon a state of ontological alienation, allows us to perceive a parallel between allegory and women, themselves often cast, like allegory, as useful, but potentially untrustworthy, intermediaries. Indeed, I argue that the allegories of kingdom and University perform the mediating functions associated with medieval (especially royal) women.

Late medieval allegorical texts evince a heightened awareness of the indeterminacy and the semantic multiplicity, the potential even for duplicity or violence, that is constitutive of allegory. In response, these texts display a tendency towards what I call auto-exegesis, the simultaneous redaction and explanation of one's own allegory in an effort to secure meaning, or to ensure correct reading. The role of the reader is of paramount importance, as the inscription of history into the allegorical works that I discuss requires the reader to engage in a quest for understanding that has both political and soteriological implications.

In chapter 2, "From *douce France* to the *dame renommée*: Figuring the French Body Politic," I concretize the analysis of metaphor and allegory carried out in chapter 1 by first exploring in specific terms the operation of metaphor and allegory in the poetic works of Eustache Deschamps, and then by examining the introduction of France as a maternal figure and the theory of allegory laid out in Christine de Pizan's *Livre de l'advision Cristine*. Deschamps was an innovative and very influential poet whose extensive and diverse body of work included many poems that staged metaphorical and allegorical representations of the kingdom, sometimes in the same poem. Deschamps uses each of these figures to shape the political consciousness of his readers, who are invited to identify with the (masculine) body politic that presents the kingdom in bounded and coherent terms, despite its actual fragmentation and internal tensions, and who are interpellated as masculine political subjects by the extravagantly feminine allegorical figure of the kingdom, movingly depicted as a beloved but vulnerable woman in need of rescue and protection.

In the *Livre de l'advision Cristine*, Christine de Pizan further enriches Deschamps's use of allegory with her own figure of France, called Libera, who is constituted in terms of her maternity. Libera's children are condemned for their abusive and unnatural treatment of their mother, and for their violent conflicts with one another, while the narrator, depicted as the kingdom's exemplary (though adopted) child, furnishes a model of correct political conduct. Christine exploits the expectations of love and loyalty associated with the mother–child relationship, on the one hand, and the historical and textual absence of the king, on the other, in order to construct an alternative site or mechanism for the production of political and social identity, as the subjects are constituted in direct relationship to the kingdom. Thus, imaginary bonds of kinship supplement or displace the biological kinship that has failed to ensure harmony within the kingdom. In Christine's hands, allegory is not only politically constructive, but also salvific. The figure of Libera is typologically connected both to scriptural events and to the fate of the French, God's new chosen people, demonstrating that allegory is not simply a rhetorical embellishment, but an instrument of political and spiritual salvation.

Chapter 3, "Jean Gerson and the University of Paris," shows how Gerson, chancellor of the University from 1395 to 1415, deployed allegorical and metaphorical representations of the University in order to fortify and defend the king's authority, as well as to ensure that the king's governance of the kingdom remained within the bounds of justice and reason. Gerson does not employ metaphor as Deschamps does, to explore the relationship of parts to one another and to the whole. Rather, his use of metaphor permits the assimilation of the collective body of the University to other bodies: those of the king and the kingdom. As an analogue of the king, the University is able to supplement the king's reason when it is wanting, while as a body comparable to and representative of the kingdom, the University can advocate for the interests of the French people.

Gerson also depicts the University in allegorical terms, as the devoted and obedient *fille du roy*. Because she is imagined as a daughter, the University cannot rival the king's authority in any way, thereby allowing her to serve as an ideal royal counsellor, more loyal and disinterested than the king's own kin, those who comprised the council that ruled during his "absences." By means of these sophisticated figural representations of the University of Paris, Gerson is able to construct a platform for political action for himself, and for the University masters generally.

The University is depicted as a unified, quasi-institutional body, one that ensures the continuity of royal rule by compensating for whatever condition might render the head of the body politic unable or unfit to rule, while preserving the authority of the king. The University's inscription into an imaginary royal lineage, as well as the bonds of kinship that unite the University to her "children," the masters and students, construct an alternative genealogical structure that is more resistant to corruption or failure than biological kinship, and that ensures the transmission over time of knowledge and of royal authority.

In my final chapter, "Envisioning the Body Politic before and after the Treaty of Troyes," I argue not only that the fabrication of Salic Law by the royal administrator Jean de Montreuil in the early fifteenth century was useful in asserting Valois legitimacy on the basis of female exclusion from rule, but more importantly that it constructed French collective identity as an effect of law. Salic Law quickly became – and has remained – one of the defining features of the French as a people, an aspect of the collective history of the kingdom of France that helped to create and shape a sense of French national identity.

I then turn to two responses to the Treaty of Troyes (1420), according to which the English king Henry V was named regent, and adopted as the heir to the throne of France.[61] In the *Quadrilogue invectif* (1422) the royal administrator and diplomat Alain Chartier stages an allegorical figure of France who angrily denounces the self-interest and inactivity of her "children," the three orders of French society, and calls upon them to mobilize in her defence. France invokes nature as a model of political conduct, and the foundation of political legitimacy and action. Jean Juvénal des Ursins's *Audite celi* (1435) written on the eve of the peace talks in Arras between France, England, and Burgundy, attempts to demonstrate the speciousness of the Treaty of Troyes in order to make possible a separate peace between France and Burgundy. Here too allegory is used to delimit political spaces and to define political actions that are presented as natural. In each of these texts concepts founded on nature – natural law, love, rights – are employed to justify the legitimacy of the Valois kings, and to constitute the basis of political allegiance. The "natural" hierarchy that is inherent in the gender binary is thus exploited to make visible and to justify political hierarchies, boundaries, and allegiances.

I conclude this study with a short reflection on Joan of Arc, a "real" person of course, but also one who, like the allegorical figures of kingdom and University, seems to overflow with an uncontainable surplus of meaning, who was endlessly reinterpreted in her lifetime and since by her various "readers," including each of the authors studied in this book who lived to witness her career. During her lifetime Joan's semantic multiplicity and indeterminacy proved threatening to a masculine political order, but once contained (i.e., killed), Joan was effectively co-opted into the fantasy of Frenchness, a constitutive element of a collective identity predicated upon female sacrifice (and the sacrifice of women's political agency to produce French exceptionalism) and love for the mother country, France.

1
Allegory Is a Woman

Every nature tells of God; every nature teaches man;
every nature reproduces its essential form,
and nothing in the universe is infecund.

Hugh of St Victor, *Didascalicon*

If allegory is a woman, it is not, as has too often been claimed, simply on the basis of grammar. Rather, it is because the very processes of allegorical writing and reading are imagined by their practitioners in gendered terms. As the above quote from Hugh of St Victor shows, allegorical reading in the Middle Ages was a generative process, one in which the (male) exegete drew forth meaning from God's fecund allegorical texts – Scripture and the world. The allegorical text[1] was often said to be veiled,[2] like a chaste or modest women, and it was the object of the (again male) reader to strip allegory of its covering, to lay bare and possess allegory's hidden meaning. The practice of allegory was also connected to a certain indeterminacy, instability, or multiplicity of meaning, suggesting that allegory, like woman, might be fickle or duplicitous. As this chapter and this study will show, gender is an extremely useful lens through which to examine the practice of allegory, and in particular the figures of kingdom and University which constitute the primary objects of this project.

The Practice of Allegory

Despite the diversity of both medieval and modern allegorical practices,[3] as well as the terms employed to discuss them, I believe that all understandings of allegory share what one might think of as an allegorical structure, predicated upon distance or difference, whether between the visible and the invisible, form and meaning, or past and present (or future). The Greek term *allēgoria* has two components: *allos*, meaning other, and *agoreuein*, meaning to speak in the public political space or forum, or in the open marketplace. Many medieval definitions of allegory, including those of Augustine, Cassiodorus, Raban Maur, Isidore of Seville, and Hugh of St Victor, focus on the fundamental difference or distance between language or form, and meaning, sometimes Latinizing the two Greek components of the word *allēgoria* in order to define allegory as *alieniloquium*, or "other-speaking."[4] In general, one can identify two broad allegorical practices. One writes allegorically by hiding or disguising one's true meaning, whether to confine knowledge to select publics, or to protect writers from the consequences of subversive or dangerous discourses. One can also read allegorically, by seeking meanings other than those which are readily apparent in an effort to supplement – or supplant – a base text.[5] We shall see that one of the most original characteristics of the works examined in this study is that they frequently combine both of these practices into a narrative mode that I will call "auto-exegetical."

As a compositional practice or strategy, one related to grammar or rhetoric, allegory enjoyed a long and vibrant medieval existence.[6] Allegorical composition often entails the use of personification,[7] that is to say, the textual embodiment of concepts, values, abstractions, or generalities, as in Prudentius's late antique *Psychomachia*, which depicts a battle between vices and virtues.[8] Personification has been characterized as both a limited figure (i.e., as the representation in human form of something that is not a person),[9] and a virtually limitless one (as a kind of master trope that undergirds all linguistic activity).[10] Demetrius of Phalerum's *On Style* (*Peri Ermeneias*) provides the first definition of personification, using the term *prosopopeia*. Demetrius writes, "the so-called 'prosopopeia' – may be employed to produce energy of style, as in the words: 'Imagine that your ancestors, or Hellas, or your native land, assuming a woman's form, should address such and such reproaches to you.'" For Demetrius *prosopopeia* includes apostrophic pronouncements of dead ancestors, as well as "the anthropomorphizing and lending of speech to a conceptually abstract, geopolitical entity."[11]

The female figures of kingdom and University discussed in this volume would appear to illustrate perfectly such definitions of prosopopeia or personification. However, I choose to refer to them as allegorical figures throughout this work in order to highlight the idea that allegory is not a thing, but a practice (not unlike gender). Allegorical meaning is not ontological or fixed, but is produced as the effect of a complex dialectic between text and reader.[12] Within the works that I examine the figures of France and the University are not static or univocal, but dynamic.[13] Kingdom and University are inscribed in specific and contingent historical circumstances which create the possibility of their transformation. Indeed, the contrast between France's past and her present is one of the most salient aspects of her literary representation, one which shows the degree to which France is subject to, indeed swept up in, the forces of history. Even if one believes that a personification can only ever enact its own meaning (e.g., Humility can only be humble), is it ever possible to say what France "means"? On the contrary, as I will show, the "meaning" of France is always under construction, subject to both synchronic and diachronic change and reinterpretation, a site of conflict and negotiation. Moreover, as we shall see, the allegorical figures of France and University themselves participate in the construction of political subjects and national consciousness. Not simply decorative figures, France and University engage their readers in a search for meaning that itself creates the opportunity for the reader to "se *refigurer*."[14]

In addition to composing allegorical texts, medieval scholars also read or interpreted allegorically, a practice that in medieval terms is often referred to as commentary or exegesis, and in modern critical dialogue might be called allegoresis[15] or interpretive allegory.[16] Like allegorical composition, the tradition of allegorical interpretation reaches back into antiquity, in the efforts of commentators such as Anaxagoras or Prodicus to provide philosophic interpretations of Homeric texts.[17] Centuries later, we see allegorical commentaries employed to recuperate pagan, antique texts for Christian publics.[18] Such allegorical interpretations point to one of the principal virtues of allegory (about which more presently): its ability to bridge or join distinct temporal moments, and to surpass the dictates of linear time.

The most developed and prestigious tradition of medieval allegorical interpretation concerned the exegesis of Scripture.[19] From the outset, readers of the Bible recognized that some passages were to be understood literally, while puzzling or unclear passages required another kind of reading.[20] The problem for Christian readers was first to recognize *when* the text demanded a non-literal reading, and second *how* to carry out such a reading. Augustine addresses this problem in his *De doctrina christiana*. Generally speaking, his default position is that Scripture should be read literally, since, if a point can be made literally, there is no need of figurative expression. When unsure of a passage's meaning, the reader should apply the test of faith, such that anything not related to good morals or the true faith should be interpreted figuratively.[21] The literal sense was by no means narrow or impoverished, however, as illustrated by Augustine's own multi-book work, *The Literal Meaning of Genesis*, as well as other literal commentaries.[22] Indeed, the temptation to move in haste past the literal in an effort to uncover allegorical meanings introduced the dangerous potential for overzealous readers to do violence to the text through their forced interpretations.[23] Scholars from Origen to Nicholas of Lyra caution their readers to attend carefully to the literal before moving, if at all, to the allegorical.[24]

Biblical exegesis, studied in magisterial fashion by Henri de Lubac, is most often discussed in relation to the four senses of Scripture as distinguished by Cassian,[25] whose schema was repeated with great regularity by a range of medieval exegetes.[26] The classic medieval example of how the four senses might illuminate Scripture, also repeated in numerous texts, is that of Jerusalem, which may be understood as a historical place, as the Church militant, the individual soul, and the heavenly Jerusalem. The example of Jerusalem prefigures and informs the allegorical figure of France, which can also signify multiply. In literal terms France is a kingdom; allegorically, it is a suffering figure; morally, it is the individual subject; and anagogically, it is the kingdom of God's new chosen people. The figure of France thus enacts a radical inscription of secular, political content within a structure that had long been associated with spiritual practices of reading and interpretation. By taking a system of interpretation used to speak of the soul's relationship to God, and using it to think about the political condition and fate of France, the authors whom I study forge a connection between one's political conduct and one's salvation, thereby instrumentalizing allegorical practice to concrete political ends.

Denys Turner has observed that this semantic agreement concerning the four senses of Scripture masks a significant semiotic ambiguity surrounding the relationship of the senses to one another, and more broadly of the allegorical to the literal.[27] In fact, despite efforts to separate the various levels of allegorical meaning, the parameters of "the allegorical" were no more clear in the Middle Ages than they are today. In a famous letter to Can Grande about allegorical interpretation,[28] Dante provides an example of fourfold biblical exegesis, using Psalm 113 to illustrate the four senses of scripture.[29] His example seems quite straightforward until he points out that the various non-literal senses "may one and all in a general sense be termed allegorical, inasmuch as they are different from the literal or historical."[30] Thus, Dante begins with the rhetorical principles of division and classification, then moves to illustration, but concedes in the end that any demarcation between the levels or types of allegory may be unimportant, or, actually, impossible to discern.

The practice of allegorical reading was not restricted to Scripture. Hugh of St Victor distinguishes between sacred and secular allegory, and discusses the kind of reading to be brought to bear upon each. He explains that Scripture contains "history, allegory, and tropology" (also referred to as letter, sense, and deeper meaning or *sententia*),[31] and not every text or passage will contain all three of these. Secular allegory, in contrast, is to be read for its letter, sense, and inner meaning, in that order. "The letter is the fit arrangement of the words ... The sense is a certain ready and obvious meaning which the letter presents on the surface; the inner meaning is the deeper understanding which can be found only through interpretation and commentary."[32]

The distinction that Hugh and others make between sacred and secular allegory, and their respective hermeneutics, invites another distinction, that between the so-called allegory of the poets and the allegory of the theologians. This difference might be mapped onto compositional allegory (a rhetorical practice employed by poets) and interpretive allegory (a hermeneutical practice employed by scriptural commentators and exegetes). The allegory of the poets is founded upon the premise that poetry is literally false,[33] but may enclose moral or philosophical ideas that are true and valuable. Scripture, in contrast, is a vehicle of literal truth, and also contains or conceals additional meanings that the attentive and devoted reader may, through careful study, reveal.

Not only texts, but the natural world, was available to allegorical interpretation. In his commentary on the *Song of Songs*, Origen explains that "Paul the apostle teaches us that the invisible things of God are understood by means of things that are visible, and that the things that are not seen are beheld through their relationship and likeness to things seen."[34] The contemplation of the created world holds spiritual value, for the soul can be guided by things seen to things unseen, and thereby elevated. Hugh of St Victor makes a similar set of claims about the hermeneutics of the created world. According to Hugh, not only words, but also things have meaning. Indeed, the significance of things is superior to that of words, because the latter are of humans, while the former are of God.[35]

The Allegorical Condition

What I have termed the structure of allegory is predicated upon the incommensurability of its parts, for discontinuity or rupture (whether temporal or hermeneutic) is constitutive of allegory. Allegory thus acts both as a barrier to understanding and an invitation to hermeneutic activity. Paul de Man writes that "it remains necessary, if there is to be allegory, that the allegorical sign refer to another sign that precedes it" and, furthermore, that "allegory designates primarily a distance in relation to its own origin."[36] Accordingly, one might construe allegory as an ontologically determined and irremediable condition of alienation from its own origins, or conversely as the effort, precisely, to bridge that distance, to make of allegory a link or intermediary, albeit a fragile and tentative one, between form and meaning, or between distinct temporal moments. As we shall see, both with respect to its ontologically determined alienation and its capacity to mediate difference or distance, we may think of allegory itself (figuratively) as a woman. Within a Christian framework, the Logos, which, according to thinkers such as Origen is incarnate in both Christ and Scripture, might be seen as guaranteeing allegorical access to truth.[37] In a post-modern context, however, what allegory may point to is a kind of infinite regress in which meaning is constantly deferred, or just beyond reach, unveiling, in the end, the contingency and the fragility of our attempts to find meaning in the world.[38]

Allegory operates independently of linear time; it has the capacity to place the past in proximity to the present, making the former recognizable and relevant. For Craig Owens, two salient feature of allegory are its awareness of the remoteness of the past and its effort or desire to "redeem it for the present."[39] Similarly, Erich Auerbach's figural typology establishes relationships between different historical moments, those of the Old Testament, of the New Testament, of the present, and of the future.[40] Auerbach distinguishes between allegory, on the one hand,[41] and figura, on the other, explaining that the latter "establishes a connection between two events or persons, the first of which signifies not only itself but also the second, while the second encompasses or fulfills the first."[42] The two are separate in time, but are within time. Figural interpretation (which he elsewhere calls typology) thus differs from allegory in the historicity of both the sign and what it signifies. Auerbach's figural interpretation functions largely, though not exclusively, with respect to the Old and New Testaments. Auerbach further suggests that just as Old Testament people or events can prefigure later ones, so too events of the present may prefigure people or events that have not yet taken place. According to Auerbach, figural interpretation permeated the medieval mindset with the idea that earthly life was thoroughly real, but might also herald the authentic, future, ultimate truth, the "real reality" that would fulfil and unveil the figure.[43] The idea that typology/allegory can join past and present, but also present and future, is what enables the figures of France and University to shape the political consciousness of their public. By deciding how these figures are connected to the future, France and University ask their readers to imagine their own prospects, to articulate and define what lies ahead. Allegory thus both presupposes, and seeks to surmount, temporal distance or rupture.

In like manner, disjuncture or discontinuity haunts the relationship of allegorical form to meaning. One notices the spatiality of the language used to talk about allegory in both medieval and modern accounts, and which conveys this sense of distance or rupture. Allegory is sometimes thought of as pointing to a meaning hidden within an exterior, or beneath an *integumentum* (veil or covering). The term *hyponoia*, or undersense, was used until the first century BC to distinguish between "what was meant (the philosophic meaning), as opposed to that which was said (the literal meaning)."[44] In addition, allegory is sometimes imagined as pointing to meaning outside of or beyond itself. This going-beyond is often conceptualized in Neo-platonic and Pseudo-Dionysian inflected terms as a vertical ascent towards the truth/God. Whether meaning is believed to reside within, beneath, or beyond the allegorical figure, semantic content or meaning is never coterminous or coexistent with allegorical form, and yet it cannot exist independently of it.[45]

In Christian Scriptural allegory, all divinely intended meanings are believed to be present simultaneously and continuously. As Origen explains, allegorical interpretation of Scripture represents an effort to return to God's speech. Divine Scripture expresses things in the manner of human speech, but only because we cannot understand the divine language. Consequently, the words of Scripture "will be well known and familiar; but our perception of them, if we give them the perception they deserve, will be of things divine and incorporeal."[46] Daniel Boyarin affirms that for Origen the Incarnation, understood both in terms of Christ's presence on earth and as Scripture, is a "hermeneutical moment of full presence of meaning," one that makes it possible for other readers to attain spiritual meaning, to effect a return to an understanding of divine speech.[47] The idea that allegory and its correct interpretation can restore "full presence of meaning" is one to which we shall return.

Despite such faith in the harmonious co-presence of allegorical language and meaning in Scripture, the apperception of the different senses of Scripture on the part of individuals remains inscribed in time. A reader first encounters the literal sense of Scripture, and only subsequently (and not even with certainty) the additional senses. Thus, while all meanings may be simultaneously present in the divine mind and in Scripture, the apprehension of allegorical meaning on the part of a given reader occurs as the result of a subsequent and sequentially ordered process of reception. This exile or distance from allegorical truth or meaning is even more pronounced when dealing with non-Scriptural texts or objects.

The modern scholar Friedrich Ohly, an attentive reader of Hugh of St Victor, distinguishes between sacred and secular allegory, in the process showing that the former had important implications for the latter. Sacred allegory awakened readers to what Ohly calls a new beauty: "A new Christian aesthetics in the Middle Ages looked beyond antiquity ... and saw that *a new beauty* had entered the world," and "what we call allegorical literature is what realizes *a new beauty* in a form that embraces meaning through the awakening of the letter to the spirit."[48] Ohly extends to secular authors not the possibility of signifying in the manner of Scripture, but that of recognizing and exploiting the potential of language to signify beyond itself.

For the art critic Craig Owens (writing, admittedly, of very different works made for very different publics), "allegory is not just something appended to the work of art, but is a structural possibility inherent in every work." He qualifies this idea slightly by asserting that "the allegory remains *in potentia* and is actualized only in the activity of reading."[49] Thus, as in Scripture, allegory inheres in the work, and yet, it can only be actualized by the reader, through the act of reading. In the case of Scripture, God guarantees allegorical meaning, but in the case of secular works, how is allegorical meaning produced? Does the reader discover, or supply, the allegorical meaning of a work? The answer, I contend, is both. Allegory is reading and writing, it exists *in potentia* in every work of art, but can be produced only as an effect and by means of an enactment of viewing or reading. It is not possible to tell the dancer from the dance.[50]

The capacity of language to point to something other than and beyond itself, as well as the unlocatability and indeterminacy of allegorical meaning, constitutes a source of anxiety for the authors in this study. In the rupture or seam between allegorical form and meaning resides the potential for perversion.[51] Late medieval authors, as we shall see, were acutely and painfully aware not only of allegory's potential, but also of its latent danger. If allegory is imagined as a supplement, it is one that displaces or reinflects the original object or sense, which no longer signifies as it did in the absence of the allegory. If, on the other hand, allegory is construed as an explanatory gloss that seeks to unveil or explicate a hidden or unclear sense, in some way to pre-empt or take precedence over an original,[52] it runs the risk of hermeneutic failure by interpreting wrongly, even unethically.

Allegory and Gender

The idea of allegory as a necessary and useful, but not entirely trustworthy, go-between, aligns allegory with medieval (and not so medieval) beliefs about women. Medieval women were deployed as mediators in many contexts. Through marriage, women could connect the family of their birth to a new family or lineage. Mothers are the absent presence in many genealogical images, in which sons appear to succeed to fathers by means of some sort of spontaneous generation. Mary mediated between God and the faithful. One of the principal functions of the queen was to serve as an intermediary, whether between the king and his people, family, or nobles, or among those subject to the king.

The role of the intermediary has received considerable critical attention as it relates to queens. In her analysis of the "mediator queen," Tracy Adams provides many late medieval historical examples of queens and other noblewomen occupying the intercessory function thought to be appropriate to women, and especially to queens.[53] John Carmi Parsons, Pauline Stafford, Louise Olga Fradenberg, Lois Huneycutt, and Paul Strohm, among others, have examined the liminal, or interstitial,[54] status of the queen, whose power and authority depended upon her relationship to the king.[55] The figure of the intermediary, whomsoever she or he might be, reinforces social order, for the fact that the intermediary can intervene with the king highlights that person's superiority over the people, while recognizing and maintaining the authority of the king.[56] At the same time, the intermediary is also powerful, "essential to petitioner and petitioned alike."[57]

It would be a mistake at any time, but especially during the reign of Charles VI "the Well-loved," but also "the Mad," to imagine power as something that might be exercised in a unilateral and uncontested manner. Rather, the exercise of monarchical power relies upon a network of relationships, what Earenfight refers to as "a dynamic and shifting set of force relations that circulated and passed back and forth among the political actors."[58] During the reign of Charles VI, the complexity of this network, the tensions between the political actors involved, and the importance of Queen Isabeau of Bavaria within the "set of force relations" are all clearly visible. These tensions are thrown into heightened relief by an examination of the councils constituted to govern the kingdom during the "absences" of Charles VI, and the series of ordinances passed in an effort to clarify and refine the duties and limits of queen and council, respectively.

Though she has been much maligned by history,[59] Isabeau was clearly deemed capable of taking part in the rule of the kingdom, and indeed was called upon to assume an increasingly important arbitrating and governing role over the course of the late fourteenth and early fifteenth centuries. In March 1402 Isabeau was accorded full powers of mediation between the rival dukes of Orléans and Burgundy, and on July 1 she was granted the authority to deal with financial and other governmental matters. Two ordinances of 26 April 1403 declared first that in the event of the king's death, the dauphin, even if a minor, was to become king, while the government would remain in the hands of the queen, advised by a council that would operate by majority vote. Second, the same distribution of authority was to obtain during the king's absences.[60] Either Isabeau was recognized by her contemporaries as a competent individual, or else it would have been deemed so inappropriate to exclude her entirely from the governance of the kingdom that it could not be done. In either case, the importance of the queen in structures of power was clearly upheld. Queens such as Blanche of Castile had previously served as regents for their minor children, or during the king's absence on crusade or as part of other military campaigns.[61] What distinguished Isabeau's role from these precedents was the ongoing – and yet intermittent – nature of her governing responsibilities. Unlike queens who governed on behalf of minor or absent kings, Isabeau's role had no foreseeable conclusion. At the same time, as Tracy Adams has pointed out, Isabeau attended council meetings only during the king's "absences." In contrast to the princes of the blood who comprised the council, she was not a permanent member of this governing body.

Christine de Pizan, whose *Livre de l'advision Cristine* will be examined in chapter 2, discussed the role of the queen in theoretical terms in several of her works, most notably the *Livre des trois vertus*.[62] There, she explains that women of noble birth are to serve as "advocate et moyenne" [advocate and intermediary] between their spouses and lords, and his subjects.[63] If the prince attempts to "grever son peuple d'aucune charge" [charge his people with some burden], or "se il avient que [the subjects] soi[ent] en aucune indignation vers le prince" [if it so happens that the subjects are angry at or resentful of the prince], or even "se ilz ont a faire d'aucune grace ou d'aucun previlege" [if they have some favour or petition to request], they will not approach the prince, but his lady.[64] She will listen with kindness and pity, such that she will help them to see their situation and the prince's actions in a more favourable light. Thus, "se ilz avoient devant aucune rancune, rebellion, ou murmure en courage, ilz seront tous pacifiéz" [if they previously had some rancour, rebellion, or sedition in their hearts, they will be entirely pacified].[65] The queen or noble lady thus serves at least two distinct intermediary functions in Christine's writings. On the one hand, she protects and serves the weak vis-à-vis the king, as when the lady goes before her husband to plead the cause of the people, and to try to obtain, at least in part, what they desire. Subject to her lord, the lady is nevertheless superior to the people, whom she protects from the wrath, or even from the injustice and the oppression, of the prince. On the other hand, the queen or lady preserves and perpetuates existing power structures by cajoling the people into accepting their place within such structures. Indeed she is herself a kind of *glossator* who reinterprets the prince's words and actions, endowing them with an alternative and more positive meaning that will sooth the people's anger. As we saw in the passage above, the threatening "murmure" of the people is calmed by the kind words and demeanour of lady, who invites them to accept the conditions of their existence with an eye towards preventing any violence that might subvert the unity and the integrity of the kingdom and the established order.[66]

The structural analogy between the cultural and political work accomplished by queenly intermediaries and that of the allegorical figures of France and University provides a partial explanation for the presence of the latter in late medieval literary works. Moreover, both kingdom and University are depicted as royal women, the former quite variously as the widow or orphan of the king, but also as the mother of the French subjects, and the latter as the daughter of the king.[67] Thus, they are not ordinary women, but women endowed with a special relationship of proximity to and intimacy with the king. Though this relationship invites us to think about allegorical figures in connection to actual women, this study is not about the latter. Many excellent works, including those cited above, have examined the roles and action of royal women. I wish here to interrogate the conceptual work performed by the allegorical figures of France and University, represented as royal women.

Female allegorical figures, in and of themselves, are not new to textual production, but several features of the allegorical representations of kingdom and University demand our attention. First, the presence of such figures in the texts I examine in this volume cannot be understood simply as an effect of grammar, that is, the fact that *France* and *université* are feminine nouns. In the wake of the extensive diffusion and enormous influence of the *Roman de la Rose*, with its male allegorical figures, including Déduit, Malebouche, and the ambiguously gendered Bel Acceuil, the presence of female allegorical figures in post-*Rose* literature must be understood as a conscious choice, rather than a default.

Moreover, the allegorical figures of France and the University are represented according to radically overdetermined gendered norms. These are not the shield-bearing, javelin-wielding female allegorical virtues of Prudentius's *Psychomachia*. Nor are they the nominally feminine figures of Philosophy or Nature. Instead, as we shall see in subsequent chapters, these figures conform to dominant models of medieval femininity: courtly beloved, damsel in distress, cherished mother, and dutiful daughter. I suggest that this highly conventional femininity inscribes the figures of France and University firmly within a gender binary that serves to interpellate, even to fashion, a male public that is asked to imagine itself and to behave in conventionally masculine terms, to adopt the masculine roles of protector and safeguard of feminine frailty and virtue.

Finally, I would propose that an explanation for the sudden emergence of allegorical representations of kingdom and University may be sought in the simultaneous "absence" of King Charles VI and the affinity I have suggested between the structure of allegory and women in the late medieval imaginary. The absence of the king is the precondition and the site of literary production. In the terms of Derrida's now-classic essay, if the supplement "represents and makes an image, it is by the anterior default of a presence." Like allegory itself, which may be understood as both ontological and performative, Derrida's supplement partakes of a double nature, for it is paradoxically both surplus and substitute. The allegorical figures of France and the University supply what the absent Charles VI cannot offer – a foundation for political consciousness and action, as well as reason, understanding, and sound judgment. As women, foreclosed from royal rule, these allegorical figures conform to the notion that the supplement be a "subaltern instance," as well as "exterior" and "alien" to that to which it adds, or for which it substitutes, itself.[68] The femininity of these figures, their apparent inferiority to the male king, masks their power to displace. Indeed, one of the most striking characteristics of the texts that feature the figure of France is the near-total textual absence of the king.[69] Thus, these allegorical figures complete, but also supplant, the absent or deficient king. By providing an alternative focal point for political loyalty and identity, the figure of France (re)defines the political subject on the basis of his or her relationship to the kingdom. The allegorical figure of France transforms concepts of social and political identity by substituting for *the vassal* – who is inscribed in vertical structures of alliance and loyalty on the basis of personal relationships, not least with the king himself – *the subject*, who is constituted in direct relation to the kingdom. The collectivity of subjects are thus configured in horizontal terms each with respect to the kingdom. The intimacy of the personal bond is not lost, however, but is preserved figuratively by means of the kinship that unites subjects to kingdom, for the figure of France is the mother of her people, an object of their devotion and loyalty to whom all owe love and allegiance.

Corporeal Metaphors

In the works that form the basis for this study, kingdom and University are not represented exclusively in allegorical terms. On the contrary, metaphor is also an important conceptual tool of the authors I consider, and consequently it is necessary to distinguish between the metaphorical and allegorical bodies that they, and I, discuss. In what follows, I shall examine the specificity of metaphor, its relationship to allegory, and the ways in which these two tropes or figures perform different and complementary cultural and political work in representations of kingdom and University.

The combined or alternating metaphorical and allegorical renderings of the kingdom of France and the University of Paris discussed in this book had a very important antecedent – the Church. The Church was given visual and textual form as a woman. One of the oldest Christian allegories, in Ephesians 1:22–3 and 2:20–2 we see the Church depicted as the body of Christ, and in Ephesians 5:24–5, the Church is represented as the bride of Christ. Similarly, in commentaries on the Song of Songs, the Bride was often understood as a figure of the Church. Beginning in the Carolingian period, Ecclesia is visually represented with, and in contrast to, her counterpart, Synagoga.[70] In later medieval art, Ecclesia was represented by herself, often as the *Ecclesia universalis*, *Ecclesia orans*, or *Ecclesia triumphans*. In the last of these postures, Ecclesia was frequently depicted as a queen, with crown, halo, and sceptre. As such, her iconography might be visually conflated with that of Mary.[71] The rise of Marian devotion in the thirteenth century[72] contributed to this increasing visual assimilation between Ecclesia and the Queen of Heaven. In the Vatican library, barb. lat. 592, for instance, Ecclesia is represented as a mother who gives birth to new souls, the faithful who constitute the body of Christ and the Church.[73] Ecclesia was also given textual representation, often during times of crisis when, like her successor France, she was presented as a victim of male aggression.[74] The Great Schism of the West (1378–1417), which overlapped the reign of Charles VI, was a period particularly rich in representations of a suffering Ecclesia.[75]

The Church was not only represented allegorically as the female figure Ecclesia, but also metaphorically, as a mystical body. Both the community of the faithful (1 Corinthians 6:15 and 12:27) and the Church (Ephesians 1:22–3 and 2:20–2) are represented as the body of Christ. In his commentary on the Song of Songs Origen writes that the faithful should love one another "not as alien bodies, but as our own limbs" (188).[76]

The classical metaphor of the body politic likewise shaped and informed understandings of the communities of kingdom and of University. In Titus Livius's fable of the stomach and the members, for instance, the limbs refuse to nourish the stomach because they believe that it profits from their labour without contributing to the good of the body. As a consequence of the limbs' revolt, the entire organism suffers.[77]

Medieval authors regularly drew upon and combined these Christian and classical traditions. In the twelfth century Marie de France composed a vernacular version of the fable of the stomach and the members in which the organism dies. In the moral of her fable Marie affirms that lords and their men ought not neglect their duties to one another. Disregard for the bonds of loyalty that unite men results not only in personal dishonour, but in the very dissolution of society. The corporeal metaphor for the polity finds its most developed expression in the *Policraticus: Of the Frivolities of Courtiers and the Footprints of Philosophers*, completed in 1159 by John of Salisbury. Books 5 and 6 of the *Policraticus*, presented by John as the text of a letter from Plutarch to the emperor Trajan, constitute an extended metaphor in which the body politic is compared to the natural body.[78] This metaphor places in parallel the various parts of the body and the diverse components of human society, and provides advice to each part. Accordingly the head is compared to the prince, the soul to the Church and its representatives on earth, the heart to the senate, and so on down to the feet, which represent the peasants and labourers, who sustain the rest. John's text was widely diffused and extremely influential. His metaphor, often still associated with Plutarch, was deployed by a range of subsequent authors, including many of those studied in this volume, such as Eustache Deschamps, Jean Gerson, Christine de Pizan, and Alain Chartier.

The translation of Aristotle's *Politics* into Latin in the mid-thirteenth century, and into French just over a century later, led to a late medieval flowering of Aristotelian-inflected political thought. This rediscovery of the *Politics* helped to ensure the continued relevance of the metaphor of the body politic because it situated the political realm within the natural world. In the prologue to the *Politics* Aristotle compared political science to medicine, thereby suggesting an analogy between the body politic and the natural body. The impact of Aristotelian thought, with its emphasis on nature and the natural world in connection to human society and political philosophy, reinforced the logic and the utility of John's metaphor of the body politic.

The University of Paris was imagined in the metaphorical terms employed within the context of corporation theory. In Roman law the corporation was comparable to a state, or, according to the metaphor that came to dominate, to a body "whose internal structure was analyzed through an analogy to the relationship of head and members."[79] In the thirteenth century the corporation theory deriving from Roman law was still rather imprecise, and a corporation might be referred to as a *corpus*, *universitas*, *communitas*, *collegium*, or *societas*. With regard to the University of Paris, initially the term *universitas* most often designated the whole body of masters and students acting as a legal person.[80] In metaphorical terms, the University made for a complex body. It was in some respects a federation of other bodies – those of the nations, faculties, and colleges – and it existed in relationship to another powerful body – that of the Church, with the pope as its head. It is precisely in its dealings with this institutional body that the University acquired the trappings of a legal body, such as the right to appoint a procurator to represent its collective interests, and the use of a seal. Gaines Post has concluded that the University of Masters was a legal corporation, fully recognized by the highest ecclesiastical authority, by 1215 at the latest.[81] It was not until the mid-fourteenth century that the University received the appellation *fille du roy* and began to be represented allegorically as well as metaphorically.[82] In the works of the University chancellor Jean Gerson, discussed in chapter 3, the University is depicted both allegorically, as the *fille du roy*, and metaphorically, as a body that may fruitfully be imagined in relation to other bodies – those of king, kingdom, and the Church militant.

What is metaphor, and how does it relate to allegory? In one of the earliest and most enduring definitions of metaphor, Aristotle says that metaphor is "the application of a noun which properly applies to something else." This may be achieved, he further explains, by substitution (for instance of species for genus, or genus for species) or by analogy (A is to B as C is to D). Aristotle affirms that "the successful use of metaphor is a matter of perceiving similarities."[83] The question of perceiving similarities is an important one, to which we shall return.

In medieval considerations of metaphor we often observe a spatial imagination of how this figure operates. Isidore of Seville says that metaphor is a word drawn across from another usage, while Bede defines metaphor as a translation between words and things.[84] In these definitions metaphor is on the move, as words leave the places they (ought to?) occupy to inhabit the spaces newly assigned to them. However, metaphor is not, cannot be, a simple substitution, transfer, analogy, or drawing across.[85] If it were, it would fail to convey or, more important, to *create* meaning. Metaphor is not an X in the place of Y operation, but rather a both/and proposition, for if, as Aristotle affirms, metaphor is about "perceiving similarities," then at least two terms are required. As Paul Ricœur has argued, "The metaphorical sense not only abolishes but preserves the literal sense, the metaphorical reference maintains the ordinary vision in tension with the new one it suggests" (152).[86] Thus, metaphor suggests a co-presence of the alike-but-different. Metaphor asks us to see a first term with or through a second term, potentially reinflecting the ways in which we imagine both.

There is another type of co-presence that I would argue is constitutive of metaphor – that of the creating and of the apprehending mind. Metaphor is shared or communal in a way that allegory is not, for in order to exist *as metaphor* it must be recognized as such. To make sense of a metaphor the reader must rely upon what Max Black calls the "system of associated commonplaces," or what Monroe Beardsley refers to as the "potential range of connotations."[87] These commonplaces or connotations determine the connections that are available to be made between unlike terms. A new or original metaphor may cause a reader to pause and reflect, it may even redefine to some degree the ways in which the terms brought into proximity are respectively understood, but ultimately the congruence must be perceptible, or else the metaphor may be identifiable as an instance of figurative language, but will not signify semantically.[88] By requiring the agreement, or at least the recognition, of similarity between unlike terms, metaphor affirms (or compels) community. The metaphor of the body politic, which required its readers to recognize the coherence and unity of the kingdom of France, was thus a particularly useful one during the Hundred Years' War, when these very qualities were cast into doubt.

Like a perceptual grid,[89] the similarities called forth by metaphor highlight certain qualities of the terms in question, while suppressing others. Whether I say that my love is a rose, or a sickness, I am invoking, in each case, different – even opposing – aspects of the amorous experience. In this manner metaphors can be used to define or to delimit the ways in which a term might be understood, at least within the framework of the discourse in question. Some metaphors may become so dominant or ubiquitous as to exclude other possible perceptions. Consequently, metaphors are instrumental in the construction of social and political reality. Because they demand acknowledgment and forge community, metaphors do not simply reflect social, cultural, or political conditions, but can influence how people think, and shape what is believed to be true about the world.[90] By calling upon readers to "perceive similarities," the metaphors of kingdom and University compel their publics to recognize and assent to a certain vision of the world, and the reader's place within it.

In theoretical terms, the distinction between metaphor and allegory is not so clear-cut. Like allegory, metaphor entails a gap or distance between what is said and what is meant, and the early rhetoricians (as well as their successors) had a difficult time demarcating the difference between metaphor and allegory, and other so-called tropes of figurative language. Quintilian uses the example of the ship of state to show that allegory may be thought of as an extended metaphor. Isidore's definition of metaphor, cited above, quickly begins to sound rather allegorical, as he goes on to explain that "these [metaphorical] expressions, and others that also use tropes, are veiled in figural garb with respect to what should be understood, so that they may exercise the reader's understanding, and lest the subjects grow common from being stripped bare and obvious."[91] The idea that meaning is covered or concealed is one of the key concepts in understandings of allegory. For some medieval scholars metaphor is a subset of allegory, referring to allegory *in verbis* as opposed to allegory *in factis*, whereas others, such as Hugh of St Victor, will claim that metaphor, as part of the language of a text, belongs to the literal and not to the allegorical. Both allegory and metaphor invite, indeed require, readers to reflect upon the relationships between literal and figurative language, between words and things, between language or form and meaning.

In practice, one can observe clear differences between the allegorical and the metaphorical representations of France and the University of Paris, and this in two principal regards. First, the narrating figure occupies a different position with respect to the metaphorical as opposed to the allegorical bodies in question. The figure of the poet, the "I" of the first-person texts examined in this volume, belongs to the metaphorical body. The "I" is part of the collective of which she or he speaks, and which the author can exhort or criticize. The reader is likewise presumed to belong to the metaphorical body, thereby forging a certain collaboration or connection between author and public, one that, as we have seen, is constitutive of the very process of metaphorical language and interpretation. In contrast, the "I" observes and describes the allegorical body from a subject position firmly outside of and distinct from the allegorical figure, which remains irremediably separate. The reader, who occupies the pronominal "I" of the narrating voice, is invited to remain, likewise, detached from the allegorical body.

This shift in perspective is accompanied by a gender transformation, which points to the second respect in which allegorical and metaphorical representations of kingdom and University differ. The metaphorical body is an unmarked one, and as such may be considered a masculine body, since the universal or the general always corresponds to the masculine. If allegory were no more than extended metaphor, if the metaphor of the body politic were simply to stand up and begin speaking and acting, then the allegorical figure of kingdom and University would likewise be a masculine one. However, such is not the case. In the passage from metaphor to allegory we observe a shift from the masculine to the feminine, from the universal to the particular, and from the intimate to the alien. As we shall see, the allegorical figures of France and University are explicitly and extravagantly feminine. Daughter and mother, eroticized courtly beloved and abject supplicant, victim of (sexual) violence and obedient helpmate, the allegorical figures of France and University occupy highly conventional feminine roles. Moreover, the feminized Other of allegory allows for the constitution of a masculine political subject by inscribing the kingdom or University on the feminine side of a clearly-demarcated gender binary, and inviting the masculinized reader to define himself in contradistinction to this figure, whom he is called upon to love, sustain, and protect.

By employing both metaphorical and allegorical figures of France and the University, the writers in this study are able to explore relationality and community in different ways. In the works of Jean Gerson, for example, the metaphorical body constituted by the University masters allows him to think about this collective in parallel with other bodies, suggesting that the University, since it is analogous to both king and kingdom, might effectively supplement royal authority during the "absences" of Charles VI. The allegorical *fille du roy*, in contrast, permits Gerson to present the University as a royal counsellor of unimpeachable loyalty, one who, unlike the king's actual relatives, does not threaten the king's authority or the royal succession. The allegorical figure of France as portrayed by Christine de Pizan, Alain Chartier, and Jean Juvénal des Ursins often interacts with other collectives, likewise represented allegorically, notably those of the three orders of French society, the Church, or polities such as England. Both figures, consequently, are essential to the cultural and political work being performed by the writers in this study, and both serve, in different ways, to establish and proclaim the coherence and integrity of the French body politic.

Not Your Mother's Allegory: Writing after the "Roman de la Rose"

The vast signifying potential and the hermeneutic possibilities of language and of the world discussed in the first part of this chapter suggest a certain promiscuity of allegorical signifying practices. From the prevalent medieval belief that people and events would find fulfilment at a future moment, and that each element of the created world exists in a meaningful relationship to the divine, it's but a short step to the perception that all texts, people, events, things, are potentially available for interpretation. I suggest that such a conviction undergirds, in part, the proliferation of allegory in the later Middle Ages. In the final part of this chapter I would like to identify and situate the specificity of late medieval allegorical literature with respect to three main areas. First, I will consider the literary consequences of the simultaneously liberating and terrifying dislocation of language and meaning effected by the *Roman de la Rose*. Second, I would like to examine the emergence of what I will call auto-exegesis, the simultaneous narration and explanation of one's own allegory. Third, I will consider the inscription of contemporary political history and concerns into allegorical structures and time.[92]

As we have observed, medieval scholars had long been aware that truth was not necessarily recuperable, and their anxiety about misinterpretation is perceptible in the many meta-hermeneutic texts executed over the course of the Middle Ages. As far back as the *Psychomachia*, often cited as an ur-text of personification allegory, one can observe a disturbing capacity of the vices to depart from or manipulate the denotative potential of their own names, to the point even of simulating the virtues. Avarice's "dubious likeness" (29) to frugality, for instance, allows this vice to infiltrate the army of virtues, nearly bringing about its defeat.[93] Similarly, at the apparent conclusion of the battle, the virtues' victory is almost undone by "a concealed Vice," Discord, surnamed Heresy, who has "feigned the shape of one of our comrades" (32) in an attempt to assassinate Concord. Here too, virtue triumphs. Yet, despite the clamorous victory of the virtues for which Prudentius's text is perhaps best remembered, the struggle is not over, for in his final paragraph Prudentius affirms that "terrible wars rage, shut within the bones they rage" as the soul toils on in its efforts to overcome sin. I suggest that Prudentius's anguished conclusion points not only to the soul's terrible struggle against its own base instincts or desires, but also to its own corruptible, frail, and limited capacity to discern meaning from form, or good from evil.

Centuries later Jean de Meun, in marked contrast to his predecessor, seems to delight in allegory's potential for indeterminacy, even for violence. The *Roman de la Rose*'s often outrageous enactments of its allegorical figures' failure to embody their names, and the doubt cast upon the capacity of language to communicate effectively and truthfully, provoke a loss of innocence on the part of his readers that can (and will) be contested and rewritten, but not regained.

The two-part, thirteenth-century, poetic summa known as the *Roman de la Rose* constitutes a turning point in allegorical writing. Many studies have been dedicated to the *Rose* itself and the nature of its allegory,[94] while many other studies either conclude before, or pick up after, the *Rose*,[95] marking it as a threshold or divide between two related, yet somehow fundamentally different, moments. This perception of difference arises, I would argue, from how the *Rose* plays with (or perverts, some might say), medieval traditions of rhetoric and hermeneutics, putting into question the very nature and operation of allegory.

For a patristic theorist of allegory such as Origen, the relationship between the literal and the non-literal, or between things and words, is not arbitrary.[96] This conviction finds its fullest expression in the work of Isidore of Seville, whose *Etymologies* was one of the most well-known and influential texts of the Middle Ages.[97] The belief in a meaningful relationship between things and words is put into question by a key episode of the *Roman de la Rose*, when the speech character Reason debates with the Lover about proper speech, literal versus figural language, and integumental poetics and hermeneutics.

Over the course of Reason's lengthy discourse to the Lover, she situates the end of the golden age at the moment when Saturn "jupiter coupa les coilles" [cut off Jupiter's balls] (v. 5533). At the time, the vulgar term *coilles* – employed at the rhyme no less! – passes entirely unremarked.[98] When later the Lover denounces Reason's uncourtly speech, she skirts the accusation of vulgarity in order to embark upon a defence of plain or literal speech.[99] Reason affirms that she is in the habit "De parler proprement des choses / Quant il me plaist sanz metre gloses" [of speaking appropriately of things, when it pleases me, without glossing them] (7075–6). Here she plays on the broad semantic field of "proprement," which can signify both literal language, and language that is appropriate or suited to its context, in order to address, albeit obliquely, the Lover's criticism, and to advance her own linguistic claims. Reason affirms that all words are equally useful and worthy, and that it is custom (acoustumance) that governs their use and determines their connotations.[100] Indeed, Reason declares to the Lover that "quant pour reliques m'oïsses / Coilles nommer, le mot prisses / Pour si bel et tant le prissasses / Que partout coilles aorasses / Et les baissasses en eglises" [if you had heard me name relics, balls, you would have deemed the word {balls} so beautiful, and so much would have esteemed it that everywhere you would have adored balls and would have kissed them in churches] (7115–19). Reason's very pointed repetition of *coilles*, her substitution of relics for balls, and her rather equivocal image of the Lover venerating and kissing *coilles*, all constitute an absolute, even violent, rejection of the notion that signifiers exist in a motivated and meaningful relationship to their signifieds.

Jean de Meun further destabilizes understandings of allegory by staging figures – such as Wealth, Hypocrisy, Reason – which, rather than embodying and enacting immaterial concepts and values, instead operate as mobile and contingent signifiers that fail to enact their own meaning in any consistent manner. The *Rose* suggests that ultimately all truth, all understanding, is necessarily partial and subjective. In this manner, Jean de Meun makes explicit what has always been a danger lurking in allegory, that of hermeneutic failure, or even of wilful perversion. If allegory is capable of redeeming, recuperating, bridging, reaching, seeing through or beyond, it is equally capable of supplanting, erasing, and suppressing, sometimes violently.

Jean de Meun's "bad" allegory will move writers such as Dante to make opposing, but equally forceful and productive, claims about the way that allegory operates in their own works.[101] In his *Convivio* and letter to Can Grande Dante suggests for his *Commedia*, and arguably for the *Vita nuova* as well, the status previously reserved for Scripture, implying that his works require the reading practice not of the poets, but of the theologians. Robert Hollander sees this claim being made in explicit terms, highlighting the radical nature of Dante's position, and also its departure from the similar and related claims of other advocates of poetry, who affirm poetry's ethical and philosophical value, but do not go so far as to insist upon its literal truth.[102] Dante's poetry and his reflections upon interpretation will provide important models and points of reference for, among others, Christine de Pizan, who, as we shall see in chapter 2, very explicitly employs Dante as an authorizing figure for her own poetic ambitions.[103]

The importance of Jean de Meun is signalled by the attention accorded him and his allegorical practice by many of the authors discussed in this study, including Christine de Pizan, Jean Gerson, and Jean de Montreuil, all of whom took part in the early-fifteenth-century quarrel of the *Roman de la Rose*.[104] In this polemical exchange of letters and treatises Christine de Pizan denounced not only Jean de Meun's poetics, but especially his misogyny, citing him as a source of violence against women. Gerson focused specifically upon Jean de Meun's misuse of language, and especially of allegory, in a manner that endangered the spiritual health of his readers.[105] Gerson put Jean de Meun on trial in his own allegorical dream vision, *Traictie d'une vision faite contre le Romant de la rose par le chancelier de Paris*. Both Gerson and Christine employ allegory to positive ends, resisting or shutting down its potential for dangerous ambivalence. Jean de Montreuil, in contrast, displays little interest in allegory, focusing instead upon issues of textual authority.

Jean de Meun's *Rose*, and the attendant quarrel, created a heightened awareness of allegory's potential to lead readers astray. This hermeneutic anxiety may well have been compounded by the social and political instability endemic to the reign of Charles VI, which, as we have seen, was marked by recurrent bouts of plague, the papal schism, as well as both civil and external warfare.[106] These factors produced the conditions of possibility for what I have identified as the second distinctive feature of late medieval allegory, namely, its near-obsessive tendency towards auto-exegesis.[107] The process of auto-exegesis involves a collapse of the distinction between what I have called compositional (illustrated by someone like Prudentius) and interpretive (as in the tradition of biblical exegesis) allegory, by staging a narrator engaged simultaneously in creating an allegorical narrative and interpreting or explaining it as it unfolds. Auto-exegesis represents an attempt to secure meaning, ensuring correct interpretation on the part of the readers.

In the vernacular allegorical poetry of the later French Middle Ages, auto-exegesis has become standard fare. Philippe de Mézières, preceptor of the young Charles VI, for instance, furnishes a table of concordances at the end of his prologue so that "le liseur seculier, aucunefoiz non fonde en clergie … entendra clerement toutes choses" [the lay reader, sometimes not well educated … will clearly understand all things].[108] It might seem that Philippe's auto-exegetical practice reduces allegory to a kind of algebraic equation. However, the sheer proliferation of allegories render a reductive reading impossible. The items in Philippe's allegorical universe signify multiply, and every person, landscape, animal, and object encountered by the narrator (himself doubly allegorized as both the Old Pilgrim and Ardent Desire),[109] seems to bloom with allegorical potential.

Like Philippe de Mézières, Christine de Pizan provides an explanatory prologue, or "glose," to her *Livre de l'Advision Cristine*.[110] She identifies the three levels at which the elements of her text might be understood – as pertaining to the individual, to the kingdom, and to the cosmos – a move which very clearly points to the multiple (also often three) levels at which Scripture might be interpreted, and which suggests thereby a parallel between her text and holy writ.[111] Moreover, she says, polyvalence is a source of aesthetic pleasure, for "est la poesie belle et soubtille quant elle puet servir a plusieurs ententes et que on la puet prendre a divers propos" [the poetry is beautiful and refined when it can support several meanings and one can take it in various ways] (3). In his *Convivio*, Dante accords beauty a very different value. At the conclusion to the *Canzone prima*, the poet addresses his work, saying to it that few indeed will understand it properly, "tanto la parli faticosa e forte" [so laborious and tough do you make it].[112] Those foreclosed from the richness of poetic meaning are invited at least to notice "com'io son bella" [how beautiful I {the poem} am]. In contradistinction to Dante, who offers beauty as a kind of consolation prize to those for whom meaning is obscure, Christine identifies multiplicity of meaning as, precisely, the source of her text's beauty. Indeed, poetry is not defined by its formal qualities, but by its use of metaphors and its availability to multiple modes of interpretation.[113] Poets speak "soubz figure de methaphore, c'est a dire de parole couverte" [by manner of metaphors, that is to say, covered words] (3), and "telle parole dicte par poisie puet avoir mains entendemens" [a given word pronounced poetically may have several meanings] (3).

Multiplicity of meaning does not, however, permit a kind of hermeneutic free for all. On the contrary, Christine shows her readers how the various components of her allegorical narrative may be understood in relation to the individual, the kingdom, and the cosmos. The "grant ymage" [great image] (3) with which her text begins, for instance, may be understood as "tout le monde ... c'est asavoir ciel, terre et abeisme" [the entire world ... that is to say, heaven, earth, and the abyss] (3), as well as "une chascune creature humaine" [each human creature] (4), and as "le royaume de France, lequel est grant et n'est que ung corps" [the kingdom of France, which is vast and constitutes a single body] (4). Christine thus provides a proleptic interpretive gloss of her allegorical narrative. Over the course of the prologue, she becomes more telescopic and formulaic in her three-part interpretive glosses, with the phrase "Item, puet segnefier" [Likewise, it may mean] employed to introduce the various interpretive levels.[114] Christine's *glose* thus enacts for her readers an educative hermeneutic performance, at the conclusion of which the reader has been habituated to a triple interpretation of allegorical elements, and is thereby invited, of his or her own accord, to subject each figure or image encountered to the same interpretative grid.[115]

The auto-exegetical impulse of late medieval authors is accompanied by a fragmentation of the first-person narrative subject[116] into an experiencing self, on the one hand, and a narrating or interpreting self, on the other.[117] The form of the dream or vision is often used to dramatize this dislocation of the subject,[118] for this duplication of the narrating *I* imposes a certain critical distance between narrator and narrative, and provides a way to testify to the truth of the vision transmitted by the narrative in an apparently objective fashion. As Margaret Mitchell brilliantly demonstrates in her analysis of 2 Corinthians, in which Paul must justify his apostolic mission, one cannot testify in one's own behalf, but "in the mouth of two or three witnesses every word shall stand" (Deuteronomy 19:15, Matthew 18:16). Accordingly, Paul invokes a series of witnesses: the fool (Paul), "a man I know" (Paul again!), and finally, God.[119] In a similar manner, the duplication of the authorial or narrative self via dreams or visions (Christine de Pizan, Alain Chartier), or by the designation of a third party as the source of a vision (Jean Gerson, Jean Juvénal des Ursins), allows the author to present the allegorical work as a true revelation to a privileged witness. In most cases, the author figure is specifically enjoined to convey the content of their text, often by the allegorical figure of France or of the University of Paris herself. This brings us to the final point that I would like to make concerning the specificity of late medieval allegorical literature, that is, the inscription of history into allegorical time and practices, and the idea that being a good political subject is instrumental to one's salvation.

Intellectuals, and especially theologians, of the later Middle Ages were strongly influenced by the thought of the so-called Pseudo-Dionysius,[120] who posited a "dynamic of procession and return, *exitus* and *reditus*, descending pluralization and ascending unification" by which the soul might return to God.[121] The authors in this study adapt the Dionysian notion of vertical hierarchy of ascent towards God/truth by incorporating the kingdom or the polity into these levels of ascent, situated between the micro- and the macrocosm, the individual and the universe, the temporal and the spiritual. In this manner the historical and political circumstances in which readers find themselves, and more importantly the ways in which readers conduct themselves within the temporal realm, have direct implications for their salvation.

The very metaphor of the body politic, which is especially prominent in the work of Eustache Deschamps, connects the individual to the social body, thus suggesting that individual morality is inseparable from ethical behaviour in the public realm. Christine de Pizan, as I have just discussed, advises her readers to interpret the elements of her allegorical narrative on three levels, as pertaining to the individual, the kingdom, and the spiritual realm. Alain Chartier, too, in his *Quadrilogue invectif*, discusses the lifespans of individuals, of polities, and of the cosmos, thereby inserting the political realm into the familiar parallel between microcosm and macrocosm. Similarly, Jean Gerson, as we shall see in chapter 3, imagines three kingdoms – personal, temporal, and spiritual – which every person both inhabits and contains within him or herself. These kingdoms are ordered and oriented towards the goal of salvation. In Gerson's writings the temporal realm, the kingdom of France, is able – indeed intended – to help the individual soul or political subject ascend to a higher order with the objective of returning to God. The earthly realm is invested with spiritual value, and the just and effective management of political affairs becomes not simply a secular preoccupation, but a spiritual one as well.

The inscription of the temporal realm within the levels of ascent towards God shows the degree to which late medieval allegory – perhaps paradoxically – has embraced historical specificity. For some scholars, allegory's turn towards history signals its demise.[122] On the contrary, I would suggest that, as the authors studied here make clear, historical and political actuality represents a new frontier for allegorical writing of the later Middle Ages, and that the confrontation of allegorical forms and specific historical content enriches and expands the potential of allegorical writing. Indeed, we might take this idea one step further, and imagine not only that the political and historical realm provides a new subject for allegorical practice, but that the circumstances of the reign of Charles VI demand an allegorical intervention.

This is not to suggest that allegory is the answer to all political chaos. If it were, we might expect to observe the allegorical representation of France emerge far sooner than we do, since previous centuries had enjoyed their share of chaos as much as did the "autumn of the Middle Ages." As the figure of Ecclesia shows us, a very pertinent model for the elaboration of the allegorical representation of the kingdom of France had existed for centuries. The necessary elements from which to construct an allegory of France had long been in place. Why, then, does the allegorical figure of

France emerge suddenly and with vigour in the late fourteenth century, followed closely by the less common, but no less interesting, figure of the University?

In part, allegorical literature and interpretation, which had a long and complex history, had reached a point by the late fourteenth century when it was prepared to take on historical and political subjects, to become a conceptual tool for the apprehension and potential transformation of actuality in the same way that it had, in previous centuries, permitted the conceptualization of questions of morality, or the psychology of the individual subject. In addition, the lack of political authority brought about by Charles VI's minority and then his madness created a kind of space or vacuum into which rushed the allegorical (and metaphorical) representations of France and of the University of Paris. The specific circumstances of both literary and social history thus intersect to give rise to a new form of expression, or rather, to transform a well-established and very authoritative one such that it is equipped to intervene in the political crises that afflicted France when first these texts were produced and consumed. Not only does the reading and interpretation of allegory generate meaning, but also the readers' engagement in a quest for understanding is potentially transformative of they themselves, as they are invited to become zealous and loyal political subjects of the kingdom, and thereby to secure the prosperity of France, as well as their own salvation.

2

From *douce France* to the *dame renommée*: Figuring the French Body Politic

ne fu pas sanz raison dame renommée seur autres nations …
Si li a Nostre Sires doué par sa grace une prerogative et un avantage seur toutes autres terres et seur toutes autres nations

Grandes chroniques de France

When Primat characterized France in the preface of what would come to be known as the *Grandes chroniques de France* as a "dame renommée seur autres nations" [lady renowned beyond other nations] he was both drawing and building upon established cultural, intellectual, and literary conventions.[1] As we saw in chapter 1, any polity or community could be thought of, metaphorically, as a human body.[2] At the same time, Primat's evocation of the *dame renommée* also fits squarely within the long tradition – both classical and biblical – of imagining cities, provinces, or kingdoms in allegorical terms, as women.[3] Isidore of Seville characterizes Spain as a queen and mother, while Vincentius Hispanus praises "blessed lady Spain"; Gallia is represented as a female figure in Ottonian art and literature;[4] Dante's *Purgatorio* 6 opens with the image of the enslaved and prostituted Italy, while Petrarch's poem 128 of the *Rime sparse* contains a long address to "Italia mia."[5]

Long before Primat's evocation of the *dame renommée*, the idea of France, shaped by a set of accepted beliefs, stories, and attributes, was slowly being accreted. Myths of origin, such as that which affirmed the Trojan descent of the Franks,[6] of divine election, exemplified by the conversion of Clovis which established France as the oldest Christian kingdom and the dove which furnished the sacred oil for his anointment,[7] and of cultural and intellectual supremacy, like that communicated by the notion of *translatio studii et imperii*, which posited France, and in particular Paris, as the successor of Greece and Rome, provided a common history and a set of beliefs about what it meant to be French. All of these and similar ideas – shared, well known, and oft-repeated – reinforced over time the notion that the French were distinct among the peoples of Christendom, and that they occupied a special place in Christian history.

The idea of France also assumed a privileged place in the rise of vernacular literature. In the eleventh century Roland, dying on the field of Roncesvalles in a text which would itself become an icon of French national identity, laments that he will never again see "dulce France" [sweet France], thereby highlighting the affective bond which united the French to France, and to one another.[8] Like Roland, Guillaume au Court Nez in the *Charroi de Nîmes* speaks warmly of "douce France."[9] Thus, Primat capitalized upon a long literary tradition of loving affection for the kingdom.

During the troubled reign of Charles VI the poets Eustache Deschamps and Christine de Pizan cultivated and enriched these cherished beliefs concerning the singularity and the exemplarity of France and its people by developing in richly textured and original terms both metaphorical and allegorical representations of the kingdom. I argued in chapter 1 that structural and functional similarities unite the figure of allegory – predicated upon and operating within the space between form and meaning – and medieval women – essential, but potentially unreliable, mediators of political power and authority. In the present chapter I shall show how, in the disquieting absence of the king, our poets reinvigorated the familiar metaphor of the body politic, and generated the allegorical figure of France – portrayed in terms of an overdetermined femininity – in order to explore, articulate, and promulgate new ideas about the respective natures of king and kingdom, and their relationship to one another. They elicited on the part of their readers a consciousness of themselves as political subjects, and an understanding of the duties and conduct appertaining thereto. By attending to the dynamics of a specific body of texts we shall be able to observe how literary works were able to shape the social, political, and cultural imaginary – making claims for the unity, coherence, and wholeness of a kingdom that in reality was fragmented and weakened by the minority and madness of its king.

In part one of this chapter I will examine the ways in which Deschamps turned poetry to concrete political ends. Nature and the natural world in general, and the human form in particular, provided an especially useful vehicle for the expression of Deschamps's political ideas, and the poet's varied representations of the body politic gave new force and relevance to a well-known metaphor. In addition, Deschamps is the first to transform the silent object of previous poets' apostrophes into a speaking, moving, living representation of the kingdom. In Deschamps's immense, heterogeneous, and dialogic corpus, the particularity of France has yet to emerge. His many poems depict her variously as the orphan, the widow, the ward, or the inheritance of the French king, and sometimes also as a mother. His innovative poetics – including his imaginative deployment of the metaphor of the body politic, his development of the allegorical figure of France, and his productive use of the dream vision – provide his readers with ways to conceptualize and articulate the considerable troubles facing the kingdom, and to imagine possible solutions to them, as well as furnishing inspiration and fertile ground for his successors.

In the second half of this chapter I will focus upon Christine de Pizan's *Livre de l'advision Cristine*, in which the maternity of France – a minor detail in Deschamps's poetry – has become constitutive of her identity. France's motherhood allows for the inscription of the French nobles, the king's subjects, Christine's very readers, into imaginary bonds of kinship with the kingdom. This model of kinship, and the concomitant appeal to natural love, provide an archetype for political community and action. France's "children" should love, respect, and protect her as a good child would his or her mother. Moreover, the maternity of France and her connection to the French people allow for the kingdom to displace the king as the focal point of the French people's affection and loyalty in the face of threats both external and internal. Christine employs and exploits the authoritative models of allegorical interpretation,[10] and of allegorical composition,[11] discussed in chapter 1. Moreover, Christine's allegory operates on three connected levels: those of the individual, the polity, and the spiritual realm. Her allegorical text is thus both politically constructive and salvific.

Eustache Deschamps and the Body of France

Eustache Deschamps (né Morel) was born in approximately 1340 in Vertus, and he died before 26 March 1405.[12] Although he produced an astonishing amount and variety of poetry, some 1500 lyric works, including over 1000 ballades, several longer *dits*, the 12,000-verse incomplete *Miroir de mariage*, and his well-known *Art de dictier*, he was not a professional writer. Instead, he occupied a series of increasingly important administrative positions during the reigns of Charles V (1364–80) and Charles VI

(1380–1422) of France, and his lyric works, composed over four decades and largely undateable, were written in the interstices of these other responsibilities.

Deschamps was not overly concerned with his own literary posterity, and it is most likely thanks to the chancellor, Arnaud de Corbie, that the Parisian scribe Raoul Tainguy copied the single manuscript of Deschamps's complete works that we possess.[13] Despite this lack of authorial management, Deschamps's poems clearly circulated among his friends and contemporaries. In his vast allegorical dream vision, the *Songe du vieil pelerin*, Philippe de Mézières recommends to Charles VI the reading of "les dictez vertueulx de ton serviteur et officier Eustache Morel" [the virtuous writings of your servant and officer Eustache Morel].[14] In addition, Deschamps engaged in literary correspondence with both Christine de Pizan and Chaucer.[15]

Deschamps travelled widely in his various administrative capacities, and with his keen satirical eye he provides invaluable testimony from the reigns of Charles V and VI. The reign of the former represents for Deschamps, as for many of his contemporaries and successors, a golden age, while the reign of the son forms a sad contrast with that of the father.[16] In addition to suffering through Charles VI's minority and madness, Deschamps was also a historical witness to the Great Schism of the West.[17] While many of Deschamps's poems attempt to think through and cope with these difficult events and circumstances, a staggering variety of other subjects find their way into Deschamps's poems. From a comic prayer that he might not lose his hair, to a joyful salute to Parisian women, Deschamps effectively redefined the scope and potential of lyric poetry, transforming it from a vehicle for expounding upon courtly love to an instrument fit to examine any aspect of the individual, social, intellectual, political, or moral life.

My analysis will demonstrate how Deschamps's poetry articulates and promulgates a set of political views concerning the nature and composition of the kingdom, and the obligations of the parts of society to one another and to the king.[18] Both Deschamps's metaphorical and his allegorical representations of the kingdom serve to conceptualize the kingdom as a bounded territorial, cultural, and political space, one endowed with a coherence and unity that, from a geopolitical standpoint, fourteenth-century France did not possess.

We shall see that corporeal metaphors provide Deschamps with a powerful and flexible conceptual instrument for thinking about human political communities, specifically the kingdom of France. The body lets Deschamps explore ideas of interiority and exteriority, as well as the function of each part and its relationship to the others, to the whole, and to the head or leader. Deschamps's metaphors of the body politic are by and large unmarked in terms of gender. Inasmuch as the words *chief* and *corps* are grammatically masculine one might imagine that the physical bodies to which political communities are compared are male bodies, but such an identification is not explicit. Consequently, the poems that rely upon metaphor emphasize inclusion, unity, and the relationship of parts to a (fantasized, masculine and thus universal) whole that displays coherence and harmony. All readers, from king to humble subject, male and female, are presumed to belong to the body evoked in such poems.

Allegories of the kingdom, in contrast, foreground alterity. The reader is invited to contemplate the kingdom of France from without. The kingdom, meanwhile, is represented in terms that are highly codified with respect to gender, cast in the familiar feminine roles of courtly lady, vulnerable widow, or intercessor and supplicant. In this way the allegorized kingdom does not threaten the social order founded upon the supremacy of the king as the head of the body politic, even though Deschamps's poems can be seen to displace the king by providing an alternative focus for the subjects' political loyalty and identification – the kingdom. In addition, the highly conventional gender binary in which the allegories are inscribed invites the reading public to assume a set of attitudes and actions that is conventionally masculine: confronted with the allegorical figure of France, the reader is to respect, cherish, and protect the vulnerable and beloved kingdom.[19]

Deschamps's work is remarkable for its dialogism; a wide range of poetic interlocutors speak within, from, and across his poems. This formal feature helps to situate the voice of the kingdom that emerges, among many others, from Deschamps's works, and lets us see how poems that do not appear to have a social or political significance may be read as such.[20] The poet's many lyric voices include those of a *preudomme* (Ballade 324), a decrepit old man (Ballade 834), a wife disappointed with marriage (Ballade 1232), a young woman proud of her beauty (Virelai 554), as well as the voices of a head which complains of its members (Ballade 978), God (Ballade 358), the city of Paris (Ballade 193), the world (Ballade 1426), the Church (Ballade 243), and the kingdom (Ballade 255). Many poems contain portions of dialogue, while others respond to one another or examine a similar issue from different vantage points. Susanna Bliggenstorfer has noted that Deschamps was the first poet to adapt the use of the *envoi*,[21] borrowed from the *chant royal*, to the ballade, and his employ of the *envoi* is very original. Even in those poems which do not contain dialogue, the *envoi* inscribes an interlocutor into the space of the poem, often shifting the perspective provided by the rest of the ballade, whether by glossing what has come before, or by casting the poem in a different light such that other meanings become apparent. The *envoi* always has an addressee, in Deschamps most often "Princes," traditionally imagined to be the Prince who would judge the *puy* or poetic contest of which the poem was a part, but which in Deschamps may easily be conflated with the figure of the king. By addressing the *Princes*, Deschamps makes possible a political reading even of poems that lack overtly social or historical content.

One of the most prominent themes in Deschamps's poetry – not surprisingly, on the part of one whose professional duties involved the administration of justice – is the importance of order. For Deschamps, the world has a fixed moral order ordained by God and which is reflected from the macrocosm of the cosmos to the microcosm of man, and including as a third term, in between and analogous to the macro- and microcosms, the political community.[22] In Ballade 377 the poet explains that people ought to remain in their places. The first three stanzas focus on the error of supposing that those born into servitude or modest positions ought to be raised above their station in life. As the refrain insists, "Serf eslever est chose perilleuse" [to elevate a serf is a dangerous thing]. Lowly people who are elevated become deviant and unnatural, a mixture of scorpion, serpent, ox, and lion (vv. 5–7): hybrid monstrosities not to be found in God's world.[23] In the fourth stanza the poet writes that Scripture has provided for three orders, all of which are necessary to the whole community: "Chevalier, prestre et laboureur qui fuet" [knight, priest, and the labourer who threshes] (v. 27). The ballade as a whole posits the divinely ordered division of society, but at the same time the fundamental unity that is created on the basis of a shared concern for and dedication to the common good; thus, the "Chevalier, clerc et laboracion, / *Deussent estre un* en œuvre vertueuse" [knight, cleric, and labourer *ought to be united* in virtuous endeavour] (vv. 42–3, emphasis added). Ballade 231 further develops the idea that each type of person has obligations to the collective good by enumerating the duties of the various divisions of society, including the nobles, knights, churchmen, labourers, and even the king, to whom the third and final stanza is dedicated. In a miniature *miroir du prince* the poet reminds the king of his principal responsibilities: cherish good men, remove the bad ones, be generous and despise greed, be courageous in pursuing war, strive to achieve honour and prowess, and beware of pride. The refrain affirms that it was to ensure the continued respect for the order described in the poem that "furent les Roys et princes fais" [king and princes were made]. Thus, the king is responsible not only for carrying out his own duties, but also for ensuring that all those below him, from nobles to the common people, do so as well.

Unfortunately for Deschamps and his contemporaries, his poems all too often depict the order of human society in theoretical or prescriptive terms, for the poet's observations show that in reality man does not behave as he ought. In Ballade 358, the four elements, the seasons, the birds and beasts, and the celestial bodies all serve and obey God. Only humankind, God laments, "contre moy ... estrive et erre" [struggles and acts against me] (refrain). Similarly in Ballades 1011 and 1102 the orderly and obedient animal world contrasts with human society. In the opening of Ballade 1011 the poet "voy faire a tout animal / Ce que Nature lui ensaingne / Fors qu'a homme" [sees every animal do that which Nature instructs it, except man] (vv. 1–3). This point of departure allows the poet to catalogue the sins he observes in his contemporary society, which range from deceptive speech to vestimentary impropriety, and which cause the poet to exclaim "Du temps qui court ay grant merveille" [I wonder at the world nowadays] (refrain).[24] Ballade 1102 is likewise structured around a contrast between nature and society, animals and humans. While each element of nature "trait a sa nature" [tends towards its nature] (v. 1) and the animals "tiennent entr'eulx leur nature ordonnée" [among themselves adhere to their fixed natures] (v. 6), mankind "se denature" [denatures himself] (vv. 2, 31). Those who do not conform to the expectations and conventions of human society are unnatural, or, as Virginie Minet-Mahy expresses it, "la dé-naturation se constitue véritablement en motif d'expression de la dégradation de l'*homo politicus*."[25]

In addition to the exemplarity of the natural world, the homology between body and kingdom, which emphasizes the clear and consistent organization of body parts and their functions, provides an apposite vehicle for the poetic expression of Deschamps's ideal of an orderly community, in which each part performs its duties to the whole. The bodies so frequently staged by Deschamps highlight the responsibilities of all parts of the organism towards the body – or the kingdom. Ballade 377, as we have seen, affirms that the three orders of society "deussent estre un en œuvre vertueuse" [should be united in virtuous endeavour] (v. 43). Similarly, Ballade 1056 reiterates the idea that the physical body, like the body politic, succeeds or fails as a whole, and that one part of the body cannot seek its private advantage without compromising the entire entity. The analogy between physical body and body politic is so frequent in Deschamps that even poems that do not seem to have a political message can be read as such. In literal terms, Ballade 958 condemns the fashion of removing one's hat – even in wintertime – when at court. The poem details the various threats posed by cold weather and bare heads, especially for an old man like the poet. However, one can also read the opening verses, "Puisque le chief qui est si precieux, / Lui malade, fait les membres doloir" [because the head is so precious, when it is ill, the limbs suffer] (vv. 1–2), metaphorically, as an affirmation of the interdependence of the parts of the social body, and the necessity of the king's or head's health to the good of the whole.

It would seem that the human body is neatly bounded, such that bodily metaphors convey the quasi-organic coherence of the political community and allow for the clear demarcation of those who are part of, or foreign to, that community. In fact, the body is disturbingly permeable, and Deschamps's poems sometimes betray anxiety about the ways in which the body is vulnerable to penetration or mutilation. For example, Ballade 398 stages the voices of feet, hands, and a mouth who reproach one another for the ills that they suffer, due, according to the members, to the gluttony of the mouth. The mouth is sovereign over the body ("Vous estes souveraine" [you are sovereign] [v. 44], the hands say), and yet this orifice, which should act as a gatekeeper, is itself responsible for introducing into the body elements that have rendered the organism unhealthy.[26] The *envoi*, addressed to "Prince," connects the voices of this dismembered and ventriloquized material body to a metaphorical body politic. As he who is sovereign over the body politic, the prince is placed in parallel with the mouth. In the *envoi* the prince is cautioned against the "desordenance" [disorder] (v. 52) of the mouth, whose gluttony causes the death of the hands and feet, and he is exhorted to exhibit "attrempance" [moderation] (v. 54) in order to preserve the body politic.[27] By showing how the integrity of the body can be breached through its orifices, this poem reminds its public of the body's susceptibility to threats from without, as well as betrayal from within.

The unity and wholeness of the body can be menaced in other ways as well. When the animate head of Ballade 1056 complains of illness, the body retorts that the head itself is to blame for having removed the members that used to support both trunk and head. In a rather Frankenstein-ish manner, it would seem that the head has amputated "jambes et bras et le destre costé" [legs and arms and the right side] (v. 7) and joined to its trunk "membres d'autre paraige" [limbs of other extraction] (v. 8). This is the head's – and the body's – problem, for "estranges piez sont comme chiens et pors … les mains aussi" [foreign feet are like dogs and pigs … the hands also] (vv. 13, 15). In order to restore its health the body advises the head to get rid of "ces membres vilz et ors, / Et me lairez les membres que j'avoye / Naturelment" [these vile and filthy limbs, and leave me with the limbs that I had naturally] (vv. 21–3). The ballade stages the opposition between the "estranges" [foreign] (v. 5) limbs, presented as self-interested flatterers of dubious loyalty, and the "droiz" [rightful] (v. 4) or natural limbs, who are "conjoins a vous et a dueil et a joye" [joined to you in sorrow and in joy], "conjoint en unité" [joined in unity], and "membres de linaige" [limbs of one lineage] (vv. 24, 26, 28). This promotion of a natural citizenry ruled by natural kings constitutes an implicit rejection of the English pretensions to the French throne within the context of the Hundred Years' War.[28] The question of how to determine who is a subject of the king or, in the language of the poem, who is a natural limb and who is not, becomes a serious problem during an era in which the fluctuating winds of war caused whole regions to move back and forth between French and English political and military control or alliance, and in which the king and his closest advisers had disparate, and evolving, attitudes towards the English. Ballade 1056, with its monstrous composite body parts and its head who does not know how to lead, reveals both a longing for organic coherence, and a tacit acknowledgment of the limits to the unity that the body – physical or political – can provide.

Deschamps's metaphors of the body also express ideas about the relationality of the parts to one another and to the whole that can be connected to ideas about human communities.[29] Some scholars have affirmed that organological metaphors were used to reinforce a hierarchical vision of society.[30] Laurence Harf-Lancner, for example, argues that the originality of the medieval interpretation of the fable of the stomach and the members resides in the fact that the prince is assimilated to the head at the summit of a social hierarchy in which each part has a precise function.[31] However, such a strict hierarchy is not what we observe in Deschamps. Although in Deschamps's corporeal metaphors the head most often rules the body, this is not always the case (as seen in Ballade 398, where the mouth is sovereign), and even when it is, the head is neither isolated nor infallible.[32]

Ballade 252 explores the relationship of the head to the members. The opening stanza institutes a parallel between the body, the family, and the political community. The notion that the individual human body constitutes a microcosm might well be familiar to Deschamps's readers, although in this poem the macrocosm is not represented by the cosmos, but by the political community, as illustrated by the terms "seignour" and "serf."

The analogy between the individual, the family, and the polity recalls the tripartite division of Giles of Rome's adaptation of Aristotle, the *De regimine principum*, in which effective rule of the self is taken as a necessary prelude to rule of the family and of the kingdom.[33] What the poet imagines as the cohesion and unity of the human body ought to be reproduced on the levels of the family and of society as a whole; however, the poetic voice observes with dismay that discord reigns between head and members, father and son, lord and vassal (see vv. 1–6). In the stanzas which follow, the poet focuses on the relationship between the head and its members, which in some senses is a hierarchical one, since the former is to "nourrir et gouverner" [provide for and rule] the latter (v. 10). However, both of these verbs are used also with respect to childrearing and fostering, and so the relationship that is suggested is one of nurture rather than simple dominion, as in Nicole Oresme's "princey paternel," or paternal rule, which is at the origin of royal rule.[34] The head should be moderate, for it is also a teacher (it "leur doit aprandre les doulz ars" [should teach them the noble arts] [v. 11]), and it should rule "cautement" [prudently] (v. 12). Should the members rebel against the authority of their "chief," the head is to punish them, but "[m]oiennement, puis qu'ilz se sont subgis" [moderately, since they are his subjects] (v. 14). If the head is so punitive that it destroys its own limbs, it will not long survive them, since "l'un sanz l'autre ne puet longues durer" [one cannot last long without the other] (v. 21). Overall, this ballade emphasizes the worth and dignity of the members, and the necessity of their good treatment by the head. Such a vision does not negate the authority of the head over the limbs and body, but it does suggest that this power is not unbounded. As in Ballade 398 the *envoi*, directed to "Princes," inscribes the consideration of the human body within a political context, and connects the ending of the poem to the family and the political community with which it opened.

Ballade 1056 also considers the relationship of a head to its body, although the vision of political community contained therein differs in important respects from that of Ballade 252. While the latter was articulated by a wise and detached poetic voice, one able to see clearly and to proffer advice, Ballade 1056 consists of a dialogue between a head and its body. Surprisingly, it is the body and not the head who displays prudence and wisdom. The authoritative head of Ballade 252 is replaced by an uncertain and ignorant one, who asks repeatedly in the refrain – "Corps, doulz amis, dy moy donc que feray ge?" [Body, sweet friend, tell me then, what shall I do?]. Jacques Le Goff has shown that in the classical tradition the trunk was more highly valorized in organological metaphors than in later Christian traditions. The stomach and intestines were thought to play a unifying, coordinating role, while the heart was understood as the seat of moral conscience.[35] Seeking and heeding the advice of wise counsellors was a standard recommendation in late medieval mirrors for princes, and here the body performs the duties of such an adviser. It is important to note, however, that the head is *not* seeking the advice of, say, its feet, which were often assimilated to peasants and which clearly occupied an inferior position in the hierarchy of the organism.[36] Instead, the body in Ballade 1056 corresponds to what some late medieval political thinkers referred to as the "wise few," those who were authorized, indeed obliged, to advise the king.[37] This integration of the head, or king, into a system or structure of rule, one in which the advice of the body is sought and heeded, can be seen as an attempt on the part of Deschamps to respond to Charles VI's lack of authority, and its dire consequences for political order and harmony. By inscribing the king into a political body in which governance is the product of a coordinated effort, Deschamps imagines, and helps his readers to conceptualize, a structural response first to the king's minority, and later to his "absences."

In addition to his frequent recourse to metaphor, Deschamps also employs allegory in order to imagine or define a political community, as in his poetic apostrophes to Flanders (Ballade 18), Jerusalem (Ballades 68 and 1139), Ghent (Ballade 94), Paris (Ballades 170, 171), and Rheims (Ballade 172). We shall see that Deschamps uses allegory in flexible and innovative ways, sometimes combining metaphor and allegory, or compositional and interpretive allegory, and at times staging masculine allegorical figures, a practice inaugurated by the *Roman de la Rose*, but still relatively infrequent.

Deschamps's allegories of political communities or institutions and his organological metaphors do not operate in isolation from one another. On the contrary, they are closely related and are sometimes even combined within the same poem. Ballade 978, for instance, opens with a first-person voice that complains of its many physical ills.[38] In the second stanza the perspective shifts as a third-person voice intervenes to ask, "qui est ce chief taint, malade et pali, / Qui au jour d'ui pour sa grant doleur crie?" [who is this head, discoloured, sick and pale, who today cries out in sorrow] (vv. 11–12), and promptly explains that it is "[l]'eglise Dieu, quant elle voit en li / Division, et que pas n'est unie" [God's church, when she sees in herself division, and that she is not unified] (vv. 13–14).[39] Thus, what was presented as a suffering physical body in the first stanza is subsequently revealed to be a metaphorical one, here representing the Church militant instead of the political community, and whose internal division is foregrounded by the enjambment of verse 14. Yet this metaphorical body is capable of perception and of speech, and the Church is both embodied and gendered in a way that solicits the readers' compassion.

Like Ballade 978, Ballade 243 also stages the first-person voice of the Church, though it is not identified as such in the opening line, "Las! je me plain, destruite et desolée" [Alas! I lament, destroyed and tormented], which deploys the conventions of the lyric love plaint. Within this framework the speaker, marked by the adjectives as female, would appear to be a courtly lady abandoned or betrayed by her beloved. The public's expectations about what may follow are quickly surprised, however, for in verse three the speaker declares, "Je fus jadis saincte Eglise appellée" [I formerly was called holy Church]. This allegorical speaker adheres to the formal demands of the love complaint in that her poem is structured around the pronounced contrast between a happy past (vv. 3, 13) and a sorrowful present (vv. 11, 23), but the content, which focuses on key moments in early Christian history, is entirely different. In semantic terms, the speaker is analogous to the sorrowful figure of Jerusalem from the Book of Lamentations. The closing stanza recalls the Bride of the Song of Songs calling to her Bridegroom, Christ, as the speaker implores her "vray espoux" [true spouse] (v. 29) to come to her rescue. Thus, in lyric terms the first-person female voice contrasts her false lover and faithful spouse, while in spiritual terms the allusions to Lamentations and to the Song of Songs inscribe Ballade 243 within a commentary tradition that itself associated these two biblical books with the allegorical figure of Jerusalem.[40]

This poem constitutes an important intervention into the practice of allegory, and an example of what I have termed the auto-exegetical mode discussed in chapter 1. Though clearly informed by the robust tradition of biblical commentary, Deschamps innovates in a radical manner. While other commentaries interpreted an anterior text that existed outside of and beyond the textual boundaries of the commentary, here what Jon Whitman has referred to as compositional and interpretive allegory inhabit the same space or textual body.[41] In other terms, Deschamps's poem both allegorizes and explains. The interpretation is not a post-facto supplement to the poem, but, in a kind of lyric auto-exegesis, constitutes the very substance of the poem itself. On one hand, the poem has collapsed, or at the very least seriously blurred, the distinction between the literal and the allegorical levels of the text.[42] On the other hand, it is possible to imagine the poem having reversed these two levels, casting the literal outside of the textual body, which remains the space inhabited by allegory. The literal or historical event or context to which the poem responds is the Great Schism of the West. In a reversal of typological readings, which take the literal or historical as a point of departure which prefigures or finds fulfilment in a later event, or in contrast to allegorical methods of reading which see in things visible and corporeal signs of things invisible and spiritual, here the text's hidden meaning is a literal and a historical event. Deschamps's poem does not provide an allegorical interpretation of a text, but of human history, of the real and material social world of his contemporaries. We can observe a similar transformation of allegorical practice in other poems by Deschamps, and in the works of his successors. His corpus thus marks a transformation in the possibilities afforded allegory, one which may help to explain the late medieval explosion of allegorical texts.

Like the poem just discussed, Ballade 112 also employs conventional lyric themes and language to suggest a political meaning. The poem opens on the "jour de l'an nouvel" [New Year's Day] (v. 1), a time associated with the courtly custom of gift-giving, whether to followers, family members, or lovers. The poet declares that he himself has long had the habit of composing, in honour of this day, "une chançon / Sur l'art d'amours, de dueul ou de revel" [a song on the art of love, whether sorrowful or joyful] (vv. 2–3). This year, however, the poet's song must be a sorrowful one, "car la belle façon / Voy deperir de celle que j'aimay" [for I see languish the fair semblance of she whom I loved] (vv. 5–6). If this text is read in isolation, no grammatical or semantic detail confirms that the poet's lady is an allegorical one; however, a reader habituated to Deschamps's creative use of allegory may suspect that this is the case. The poet describes his lady's pale face, languid body, and other symptoms caused, he says "Par le default d'estre bien *gouvernée*" [for lack of being well *ruled*] (refrain, emphasis added), a verb which could be employed with regard to political entities or to women and children.[43] He then explains that "Convoitise la ferit d'un canon / Car riche fut" [Covetousness struck her with a piece of artillery, for she was powerful] (vv. 15–16) and that "depuis oy dire ay / Qu'Envie y vint disant: 'Je la guarroy'" [I have since heard that Envy went there saying, "I will make war on her"] (vv. 16–17). Thus, the lady, whether real or allegorical, has been assailed by allegories. Her woes could be attributed either to the war with England, or to the *jaloux* and *medisans* who typically surround the courtly woman. The *envoi* directed to "Prince" does not resolve the poem's ambiguity, since we have seen that this conventional address could refer to the king, or to the prince called upon to judge a poetic contest. The conflation of a beloved woman and a place, often identified simply with a feminine pronoun, belongs to a lyric tradition reaching back to the troubadours, and it allows Deschamps's poem to signify on multiple levels. The implication that the kingdom lurks behind the courtly lady highlights the affective – even eroticized – bond that unites the poet to France. The kingdom here is a courtly lady, object of the poet's love. Needless to say, the relationship between subject and body politic suggested by a poem such as this one is radically different than the relationship that we observed in ballades based on metaphors. While the latter stressed duty, reciprocity, order, and also integrity, for the subject is incorporated into the body, a poem like Ballade 112 emphasizes affective bonds and alterity, as the subject is situated at a remove from the representation of the polity. We shall see that in other allegorical poems the political body is understood in similarly feminized terms, often ones that emphasize the king's power and authority, and the weakness, dependence, and subservience of the kingdom or city.

As I shall show in connection to two poems that stage the speech of Paris, Deschamps's use of allegory inscribes a political community on the feminine side of a firmly articulated gender binary, while inviting the poem's privileged reading public, the king, to assume the masculine role of judge and authority figure, one who is just and merciful, assures social order, and is the object of his subjects' respectful love. In Ballade 193 nothing within the poem explicitly identifies the lyric voice as that of Paris.[44] In fact, throughout the first two stanzas the reader is not necessarily aware that the first-person poetic voice belongs to a city and not a person. As in the plaint of the Church discussed above, the speaker of Ballade 193 contrasts past and present, but whereas the Church was a victim, the city is to blame for her present "provreté" [poverty] (v. 1), "plour" [cries] (v. 2), and "adversité" [adversity] (v. 3). The speaker's crime is of the most serious nature ("crime commis de lese magesté" [I committed the crime of lèse majesté] [v. 11]), and although her degradation is not a fait accompli, it will become one "Se Pitié n'est, Grace et Misericorde" [if there is no pity, grace, or mercy] (refrain). This poem likely refers to the Maillotin revolts of 1382, which occurred in Paris and other parts of France during the minority of Charles VI and the government of the royal uncles.

The purposeful ambiguity surrounding the identity of the speaker combined with the first-person poetic voice allows for individual readers and inhabitants of the city of Paris to pronounce the words of the city's confession, to admit their wrongs towards their "droit seignour" [rightful lord] (v. 10), who is "chief du regne et la flour" [the head and flower of the kingdom] (v. 12). In this way the city's act of contrition becomes a script or discursive model that may be actualized by any who recognize and repent of their misdeeds towards their lord. The first two stanzas are not grammatically gendered, thereby readily including men among the potential "performers" of the poem.[45] In the third and final stanza the speaker establishes her civic identity and her exemplarity by soliciting the attentive gaze of other cities: "En moy se doit mirer toute cité" [every city should observe itself in me] (v. 17). Hers is a cautionary tale that should be heeded by other cities who might be tempted to rebel against their rightful lords. In this way the utility of her example, which in the first two stanzas provided a confessional script that might be performed or enacted by any reader of the poem, is now carried abroad.

This revelation of poetic identity at the ballade's conclusion inscribes within the very reading of the poem a necessary rereading, and a reinterpretation. That which had been understood according to the letter must now be thought of in allegorical terms. Yet, the first, literal reading is not invalidated, but supplemented by the second. As in the lament of the Church, the literal may be understood in textual terms, by imagining the repentant lyric *je* as an actual woman, or in historical terms, by connecting this *je* to the rebellious inhabitants of Paris, and to the city as a social and political body. By forcing its readers to reread, the poem helps to shape a public that is attentive to the multiple meanings suggested both by texts and by the material world. The imagined perfectibility (or at least improvement) of readers has both socio-political, and soteriological, implications. From the neo-Platonists of late antiquity, to Victorine thinkers such as Hugh of St Victor, to the Pseudo-Dionysian inflected intellectual milieu of late medieval France, and in the works examined in this volume, one sees persistently articulated the idea that careful reading and contemplation can elevate the soul to God and can lead the spiritually striving individual to salvation.[46]

Ballade 385 functions as a clear counterpart to Ballade 193, though here the poem's female speaker is explicitly identified as Paris (see vv. 18–23), and she has a specific addressee: the king. The refrain, "Sire, fay moy grace et misericorde" [Sire, accord me grace and mercy], echoes the pity, grace, and mercy that the city sought in the refrain of Ballade 193, and emphasizes the power of the king to punish or forgive his wayward city. Paris compares herself to other biblical cities, including Nineveh, Babylon, and Gadara – and also to Lucifer, the figure of pride par excellence – thereby inscribing her rebellion in a tradition of disobedience to legitimate authority, and suggesting that the king's power over his city is like that of God over humankind. Paris freely admits her sins (vv. 6, 9, 25, 26), depicting herself as a tearful and repentant "pecheresse" [sinner] (v. 25) who begs for the pity of the king (vv. 20, 33, 36, 41). The *envoi*, directed towards "Prince piteux" [merciful prince], reinforces the authority of the king, and appeals to him as a loving and merciful lord. The theatrical first-person staging of the city's repentance places her guilt beyond doubt, while the collective representation of the city's male and female inhabitants, perpetrators of a rebellion against royal authority, as a tearful, supplicant woman emphasizes their humility and abjection, and invites the king to turn his righteous anger into mercy and forgiveness without any loss of honour.[47]

Thus gendered, Deschamps's allegorical representation of the city is able to serve as an intercessor between the city's real citizens and its king. As I showed in chapter 1, allegory and women are both mediating figures, capable of overcoming distance or difference. Here we observe an example of this phenomenon, as the allegory of Paris plays the social and political role assigned to actual women in, for instance, Christine de Pizan's *Livre des trois vertus*, wherein Christine states that "nature de femme est plus paoureuse et aussi de plus doulce condicion, et pour ce ... estre puet le meilleur moyen a pacifier l'omme, qui soit" [woman's nature is more timid and also softer, and for this reason ... she can be the best means of pacifying man that there is].[48] The tearful lyric *je*, one that is overdetermined in its conventional femininity, both figures the (male and female) inhabitants of Paris and serves as an intermediary on their behalf in an effort to transform civil unrest and rebellion into social order and peace.

Deschamps's allegorical representations of the kingdom function in similarly complex ways. A figure that may be assimilated to France appears in a number of poems scattered throughout Deschamps's corpus, though the specifics of the kingdom's representation are not yet fixed as they will be in the works of later authors.[49] In Ballade 1142 the identity of France is clear from the opening lines, "Douce France, pran en toy reconfort, / Resveille toy, soies de joie plaine" [Sweet France, take comfort, awaken, rejoice] (vv. 1–2). Ballade 1317, in praise of France, opens in a similar way: "O doulz pais, terre treshonourable" [O sweet country, very honourable land] (v. 1). These poems belong to the literary tradition that establishes "douce France" as an object of affection. In Ballade 1142 the poet celebrates the birth of a son to Charles VI, and predicts the child's glorious future. Not only will he restore the kingdom to her original splendour, but he will be crowned emperor, and will lead Christendom against the Saracens. As in Ballade 112, which described the suffering of an unnamed lady, France is depicted as a woman with a specific lack: that of effective leadership. However, in Ballade 112 lack of good government causes the lady's illness, while Ballade 1142 imagines that the infant son of Charles VI will supply this necessity.

In other poems, a figure that might be understood as the kingdom is herself given a voice.[50] In Ballade 141 the first-person poetic voice (never explicitly identified as that of France) regrets the lack of a hero capable of restoring and protecting the kingdom. The refrain laments the passing of Charlemagne and Roland, and the nine worthies are also gone.[51] The second stanza praises the kingship of Alexander, who "ot a justicier / Tout le monde par sa bonne ordonnance" [provided justice to the whole world by means of his good order] (vv. 9–10) and who recognized and rewarded good knights. The third and final stanza, in contrast, criticizes very harshly "Cellui qui doit en moy faire deffense" [he who should defend me] (v. 20). He lacks "vraie congnoissance" [true understanding] (v. 18), is held captive by Deduit or Pleasure (v. 19), and is compared to Roboam, the biblical figure who represented disregard for tradition and for wise counsel. The speaker's anonymity serves a purpose; because the lyric voice is never explicitly identified as that of France, the connection between the individual who has failed to protect the speaker and Charles VI also remains unarticulated.

Ballades 159 and 164 are twinned poems, both of which stage a female lyric voice that has traditionally been understood as that of the kingdom, though this identification is not explicitly made in either poem. In fact, the third-person reference to the kingdom in the refrain of Ballade 159, "Qui jadis fui la lumiere de France" [Who formerly was the light of France], creates a disjunction between the lyric *je* and the kingdom. In Ballade 164, as in the poems studied above, France is never named, and thus the reader can interpret the speaker as an actual woman or, reading allegorically, can imagine the speaker as a representation of the kingdom. The speakers of Ballades 159 and 164 find themselves in nearly identical circumstances. "Povre d'amis, deffaillant de confort" [friendless, lacking comfort] (v. 1) begins the speaker of Ballade 159, while her counterpart describes herself as "Lasse, lasse, chetive et esgarée / Povre d'amis, defaillant de seignour" [Alas, alas, weak and troubled, friendless, lacking a lord] (vv. 1–2). In Ballade 164 the word "seigneur" has replaced "confort" in an otherwise identical verse, thereby showing that the latter is provided by the former. This loss has led to a transformation in the conditions of the speakers, and the contrast between glorious past and turbulent present forms the subject of the opening stanza of each poem. In Ballade 159 the speaker is "Vefve au jour d'ui et dolente orpheline / Pleine de plour et de tout desconfort" [widowed today, and a sorrowful orphan, full of tears and entirely discouraged] (vv. 2–3). She continues describing her troubles in the present tense (vv. 4–7), and her accumulated ills contrast all the more sharply with the nostalgic refrain "jadis fui la lumiere de France." In Ballade 164 the speaker likewise opposes a past in which she was "partout si renommée, / Riche d'avoir, franche et digne d'onnour" [everywhere so renowned, wealthy, free and worthy of honour] (vv. 3–4) to a present which finds her "si plaine de plour / Serve en tous cas et presque anientie" [so full of tears, enslaved in all circumstances and almost destroyed] (vv. 5–6). The temporal indicators "au jour d'ui" and "jadis" mark the passage from one era to the next. It is especially noteworthy that the speaker of Ballade 164 was "franche" (v. 4) in the past, but today finds herself "serve" (v. 6). This transformation signals a loss of identity which is reinforced by the fact that the speaker is never named in the poem. Deprived of her lord, the speaker cannot consider herself *franche*, or *France*, a play on the etymological origins of France, the kingdom of the Franks or the free people.[52]

While the speaker of Ballade 159 looks regretfully towards her past, both in the refrain and in subsequent stanzas, that of Ballade 164 thinks of the future, wondering "Que devendra la dolente esbahie?" [what will become of the sorrowful stunned one] (refrain). As both widows and orphans, the speakers' vulnerability is radically overdetermined. One of the most fundamental obligations of kingship was the protection of the defenceless, epitomized by widows and orphans, yet here the kingdom is herself bereft and abandoned, utterly without protection. Though the speaker of Ballade 164 recognizes how she ought to be treated – "Je deusse estre comme vefve gardée / Et cherie comme la douce flour" [I ought to be protected like a widow, and cherished like the sweet flower] (vv. 9–10) – her use of the subjunctive mood to express her hopes for the future – "Que je sois saigement gouvernée" [that I might be wisely ruled] (v. 19) – indicates that such solicitude is not a foregone conclusion.

The metaphor of the body politic borrowed from, and owed much of its symbolic resonance to, similar metaphors concerning the mystical body of the Church.[53] Deschamps's staging of a female allegory of the kingdom, a widow and orphan who laments the loss of her father, husband, lord, and protector, creates a parallel between this figure and Mary, specifically the *mater dolorosa*, daughter, sister, spouse, and mother of her lord. This allegorization of the kingdom coincides with the rise of the cult of Mary, while the inscription of the kingdom into a set of imaginary familial and domestic relationships parallels the increasing focus on the holy family and Mary's central place within it.[54] Such a depiction presents France as an object of veneration, like the Virgin. The importance of the king or head to the well-being of the kingdom or the body connects these ballades to those that feature metaphors of the body politic. However, the appeal to order and reason that structured the organological poems is here replaced by the tearful lament of the allegorized kingdom. The kingdom's vulnerability and her association with Mary form a powerful emotional appeal to the readers, who are called upon to rescue and protect the worthy and beloved lady France.

The final poems that I will examine are another set of twinned *chansons royales* which combine in extraordinary ways allegorical figures with the organological metaphor for the kingdom. Poems 387 and 388 are both dream visions, a well-established genre in the later Middle Ages, and one closely associated with allegory.[55] One of the Middle Age's most important authorities on dreams was Macrobius, whose commentary on the dream of Scipio was often cited.[56] In his commentary Macrobius discusses not only dreams, but also allegory, or *narratio fabulosa*, and in very similar terms. The latter is appropriate for explorations of certain philosophical truths, while dreams, if they are of the type that "conceals with strange shapes and veils with ambiguity the true meaning of the information being offered ... requires an interpretation for its understanding."[57] As Peter Struck has observed, Macrobius does not feel the need to clarify "whether he considers himself doing literary allegory or divinatory dream interpretation," which shows how little separates the two.[58] This hermeneutic affinity between certain kinds of fictions, and certain kinds of dreams, gave rise to amorous or courtly dream visions, like the thirteenth-century *Roman de la Rose*, and to the political dream visions of the later Middle Ages, such as Philippe de Mézières's *Songe du vieil pelerin* (c. 1389), Honoré Bouvet's (or Bonet's) *Apparition Maître Jean de Meun* (c. 1399), and the *Songe véritable* (1406), not to mention Christine de Pizan's *Livre de l'advision Cristine*, to which we shall turn shortly.

Deschamps's political dream visions – among the first of their kind, and another example of Deschamps's poetic creativity – stage the observations of a narrator figure who witnesses a set of allegorized virtues and vices. In each poem the poet-narrator falls asleep in the opening stanza. In Chanson royale 387 the narrator is sleepy "par trop veiller" [for having stayed up too late] (v. 2), a suggestion that the troubles facing the kingdom have preoccupied him, disrupting his sleep.[59] He falls asleep outside, "prés d'une voie" [near a path] (v. 3), and in this public and liminal space he experiences "une avanture" [an adventure] (v. 4), a term typically associated with romance conventions,[60] but which is often used in dream visions to describe the experience of the dreamer.[61] The opening of Chanson royale

388 is different, though also conventional. The poet, who is already sleeping in the opening verse, is ravished, "ravis" (v. 1), to another kingdom, not unlike Paul, who was granted a vision of God (Acts 9). This allusion to Paul highlights the perceived proximity of the dream vision to the prophetic vision. In this way the dream vision establishes the authority and the authenticity of its content, without, however, attributing it to the poet, who functions as the chosen witness and transmitter of a divinely revealed truth.[62]

In neither poem does the dreaming poet-narrator interact with the figures he encounters; instead, his role is limited first to observing, and then to recording what he has seen and heard. In poem 387 the poet-narrator sees a richly armed figure lying on the ground: "Ce fu un corps, comme de creature, / Qui armez fu richement" [it was a body, as of some creature, which was richly armed] (vv. 5–6). This figure is possessed, as one might expect, of legs, a midriff, arms, and a neck but, as it laments in the refrain, "Riens ne me fault, mais que j'aye bon chief" [I lack for nothing, but that I might have a good head]. This headless knight recalls the fragmented or malformed bodies that populated some of Deschamps's other poems, though here the body is animate. The knight may allude to Charles VI's madness, though without a confirmed date of composition this proposition is speculative. The headless knight could also suggest the minority of Charles VI and the government of the royal uncles, who were each more concerned with their personal advancement than with the administration of the kingdom. In either case, the knight's lack of a head renders it incapable of putting to good use its many resources; though richly endowed with money, land, and people, it lies "comme mort" [as though dead] (v. 15) on the grass. The poet-narrator watches as a sort of political psychomachia unfolds over and on behalf of this figure. The "creature" is beset by the figure of Cowardice, and saved by that of Reason, who enjoins Nature to restore the armed figure's head. Within the dream there is hope and rejoicing as the armed figure rises and vows to satisfy the exhortations of Honour, who has enjoined him to "fais hardiement" [act boldly] (v. 47) and "estre vaillant et brief" [be brave, and promptly so] (49). In the *envoi*, however, pronounced from the perspective of the poet's waking state, the armed figure of the vision is explicitly identified as France, and no such restoration has occurred. In a striking prolongation of the dream, the poet continues to see the figure after he has awoken: "quant je m'esveilloie / Je vy ce corps par lequel figuroie[63] / France" [when I awoke I saw that body by which I represented/figured France] (vv. 52–4). Thus, the headless knight of the dream vision corresponds to the kingdom which the poet-narrator continues to see even after the conclusion of his dream. Salvation lies yet in the future, as the figure intones, "J'aray encor soulas et joye; / Riens ne me fault, mais que j'aye bon chief" [I will yet have solace and joy; I lack for nothing, but that I might have a good head] (vv. 56–7).

In poem 388 the poet-narrator again observes a scene, this time one in which Nature derides ("laidangoit fort" [v. 7]) a "creature" (v. 7) who, like that of poem 387, is tall and comely.[64] However, in spite of his physical and material advantages, this figure, like his counterpart, lacks an essential body part: "J'ay terre et corps, mais je n'ay point de cuer" [I have land and a body, but I have no heart] (refrain). Whereas in Chanson royale 387 Nature, Honour, and Virtue were blamed for that figure's lack of a head, here Nature places the fault squarely on the shoulders of the heartless creature, whom she harangues mercilessly: "tu as sens pour congnoistre et aprendre / Bien et honneur, mais du faire n'as cure" [you have sense in order to know and learn honour and the good, but you don't care to do anything] (vv. 15–16), Nature cries, and so "Pourquoy es tu lasches et desconfis?" [why are you cowardly and discouraged?] (v. 21). The heartless figure, shocked to find himself upbraided thus, "maudisoit ceulz dont il fu nourris, / Qui ont son cuer plus amoli que cendre" [cursed those who raised him, who weakened his heart/courage more than ashes] (vv. 43–4). The outlook is considerably more bleak than in poem 387, for here are no promises of reform on the part of the heartless figure, but only blame for others, and a final remonstrance from Nature: "Use souvent de vaillance la fleur; / Vaillans seras" [make use of the flower of bravery, and you will be worthy] (vv. 48–9). In the *envoi* the poet-narrator, now awake, reflects upon "ce debat en mon memoire mis" [this quarrel put into my memory] (v. 52), and concludes that "dire puet maint hault homs qui est vis: / J'ay terre et corps, mais je n'ay point de cuer" [many a noble man alive can say "I have land and a body, but I have no heart"] (vv. 55–6). As noted previously, the poet-narrator seems to hesitate before providing too close an identification between the heartless body and the king or kingdom, perhaps because of the very harsh criticisms Nature levels at the "creature." Moreover, the passivity and laziness of the "creature" are shared by "maint hault homs," suggesting that the ills facing the kingdom are not wholly of the king's making, but reflect a general dereliction of duty on the part of the entire knightly class.[65]

In these two remarkable dream visions Deschamps combines aspects of the organological metaphor with the allegorization of the kingdom.[66] The poet-narrator insists upon the very bodily presence of the figures in each poem by referring to them not as people, but as "corps," and by enumerating their body parts.[67] The many poems that forge links between the kingdom and the human body invite us to understand the malformed bodies of Chansons royales 387 and 388 as metaphorical representations of the kingdom, though here the human bodies which can be understood to represent the body politic are animated as though they were living individuals; they are clothed and armed, rendered capable of speech and movement. In this respect Deschamps's dream visions resemble Ballade 278, in which the allegorized Church complained of her ailing physical – and metaphorical – body. However, the gender dynamic that we have observed in many of Deschamps's allegorical poems, in which the Church, France, or Paris are cast in conventional feminized roles such as beloved, intercessor, or victim, functions quite differently here. The allegorical figures of pieces 387 and 388 are both identified, through the use of masculine pronouns and adjectives, as male, inviting us perhaps to interpret them as allegories of the king rather than the kingdom, although the narrator of Chanson 387 states that the body in the poem "figuroie / France" (vv. 53–4).[68] The use of masculine allegorical figures represents a departure from allegorical conventions, and reminds us that the staging of female allegories is not a phenomenon to be chalked up to grammar, but a choice whose implications must be interrogated.

An important difference between Deschamps's masculine and feminine representations of the kingdom concerns the question of accountability. The male figures of Chansons 387 and 388 are upbraided, held responsible for the state of their kingdoms, while the female figures of Ballades 159 and 164 are cast as victims of abandonment through death or disregard. The other allegorical figures featured in the dream visions, such as Reason, Honour, and Nature, push the knight-kingdoms to act, while the female allegories of the kingdom themselves serve as instruments to instigate action on the part of the poems' publics, including and especially the king.

It is quite striking to observe that these masculine representations of the kingdom did not give rise to literary posterity, as the feminine representations did. I contend that the weakness and apathy of the malformed knight-kingdoms put into question an essential component of masculine chivalric identity, and may have provoked unease among Deschamps's reading public. In contrast, the vulnerability of the female allegories of the kingdom accords with medieval gender conventions, which declared women to be frail and fearful, and these allegories were able to inspire compassion and protectiveness in a masculine (knightly) public, while confirming their own strength and power.

The richness and complexity of Deschamps's ideas concerning the nature of the political community, the relationships that governed its various components, and the place of the king within this system made him a productive point of reference for his contemporaries and successors. He provided a lasting legacy in the form of his remarkable literary creativity. Deschamps's adaptation of the conventions of courtly love poetry to the political realm, his exploitation of the possibilities inherent in the *envoi*, his use of dialogue, of prosopopeia, of the allegorical dream vision, and not least his creation of the dramatic and vivid beloved, France, would prove to be fertile ground for his successors. Among the many possibilities Deschamps provided for thinking and talking about the kingdom, those upon which his successors would seize and dramatically expand are the dream vision and the idea of France as a mother.

The dream vision is the basis, as we have seen, for two of Deschamps's most fascinating ballades, and provides the framework for representations of France found in Christine de Pizan (to be discussed presently), Alain Chartier, and Jean Juvénal des Ursins (both examined in chapter 4). The significance later accorded France's maternity, however, has cause to surprise us, for France's motherhood is hardly a central aspect of her representation in Deschamps. The idea of France's marriage, which is established by her widowhood in Ballades 159 and 164, provides the possibility that she might be envisioned as a mother. France's potential maternity is realized in at least two other poems in which she mentions or addresses her children. In Ballade 255 the voice of the kingdom refers to her children who "chascun veult par force estre mon hoir" [each one wants by force to become my heir] (v. 22), suggesting that her offspring are the king and princes of the blood who are struggling for control of the kingdom, while in Ballade 1430 she begs: "Tous mes enfans, vueillez a ce [i.e., the imminent danger in which the kingdom finds itself] penser" [my children, do think of this] (v. 29). Here "mes enfans" seems to refer more broadly to all of the French subjects, each of whom can do his or her part to support and safeguard the kingdom. Beyond these rather oblique references France does not specify the identity of her children, or engage in dialogue with them, and within the confines of the text France's relationship to her children goes largely undeveloped. Responsibility for her present condition is only implicitly attributed to them. What is noteworthy about France's children is the fact that they are not presented as allegories – they are not, for instance, Discord, Selfishness, and Pride – but *people*. France's children, then – understood variously as the princes of the blood, nobles, or all the subjects of the kingdom – are also, potentially, her readers. In this manner Deschamps's allegorized France reaches out of the pages of his manuscript directly to her public. She lays claim to kinship with them, and it is on the basis of this relationship that France demands their loyalty and their aid. Christine de Pizan recognized the immense rhetorical potential of this affective relationship between France and her children/readers, and she vastly expanded the role of France's children, and that of the narrator as the chosen child – and voice – of the kingdom.

Christine de Pizan, *poeta theologus*

Christine de Pizan was born c. 1365 in Italy, and at a young age she moved with her family to the French court of King Charles V (r. 1364–80), where her father, Thomas de Pizan, had been named royal physician and astrologer.[69] Christine, like Deschamps, represents the reign of Charles V as a golden age. Following the deaths of her husband and father, Christine turned to study and writing, in part as a form of consolation, and in part from financial necessity. In the early years of the fifteenth century she took an active role in the so-called quarrel of the *Romance of the Rose*, an exchange of letters among a set of well-known intellectuals, including Jean Gerson (see chapter 3), the chancellor of the University of Paris, who shared Christine's low opinion of the *Rose*, and the royal secretaries Jean de Montreuil (see chapter 4) and Gontier Col, and the canon of Notre Dame de Paris, Pierre Col, who supported the famous work.[70] In 1402 Christine assembled the documents associated with the quarrel into a manuscript which she presented to queen Isabeau. Christine's presence among such illustrious company, and the publicity that she herself accorded the quarrel, propelled her to the forefront of the intellectual public stage.[71]

In the quarrel Christine took issue with the *Rose*'s misogyny, as well as with Jean de Meun's dangerous use of allegory. In Christine's view, his disordered jumbling of good and ill, truth and lies, was more harmful than a text that one might denounce in its entirety. In a letter to Pierre Col Christine says that if the champion of Jean de Meun wishes to hear theology spoken of "plus prouffitablement, plus poetiquement et de plus grant efficasse, lis le livre que on appelle le Dante ... la oyras autre propos mieux fondé plus subtilment, ... et ou tu pourras plus prouffiter que en ton Romant de la Rose, – et cent fois mieux composé ; ne il n'y a comparison" [more profitably, more poetically, and more effectively, read the book that people call the Dante ... there you will hear other speeches, better and more carefully founded, ... and whence you might profit more than from your Roman de la Rose – and a hundred times better written, without comparison] (142).

In this section I shall argue that, in addition to this praise of Dante's *Commedia*, and the systematic critique of Jean de Meun carried out in the letters of the quarrel, Christine also provides her *own* corrective to Jean de Meun's misuse of allegorical language in her *Livre de l'advision Cristine*. Allegorical narrative, in Christine's hands, is both a politically constructive and a salvific discourse, and we shall see that Dante's works and his poetics provide an important point of reference throughout the *Advision*. As I shall show, Christine refers directly to the *Commedia* at key moments in her text, and develops what we might call a Dantean hermeneutics, in order to advance and authorize her own poetic claims and to create a powerful allegorical figure capable of filling the void left by the absent Charles VI.

The *Livre de l'advision Cristine* is a three-part allegorical dream vision in which the narrator travels to the "maistre cité" [master city] (15) of a prosperous kingdom, called "la seconde Athenes" [the second Athens] (15).[72] Part one of the *Advision* features a lengthy dialogue between the narrator and the princess of this kingdom, called Libera, in which the latter recounts her history. In part two the narrator visits the "noble université" [noble university] (51), where she speaks to a figure comprised of an apparently infinite number of individual shadows, who reveals herself to be Dame Opinion. In the final part of the *Advision* the narrator finds her way to the highest and most secluded part of the University, where she enters into conversation with Philosophy. A new Boethius, the narrator first recounts her sorrows and misfortunes, and then is comforted by Philosophy, who, in the conclusion, is addressed as Holy Theology.

The *Advision* is what I call an auto-exegetical text,[73] one that simultaneously narrates and glosses the narrator's allegorical journey, and that invites reflection on both the theory and the practice of allegory. Christine explains her approach to allegory in the preface that appears in one of the three known surviving manuscripts of the *Advision*, ex-Phillipps 128.[74] Entitled *Glose sur la premiere partie de ce present volume* [Gloss on the first part of this present work] (3), this preface is explicitly directed towards the interpretation of part one of the *Advision*; however, it invites us to think about Christine's understanding of allegory and of poetry with respect to the entire *Advision*, and indeed vis-à-vis her allegorical production as a whole. Christine imagines those readers who might wish to clarify ("declairier") what she has written "soubz figures" [by means of figures] in the first part of her book, and who might wish to interpret

> selon la maniere de parler des pouetes, que souventesfois soubz figure de methaphore, c'est a dire de parole couverte, sont muciees maintes secretes sciences et pures veritez. Et en telle parolle dicte par poisie puet avoir mains entendements, et lors est la poisie belle et soubtille quant elle puet servir a plusieurs ententes a que on la puet prendre a divers propos. (3)
>
> [according to the poets' way of speaking, for often under the figure of metaphor, that is to say, covered words, are hidden many secret sciences and pure truths. And in such a word pronounced by poetry there can be many understandings, and then the poetry is beautiful and subtle, when it can serve several meanings and one can understand it in different ways]

Christine does not define poetry by formal features such as verse, but rather by its semantics, and in particular its deployment of figural language, or "figure de methaphore."[75] In poetry, meaning is cloaked or hidden, perhaps, as Isidore of Seville proposes, in order to "exercise the reader's understanding, and lest the subjects grow common from being stripped bare and obvious."[76] In defining poetry in semantic and hermeneutic rather than formal terms, Christine situates herself within an important late medieval literary and intellectual current, according to which, as Sarah Kay and Adrian Armstrong have shown "*poetrie* [is] broadly understood as a style of writing that relies on *figural* complexity, and is potentially expressive of *philosophical* meaning."[77] In addition, Christine identifies polyvalent poetic language as a source of aesthetic pleasure, in contradistinction to Dante, who, in his *Convivio*, defines beauty as a compensatory quality of poetry available to those for whom meaning is obscure.[78]

Though she insists upon the aesthetic and philosophical value of multiplicity of meaning, Christine does not allow her readers complete hermeneutic latitude. On the contrary, as we saw in chapter 1, in her preface she shows her readers how the various elements of book one of the *Advision* may be understood with respect to the individual, the kingdom, and the cosmos. This demonstration of productive hermeneutic activity guides her readers in interpreting the entire text according to the threefold schema Christine provides.

Part one of the *Advision* begins with a Dantean reference that invites Christine's readers to think about her text in relation to that of her predecessor: "Ja passé avoye la moitié de mon pelerinage" [already I had passed the midpoint of my pilgrimage] (11), a clear nod to the opening verse of the *Commedia*, "Nel mezzo del cammin di nostra vita."[79] The narrator then retires to bed; "Et comme tost aprés, mes sens liez par la pesanteur de somme, me survenist merveilleuse advision en signe d'estrange presage, tout ne soie mie Nabugodonozor, Scipion ne Joseph" [and soon afterwards, my senses bound by the weight of sleep, there came upon me a marvellous vision in the form of a strange prophecy, albeit I am not Nebuchadnezzar, Scipio, or Joseph] (11–12). The distinction between the waking world and the realm of the dream vision cues the reader to interpret the text allegorically, while the words "advision" and "presage" mark the narrator's experience as a true one.[80] The narrator's protest of unworthiness again points to Dante the pilgrim who, when informed of his otherworldly itinerary, cries "Io non Enëa, io non Paolo sono" [I am not Aeneus, I am not Paul] (Inf. 2.32). In fact, the *Advision*'s narrator is suggesting precisely that she *is* like Nebuchadnezzar, Scipio, and Joseph, while the allusion to Dante's words to Virgil signals the important relationship that will be developed between the poetics of the *Advision* and those of the *Commedia.* While the figures cited by Dante were people who had made otherworldly journeys, the figures referenced by Christine are ones known for their prophetic dreams. Nebuchadnezzar, although he had a prophetic dream, was unable to interpret it, and consequently his vision is of an inferior sort, according to the hierarchy of visions laid out by Augustine in his *Literal Meaning of Genesis.* Indeed, Nebuchadnezzar is cited by Augustine as an example of a person who sees images in his imagination but who lacks understanding.[81] The dream of Scipio is recounted at the end of book 6 of Cicero's *De re publica.* In this dream, Scipio meets his grandfather, who reveals to him both his personal and political future. The book concludes with Scipio's awakening, but with no interpretation, either by Scipio or by another figure. The dream would have to await Macrobius and his famous commentary to achieve semantic clarity. Finally Joseph, whose dreams and dream interpretations are narrated in Genesis, provides an example of one whose visions are sent by God, and who both sees and understands. The visionaries to whom Christine compares, and yet distinguishes, herself, are inscribed in a hierarchy, in which she, as we shall see, appears favourably. Thus, in this passage Christine establishes herself and her visionary text in relation to Dante and his *Commedia*, while marking the difference that separates her from her illustrious forebear and compatriot.

In her vision, the narrator seeks out and becomes the confidante of "une princesse de grant auctorité couronnee de precieux dyademe a septre royal de grant ancienneté et richesce" [a princess of great authority crowned with a precious diadem and holding a royal sceptre of great age and richness] (15) who calls herself Libera, and who rules over the second Athens.[82] Unlike the narrator/scribe of Deschamps's dream vision ballades, who was a detached observer, the narrator of the *Advision* remains at the centre of the text, the principal character and the privileged interlocutor of the allegorical figures she will encounter. The relationship between the narrator and Libera, who are placed in parallel with one another, is an affective one that makes possible the verbal exchange that the narrator records in part one.[83] The crowned princess enjoins the narrator to become the "antigraphe de ses aventures" [recorder of her adventures] (16),[84] and consequently Libera's harsh denunciation of her children corresponds to what Macrobius calls the oracular dream, one in which an authoritative figure transmits truths to the dreamer that otherwise would be unavailable to her.[85]

The figure of Libera owes a clear debt to Deschamps, whom Christine may well have met through her family connections to the royal court and chancery.[86] As in Deschamps, the crowned lady is a tearful victim who laments her present troubles, contrasting them to her glorious past. Yet unlike Deschamps's figure of France, Libera is depicted as a maternal being who solicits the sympathy and aid of her children.[87] As we shall see, Libera's maternity allows Christine to reimagine the relationships between the members of a political community. The bonds of affection and the duties of protection and loyalty upon which the mother–child relationship was predicated are deployed here in favour of the kingdom. In addition, King Charles VI, the head of the metaphorical body politic, is displaced by the kingdom itself, given form, coherence, and unity by the moving allegorical figure of Libera.

Libera begins her story with her descent from a golden tree which was uprooted, but whose branches and shoots were preserved and transplanted in other locations, including one plant which "parcruit tant que de la beauté d'elle je pris mon nom et fus 'Libera' appellé" [grew such that from its beauty I took my name and was called Libera] (18). The golden tree recalls the golden bough that granted Aeneus access to the underworld, and to privileged knowledge of the afterlife and the future. Despite her youthful appearance Libera has a long history, and she describes its ups and downs using metaphors of gardens and cultivation, from an early king who bore a "fruit de grant digneté" [fruit of great worth] (18) to an unfortunate period of care under "cultiveurs mau diligens" [less diligent gardeners] (19).[88] Finally, Libera describes her recent past, including her premature widowhood following the death of the "tres saige amenistreur" [very wise administrator] (23), a clear reference to Charles V, and concluding in the present, which is characterized by "erreur" [error], "pestillence" [pestilence], and "yre et contens" [anger and strife] (25).

Having concluded her personal history, which, in accordance with the hermeneutic directives laid out in the preface, may also be understood as the history of the kingdom, Libera then articulates her views on maternal duty. The two principal obligations of this role, as she presents it, are to love one's children, and to pursue their well-being. What "cuer de mere" [mother's heart] (25), she asks, would not suffer to see her legitimate and beloved children fight?; and what is more, to see her attempts at intervention, unlike those of the Sabine women, spurned such that the children "debrisent et mahagnent" [break and wound] (25) their own mother? The violent conflict between Libera's children, with its disastrous effects for the kingdom, would have suggested to Christine's readers the enmity between Louis d'Orléans and Jean sans peur, brother and cousin of King Charles VI, who were locked in a contest for political supremacy.[89] Libera's inability to (re)establish peace between her children is, she affirms, the "supellative des douleurs" [greatest of sorrows] (26),[90] for she has failed to fulfil the very intercessory and peacemaking roles that Christine de Pizan assigns, in other of her writings, to women.[91] Here, the love owed to mothers, and their powers of mediation, are presented as even greater than those of ordinary women, thereby making Libera's unsuccessful efforts to restore harmony all the more painful. "Lasse! lasse!" Libera cries, "je suis celle mere amere" [Alas, alas! I am that bitter mother] (26).

Christine's depiction of the body politic as a female, maternal body has important political and cultural consequences. Mothers were conventionally expected to be honoured by their children and within society.[92] Here, Libera's children may be identified in limited terms as the princes of the blood, or in broad terms as the French people. In both cases, imagining Libera as a maternal figure imposes a bond of natural love among her children, and between the children/subjects and the kingdom. Ernst Kantorowicz has observed that after the advent of Christianity, dying for the *patria* lost the religious flavour it had enjoyed in classical Rome, and he describes the process of sacralization of the body politic by which the notion of *patria* was gradually reinvested with emotional content.[93] In the *Advision* Christine de Pizan takes a different route than that charted by Kantorowicz, though, I would argue, towards a similar end. The relationality suggested by structures of kinship allows for the exploration, and potentially the redefinition, of relationships within the political community. The bonds – of affection, loyalty, gratitude, honour – that are supposed to link mothers and children are deployed here on behalf of the kingdom in order to prescribe the feelings and conduct that (ought to) join subjects to their kingdom, for it is not only mothers who have duties – children do as well.

If Libera has failed in her feminine and maternal duty to reconcile her children, they have likewise neglected to honour and respect her as good children ought. Indeed, they have not simply disregarded, but have actively injured their mother. In a demonstration of her own victimization, Libera lifts the edge of her robe to reveal "les costez blans et tendres par force de presse et de deffoulement noircis et betez et par lieux encavez jusques aux entrailles, non mie trenchiez de coups d'espee maiz froissiez par force de grans foules" [the white flanks, made tender by the pressure of the crowd and blackened and beaten from trampling underfoot, and in places caved in as far as the innards, not cut by blows from a sword, but broken by the force of great crowds] (26).[94] Like Christ commanding Thomas to touch his side (John 20:19–29), Libera displays the physical evidence of her persecution in order verify its existence, so unbelievable is the conduct of her children. The radical opposition between Libera's refined and beautiful exterior and her naked body, bruised and disfigured, reinforces the opposition between the treatment that Libera merits and that she actually receives. Moreover, the disjuncture between interior and exterior, meaning and form, what is covered and what is revealed, invisible and visible, allows Libera to figure the operation of allegory itself. Christine-narrator is one of the elect readers able to penetrate Libera's spiritual (in the sense of non-literal) meaning and to understand the (moral and political) truth that she incarnates. The meaning of Libera, and its implications for her reading public, are communicated in the *Advision*.

Horrified by the shameful sight of Libera's battered flanks, the narrator can only reply "Dame, pour Dieu, couvrez cheus" [Lady, by God, cover them]. The narrator's sickened reaction to this evidence of abuse on the part of Libera's own children provides a model for her reading public, who ought to be similarly repulsed by this treatment of their "mother," France. After the revelation of her children's ill treatment, Libera further details their misconduct and predicts God's eventual retribution for their misdeeds. Yet despite their brutal disregard for her, Libera, "naturellement ... amoureuse de sa porteure" [naturally ... loving her offspring] (39), continues to desire their well-being. Libera's own maternal love enables her to turn the other cheek, thereby further highlighting the degree to which her children act unnaturally.

Given the significance accorded to Libera's motherhood, it is surprising that her children are absent from the text.[95] They are not present even as auditors to her reproaches, much less as respondents. Indeed, their very identity is vague. In how broad or restricted a sense are Libera's children meant to be understood? as the French subjects? the nobility? the princes of the blood? This ambiguity allows Libera's reproaches to apply to anyone who does not honour and protect Libera as they ought. Given the "presse" held responsible for Libera's injuries, it would seem that this group is quite numerous. Libera's "real" children, a violent, faceless crowd, reminiscent perhaps of those Christine witnessed during the popular rebellions that periodically shook Paris, stand in contrast to the figure of the narrator, who comes to occupy the place of Libera's good child.

The revelation of Libera's motherhood precipitates a profound shift in her relationship to the narrator. The distance which had marked their initial encounter, in which the renowned princess favoured the humble foreigner with her attention, has closed. No longer simply the lady's scribe, charged with recording her history, the narrator has become Libera's "bonne nourrie" (26), a suggestive expression that lends itself to a variety of interpretations. The verb "nourrir" can be employed in the context of child-rearing and systems of fosterage common among noble families. The term can also bear connotations of patronage or mentorship. Deschamps, for instance, refers to himself as the "nourry" of Guillaume de Machaut (Ballade 447). While he might have financed Deschamps's education, Machaut's support may have been limited to encouragement of the younger poet's literary undertakings. Used in this sense, the word suggests a relationship of nurture and protection, on one hand, and gratitude and affection, on the other, similar to the ideal of the parent–child relationship. Finally, the term "nourrie" implies physical nourishment, and in this way connects to Libera's metaphors of cultivation. Libera is a kind of earth mother, whose bounty has nourished the narrator and enabled her to thrive, and the idea of Libera as representative of a political entity – the kingdom – is thereby grounded in a geographic and material reality. The expression "bonne nourrie" is used to distinguish the narrator from those Libera calls her children, for the narrator, though "mie du fruit de ma terre" [not of the fruit of my land] possesses a heart "de noble nature, non ingrate des biens que y a receuz" [of a noble nature, not ungrateful for the good it has received there] (26).

The failure of what is presented as the biological kinship that unites Libera and her children to preserve peace or to create cohesion may be understood in relation to the events of the early fifteenth century, which demonstrated the inadequacy of consanguinity as a stable foundation for political relationships or action. At the same time, the presence of the narrator, Libera's "bonne nourrie," creates and defines a model of imaginary kinship capable of supplementing or replacing the imperfect connections forged by blood. The narrator is the ideal child – or subject – of the kingdom, one who is grateful for her "mother's" bounty, and anxious to promote her well-being. In this way the narrator provides an exemplum of political conduct for her public.

At the same time, the representation of Libera as a mother substitutes the kingdom for the king as the appropriate object of the subjects'/children's reverence and loyalty. In fourteenth-century manuscripts of the *Avis aus roys* and in Nicole Oresme's *Livre d'Ethiques*, the king is represented using the iconography of the Madonna of Mercy, sheltering the French beneath his outstretched outer garment. As Michael Camille has pointed out, this image "depicts not just the king as guardian of his people but as administrating and containing an envelope of a space – the kingdom of France."[96] In the *Advision* this notion of a maternal and protective king, one whose visual representation also suggests the space of the kingdom, has been displaced by the allegorical representation of the kingdom, figured in feminine, and specifically maternal, terms. The historical "absences" of Charles VI, like the textual absence of the king from the *Advision*, allow Christine to develop an alternative site and mechanism for the production of political and social identity. Through the figure of Libera Christine provides her public with the means to preserve unity despite the centrifugal forces at work in the kingdom, and the kinship she creates through language displaces the biological kinship which has so manifestly failed to preserve political harmony.

The three levels or modes of interpretation – individual, political, and spiritual – that Christine discussed and demonstrated in her preface, allow her to further explore the potential of a kinship imagined in relation to the public and spiritual realms. Just as Libera's story may be interpreted as pertaining to an individual noble woman, or to the kingdom of France, so too Christine's own autobiography, recounted in book three, may be interpreted on multiple levels. In the final book of the *Advision* Lady Philosophy reminds the narrator that the three most prized earthly goods are noble ancestors – "laquelle noblesce je tiens des vertus" [by which nobility I mean of virtues] (120), Philosophy quickly specifies – a sound and healthy body, and moral, God-fearing children, all three of which Christine possesses. The three prized goods mentioned by Philosophy – lineage, health, and progeny – may each be understood precisely on the three levels identified in the prologue. According to this interpretive schema lineage can refer to one's personal ancestors, one's forefathers, or one's spiritual genealogy; health to one's physical body, the body politic, or the mystical body of the Church; and god-fearing progeny to the members of the Church militant, the political subject, and the spiritually striving soul. I propose that the successful maternity exemplified by Christine in book three has both political and soteriological implications, providing her readers with an image of the ideal subject, and directing them towards the political conduct that would lead the soul to salvation.[97]

At first it appears that Christine's use of allegory in part one of the *Advision*, of the things she has written "soubz figures," corresponds to what one might call an integumental poetics, or the so-called allegory of the poets, in which fictions or *fabulae* contain or conceal a hidden truth.[98] Within this framework the story of the crowned princess would constitute a fiction or fabulous narrative by means of which one might nonetheless recognize certain moral truths pertaining to the kingdom of France (or to the individual or the cosmos). However, the story of Libera is presented to the reader not as *fabula*, but as *historia*, one which, like the true histories of the Bible, conveys a true sense that is different from its literal or apparent sense. Libera's story thus corresponds to what Bernard Silvestris calls allegory, or what Auerbach refers to as figura or typology.[99]

Libera performs an exegesis of her own history, systematically relating her history to Scripture in ways that reveal her experiences to be a fulfilment of God's word. In chapter 17, for instance, Libera refers to Daniel's interpretation of the dream of Nebuchadnezzar. The dream begins with a tree so tall and grand that its outstretched branches touch the heavens and extend to all parts of the world.[100] In the dream the tree is filled with fruit and birds, and beasts of all sorts are gathered below it. A voice is heard which says that the tree must be cut down and its branches stripped off. Libera explains that the biblical tree of Nebuchadnezzar's dream "segnefie les enflez devant dis tres puissans qui sont logiez es haulz dongions de ma terre recevent le vent de perdicion" [signifies the aforementioned puffed up ones, the very powerful who are lodged in the high towers of my land receiving the wind of perdition] (32), and she predicts their downfall and humiliation. In chapter 18 Libera says that the woman who has lulled her handmaiden, Chivalry, to sleep was seen by Zechariah in a prophetic vision. She summarizes Zechariah's vision and relates each of its elements to her own story. These examples are not isolated, for Libera continues to link her story to prophecies from the Bible and to episodes from sacred history.[101] In this way Libera's history constitutes a fulfilment of Old Testament events and prophecies, and consequently Libera's own prophecies for her "children" partake of the authority of Scripture.[102]

The truth of Libera's story is also founded upon the authority of lived experience. At the end of the scene in which Libera recounts her history, culminating in the revelation of her sorrowful maternity, the narrative perspective shifts back to the narrator, who declares "je vy ... sa belle chiere, qui estre souloit clere, fresche et coulouree, toute destainte et noircie" [I saw ... her fair countenance, which used to be clear, fresh, and rosy, all discoloured and darkened] (26). The narrator's interjection and her use of the verb "vy" reminds the reader that the *Advision* purports to be an eyewitness account, that is to say, one based upon experience. Libera is anxious to prove to her *antigraphe* the truth of her narrative. It is quite remarkable in fact that Libera is worried about confirming the authenticity of *her* account, while the true and prophetic nature of Christine's *Advision* is never placed in doubt. Libera repeatedly highlights the importance of visual perception as the basis for experiential knowledge, and hence for the apprehension of truth. Indeed, Libera displays her wounded body precisely so that "experience te face certainne de la verité de mes narracions" [experience might make you certain of the truth of my account], and she directs the narrator to "regarde et avise les plaies de mes costez et de mes membres" [observe and consider the wounds of my flanks and my limbs] (26). Later, before showing the narrator the imprisoned figures Reason, Justice, and Knighthood (Chevalerie), Libera explains that "que mieulx me croies, vueil que le sens de ta veue ait experience du vray de ma parole" [so that you might better believe me, I want your sense of sight to have the experience of the truth of my words] (29–30), thereby connecting vision, experience, and truth.

When Libera points out the figure of Fraud, who has imprisoned Reason, the narrator cries out, "Ha! desloial ennemie de verité, qui cy t'a menee? Ne te vid pas en fourme d'orrible serpent a longue queue jadis le tres saige pouete Dant de Florence sus les palus d'enfer quant la le convoia Virgile" [Ah! disloyal enemy of truth, who has led you here? Did not the very wise poet Dante of Florence see you in the form of a horrible serpent with a long tail in the swamp of hell when Virgil conveyed him there?] (30). This allusion to Geryon directs the reader to a key moment in the *Commedia*, for the appearance of the beast, the "imagine di froda" [image of fraud] (Inf. 17, 7), at the midpoint of the *Commedia* moves Dante to address his readers, swearing to them "per le note / di questa comedìa" [by the notes of this comedy] (Inf. 16, 127–8), just as one might swear on the Bible, that he beheld this marvellous creature.[103] The figure of Geryon in the *Commedia* is not presented as a fictive veil which conceals a hidden truth. Rather, Dante insists upon the monster's referential and physical reality or truth. It is precisely this moment that led Charles Singleton famously to declare that the principal fiction of the *Commedia* is that it is not a fiction.[104] Whether one agrees with this interpretation or not,[105] it is certain in any case that Dante's poetics made (and continue to make) possible a set of conversations about what is possible for poetry, whether poetry is able to signify in the manner of Scripture, and what the relationship might be of truth to fiction, allegory to fraud, the literal to the spiritual. It is the difficulty of navigating these waters, I would argue, that makes Dante's text of enduring and intense interest to its readers, and these are the questions that Christine likewise raises and explores in her *Advision*.

We see then that Libera's story functions typologically with respect to Scripture, and that throughout her narrative Libera "establishes a connection between two events or persons, the first of which signifies not only itself but also the second, while the second encompasses or fulfills the first."[106] In addition, the *Advision* itself, the interaction between Libera and the narrator, is presented as the product of vision and of experience, and consequently as true. Sacred history, the history of the crowned princess, and the visionary experience of the narrator, are all connected. By showing the typological connection between Libera's history and Scripture and by insisting on the status of the vision as lived experience, Christine is not just imagining or reflecting upon moral truths that she imparts in the form of a poetic allegory. Like Dante, she is suggesting, at the very least, that her allegorical narrative functions scripturally or theologically.[107]

Christine's reformulation of allegory and her self-presentation as a divinely sanctioned prophetic voice are not limited to part one of the *Advision*. In the university setting of part two the narrator encounters a second allegorical lady, identified as Opinion.[108] Dame Opinion explains that she is the source of both knowledge and error, and it is she who causes humans to "haïr et amer sans cause" [to hate and to love without cause] (56). Indeed Libera, who does not blame her children for their actions, attributes their discord to their mistaken opinions (1: 14, lines 52–67). Even intelligent and well-intentioned thinkers are sometimes mistaken in their beliefs, and to illustrate this point Dame Opinion reviews for the narrator the early philosophers' theories about the origins of the world. This section, beginning in chapter 6 and concluding in chapter 13, is a translation and adaptation of Thomas Aquinas's *Metaphysicorum Aristotelis Expositio*.[109] This scholarly tour de force allows Christine to demonstrate to a potentially doubting public her considerable erudition.[110] Those who wish to know more about the ancient philosophers, Opinion says, can read Aristotle's *Metaphysics* for themselves, but "comme la matiere soit obscure, de ce atant souffise ... soient ycestes choses ou tresor de ton volume reservees aux hommes scienceux de soubtil entendement, et passent oultre les moins expers aux choses plus legieres et communes" [as the subject is difficult, let this suffice ... may these things be reserved in the treasure house of your volume for knowledgeable men of subtle understanding, and may those who are less expert pass them by in favour of things that are lighter and more common] (74–5).[111] Christine's choice of text and specific passage to adapt is not gratuitous, for the section of the *Metaphysics* that she incorporates into the *Advision* contains important reflections on the relationship of poetry to philosophy and on the status of the theologian-poets.[112] As Ernst Curtius has pointed out, the Middle Ages did not know Aristotle's *Poetics* and had access to his theories of poetry only via the *Metaphysics*.[113] It is precisely these views, I propose, that interest Christine.

As part of her discussion of ancient philosophy and first causes, Opinion examines the beliefs of Thales, who was one of the seven sages, "qui plus proprement furent dis theologiens pouetes" [who more properly were called theologian-poets] (61).[114] Opinion highlights the superiority of Thales, who alone "se transporta a considerer les causes et les principes des choses, les autres seulement demourez occupez es morales sciences" [was moved to consider the causes and the origins of things, the others remaining occupied only with moral sciences] (61), and who believed that water was the generative principle of all things. Thales so believed, Opinion says, "par l'auctorité des anciens" [based on the authority of the ancients], and in particular the opinion of those "pouetes theologisans" [theologizing poets] (63) who had preceded him. Opinion explains that poet-theologians were "ainsi dis poetes, car de ce qu'ilz disoient ils formoient dictiez et parloient saintement, theologisans aussi, qu'ilz parloient des dieux et des choses divines" [thus called poets because of what they said they formed poems and they spoke in a saintly manner, theologizing also, for they spoke of the gods and of divine things] (63). Some scholars have interpreted "theologiens pouetes" as a limited, or a limiting, category, one which accounts for the errors of the so-called ancient philosophers who, unlike Aristotle, were not true philosophers but only theologian-poets.[115] I propose instead that Christine redeems this category by showing that inasmuch as the early philosophers erred it was not because they were poets, but because they "semblent philosophes et sont hors de verité" [seem to be philosophers but are outside of the truth] (65). They are not to be condemned for their errors, however. As Opinion tells the narrator, inasmuch as these poets and philosophers "des sciences les portes vous ouvrirent, vous les devez excuser, amer et supporter" [opened the doors of knowledge to you, you should excuse, love, and support them] (64).

This passage, together with the preface in which Christine defined poets as those who spoke "soubz figure de methaphore" of "secretes sciences et pures veritez" (3), constitutes a powerful valorization of poetry as a discourse that is capable of transmitting the highest truths, and in particular of what Christine has here called theologizing poetry, or the works of the poet-theologians. It is particularly striking that Christine's defence of poetry unfolds within an adaptation of a text by one of poetry's principal detractors. For Aquinas poetry was an "infima scientia."[116] Indeed, in a passage preceding the one Christine translates (to which she pointedly does not allude), Aquinas details the metaphysical errors promulgated by poets, concluding that "poetae non solum in hoc, sed in multis aliis mentiuntur" [poets not only in this, but in many others things lie] (1, 3, 61–2). Thus, Christine is not only translating the Doctor Universalis, she is effecting a radical realignment of his thought such that it appears to support her own views on poetry. In composing her *Advision* Christine provides a corrective to the deficiencies of the early "theologiens pouetes." Like them she speaks "soubz figure de methaphore" and "saintement" of divine things. Establishing herself as a poet-theologian allows Christine to claim for poetry – and the poet – the right to take on the highest philosophical, moral, and theological subjects. In addition, her use of this term situates Christine at the heart of a fourteenth-century debate over the relationship of poetry to theology, and inscribes her in an intellectual and literary genealogy that includes Dante.[117]

Unlike the ancient philosophers, Christine's philosophy wears the face of theology, and her writings are illuminated by the divine truth of Scripture. In the final chapter of the *Advision* the narrator effects a kind of displacement of Philosophy by Holy Theology.[118] Though in the beginning of her thanks to lady Philosophy the narrator calls her "l'armoire et corps de toutes sciences, lesquelles sont tes membres" [the container and the body of all sciences, which are your limbs] (140), she then affirms that Philosophy reveals herself to her followers "telle qu'il te plaist selon la voie qu'ilz te veullent enquerre" [as it pleases you, according to the path along which they wish to seek you] (140). To the narrator, "simple" and "ignorant" (140), she has revealed herself as theology, and it is to Holy Theology that the narrator addresses the remainder of her thanks.[119] This elevation of theology makes Christine's assimilation of poetry to theology all the more remarkable. Her poetic allegory does not simply possess a multiplicity of possible meanings or interpretations. By defining poets as those who speak "soubz figure de methaphore," by problematizing the distinction between the allegory of the poets and that of the theologians, by defining herself as a "poete theologisan," and finally by making theology into an aspect or face of Philosophy, and as such able to encompass all forms of knowledge and hermeneutical inquiry, Christine is able to present the *Advision* not only as an autobiographical, or a political, but also a theological text. Like the ruby to which the narrator compares part three of her text, the entire *Advision* "a proprieté de tant plus plaire comme plus on le regarde" [has the quality of pleasing more the more one looks at it] (142).

At the conclusion to her dream, the narrator does not return to her waking state, or to the narrative frame with which she had opened. Rather, she says, "[a]insi me depars de mon advision" [in this manner I leave my vision] (142). Thus, the narrator elides the distance between the "real" or waking world and the dream landscape which is normally an aspect of the dream vision and which had informed the start of the *Advision*. This passage from waking to dream realm normally signals the entrance into allegory, and the two sides of this passage are to be read differently, the one taken at face value, the other mined for hidden meaning. By erasing this boundary the narrator remains fully in control of her vision, with the ability to conclude, or step outside of it. The idea that Christine's vision was perhaps not a dream had been suggested in the preface, in which Christine writes that "songe puet estre pris pour pensee" [dream can be taken for thought] (3). From this perspective the *Advision* would not be the product of the narrator's unconscious, but of the author's intellect. According to Augustine's *Literal Meaning of Genesis*, intellectual visions occupy the highest place in the hierarchy of visions. As Augustine explains, there are three different types of vision: by means of the body one perceives corporeal objects; with the spirit one sees likenesses of bodies; with the mind one understands those realities that are neither bodies nor likenesses of bodies. In order to evaluate corporeal vision, one should consider the testimony of the other senses, and of the mind and reason. Sometimes the soul is removed from the senses of the body, more than in sleep but less than in death. In such cases, "it is by virtue of divine guidance and assistance that it [the soul] realizes it is seeing in a spiritual way not bodies but the likenesses of bodies." The ultimate vision is intellectual, for "in such a vision God speaks face to face to him whom He has made worthy of this communion."[120] This, I propose, is the type of visionary experience and authority that Christine claims for herself and for her allegorical narrative.

Christine's redefinition of poetic discourse and assimilation of poetry and theology have important implications for the kingdom of France. Libera is not just a trope. Her true significance lies in her relationship to the individual human soul, on one hand, and to the fate of God's chosen people, on the other. In the *Advision* Christine suggests that each individual soul and subject may him or herself be understood as the equivalent of the kingdom.[121] Consequently, the protection of the kingdom is more than simply an aspect of good conduct; it is rather an alternative way of understanding or apprehending the journey of the soul towards salvation. By forging an ontological identification between kingdom and subject, Christine obviates the possibility of conflict between self-interest and the public good. In addition, the temporal realm is invested with spiritual value, and the just and effective management of political affairs becomes not simply a secular preoccupation, but a spiritual one as well. From a rhetorical perspective Christine's Libera is a memorable and moving figure who appeals to readers' emotions. But she is also the keystone to Christine's comprehensive reconceptualization of allegory as a powerful moral discourse with the signifying power and authority of Scripture.

The proliferation both of organological metaphors of the body politic and of allegorical representations of the kingdom as a mother constitute different, though related, attempts to refashion ideals of royal rule and conduct such that kingdom could continue to exist and to function, even in the absence of the king. Deschamps's corporeal metaphors inscribe the king within an organism that supports the kingdom and allows it to operate without – or despite – its head. His metaphorical bodies promote cooperation and emphasize the dependence of the organism or kingdom upon all parts of the body. His allegorical representations of the kingdom, in contrast, exploit the conventions associated with a range of feminine roles in order to solicit the sympathy, and hopefully the effective intervention, of his public.

Christine de Pizan, an attentive reader and a correspondent of Deschamps's, further develops the allegorical representation of France. In the *Livre de l'advision Cristine* she significantly expands what had been a minor aspect of Deschamps's allegory of the kingdom: the motherhood of France, here called Libera. Libera's children are condemned in the text for their abusive and unnatural behaviour towards their mother, while the narrator's gratitude towards Libera, her adoptive mother, provides a model of political conduct for the French subjects. Christine exploits the conventions associated with the mother–child relationship, effectively substituting the kingdom for the king as the focal point for the loyalty, gratitude, and love of the French subjects. Indeed, the figure of the king is largely absent from the *Advision*, and the supposedly seamless dynastic continuity that characterized and legitimized the kings of France is supplemented by an alternative, imaginary genealogy in which the French subjects are the children of the kingdom. Moreover, Libera possesses a typological relationship to the individual human soul, on one hand, and to the fate of the French, God's chosen people, on the other. This polyvalence is an essential component of Christine's comprehensive reconceptualization of poetry, which is defined by its use of metaphorical language and figures, and which functions as an ethical and spiritual discourse to which might be applied the interpretive strategies normally reserved for Scripture.

3
Jean Gerson and the University of Paris

Today we gladly sing the praise of her whose daughters and whose sons
now loyal voices proudly raise to bless her with our benisons.
Of all fair mothers fairest she, most wise of all that wisest be,
most true of all the true say we,
is our dear Alma Mater.

University of Chicago anthem

In chapter 2, we considered the relevance and utility of the metaphor of the body politic in the poetry of Eustache Deschamps for conceptualizing the obligations and relationship of the elements of French society to one another and to the kingdom as a whole. In addition, we saw how the allegorical figure of the kingdom in the works of Deschamps and Christine de Pizan – depicted in feminine terms as fair beloved, honoured mother, vulnerable widow – served both to reorient political affection and loyalty from the absent king to the kingdom, and to confer a coherence and unity upon the latter that, in geopolitical terms, it lacked.

In the present chapter, I will show how the theologian and university chancellor Jean Gerson exploited the rhetorical and hermeneutic potential of both metaphor and allegory in order to construct within the political imaginary an alternative to the royal body – the University of Paris. In the vernacular sermons that I shall examine here, Gerson represents the University of Paris in metaphorical terms as a mystical body analogous to those of the king and the kingdom, and in allegorical terms as the *fille du roy* – an authoritative and determined advocate of king and kingdom, capable of ensuring the stability and good governance of France during (or despite) the absences of its king.

The University of Paris had long benefited from close connections to the kings of France. In 1200 Philippe Auguste conferred upon the University its first royal privileges, and subsequent kings routinely protected the University, and confirmed the fiscal and legal privileges enjoyed by its masters and students.[1] In 1358 the future Charles V formalized and broadcast the privileged relationship that united University and crown by referring to the institution, in a royal charter, as the "eldest daughter of the king."[2] Gerson hails the *fille du roy* as the light of knowledge, the mother of learning, the *deffenseresse* of the faith, and the light of the holy Church.[3] In his many vernacular sermons preached before both royal and popular audiences,[4] Gerson endows the University with voice and body, intellect and affect, often making her, rather than himself, the interlocutor of king and nobility.[5] The Great Schism of the West introduced new tensions among the masters and students of the University,[6] as well as between the University and the kings of France who, in 1379, pressed the University to accept the legitimacy of the Avignonese Pope Clement VII, and who in 1381 ordered the University to desist from further debate on the question.[7] Some years later the controversy surrounding the subtraction of obedience – according to which France would withdraw its obedience from both popes in order to force a conclusion to the Schism – which was officially supported by the University, put Gerson at odds with many of his University colleagues.[8] Such tensions and dissent notwithstanding, Gerson's use of allegory permitted him to ruthlessly suppress the heterogeneity, even the fractious internal struggles, of this composite institutional body,[9] for Gerson's *fille du roy* acts with a single purpose, and speaks with one voice to achieve her spiritual, political, and social ends: the clarification and promulgation of theological truths, the good governance of France, and the salvation of king and kingdom.

The eldest of the twelve children of Arnould Charlier, Gerson was born in 1363 near Rheims, in Champagne, near the Benedictine priory of Rethel, where he likely received his early education before beginning his study of arts and theology at the Collège de Navarre. In 1395 Gerson succeeded his benefactor Pierre d'Ailly to become chancellor of the University of Paris, a position which he retained until his departure for the Council of Constance in 1415. As chancellor, Gerson not only established his personal authority, as Daniel Hobbins has shown,[10] but also vigorously defended the privileges of the University as an institution, and the rights of its masters and students.[11] In addition, Gerson carved out a role for the University as a quasi-institutional and representative governing body, one that both ensured and checked the power and authority of the king. The

Burgundian takeover of Paris, which occurred in 1418 during Gerson's absence, made it impossible for him to return to the city. Gerson went back to France only after the death of Jean sans peur in 1419, and even then, not to Paris but to Lyon, where he remained until his death in 1429.[12]

In this chapter, I shall examine how Gerson used the authority of the University to intervene directly in the most pressing issues of his time, from the resolution of the Great Schism of the West, to coping with the "absences" of King Charles VI, the moral dissipation and political unruliness of the nobility, and the tension and eventual civil war between factions led by the king's brother and his cousin.[13] I shall first consider Gerson's depictions of the University as the *fille du roy*, in order to observe how an imaginary lineage modelled on the adoption of Jesus by Joseph supplements (or supplants) the actual bonds of kinship that have failed to ensure political harmony. The use of the formula *fille du roy* highlights the genealogical and affective bond between Charles VI and the University, and Gerson exploits conventional notions about filial duty in order to show that the king's "daughter" best serves her father by revealing injustice and misconduct. The kinship upon which Gerson insists allows him to associate the interests of the University with those of the king, making the University an ideal royal adviser, and turning the defence and promotion of the University's rights and privileges into a matter of the king's honour. Gerson's representation of the University as both a daughter (of the king) and a mother (of the masters and students) suggests the idea of *translatio studii et imperii*. Just as real women served as instruments in the transfer of secular power, so too the female-gendered University reproduces knowledge, ensuring its transmission from one generation to the next. The position of the University at the centre of these intersecting lines of knowledge and power allows us to consider how Gerson employed gendered constructions of the University of Paris in his efforts to ensure that the political power of France would continue into the future.

In the second part of this chapter I shall turn to Gerson's depiction of the University in metaphorical terms. Gerson does not employ metaphor as Deschamps had done, to explore the relationship of the parts of the kingdom to one another and to the whole. Instead, metaphor permits Gerson to create an analogy between the University, the king, and the kingdom of France, for the University is a mystical body that is at once a homologue of the king and a microcosm of the kingdom. The king possesses what Gerson calls three lives – individual, political, and spiritual – and these correspond to the faculties of the University such that the institution constitutes a perfect analogue of the king. As such, the University can supply reason when the king's might be wanting, thereby ensuring that the ruler's actions do not transgress the bounds of reason and divine law. In addition, Gerson affirms that because the students and masters who comprise the mystical body of the University are geographically and socially representative of the kingdom, the University is thereby authorized to represent the interests of the kingdom as a collective. These two distinct, but related, metaphorical representations of the University allow this institution to speak on behalf of king or kingdom, or both. They also account for the University's important role in forging a sense of national identity. The University of Paris during the time of Gerson's chancellorship was not the international *studium* or institution that it had been in the decades preceding or following its inception.[14] On the contrary, for Gerson, the University's very identity and aims are intimately bound up with the kingdom and the fate of France.

Although Gerson's understanding of the University's role in royal politics and administration developed in response to a specific set of challenges to the kingdom of France, the solutions he imagines have the potential to surpass the limits of his own time and place. Gerson's University is capable of ensuring the administration of justice, protecting the rights of France's subjects, promoting the harmonious order of king and subjects in society, and making possible the salvation of same.

On Kinship

Since Gerson claims that the University's exemplary loyalty to the king and dedication to the *chose publique* is founded upon her status as *fille du roy*, it will be useful to see how the chancellor conceptualizes this relationship, as well as how he understands kinship in more general terms. Gerson refers to the University as the *fille du roy* from the time of his earliest sermons. In *Adorabunt eum* (1391) he cites as evidence of the king's deep faith the solicitude Charles has always manifested for his "tres humble et tres devote fille, l'Universite de Paris" [very humble and very devout daughter, the University of Paris] (7.2.530), while in *Ecce rex tuus* (1395) Gerson prays for those responsible for bringing peace and unity to the Church, including "la fille du roy, l'Universite de Paris" [the daughter of the king, the University of Paris] (7.2.621). In turn, the University acts out of "amour filiale et loyale au roy mon pere" [filial and loyal love for the king my father] (7.1.330). These allegorical representations of the University of Paris may well have been inspired by the work of Gerson's "pere en Jhesu Crist" [father in Jesus Christ],

Philippe de Mézières.[15] In the *Songe du vieil pelerin*, a vast allegorical dream vision and treatise on good kingship completed in 1389, Philippe de Mézières identifies the University of Paris as the daughter of King Charles VI and Queen Truth, an ardent defender of the faith, and a supporter of the "ship of France."[16]

In order to examine the precise nature and explore the effects of the imagined filiation between the University and the king, let us situate Gerson's *fille du roy* within the broader context of medieval genealogical and kinship structures. Gabrielle Spiegel has argued that genealogy constitutes a "perceptual grid" by means of which medieval historians represent and shape the past.[17] Similarly, I would argue, lineage and kinship – whether real or imagined – provide the means to understand, articulate, and define relationships between individuals and groups. Networks of kinship shaped the medieval world, from the configuration of society itself to an individual's place within it. Medieval kinship structures were carefully assembled and maintained, and highly complex. They were comprised not only of biological, but also of spiritual and legal family members, and were able to be (re)formed and modified in response to changing needs.[18] Consanguinity formed a point of departure for the constitution of one's family, but as Constance Brittain Bouchard has pointed out, one's closest kin were also, potentially, one's most ardent rivals.[19] This observation is amply illustrated by the conduct of Charles VI's brother, uncles, and cousins, many of whom were at least as interested in extending their own influence as they were in supporting the king and protecting the kingdom.

Bonds of kinship were supple. Among one's extensive network of biological kin, a restricted subset of family members were routinely recognized as friends – chosen as godparents or as witnesses to charters or donations – while others were not.[20] As Xavier Hélary aptly quips with respect to the family-influenced politics of Philippe III le Hardi, "certains cousins l'étaient plus que d'autres."[21] An individual might supplement his or her network of biological kin with spiritual kinship, created when a person stood as godmother or -father to the child of another, or through marriages, which joined the families of husband and wife through bonds of affinity.[22] The resulting relationships could serve to broadcast or fortify an existing bond of friendship or alliance, or to forge a new one. As Zrinka Stahuljak has observed, even consanguinity required confirmation. Indeed, it was the mutual recognition of a bond of kinship ("linguistic alliance"), rather than blood, that constituted the operative link between two individuals.[23]

Kinship networks furnish a sensitive and revealing model for, and reflection of, social relationships. By defining and delimiting one's family, a person is also defining him or herself, and their place in the world. Given the power of kin networks to shape individual and group identity, it is not surprising that social bonds and structures of all sorts – including guilds, confraternities, the Church, and the polity itself – were modelled upon, and employed the vocabulary of, kinship in order to articulate the relationship between their various members.[24] Indeed, kinship may be viewed in a broad sense, as Paul Hyams has proposed, as "an ongoing metaphor for social life."[25] Since the language of kinship provides an ordering paradigm or structuring principle for systems of thought as well, and an optic through which to view and understand the relationship of concepts to one another, we may likewise consider it an ongoing metaphor for moral and intellectual life.[26]

Gerson uses the language of kinship to explore questions of relationality, and to situate people and groups within structures of power. In the *Poenitemini* sermon on conjugal chastity (January 1403) Gerson stages a question-and-answer on the advantages and obligations associated with various sorts of love and kinship.[27] Whom should a man love more, Gerson asks his public, his wife or his mother? Though he should honour his mother he should love his wife more. Similarly, he should love his wife more than his children, and the wife likewise. Who loves more, the mother or the father? The mother more ardently, Gerson replies, and the father more constantly. Moreover the child loves his mother more in his youth, and his father when he's grown. Who loves more, children or parents? Parents, Gerson affirms. This passage not only provides insight into medieval beliefs concerning different bonds of kinship and the affective capacities of men and women, it also reveals the degree to which kinship both reflected and shaped structures of power and hierarchy. Gerson's ordering of family members in terms of who loves more, and whom they love, depicts kinship as a kind of contest, one subject to a continual renegotiation of roles and ranks. From this perspective the wrangling going on at the royal court, where kinship and politics were so closely imbricated, may be seen as comparable to and a projection of the struggles being enacted on the level of the family.

In the sermon *Poenitemini, pour la fête de St Antoine* (17 January 1396) Gerson defines two kinds of birth, the first of which is physical.[28] As discussed in the previous chapter with respect to Christine de Pizan's Libera, the connections created by biological kinship come with expectations of friendship, love, and loyalty, often conveyed by the use of the words "natural" or "naturally," as in "icelle amour naturelle qui doit estre entre freres et seurs tout d'un sang, d'une char" [that natural love which should exist between brothers and sisters of one lineage, of one flesh] (7.2.549). Claude Gauvard has shown that an alleged bond of *amour naturel* constituted a legitimate justification for an individual's intervention in a conflict that did not, a priori, concern them.[29] Natural love likewise provides the foundation for the closest possible affective relationships.[30] In *Beati qui lugent* (2 November 1401) Gerson imagines a mother in purgatory begging her still-living child to pray for her, for if he does not remember and help her, she asks rhetorically, from whom might she expect comfort? (7.2.553). Because the love between parent and child is imagined to be so profound, no sacrifice can be envisioned that is greater than God's sacrifice of his only son (7.2.640). Like filiation, brotherhood is also envisioned as a bond that ensures friendship and loyalty, as evidenced by the proliferation of ritual brotherhood in the later Middle Ages.[31] Accordingly, Gerson affirms that he who is helped by his brother is like a strong tower (7.2.441). Gerson is well aware, however, that the perfect friendship ensured by brotherhood, like the perfect solicitude produced by filiation, represents an ideal rather than reality. Yet these ideals are so powerful that the language of physical kinship is used also to conceptualize and define the relationship of the individual soul to God. Paradoxically, physical kinship is at once an archetype for, but a degraded version of, spiritual kinship.[32]

The second type of birth in this world, as defined by Gerson, is gracious or spiritual. This second birth is sacramental, brought about through baptism and penitence, and it makes possible the spiritual (re)birth of an individual and their inclusion in God's family.[33] Thanks to this second birth each person becomes a child of God and of the Virgin, brothers and sisters of Christ and of one another, and Gerson frequently reminds the king and nobles of their kinship with the humblest of the kingdom's subjects so that they will be just and charitable towards them.[34] Gerson stresses the profound connection between all Christians, as well as the divinity's likeness to all people, in order to promote Christian unity and each soul's intimacy with God. In the sermon *Puer natus est* (before 1389), for instance, the holy family provides figures with whom any type of person could identify. Men are encouraged to turn to Christ as to a brother. The Virgin provides a model for young girls, Mary as mother for wives, Christ as sovereign doctor for clerics, and Christ as king of kings for earthly princes and kings (7.2.965). It is important to recognize that for Gerson spiritual birth and the relationships constituted thereby are not metaphorical. On the contrary, they are every bit as real as the facts of physical birth; they are simply operative in a different realm.

Just as the soul is superior to the body, so too spiritual birth is superior to physical birth. Gerson uses the example of Mary, who stands in both physical and spiritual relationship to God, to illustrate this point. Because of her grace and faith Mary "fut mere de Jhesucrist plus dignement en gardant sa doctrine que s'elle eust este mere charnele tant seulement sans garder sa doctrine" [was the mother of Jesus Christ more worthily in keeping his doctrine than if she had been only his carnal mother, without keeping his doctrine] (7.2.761). And yet the affective power of physical kinship is indisputable. The very fact that the terminology of biological kinship is carried over into the spiritual realm and used to articulate spiritual relationships reveals the considerable force of these bonds of the flesh. The Virgin is God's daughter, spouse, sister, and "amie" (7.2.1057).[35] In *Accipietis virtutem* (2 June 1392) Gerson explains that the apostles were made as brothers to one another so that they might aid and comfort each other (7.2.441). And of course, as Gerson reminds his public repeatedly, all are brothers and sisters in Christ (*Ibi eum videbitis*, *Quaerite Dominum*).

Spiritual birth, unconstrained by the facts of human physiology, is able to create kin relationships that are not possible within a biological framework. The best example of such relationships is provided by Mary, daughter of her son, mother of her father and brother. Spiritual kinship also allows men to assume roles that are most often thought of primarily or exclusively in feminine terms. In the sermon *Nimis honorati sunt* (before 1394) Gerson evokes the humility, pity, and kindness of St Paul. Moreover Paul, he says, "se nommoit mere et nourice qui enfantoit et allaictoit tous ceulz qui se convertissoyent" [was called the mother and nurse who gave birth to and nursed all those who converted] (7.2.735). To hear St Paul called a mother and to have ascribed to him in vivid terms the biologically female capacities to give birth and to lactate may surprise us. We could interpret this statement metaphorically. Paul was *like* a mother because he was so kind and merciful. However, while this statement functions in part as a comparison between Paul and the presumed characteristics of biological mothers, it is also an expression of the relationship between Paul and those he converted. Paul was the means of the spiritual birth, through conversion and baptism, of other individual souls, and therefore stood in the relationship of mother to those souls.[36] The image of Paul as mother helps us to imagine the maternal and paternal functions or relationships independently of reproductive processes. This separation is useful when thinking about the University, a metaphorical or mystical body that represents a collective comprised entirely of men, one that is allegorized in Gerson's sermons as both a daughter and a mother.

We can see thus that Gerson and his contemporaries relied upon kinship as a cognitive structure and as one of the ordering principles of society. From a political perspective Bernard Guenée has shown that an individual's royal blood, and their relative proximity in degrees of kinship to the king, determined to a significant degree the extent of their power.[37] For one thing, close kinship to the king determined the membership of the royal council that advised the queen during the absences of Charles VI. After the death of the king's uncle Philippe de Bourgogne (27 April 1404), for instance, Louis d'Orléans's status as brother of the king gave him more authority than his rival Jean sans peur, the new duke of Burgundy, who was only the king's cousin. Indeed, Jean sans peur's presence on the council was not a given, and he resorted to a display of military force in order to obtain for himself the place on the council that his father had held. The late summer and fall of 1405 saw the kingdom on the brink of civil war. Jean sans peur came to Paris in August 1405 in order to swear homage to Charles VI for the county of Flanders, but he arrived at the head of a considerable armed force. This provoked the flight from Paris of Louis d'Orléans, the queen, the dauphin, and the other royal children, who sought refuge in Melun. After a tense stand-off lasting several months, the queen and other members of the royal family succeeded in reconciling the dukes, at least temporarily.

The multiple ordinances issued during the early years of the fifteenth century testify to the struggles being enacted over participation on the council, and the responsibilities of individual members and the council as a body.[38] The ordinance of 26 April 1403 declared that in the event of Charles VI's death the dauphin, even if a minor, would immediately become king. For this reason the physical possession of the dauphin's person was essential for anyone who might try to exercise power through him, as evidenced by the aforementioned flight to Melun, as well as other displacements of king and dauphin effected by the rival princely factions. One could not presume to exercise royal power at a distance from the person of the king or the dauphin. However, despite the political authority conferred by consanguinity, Gerson and his public were confronted with the manifest failure of biological kinship to establish or to maintain peace within the kingdom of France.[39] The fact that the king's council was comprised of members of his family should theoretically have made them especially dedicated to king and kingdom, yet many of those in Charles's entourage were clearly more devoted to their private advantage than to the protection of the king's authority.

I suggest that it is in response to this failure that Gerson endows the king with figurative kin more faithful, dedicated, and selfless than his own brother, uncles, or cousins – the University of Paris. Tracy Adams has argued that Isabeau de Bavière held appeal as a regent precisely because she had no personal political agenda.[40] One could make similar claims with respect to the University, whose aims – as Gerson presents them – consist entirely of promoting and protecting the king's authority and the security of the kingdom. By casting the University in the role of royal daughter, Gerson stresses the University's subservience to king and crown. Daughters could not usurp their fathers, or compromise the purity of the royal bloodline, since they were not implicated in the transmission of royal power.[41] Like Charlemagne's daughters, who, as Janet Nelson has shown, provided the emperor with information, perfect obedience, and unofficial influence over court factions, all the while "offering no rivalry as potential heirs to formal power, nor producing offspring with claims to a share in rulership or patrimony," the University of Paris is the perfect royal child.[42] Perfect, indeed, because she is a *daughter*, because unlike sons she does not challenge or rival her father's authority.[43] We shall see presently that although the University is also portrayed as a procreative body, involved in processes of reproduction, she does not generate potential rivals to royal power. What she (re)produces and transmits instead is a culture of perfect loyalty to the king and a cadre of royal servants. This good daughter engenders (and represents, metaphorically) a group of very real people, of whom Gerson is the leader.

The University as "fille du roy"

Throughout his sermons Gerson insists upon the genealogical bond that unites University and king. He affirms that loyalty and filial gratitude prompt and justify the University's intervention in public affairs, for the University "considere et scet bien ... que son bien, son avenement, son honneur, sa garde et sa protection despend du roy" [considers and knows well ... that her well-being, her propriety, her honour, her safekeeping and her protection depend upon the king] (7.2.1138). The parallel that this metaphor suggests between the king as father and the subject as child reflects an established tradition in late medieval political thought. In Nicole Oresme's translation and commentary of Aristotle's *Politics*, carried out during the reign of Charles V, Oresme affirms that "le pere est comme roy, et le roy comme pere" [the father is like a king, the king like a father].[44] Accordingly, the University speaks "comme fille tres obeissant au pere et du pere, comme subiecte loyalle de son souverain et droicturier seigneur" [as a very obedient daughter to her father and about her father, like a loyal subject of her sovereign and rightful lord] (7.2.1137).[45] In her recognition of and subservience to royal authority, the king's imagined daughter furnishes a model of conduct for Gerson's public, from the king's kin to the most humble listeners.

Since clearly the University is not the literal daughter of the king, nor is she a spiritual child in the same sense as a baptized soul, it is important to see in what ways she is constituted as a daughter. The figure of the University herself provides the response to this question when she affirms that the king is like "son vray pere, par benigne, civile et dignative adopcion" [her true father, by benevolent, civil and worthy adoption] (7.2.1138). Thus, the relationship that the University posits is both a legal and an affective one.

I contend that Gerson's idea of adoption, and consequently the University's "adoption" by the king, is modelled upon the chancellor's understanding of the relationship between Joseph and Jesus. Gerson was dedicated to the rehabilitation of the figure of Joseph, who throughout much of the Middle Ages was depicted, as Rosemary Drage Hale has shown, either as a cuckold or a wizened church father.[46] Gerson wrote two vernacular *Considérations sur Saint Joseph* (c. 1413–14) and preached the sermon *Jacob autem genuit* in an effort to have a new feast day honouring the marriage of Joseph and Mary recognized by the Church.[47] During the years of the council of Constance and his later exile Gerson worked on his epic poem of salvation, the *Josephina*.[48] For Gerson the marriage of Mary and Joseph provided a model for all human marriage. Their friendship and mutual support was very real, as was their shared loving care of the infant Jesus. In his *Considérations sur saint Joseph*, Gerson discusses the relationship between the members of the holy family and demonstrates why Joseph should be considered the father of Christ, including the idea that "Jhesus estoit filz de Joseph par legale ou civile adoption" [Jesus was the son of Joseph by legal or civil adoption] (7.1.70). Gerson goes on to observe that this understanding of Jesus's and Joseph's relationship "ne plaist mie a aucuns, car selond leur advis ce eust esté presumption que Joseph eust fait du Filz de Dieu tele adoption qui sonne en subiection" [is not pleasing to some, for according to their opinion it would have been presumptuous that Joseph might make, of the Son of God, such an adoption that smacks of subjection" (7.1.70). The very idea that Jesus might be subjected to a mere human being offends such critics. Gerson does not adhere to this view, but says quite clearly that a child's obedience to his or her parent does not constitute subjection, and that Jesus's adoption by Joseph provided another manifestation of the former's sublime humility. Moreover, from a functional perspective Joseph "accompli toute la cure que bon et loyal et saige pere peut et doit faire a son vray fils" [accomplished all the care that a good and loyal and wise father can and should perform for his true son] (7.1.66), and in turn Jesus "honora Joseph comme son pere, son nutriteur, son conduiseur et deffenseur, son docteur et instructeur" [honoured Joseph as his father, his provider, his guide and protector, his professor and instructor] (7.1.66). Gerson posits a similar relationship, I would argue, between the figure of the University and the king, one in which the duties associated with the father–daughter relationship are incumbent upon both parties. The *fille du roy* is bound to honour and serve her father, while the king is obliged to protect and care for his "daughter."

Gerson's public would surely have agreed that daughters ought to obey their fathers, but what duties exactly was the University of Paris to carry out on behalf of her father, the king? Daniel Hobbins has discussed the functions performed by the medieval university in terms of those that are "internal," such as collecting and preserving texts, as well as reading, interpreting, and writing them, and "external," including preaching, advising the king on spiritual matters, and furnishing the royal and papal bureaucracies with cadres of educated servants.[49] These and other similar functions were certainly performed by the University of Paris. Indeed, Gerson was particularly concerned about lay spirituality, and works such as the *Montaigne de contemplation* (1400) and the *ABC des simples gens* (1401/2), as well as the many vernacular sermons Gerson preached, attest to his efforts to extend religious instruction and a better understanding of Christian precepts to as wide a public as possible.[50]

Yet, Gerson's concern for practice and his desire to effect material improvements in the lives of the French subjects move him to assign to the University an even more active role than Hobbins's "external" functions suggest. For Gerson, the knowledge preserved and promulgated by the University masters, if not employed to bring about positive material and political change, is of little value.[51] Indeed, sermons are not simply for teaching the good, but "pour esmouvoir le cuer et l'affection a amer et desirer et acomplir ce qui est bien" [for moving the heart and the affections to love and to desire and to accomplish that which is good] (*Hoc sentite* 7.2.651). Similarly, in *Vivat rex* Gerson asks rhetorically, "Que vouldroit science sans operacion? On ne aprent pas seulement pour scavoir, mais pour monstrer et ouvrer" [What good is knowledge without action? One does not learn simply to know, but to enact and to work] (7.2.1145). The knowledge represented and imparted by the University must provide the foundation for actions that will improve the spiritual lives and the material conditions of the king, nobles, and subjects of France.

Though the University's obligation to intervene in the affairs of the king, queen, and princes of the realm was perfectly obvious to Gerson, it was not so clear to certain of his contemporaries, who would have preferred that the masters limit their activities to theological inquiry and teaching, or charitable works. In August 1405 and in response to the University's efforts to restore peace between the feuding dukes, Louis d'Orléans dismissed the University rector, saying that "[b]y returning [to their schools] you will then through your studies rightly fulfil your ministry, for if the university is called the daughter of the king, then it has no business in dealing with the government of the kingdom."[52] Gerson alludes to this episode in *Vivat rex* when he imagines the indignation of the University's opponents: "de quoy se veult elle [i.e., the University] entremettre et mesler; voise estudier et regarder sez livrez" [in what does she want to meddle and insert herself? Let her go study and examine her books] (7.2.1145). With all due respect to his noble interlocutors, Gerson refuses quite firmly to stick to his books. Instead, he exploits the notion of filial duty in *Vivat rex* precisely in order to establish a public sphere of action for the University.

Vivat rex was preached on 7 November 1405 in the hotel of the queen (though she herself was not present), before the royal counsellors and prelates, as well as the kings of Navarre and Sicily – both second cousins of the king – the royal uncles, the dukes of Berry and Bourbon, and the king's brother and cousin, the dukes of Orléans and Bourgogne.[53] The immediate context for this sermon was the fragile and uneasy peace that followed the first major confrontation between Louis d'Orléans and Jean sans peur. In this sermon the imaginary "fille du roy" provides an example of the love and loyalty to her father and king that was so clearly lacking among Charles VI's actual brother, cousins, and uncles.

"Vivat rex, vivat rex, vivat rex," Gerson's sermon begins, "vive corporelment, vive civilement et politiquement, vive espirituellement et pardurablement" [Long live the king! may he live physically, civilly and politically, may he live spiritually and everlastingly] (7.2.1137). This salutation is voiced by the chancellor Gerson in his capacity as spokesman for the "la fille du roy, la mere des estudez, le beau cler soleil de France voir de toute chrestiente, l'Universite de Paris pour laquelle nous sommes icy envoyez en la presence tres honnourable de vous" [the daughter of the king, the mother of study, the fair clear sun of France, indeed of all of Christianity, the University of Paris on whose behalf we have been sent here, into your very honourable presence] (7.2.1137). The chancellor punctuates his sermon with continual reminders that he speaks at the behest and on behalf of the University in order to insist upon the objectivity, good intentions, and utility of his speech. At one point he asks his public to "tournes s'il vous plaist ung peu les yeulx de vostre consideracion envers la fille du roy et les ostez de moy " [turn a bit, if you please, the eyes of your contemplation towards the daughter of the king and remove them from me] (7.2.1144).[54] Gerson constantly focuses the attention of his public upon the University, paraphrasing her words, explaining her position, and staging her repeated proclamation "vivat rex."

The phrase *vivat rex*, repeated throughout the sermon, regulates its rhythm from start to finish like the tolling of a bell. Moreover, its repetition, always attributed to the University, inscribes the *fille du roy* within a relationship of harmony, rather than antagonism, with her illustrious public, who clearly cannot dispute the authority of this scriptural passage or the praiseworthiness of the sentiment *vivat rex*. On the contrary, since all power comes from God, and since the king of France is especially beloved of God, a person would have to be both "scismatique et sedicieux qui ne se consentiroit a ceste priere et a ce beau cry que faict tousiours la fille du roy, sa tres loialle et tres devote, vivat rex" [schismatic and seditious, who would not consent to this prayer and to this fair cry that the daughter of the king, his very loyal and very devout {daughter} always makes, long live the king] (7.2.1140). Gerson places the king and his interests at the centre of the sermon, thereby allowing the University to transcend any partisan quarrelling and compelling the agreement of the public. Gerson's skilful staging of the University's voice serves in part to deflect accusations of partisanship that had been levelled at the chancellor himself.[55] Through his use of allegory, Gerson is able to draw heterogeneous voices into a harmonious whole, one which transcends the partisan conflicts that divide the kingdom in order to perceive and proclaim the truth.

In *Vivat rex* Gerson portrays the University as a model of obedience for her listeners. His careful definition of loyalty, and of what actions constitute the University's duties, allow him to present the forceful denunciation of disunity, profligacy, and injustice contained in this sermon as evidence of the University's love for her father. If she did not speak out, "ou seroit la loyaulte de la fille subiecte au pere?" [where would be the loyalty of the daughter subject to her father?] (7.2.1145). The University is the clear eye and the mirror of the kingdom, able to see in all corners of the land and to show what is to be done. "Ce service singulier doit la fille du roy a lui et a tous les seigneurs: plus bel service ne pourroit elle faire que de leur monstrer constamment la verite de la foy, sainne doctrine es bonnes meurs" [This unique service the daughter of the king owes to him and to all lords: she could not perform a more fair service than to constantly show them the truth of the faith, holy doctrine, and good morals] (7.2.1155). Thus, the sermon itself is evidence of the University's loyalty to the king and adherence to her filial duty.

The University has other obligations besides revealing and proclaiming the truth. She is also to combat the sins that injure the body politic, protect the king from the false and misleading speech of flatterers, and advise him on matters touching the faith.[56] Gerson places potential detractors in a rhetorically untenable position. Either they must affirm that daughters need not be loyal and obedient, or that the University's duties do not include speaking the truth and explaining the faith. Gerson's allegorical representation of the University as the daughter of the king, one who speaks out precisely *because* she is faithful and obedient, allows Gerson to claim a place for the University in the administration of the kingdom.

While *Vivat rex* exploits conventional ideas about filial duty in order to carve out a political role for the University, the discourse *Contre Charles de Savoisy* emphasizes the natural love that governs the parent–child relationship in order to claim the king's protection of his "daughter." The conflict between the knight and royal chamberlain Charles de Savoisy and the University began on 14 July 1404. The four faculties and the four nations of the University assembled on this date at the church of St Mathurin to pray for the king's health, and then processed across the Seine to the church of St Catherine. There, a young valet lost control of his horse and injured some of the students. In response he was insulted by the students, even slapped, and he returned in distress to the house of his master, Charles de Savoisy. Savoisy's men returned to the scene of the procession, where they attacked the students with weapons, pursuing them into the church of St Catherine, where their violence disrupted the mass.[57] On 19 July Gerson addressed the Parlement of Paris in an effort to obtain justice for the University.[58] The discourse that he delivered on that occasion, *Contre Charles de Savoisy*, conjoins the interests of king and University, and draws upon the expectations associated with kinship in order to obtain royal justice for the University.

Gerson employs two distinct, but related, strands of argumentation to procure justice for the University. The first is based upon natural love, which is recognized and displayed by all, from his esteemed interlocutors to the animals of the earth. As he says to the men of Parlement, "[v]ous savez quelle amour c'est de peres et meres aus enffans; plusieurs de vous l'espreuvent en leurs propres enffans ... Les bestes meismement nous montrent cecy, car elles exposoient leur propre corps a feu et a flamme et a glaive et a toute maniere de mort pour leurs faons" [you know what love fathers and mothers bear their children; many among you experience it in their own children ... even animals show us this, for they expose their own bodies to fire and flame and sword and all manner of death to protect their young] (7.1.333).[59]

Gerson's second argument is founded upon legal and institutional considerations; this dishonour is your own dishonour, he says to the king, via his representatives, and as such it is the legal right and duty of the men of Parlement, acting on behalf of the king, to punish the aggressors accordingly. A series of equivalences – between the honour of real fathers and daughters, between real and figurative daughters (like the University), between figurative daughter (the University) and her real children (the students and masters) – allows Gerson to construe the beating of a group of students as a crime against the king's very person. From there, Gerson can argue that the redress of this crime is the king's exclusive right and responsibility. Both of these rhetorical strategies hinge upon the University's privileged status as *fille du roy*.

Gerson's discourse opens under the rubric of a series of kin relationships – son to mother, daughter to father – and a set of obligations. The chancellor explains that his purpose is to present "la piteuse et tres miserable complainte de la fille du roi ma mere, l'Université de Paris" [the piteous and very dolorous complaint of the daughter of the king, my mother, the University of Paris] (7.1.326–7). As the *fille du roy* the University may legitimately claim the protection of the king, while Jean Gerson, a model son who illustrates his conformance to the biblical injunction to "honour thy father and thy mother," seeks to bring his mother's persecutors to justice. Gerson suggests that to have a jurist represent the University before Parlement would constitute an insult to the University on the part of her children, the masters. Gerson would rather be accused of ignorance or presumption than that any of the "adversaires ou malveillans de la fille du Roy, de la mere qui entre les autres m'a nourry des mon enfance, peussent reproucher que pour elle et en son affliction on ne trouve en ses filz aucun qui en aist pitie et misericorde et qui en veille ou sache ou ose parler" [the adversaries or ill-wishers of the king's daughter, of the mother who nourished me, among others, from my childhood, might be able to allege that on her behalf and in her affliction one cannot find among her sons a single one who has pity and mercy on her and who wishes, or knows how, or dares to speak for her] (7.1.329). The imagined insults of *adversaires* and *malveillans* highlights the link between slander or rumour, and dishonour.[60] By speaking in defence of his mother's honour, Gerson provides a model of conduct for the king, whom he calls upon to avenge the dishonour perpetrated upon his daughter's body. By fulfilling so scrupulously his own duties to his "mother," Gerson suggests that the king's representatives ought do no less for his daughter.

As in *Vivat rex*, Gerson stages the first-person voice of the University, who here describes the "amour filiale et loyale" [filial love and loyalty] (7.1.330) that moved her to organize the procession on behalf of her father, the king. The University is not only the king's beloved daughter, but also the loving mother of the masters and students of the University, and she emphasizes the students' youth and vulnerability in order to portray the events of 14 July as a fifteenth-century massacre of the Innocents. Horses pressed into "les enfans" [the children], crushing "indifferamment tous mes fils les escoliers" [indifferently all my sons, the students] (7.1.330). The air was full of the lamentations of the "petit et foibles enfans" [weak little children] and "les petis enfans" [the little children] cried for mercy, but their attackers pursued them as they would enemies of king and kingdom.

The University herself may be included among the Innocents. Like the allegorical representations of France discussed in chapter 2, which depicted the kingdom in overdetermined feminine terms by highlighting France's beauty, vulnerability, and dependence upon male protection, Gerson's allegorical representation of the University portrays this institution as simple and pure, as well as defenceless. She does not look in the least like a University master, nor does she insist upon or seek to demonstrate the extent of her learning. On the day in question she proceeded, she says, "par devote religion en ma bonne simplesse" [by devout religion and in my good simplicity], and "aussy alloye je en ma simplesse, en l'innocence de mes suppos" [also I went in my simplicity, in the innocence of my students] (7.1.330).

This emphasis on the University's "simplesse"[61] places her in parallel with the "simples gens" [simple folk] (7.1.16) to whom Gerson addressed one of his most well-known treatises on mystical theology, the *Montaigne de contemplation*. Particularly accessible to women,[62] but necessary to men as well, mystical theology is presented by Gerson as an antidote to the sterile intellectual curiosity and pride that pervades the University and that risks undermining the spiritual journey of the University masters and those in their pastoral care.[63] Thus, we see that in *Contre Charles de Savoisy* the allegorical figure of the University is purposefully disassociated from the older, male University masters, from Gerson himself, and is presented in a sympathetic and appealing light, moved by love, and characterized by simplicity and humility. The specificity of this allegorical figure, with its overdetermined femininity, allows Gerson to appropriate, on the University's behalf, a branch of theology that previously had not been associated with the speculative, scholastic theology practised at the University of Paris.

In addition, the University's tearful, first-person account of her inability to protect her "children," recalls the failure of Libera, discussed in the previous chapter, to ensure peace between her own "children," understood either as the princes of the blood or as the French subjects as a whole. In both cases the weakness and vulnerability of kingdom and University, depicted in postures of lamentation, constitutes a call for male intervention and aid.[64] In the case of *Contre Charles de Savoisy*, this call for help is explicit, since the University occupies the conventionally feminine position of supplicant and intercessor. Given the University's failure to defend her children, it is to Gerson and especially to his interlocutors, the men of the Parlement of Paris, that the duty of protection will fall. By casting the allegorical University and the students in the role of the Innocents, Gerson suggests that should the king and his representatives fail to redress the wrongs perpetrated against his daughter, they will be obliged to assume the unsavoury role of Herod.

Following the University's moving description of the day's events and her plea for justice, the remainder of the discourse is delivered by Gerson in his own voice. He reintroduces the theme of his discourse, "be merciful," by asking for mercy for "la fille du roy en son oppression" [the daughter of the king, in her oppression] (7.1.330), and he continues to emphasize the students' vulnerability. The "josnes escoliers" [young students] sought refuge in the church of St Catherine, like "agneaus innocens" [innocent lambs] who run from a wolf, or "poussins fuyent dessoubz les aisles de leur mere" [chicks fleeing beneath the wings of their mother] (7.1.330). Following the incapacity of the University's allegorical body to offer physical protection, once in the church the children seek the protection of real women: "les bonnes dames qui y etoient venues cachoient les enffans dessous leurs manteaux" [the good women who had come there hid the children beneath their cloaks] (7.1.331). However, these attempts do not prevent bloodshed either. The image of the women shielding children beneath their cloaks evokes that of chicks running beneath their mother's wings, and both recall the prayer of St

Anselm to St Paul, "Are you not a mother who like a chicken collect your chicks beneath your wings?"[65] This allusion to the successful protection provided by St Paul contrasts with and highlights the ineffective defence offered both by the allegorical University and by the real women in the church. Despite the profusion of maternal imagery in this passage, the scene is marked by the absence, limits, or outright failure of the feminine: the University, imagined as the students' mother, possesses no material reality, while the actual women in the church are unable to defend the children.

"C'estoit droitement une perseqution telle comme vous regardes en ces painteures quand Herodes fait occire les Innocens" [It was truly a persecution such as you see in those pictures where Herod has the Innocents slaughtered] (7.1.331), Gerson continues, making explicit the comparison suggested by the University between the students and the biblical innocents. His reference to paintings rather than to a biblical passage contributes to the ekphrastic quality of this scene, as Gerson calls upon his interlocutors to envision the violence, to imagine the University students as innocent babes and their persecutors as the instruments of a tyrant. Arrows flew everywhere, and the wounded students fell even on the altar. No one in the church was safe, "fust maistre ou escolier, fust noble comme estoient les plusieurs fust non noble, *fussent de vos enffans*, Messeigneurs" [be he master or student, be he noble, as were many of them, be he non-noble, *be they your own children*, my lords] (7.1.331, emphasis added). With this last phrase Gerson reminds his public that some of their very own children may be numbered among the University's students. By appealing to the men of Parlement not only as representatives of the king's justice, but also as fathers, Gerson invites his interlocutors to imagine the violence suffered by the University and her children as an issue that might touch them personally. In addition, his evocation of the men of Parlement as fathers shifts the focus of his discourse from failed maternity to the paternal power of redress and protection. Like St Paul, or like Joseph, whose primary duty was the protection of the infant Jesus, the king and his representatives in Parlement have the authority, power, and duty to protect their daughter, the University, represented here by her youngest children.

Gerson's discourse next moves from the attack against the University's innocent children to a closer consideration of the king's own child – the University herself – and the protection owed her honour. The assault against the University touches the very integrity of the king and the kingdom, for the body of his daughter has been violated. Gerson presents the University's body as a material and female one that has suffered sexual injury and dishonour. "[L]a fille du roy est vilenee et violee" [the daughter of the king is defiled and violated], Gerson declares, and "comme l'onneur de la fille tourne l'onneur du pere, pareillement la fille ne peut estre deshonnouree sans deshonneur du pere" [since {upon} the honour of the daughter turns the honour of the father, so too the daughter cannot be dishonoured without the dishonour of the father] (7.1.332). It is precisely the relationship of filiation, upon which Gerson insists, that allows him to argue that the violation of the University casts shame upon the king, because the purity of the daughter is the responsibility of the father.[66] Since a proven affront to the king's honour could be prosecuted as a crime of lèse majesté,[67] the men of Charles de Savoisy have not simple beaten and injured a group of students, they have committed a crime against the king himself in the body of his daughter, the University. Therefore, the attack of Charles de Savoisy's men was not a personal or private settling of scores, but a matter that fell under the jurisdiction of the king.[68]

If the men of Parlement do not now avenge the king's daughter, Gerson declares, then they risk committing a crime comparable to that of Charles de Savoisy with respect to the University and the king. This is because "quiconque blesse justice, il blesse l'honneur du roy" [whosoever injures justice, he injures the honour of the king] (7.1.332). In her analysis of the development of the *amende honourable* as a means of regulating violence, Claude Gauvard observes the increasing juridical importance attached to the king's honour. Disputes between individuals that resulted in crime and injury came to be represented as crimes against the king, and guilty parties were required first and foremost to acknowledge and seek pardon for their injury to the king's honour, such that the legal interests of the injured parties themselves were subordinated to those of the king.[69] In his efforts to show that justice is strictly the purview of Charles VI, not of private citizens, however illustrious, Gerson's discourse serves to strengthen the authority of the kings of France, who had long sought to exercise control over violence, by substituting royal justice for private vengeance, by representing the king as the figure entitled to pardon crimes committed against others, and by seeking to distinguish licit from illicit violence and punishing the latter.[70] By taking the University's case to the Parlement Gerson is both appealing to and reinforcing the king's monopoly on the administration of justice.

Ensuring justice is perhaps the foremost duty of the king. Citing Aristotle, Gerson reminds his public that "royaulme se transporte de gent a aultre par injustices quant elles y sont faites" [a kingdom is transferred from one people to another because of injustices, when they are perpetrated there] (7.1.332), and the actions carried out against the University constitute the most blatant example of injustice imaginable. Implicit in *Contre Charles de Savoisy* is a warning: if the king or his representatives neglect to administer justice, people may resort to the "voye de fait" [path of action] (7.1.333), the private, ad hoc, often violent, means of redressing wrongs – real or perceived – that so often resulted in disruptions to the public order such as the one Gerson is seeking to avenge.

In the discourse *Contre Charles de Savoisy* Gerson begins to grapple with what he will come to see as the central and underlying problem of Charles VI's reign: the administration of justice. On one hand, Gerson wants judicial authority to be concentrated in the person of the king. As he will assert years later in *Rex in sempiternum vive*, "l'authorité royale ne doit point constituer an plusieurs cours souveraines de sa justice en laquelle est la valeur de sa vertu dominative" [royal authority should not be constituted in several sovereign courts of his justice, in which reside his authority to rule] (7.2.1017). On the other hand, investing justice in the person of the king presents its own set of challenges, since Charles VI was incapable, much of the time, of ensuring that justice was done. Yet somehow justice must be maintained, as Gerson says in *Vivat rex*, whether the king is absent or present (7.2.1175). *Contre Charles de Savoisy* represents one attempt to resolve the problem of the king's absences. In this sermon Gerson employs the allegory of the University depicted as a humble supplicant and presented as the *fille du roy* to align the interests of the University with those of king, and on this basis he appeals to the king's representatives, "cette cour tres honnorable de Parlement" [this very honourable court of Parlement] (7.1.327), which embodies "son hault throne de justice ou siet et se repose son autorité royalle" [his lofty throne of justice whereon is seated and resides his royal authority] (7.1.327). We shall see that Gerson will develop another solution to the difficult problem of how to ensure justice in the intermittent presence of the king, and his response, once again, will be founded upon the University of Paris.

The University as Metaphor for King and Kingdom

During the opening years of the fifteenth century the still unresolved Great Schism of the West, the king's continued absences, the deepening and increasingly violent rift between princely factions, and the renewal of the war with England all provoked anxiety and instability among the French people. Within this fraught context the University, as Gerson observes in *Vivat rex*, advances the king's interests by disseminating and reinforcing adherence to royal ideology, in particular by emphasizing the idea that the king's subjects owe him loyalty and obedience. As Christendom's recognized authority on theological questions, the University policed the boundaries of religious orthodoxy, effectively controlling the path to salvation. In the exercise of their pastoral functions University masters were able to use their spiritual authority in order to ensure the political and civil compliance of those under their care. As Gerson says, the University "inhort tousiours pacience et bonne obeissance au roy et aux seigneurs" [always enjoins patience and good obedience to the king and the lords] (7.2.1146). The University thus serves as an instrument for the transmission, reproduction, enforcement, and social acceptance of existing structures and relationships of power.[71]

Patience is a tough sell, however, when the king and nobles fail to conduct themselves justly towards the people. Implicit in Gerson's emphasis on the University's efficacy in maintaining public order, and therefore its utility to the king, is an admonishment: if the king wishes to preserve the University's support, he himself must conform more closely to the ideal of kingship which demands that he protect those entrusted to his care. Gerson is clearly aware of the power of the University to influence and disseminate royal ideology, and he wishes his illustrious public to understand that this power may be placed at the service of the king, or, as he stops just short of saying, not. What is highlighted here, as throughout Gerson's works, is the formidable power of the University, which has the capacity to shape the conduct of the vast and protean mystical body of the kingdom, and also and more importantly, to instruct and guide that body's head.

In what follows we shall see how Gerson's University functions not just as an allegorical figure, the *fille du roy*, but also as metaphorical body, one that, like the metaphors of the kingdom examined in chapter 2, is both whole and composite, single and many. As we saw in *Contre Charles de Savoisy*, an injury inflicted upon one or some is an injury endured by all, for the University suffers not just in one of her members, "mais en tout et par tout [s]on corps" [but in everything and throughout all of her body] (7.1.329). As a metaphorical body the University is analogous to both king and kingdom. As such, it is able to step into the king's place, safeguarding royal rule both from the predations of the nobility, who were eager to disperse the power of the king, and from the disobedience of the people, who sought to oppose the king's authority. At the same time, the University is broadly representative of the kingdom in its make-up, and consequently is able and entitled to serve as the French subjects' intercessor and advocate vis-à-vis the king. Because metaphor relies upon perceptions of likeness or similarity,[72] Gerson is able to suggest that the mystical body of the University is comparable to those of the king and kingdom. This series of parallels enables him to pursue apparently incompatible efforts both to fortify the king's authority, and to protect the French subjects by maintaining the king within the bounds imposed by God and reason.

What permits the University to serve as an analogue of both king and kingdom is its singular relationship to what I shall call Gerson's three realms. As Louis Pascoe has observed, "What is especially characteristic of Gerson's thought on reform is its triadic and, for the most part, trinitarian orientation."[73] This triadic or trinitarian thought structures Gerson's formulation of the relationship between the individual, the polity, and the soul. One of the foundational premises of Gerson's political thought is the idea that individuals are inscribed in three connected and comparable kingdoms or realms. In one of Gerson's earliest sermons (*Adorabunt eum*, 1391) he explains that just as three kings came to adore the infant Jesus, so too there are three kingdoms: personal, temporal, and spiritual. Each individual has, or is, their own personal kingdom which they should rule well. The temporal kingdom consists of the individual governed "en commune police" [in a shared polity] (7.2.521), while the spiritual kingdom concerns the government of the Church. These kingdoms may be observed within each individual, as well as on the level of human society and the cosmos. In the sermon *Omne regnum* (1402?) Gerson affirms that each person has a kingdom inside of them comprised – like the kingdom of France – of three orders: the clergy, the chivalric class, and the bourgeoisie, and these orders plainly correspond to the spiritual, temporal, and personal kingdoms of *Adorbunt eum*.

Gerson's thinking was shaped in part by the hierarchical principles found in the works of Pseudo-Dionysius.[74] In discussing Gerson's efforts at church reform, Louis Pascoe argues that the chancellor viewed the Church as an image of angelic hierarchies, patterned upon a celestial archetype.[75] Similarly, with respect to Gerson's ecclesiology G.H.M. Posthumus Meyjes has shown that Gerson understood hierarchy in both distributive and in collective terms.[76] That is to say, "He imagined the hierarchy as a collective body, in which authority was not found only in the highest hierarchical regions but was distributed equitably among all its organs."[77] These ideas might fruitfully be applied to the political realm as well. Thus, Gerson's three kingdoms are not simply analogous, but ordered, and directed towards the ultimate purpose of salvation, and each possesses its own legitimacy that proceeds directly from God. From this perspective the temporal kingdom can be seen to serve as an intermediary between individuals and salvation. Indeed, the peaceful ordering of individuals in civil society is what permits their movement towards the spiritual kingdom.

Because the king is not an ordinary person, his relationship to the three realms is unique. In *Adorabunt eum* Gerson affirms that while ordinary individuals govern only their personal kingdom, the king rules all three, including the spiritual kingdom. Gerson justifies this claim based on the king's anointing with oil from the holy ampula, the shield sent from heaven to St Denis and adorned with three lilies – one for each kingdom – and the fact that the king of France is called the very Christian king (7.2.522). The king's relationship to his three kingdoms is not static, but evolves in ways that reflect the development of Gerson's political thought. In *Vivat rex*, preached over a decade after *Adorabunt eum* in circumstances that had considerably deteriorated, Gerson does not speak of the king's rule over three realms, but rather of the type of union that characterizes his three modes of existence. The king's individual, corporeal life is founded upon the union of body and soul, his civil life upon "la conionction et unite du seigneur et du peuple en une loy et juste ordonnance" [the conjunction and unity of the lord and the people in one law and rightful order] (7.2.1144), and his spiritual life upon the union of God and the soul in charity and love.

The sermon *Rex in sempiternum vive* further modifies the connection between the king and his lives. This sermon was preached on 4 September 1413 following the so-called Cabochien revolts of the spring and summer. These uprisings, in which the king's cousin Jean sans peur first allied himself with, and later distanced himself from, the Parisian butchers and other populist factions, had as one of its declared purposes to free the dauphin from his bad counsellors. The leaders of the revolt produced 258 articles related to administrative reform, the *ordonnance cabochienne*, which they obliged the beleaguered king to approve.[78] As the summer wore on and the revolt grew more radical and violent, some within the movement felt that they had gone too far. A backlash developed within the rebellion, and peace was declared on 6 August. *Rex in sempiternum vive* was preached on the eve of the public revocation of the *ordonnance cabochienne*.[79] In this sermon Gerson proposes his own project for the reform of the king's household and the kingdom, based on a series of considerations that he directs at the king and the three orders of French society. As in *Vivat*, the king's lives are physical, civil, and spiritual, but here the language of union has become that of donation. The first life is given to the king's body by his soul, the third is given to the soul by the grace of the Holy Spirit, and the second is given to the king "par loïal amour du bien public et commun" [by loyal love of the public and common good] (7.2.1006). The events that had transpired in the years separating *Vivat rex* and *Rex in sempiternum*, notably the assassination of Louis d'Orléans by Jean sans peur, which led to the outbreak of civil war between the Bourguignons and the Armagnacs,[80] highlighted the failed union of the king and his subjects "en une loy et juste ordonnance," and as a consequence the king's connection to his three lives seems here more tenuous and fragile than previously.

Several years later, in letters to the dauphins' preceptors, Gerson speaks not of three lives or modes of existence, but instead of four kingdoms, the personal kingdom, the kingdom of France, the Church militant, and the kingdom of heaven.[81] The heavenly kingdom, Gerson says to the king, is *supra te*, and the kingdom of the church *circa te*, that of France *sub te*, and the personal kingdom *intra te*. In these later letters Gerson assigns a much more modest place to the king, emphasizing his fundamental humanity and equality with other Christians. Indeed, Jacques Verger notes that Gerson is careful not to attribute any authority to the king that might be interpreted as sacerdotal.[82] The king's changing relationship to the three, then four, realms highlights the evolution of Gerson's political thought. The king's authority achieves its greatest extent in *Adorabunt eum*, a sermon that predates the onset of Charles's mental illness, while long years of experience of the king's absences led Gerson to reconsider the king's place in relation to the three realms.

Like the king, the University can be seen to have three lives or modes of existence. The University's corporeal life is represented by the parallel Gerson institutes between the king and the faculties of the University. The faculty of medicine corresponds to the king's physical life, the faculties of arts and law, which treat the subjects of moral philosophy, ethics, economics, politics, and justice, to his political life, and the faculty of theology to his spiritual life (7.2.1145). In this manner the University constitutes a kind of double or analogue of the king as he exists triply.

The University's second or civil life is represented by the association Gerson establishes between University and kingdom. The University, Gerson asks rhetorically, "ne represente elle pas tout le royaulme de France … en tant que de toutes parts viennent ou pouent venir suppoz pour acquerir doctrine et sapience?" [does she not represent the entire kingdom of France … inasmuch as from all parts come, or could come, students to acquire learning and wisdom?] (7.2.1146). The mystical body of the University mirrors the composition of the realm itself, thereby giving it a vested interest in the affairs of the kingdom, and a privileged speaking status with respect to the king. In an atmosphere of division and dissent, the University represents and gives voice to the rights and opinions not just of one political faction or segment of society, but of the entire kingdom. In comparison to Deschamps,[83] whose deployment of the metaphor of the body politic focused upon questions of relationality, Gerson displays a notable disinterest in the relationship of the parts of the University to one another, or to the institution as a whole. Indeed, he exploits the notion that the masters and students hail from all parts of the realm in order to claim a quasi-official representative status for this body, but does not acknowledge the diversity of opinions held by the various members of the mystical body of the University.

As for the University's third or spiritual life, Gerson's claims go well beyond depicting the University as a privileged place for theological inquiry. In the sermon *Pax hominibus* (1409) Gerson evokes the twelve stars of the Apocalypse, and then, glossing his own allegory, he says that the heavens may be understood as the "saincte Eglise universelle, ou l'Esglise de France, ou de l'Université de Paris ou sont saiges qui resplendissent dans le firmament" [holy universal Church, or the church of France, or the University of Paris where there are wise men who shine in the firmament] (7.2.765). This set of parallels establishes a remarkable equivalence first between the Church militant and the Gallican church, but more importantly between the latter and the University, which is equated with the entire spiritual realm. Thus, the University, like the king, possesses three lives or modes of existence, and the first two of these – the physical and the temporal – correspond precisely to the king and kingdom. The University's third or spiritual life is founded upon its homology to the Church. Taken together, this powerful set of comparisons suggests that the University is capable of leading the French subjects, together with their king, to salvation.

The University's three modes of existence – individual, political, and spiritual – may be ordered hierarchically, such that the spiritual directs and orders the actions and aims of the individual and the political modes of existence. In *Accipietis virtutem* (June 1392), for instance, Gerson explains that the laws of nature and those of scripture are instituted by the same prince, God, and that since Christ is the king of kings all laws ought to be in accordance with his. Therefore, Gerson concludes, "la science de sainte escripture est necessaire entre crestiens pour bien gouverner la chose publique" [the knowledge of holy scripture is necessary, among Christians, to govern the public realm well] (7.2.439). Scripture is the basis not only for governance and what we might call political philosophy, but also for law. In *Diligite justiciam* (between 6 April and 4 May 1408) the chancellor protests the provost of Paris's infringement of ecclesiastical privilege by affirming that law is founded upon justice, and moreover that "a la saintte escripture appartient monstrer et endoctriner aux juges terriens quelle chose est justice et comment ilz la doivent amer et garder" [it belongs to holy scripture to show and to teach to earthly judges what justice is, and how they should love and preserve it] (7.2.600).[84] In a manner consistent with his predilection for Dionysian hierarchy, Gerson does not simply reaffirm the separation of civil and ecclesiastical justice, he orders the branches of law to show that God and Scripture provide the foundation for canon and positive law.

For Gerson theology is clearly the *regina artium*, the source of all knowledge, and his version of the University's origins highlights this idea as well.[85] In *Contre Charles de Savoisy* (1404) the University says, "je suis celle qui en Adam fus premierement inspiree en sa nouvelle creation; je suis celle qui depuis par successions feu fondee et renouvelee en Egypte par Abraham et autres filz de Noe, puis feus transposee a Athenes et nommee Pallas ou Minerve; puis vins a Rome quant la chevallerie y seignorisoit. Puis par Charles Magne le grand, feus plantee a grans labeurs en France en la cité de Paris" [I am she who was first inspired in Adam at the moment of his creation; I am she who since, by succession, was founded and renewed in Egypt by Abraham and the other sons of Noah, then I was moved to Athens and named Pallas or Minerva; then I came to Rome when chivalry reigned there. Then by Charlemagne the great I was established with great effort in France in the city of Paris] (7.1.329).[86] In Gerson's strikingly original version of *translatio studii*, all skills and knowledge are represented by an institution, the University, whose creation was virtually coterminous with that of Adam. By connecting Old Testament figures and locations to the usual trajectory of learning from Greece, to Rome, to France, Gerson combines the topos of *translatio studii* with a distinct but related tradition concerning the preservation and transmission of knowledge after the flood.[87] Classical Greece is therefore not the source of a kind of learning that is potentially at odds with the knowledge to be found in Scripture. Instead, Gerson integrates all forms of knowledge into a single seamless genealogy, with God as the point of origin.

Present from the moment of Adam's creation, the University contributes to humankind's salvation by helping to ensure the just and peaceful rule that makes it possible for individuals to pursue their spiritual goals. In those places and times where warfare disturbed the peace and order of society the University was forced to leave, with the consequence that temporal power declined as well. After all, Gerson asks rhetorically in *Veniat pax*, "pour quoy se transporta l'universite d'Athenes a Romme et de Romme a Paris se non par deffault de paix?" [why else was the University transported from Athens to Rome and from Rome to Paris if not for lack of peace?] (7.2.1115). Gerson sees Paris in danger of going the way of Athens and Rome, and the University's departure could provoke the demise of the kingdom, or at least of France's political and cultural hegemony. Gerson would like to see the University allowed to serve the public good, though he does not rule out the possibility that instead the University may be driven from France.

The sermons *Vivat rex* and *Rex in sempiternum vive*, both preached in the vernacular to noble and royal audiences and in contexts of political crisis, represent Gerson's most fully articulated efforts to head off such an eventuality by outlining programs for the reform of the kingdom. The solutions that Gerson imagines to the problems of injustice, disorder, and self-interest rely upon his concept of the three realms, and upon the University's unique place both within them and in relation to the king and kingdom. We shall see that Gerson uses the familiar medieval metaphor of the body politic in order to limit the power of the king, while the University's homology to the king allows it to supplement and correct the king's reason without challenging his authority.

Gerson's comparable and connected kingdoms or realms allow for conceptual movement from one to another. Indeed herein, for Gerson, lies the interest of metaphor, which is not about exploring the connections of parts to each other or to a whole, but rather the affinities between a series or set of mystical bodies.[88] On this basis it is possible to apply to the kingdom of France the exhortations towards peace and unity in a sermon such as *Pax hominibus*, ostensibly directed towards the resolution of the Schism, because principles derived from one kingdom are equally valid for the other two. Thus, we see Gerson affirm that the spiritual kingdom that exists within each individual, analysed in *Omne regnum*, may be likened to any community (7.2.759). In *Adorabunt eum* Gerson uses the example of the personal kingdom to prove that charity or love, not fear, is necessary to rule the secular kingdom. This is clear because "se lez membres et les partiez de l'omme estoient contrairez l'une a l'autre, tellement que les mains crevassent les yeulx et les piez tresbuchant le corps, et le cuer n'envoyast pas sa chaleur aux aultrez membrez, le royaulme personnel de l'omme seroit bientot mis a perdicion" [if the limbs and the parts of man were contrary to one another, such that the hands tore out the eyes or the feet trod upon the body, and the heart didn't send its warmth to the other members, then the personal kingdom of man would soon be sent to its perdition] (7.2.528).

Moreover, the metaphor of the human body possesses prescriptive power, because the body natural was created by God in his image, and thus the order and functioning of the human body provides a valid model for the organization and action of the body politic. The Augustinian belief that human beings bear an image or *imago* of the divine is extremely prominent in Gerson's thought. All of creation reflects the Trinity, that is, bears a *vestigium* of the divine, but only humans are capable of participating in the divine nature; hence, the human soul may be thought to possess an *imago* of God.[89] To pervert the body politic by allowing it to behave in ways that are unnatural would be analogous to the harm a person might inflict upon their *imago dei* through sin.

Vivat rex is rhetorically structured around the king's three modes of existence, and in particular the preservation of the king's second, or civil, life. Though all people exist triply, as it were, the king's civil life is unlike those of his subjects because it is sempiternal. The king's second or civil life "se derive par succession legitime de royale lignie et est plus a aymer que la premiere de tant que le bien commun vault mieulx que le propre" [is derived by legitimate succession of the royal lineage and is more to be loved than the first inasmuch as the common good is worth more than the individual {good}] (7.2.1144). The same care and precautions taken to safeguard the physical life of the king must also be taken with regard to his eldest son, and the dauphin, despite his youth, must be educated and treated like a king for "il est comme une mesme personne avecquez le roy" [he is like one and the same person with the king] (7.2.1147). The king, together with his heirs, form what Ernst Kantorowicz called a corporation by succession. Moreover, the perpetuity that Kantorowicz believed to be lacking in medieval conceptions of the head of the mystical body of the kingdom is achieved precisely by means of Gerson's conceptualization of a civil or political life which unites the king and his heirs across time.[90]

In order to convey the importance of unity and order within the mystical body of the kingdom, to promote the union "en une loy et juste ordonnance" [in one law and rightful order] (7.2.1144) that provides the basis for the king's civil life, Gerson declares that he will structure his discussion around "la similitude de ceste vie mistique a vraye" [the resemblance between this mystical life and the true {life}] (7.2.1149). Accordingly, *Vivat rex* presents the familiar idea that the king corresponds to the head in the body politic, because the king in his civil life is not just "une personne singuliere, maiz est comme une puissance publique ordonnee pour le salut de tout le commun, ainsi comme de chief descent et despand la vie par tout le corps" [an individual person, but is like a public power ordered for the good of the community, just as from the head descends and is distributed life throughout the body] (7.2.1155).

It has become something of a scholarly commonplace to assert that the metaphor of the body politic was employed in the Middle Ages to promote hierarchy or, sometimes, reciprocity and cooperation.[91] While these elements are not absent from Gerson's conceptualization of the relationship of head to body, I would argue that his use of the metaphor is more complex than either of these suggest. As Alcuin Blamires has shown, the Pauline passages that constitute one of the principal sources for the medieval metaphor of the body politic (1 Romans 12:4–5, 1 Corinthians 12:12–27) and for the relationship of head to body (1 Corinthians 11:3–12, Ephesians 5:22–31) are hardly straightforward, but are comprised instead of a network of overlapping analogies that establish no clear-cut or fixed relationship between the head and the body.[92] Gerson deploys a similarly polyvalent set of overlapping analogies in his own use of the metaphor of the body politic. The passage cited above suggests that the head serves as a point of origin for political life, as well as a shared good of the community. Gerson very definitely claims that reciprocity is to govern the relationship of head and body. The limbs should expose themselves in order to protect the head, but in turn "le chief doit adrecier et gouverner les aultres membres" [the head should guide and govern the other members] (7.2.1155), for a head without a body cannot last long. Similarly, "comme les subjects doivent foy, subside et service a leur seigneur aussi le seigneur doibt foy, protection et deffence a sez subjectz" [just as the subjects owe faith, material aid, and service to their lord, so too the lord owes faith, protection, and defence to his subjects] (7.2.1155). What is more unusual than the notions that the head ought to govern the body, or that it is in the interest of each body part to fulfil its duties to the organism as a whole, is the idea that the head must be controlled or kept in check. We shall see that it is the University, which is analogous simultaneously to the head and to the entire body, which serves this function.

In *Vivat rex* Gerson further develops the metaphor of the body politic by explaining that that just as physical health depends upon the equilibrium of the four humours, so too the well-being of the body politic requires the balance of four virtues: prudence, temperance, strength, and justice.[93] These virtues are systematically opposed by four vices, which it is the duty of the University to combat.[94] In part, vices can be defeated by exposing the truth, as Gerson does in *Vivat rex* and elsewhere. In order to resist deceitful flattery, for instance, the vice which is opposed to prudence, the king needs to know about the actual condition of his kingdom and his subjects. The notion that the French subjects possess views and experiences that deserve to be made known suggests that the body does not just obey or follow its head, but that it might instead engage in dialogue with the head, and that this exchange will benefit the entire organism.[95] That it is the University who should convey the subjects' views to the king is based upon its status as a collective and representative body. As we have seen, the masters and students who comprise this collective body represent the kingdom in its entirety, both from a geographic and a social perspective, for the students hail from all parts of the kingdom and from every level of society. The University's representative status also authorizes – indeed compels – Gerson's present intervention, the very sermon that he is pronouncing: "Si doit l'Universite comme pour toute France, comme pour tous les estas desquelles elle a aucuns estudians, comme pour tous leurs parens et amys estans en griesves afflictions qui ne puent venir ycy ou estre ouis en leur douloureuse lamentacion, doyt, dy je, prier et dire Vivat rex; vive le roy" [And so the University ought, as for all of France, as for all of the estates from which she has some students, as for all their parents and friends in grave affliction who cannot come here or be heard in their sorrowful lamentation, she ought, I say, to pray and to say "Vivat rex," long live the king] (7.2.1146). The idea that the University represents the kingdom is quite striking, for the University masters and students were not exclusively French.[96] Moreover, the University masters and students could also be viewed as members of another mystical body – that of the Church. By refusing to acknowledge this other possible allegiance, Gerson is effectively creating a national university, one that is representative of the kingdom's subjects and that functions as a kind of standing body or institution authorized to advise the king on matters touching the affairs of France.

In addition to furnishing a basis for Gerson's discussion of the four principal virtues needed for good rule, the four humours are also imagined as part of the material wealth of the kingdom and its subjects, which serve to nourish the body. The head cannot reserve for itself all of the goods of the body, "le sang, l'humeur et la substance des aultrez membres" [the blood, the humour, and the substance of the other members] (7.2.1156), or the organism will perish. Gerson's image of the head, unjustly and grotesquely inflated with the material wealth of the kingdom, recalls a passage from Nicole Oresme's *Traictie sur les monnoies*: "quant le prince ... veult attraire à luy et de fait parvient à ce qu'il assemble en grande multitude par dessus ses subgectz ou ses semblables, ou préjudice de eulx, plusieurs richesses, il est comme ung monstre à nature, si comme ung corps duquel la teste est si grosse que le residu d'icelui est si foible qu'il ne la peut soustenir" [when the prince ... wants to draw to himself, and in fact succeeds in assembling many riches in great multitude, far above his subjects or his peers, and to their prejudice, he is like a monster of nature, like a body of which the head is so swollen that the rest of {the body} is so weak that it cannot support it] (lxxviii).[97] This hydrocephalic prince, in Oresme's treatise, is none other than the tyrant.

For Nicole Oresme and other post-Aristotelian thinkers the tyrant is the perverted analogue of the king, and anxiety surrounding the potential of any king to slip into tyranny haunts many medieval *miroirs du prince* and other works of political philosophy, Gerson's sermons included.[98] In *Vivat rex* Gerson defines tyranny as a malady that afflicts the head, it is "le venin et la poison et la maladie qui met a mort toute vie politique et royale" [the venom and the poison and the illness that puts to death all political and royal life] (7.2.1158). The tyrant desires his subjects to act little, know little, and love little. "Si est bien chose contraire a bon gouvernement royal qui tent que ses subgietz soient puissance, sapience et amitie; a la belle ymaige, ymitation et exemple de la benoiste Trinite" [And so it is indeed a thing contrary to good royal government which tends towards the power, knowledge, and love of the subjects, according to the image, imitation, and example of the blessed Trinity] (7.2.1158).

The triad power, knowledge, and love corresponds to the *potentia*, *sapientia*, and *bonitas* that characterize the three persons of the Trinity, and it maps onto other Gersonian triads, such as memory, intellect, and will, or justice, order, and peace. These triads and others enable the soul to obtain self-knowledge and knowledge about the Trinity, thereby helping it to return its *imago dei* to as pristine a state as possible, given original sin.[99] In his discussion of Gerson's three realms, Louis Pascoe concludes that the second is the least important because it is concerned with man's political life. I would argue, on the contrary, that political order has an essential role to play in salvation, as Gerson's identification of good government with the persons of the Trinity demonstrates. In the hierarchical model that dominates Gerson's thought, the well-ordered polity has an indispensable role to play in guiding the individual soul to the third or heavenly realm.

Given the prominence accorded the four humours in this sermon, it is important to note that tyranny does not arise from a humoral imbalance, but from a poison or venom, administered or contracted from without. Tyranny is not, then, a sign of moral depravity, but of illness, and the head is not to be cut off, but treated. How is tyranny to be extirpated from the organism? Not, Gerson states firmly, by sedition, "rebellion populaire sans rime et sans raison" [popular rebellion without rhyme or reason], but by "bonnes parolles" [good words] (7.2.1159), such as those proffered by wise people like the University masters. Indeed, the University is the kingdom's first and best line of defence against tyranny, for "le royaume de France n'est point gouverné par tirannie quant il aime les estudes" [the kingdom of France is not governed by tyranny as long as it loves study] (*Pax hominibus* 7.2.773). For Gerson the University represents reason, and it is reason, as we shall see, that ensures the king's just treatment of his subjects and his respect for their rights.

Gerson affirms that those who wish to flatter the king might claim, based on the biblical phrase *hoc erit jus regis* [this will be the right of the king] (1 Samuel 8:11), that the king can dispose at will of the material goods of his subjects and the kingdom. This is a grave misunderstanding, Gerson cautions, one based upon an overly literal reading of the passage. Scripture is indeed the basis for good government, as we have seen, but the language of Scripture is not transparent, indeed "[l]es moz de l'escripture sont souvent equivoquez et se prennent aultrement en ung lieu qu'un ung aultre ou que en commune gramaire" [the words of scripture are often equivocal and can be taken differently in one place from another, or in common usage] (7.2.1157).[100] For this reason linguistic competence alone is inadequate to the work of interpretation, and kings need learned theologians – like the masters of the University of Paris, like Gerson himself – to interpret and explain how the words of Scripture are to be understood in relation to the practical problems of secular rule.

Gerson argues in *Vivat rex* that the biblical passage *hoc erit jus regis* does not justify the king's right to his subjects' goods. On the contrary, he uses the metaphor of the body politic to show that it would be unnatural for the king to control his subjects' material wealth, instead affirming the right of individuals to possess and control their private property. In this way Gerson suggests a theory of subjective property rights, defined by Cary Nederman as "defensible entitlements to independent full ownership (including alienation and enjoyment) of some tangible good exercised by an individual as an individual."[101] In *Vivat rex* Gerson does allow the king the latitude to claim the goods of his subjects in exceptional circumstances, which he defines as "la juste et necessaire deffence de son peuple" [the just and necessary defence of his people] (7.2.1158), but never for his personal use or pleasure. We shall see that in the later sermon *Rex in sempiternum vive* Gerson states in more absolute terms the king's obligation to respect his subjects' property.

In *Rex in sempiternum vive* Gerson reinflects the metaphor of the body politic by connecting it to the book of Daniel and to the statue of Nebuchadnezzar. Gerson identifies the statue's chest and arms with knights, the stomach and thighs with the clergy, and the legs and feet with bourgeois, merchants and labourers. The statue's golden head represents the king, but not only the king. In the opening to this sermon Gerson had declared that he was directing his words also "a la Reine notre dame souveraine, et a Monsieur de Guyenne qui sont comme un membre avec vous" [to the Queen our sovereign lady, and to my lord de Guyenne, who are as one member with you] (7.2.1010), and in his interpretation of the statue he affirms that "vous qui etes roi etes le chief d'or avec tous ceux de votre sang roïal" [you who are king are the golden head with all those of your royal blood] (7.2.1013). It is not surprising to see that the head of the statue includes the dauphin, since "legitime succession de la lignie roïale" [legitimate succession of the royal lineage] (7.2.1006) provides the basis for the sempiternity of the king's second life, and concern for his posterity or lineage (7.2.1011) explains the king's attachment to the polity.[102] It is more surprising to see that the head includes some who are not and will not be king, that it has become a corporation constituted synchronically as well as diachronically.

By mapping the divisions of French society onto a human form Gerson is glossing Nebuchadnezzar's statue, he says, "conformement a la sentence d'Aristote et de saint Paul et de Plutarque qui comparent un roiaume a un corps humain et a ses membres" [according to the words of Aristotle and Saint Paul and Plutarch, who compared the kingdom to a human body and its limbs] (7.2.1013).[103] Highlighting the originality of his own approach, Gerson notes that it is more usual to connect the four parts of the statue poetically to the four seasons or the four ages of mankind, or literally to the four principal kingdoms, and these latent meanings shape the significance of Gerson's use of the statue. Discussions of Nebuchadnezzar's statue that identify its four parts with successive kingdoms contributed to the establishment of the book of Daniel as an important medieval source for the idea of *translatio imperii*, which posits the contingency of secular rule and the transfer of power, often as the result of injustice. Thus, the four-part program for reform contained in *Rex in sempiternum vive* and rhetorically structured by the four parts of the statue, also conveys a warning to Charles VI, whose civil life is threatened: if Charles and the others who comprise the golden head do not now enact Gerson's reforms, the kingdom may not survive its present king. Indeed, one of the recurring themes in this sermon is the idea that kingdoms are lost through injustice. St Remy pronounced the salutation "rex in sempiternum vive," during the anointing of Clovis, Gerson says, "car dit l'histoire que saint Remy rempli du saint Esperit lui denonça que sa roïale seignorie dureroit tant que vraye foy et justice domineroit en son rouyaume" [for history tells us that Saint Remy, filled with the Holy Spirit, warned him that his royal lordship would endure as long as truth faith and justice might rule in his kingdom] (7.2.1006). The sombre caution attributed to St Remy in *Rex in sempiternum vive* differs markedly from the saint's affirmation of the superiority of the French king in the earlier sermon *Vivat rex*, where he is said to have anointed the king "en signe de royale puissance et comme sacerdotale ou pontificale dignite" [as a sign of his royal power and as with sacerdotal or pontifical dignity] (7.2.1140). Having witnessed political assassination and popular revolt during the years that separate these two sermons, Gerson seems less optimistic in *Rex in sempiternum vive* that the king will be able to meet the challenges of his reign.

Given this evolution in Gerson's attitude towards kingship, it is significant that in *Rex in sempiternum vive* he also defends in more absolute terms than he had previously the subjects' rights to own and control their property. He criticizes the custom of purveyance, according to which knights took the goods they needed from the people whose lands they traversed. This practice was often held up as evidence of the injustice and corruption of the king's armed forces. Even when the peasants were compensated, they were denied the right to choose whether to sell or withhold their goods, and also to determine their price, and so were not truly exercising control over their property.[104] Gerson declares such actions unacceptable; moreover, "le roy meme ne puet donner le congié en tous cas et selon son plaisir, car *le roy est subjet a raison et a la loy de Dieu et a justice*" [the king himself cannot give permission in all cases and according to his fancy, for *the king is subject to reason and the law of God and justice*] (7.2.1027, emphasis added).[105] Here Gerson upholds the subjective natural rights according to which individuals are entitled to control their goods, while raising the question of the relationship between the king and the law, often framed in the Middle Ages as the debate concerning whether it was better to have a *bon roi* or a *bonne loi*.

Ernst Kantorowicz discusses this problem extensively in chapter 4, "Law-centred Kingship," of his *King's Two Bodies*, wherein he defines the king as a liminal figure, the father and the son of justice, the *imago* and the *servus aequitatis*. In the *De regimine principum* Giles of Rome takes up the question of whether it is better to have a good king or a good law by first examining Aristotle's arguments for one and the other, and then concluding that the king is subject to natural law – which for him is indissociable from reason – but above positive law.[106] However, Giles does not address the question of how to enforce the king's adherence to positive law, which remained a problem. Cary Nederman has argued that the medieval conception of law was founded upon the understanding that law was a manifestation of divinely ordained precepts of justice, and as such obeying the law was a moral, but not a legal, obligation.[107] The king, like all individuals, was morally obliged to obey the law, but unlike ordinary people he could not be legally constrained to do so. Because the king's relationship to the law was founded upon personal morality rather than legal or institutional principles, scholars have argued that medieval responses to tyranny, the manifest failure to respect the law, were forced to be local and ad hoc in nature.[108]

I would argue, however, that Gerson clearly understood the need for an institutional response to this problem. One might debate whether he was successful in his efforts to limit the authority of the king, but I contend that Gerson at least recognized that a range of circumstances – minority, personal depravity, mental incapacity – might render the king unable to ensure the administration of justice, and that therefore structural means had to be devised and implemented to guarantee justice in the kingdom. In *Rex in sempiternum vive* Gerson holds the king to the same legal standards as his subjects. The king cannot authorize exceptions to the law, nor is he himself outside of or free from its dictates. In this respect we see Gerson moving away from a conception of law in which the king's obedience is a moral – but not a legal – imperative, and towards the idea that the law provides an objective standard to which all are legally obliged to adhere.

It is important to observe in the passage cited above that reason is yoked to "la loy de Dieu" and to "justice," and we shall see that reason is Gerson's most powerful tool for attempting to circumscribe the power of the king, and the one that justifies the University's involvement in governance. In response to the threat of tyranny imagined in *Vivat rex*, Gerson had affirmed that it would be better for kings and princes "qu'ilz aient mendre seignourie qui soit raisonnable, sainne et durable par baillier aucun restraintif, que le chief ne traie trop a soy l'umeur et le sang des aultrez membrez. Ce n'est pas grever le chief mais l'aidier" [that they have more modest lordship and that it be reasonable, healthy, and durable by placing some restraint {upon it}, so that the head might not draw to itself the humours and the blood of the other members. This is not burdening the head, but helping it] (7.2.1159). Somewhat paradoxically, the very restrictions Gerson would like to impose upon the head constitute an expression of his support for the institution of kingship. By accepting restrictions on his authority "le seigneur ne se soubmect point a sez subgetz, mais a raison" [the lord does not submit himself to his people, but to reason] (7.2.1159–60).[109] It is important to note that Gerson speaks in general terms, addressing his remarks to "kings and princes" and imagining a structural response to the danger of tyranny. His solution, in other words, is not an ad hoc one, but is designed to apply to kingship as an institution. Gerson absolutely upholds royal rule, while at the same time affirming that lordship should be *raisonnable* and that the king is subject to reason.

The primacy of reason is most pronounced in the later sermon *Rex in sempiternum vive*. Here Gerson affirms that no party should be able to carry out acts of war "sans le congié du roy expres ou entendu" [without the express or implied permission of the king] (7.2.1019), a clear reference to the civil conflict between the Armagnacs and the Bourguignons, and their repeated failure to adhere to treaties of peace. The express consent of the king is only legitimate if it is granted "selon raison" [according to reason] (7.2.1020). If people lie to the king in order to obtain his accord, Gerson warns, the resulting war will not be a just one. The University, whose job it is to tell the truth and whose interests, as we have seen, are perfectly aligned with those of king and kingdom, can prevent the king from erring based on misinformation. Indeed, the University has more eyes than Argus, Gerson affirms, and if anyone should prevent one of the University masters from telling the truth, another master, hydra-like, will present himself (7.2.1027).

By implied permission Gerson means "quand selon les loix royalles justes et raisonnables aucune chose se fait au royaulme, car le roy parle en ses loix" [when according to just and reasonable royal laws something is done in the kingdom, for the king speaks through his laws] (7.2.1019). This statement represents yet another effort to cope with the king's absences, for his laws ought to be respected at all times and places. The stability of the law compensates to some degree for the king's inability to maintain order, while their institutionalized authority supplements the contingent authority of any given king. It is important to note that only laws that are "justes et raisonnables" are able to stand in for the voice of the king. Similarly, the nobles should not make war on a king "qui se porte *justement*" [who conducts himself *justly*], for the "commandement *raisonnable*" [*reasonable* command] of the king supersedes all others (7.2.1028, emphasis added). Gerson's addition of qualifiers such as *justement* and *raisonnable* suggests that in fact there may be times when the king should not be obeyed, not because his temporal authority is not supreme, but because he is not conducting himself in accordance with the higher authorities of God, reason, and justice.

Some scholars have expressed surprise at the prominence Gerson accords to reason, expecting instead to see grace predominate in his political thought.[110] In fact, these are not antithetical qualities. In Gerson's verse dialogue *L'école de la conscience* he stages a debate between the conscience, reason, the heart, and the senses, in which the latter are depicted as unruly students who require a firm master, reason, to keep them in check. Reason, however, is powerless to control the senses "Se Dieu, le docteur souverain, / de sa grace n'y met la main" [if God the sovereign doctor does not, by his grace, lend a hand] (7.1.8). In a similar verse dialogue, *L'école de la raison*, Gerson defines reason as the spouse of God (7.1.107). These dialogues suggest that reason, the heart, and the senses may be placed in parallel with the three orders of French society as they are discussed in *Omne regnum*. In this sermon Gerson affirms that the personal kingdom contained within each person is comprised of three estates: "de clergie, de chevalerie et de bourgeoisie. Raison represente l'estat de clergie; franche voulente de chevalerie et seigneurie, sensualite de bourgoisie" [of clergy/learning, of chivalry, and of bourgeoisie. Reason represents the order of clergy, free will of chivalry and lordship, and sensory perceptions of bourgeoisie] (7.2.753). *Clergie* refers to the clerical order, but also to learning more generally, and here Gerson may be suggesting that the role of *clergie* within society falls more specifically to the University masters, especially the theologians. Just as Gerson explicitly aligns reason with *clergie*, so too we may align the heart with "volonté," or the knightly class, and the senses with "sensualité," which corresponds to the merchants, bourgeois, and people. Before the fall, Gerson explains, each person's reason obeyed God perfectly, and reason in turn was obeyed by the will, and the will by the senses. Gerson discusses the ways in which individuals should strive to re-establish this prelapsarian order within their personal kingdoms. Since in *Omne regnum* the personal kingdom is said to be analogous to any community or assembly, we may understand the role of *clergie* within the body politic as comparable to that of reason within the body natural. In this way Gerson privileges the clergy – or, as I've suggested, the theologians of the University – over the nobles in their involvement in government. It is the learned men of the University, those who embody reason and who are closest to God, who should take the lead in helping the king to rule. Of irreproachable loyalty, dedicated to teaching truth and upholding justice, the University can help the king to rule in accordance with reason, thereby preserving him – and his subjects – from tyranny.

By developing in tandem the representations of the University both as an allegorical body – the *fille du roy* – and as a metaphorical one – analogous to king and kingdom – Gerson tries in all the ways imaginable to establish the University's role within a kingdom governed by the rule of law, in which reason ensures justice and the peaceful ordering of society, so that king and subjects might all attain the ultimate goal of salvation. If the king is the head of the mystical body of the kingdom, the University is that body's reason, and as such it directs the head and coordinates the body's actions in order to ensure the physical, material, and spiritual health of the whole. Those familiar with John of Salisbury's *Policraticus* (1159), which asserted that "anima tocius habet corporis principatum" [the soul has supremacy over the entire body] and "in humano corpore ab anima vegetatur caput et regitur" [in the human body also, the head is animated and governed by the soul] (462), might have been surprised to see the Church given no authority over the body politic in Gerson's works.[111] In his fourteenth-century translation and adaptation of the *Policraticus* Denis Foulechat had already distanced the Church from temporal rule, affirming that "ceulz qui sont presidens ou service de la religion" [those who preside over religious services] (271) are dedicated to the "bien et fait commun" [the common good and activities] (271) and "le corps du bien commun" [the body of the common good] (272), but are not set above the secular ruler within the body politic. This distancing of the Church from secular rule is far more pronounced in Gerson's works, where the Church is never assimilated to the soul of the body, or given a role in governance. Instead, the University and reason will lead the king and his subjects towards peace and order on earth, and to heaven in the afterlife.

Gerson's rich and diverse representations of the University of Paris allow him to assert the authority of this institution to represent the kingdom and to guide the king's rule according to principles of justice and reason.[112] Metaphorically, the University is a mystical body that is analogous to both king and kingdom, and serves as an intermediary between the two. As an analogue of the king, the University pursues an agenda entirely consistent with the king's honour and eventual salvation. It is as a representative body that the University may be seen to drift towards allegory, for although Gerson highlights the diversity of the students and masters in order to claim an institutional role for the University in the administration of the kingdom, he nevertheless suppresses the heterogeneity of opinions within this body, permitting it to speak with just one voice – his own.

As the *fille du roy*, the University fulfils the conventionally female role of supplicant and intercessor, speaking on behalf of the University masters and students, but also more broadly, on behalf the subjects who are oppressed and deprived of a voice. The *fille du roy* is a model subject and an ideal royal daughter. The University's imagined descent from the king allows her to displace the king's biological relatives, her loyalty and obedience standing in stark contrast to their naked ambition and self-interest. Moreover, the filiation between king and University suggests that the latter is, like the dauphin, descended from and also "une mesme personne avecquez" [one and the same person with] (7.2.1147) the king. The University thus serves as a repository of and heir to the king's political authority, but one who does not threaten the literal, biological lines of succession that ensured the transmission of political power from one generation to the next.

Though the University does not produce rivals to royal succession, her mystical body *is* a procreative one. In *Vivat rex* Gerson depicts the University as a kind of bride of the kingdom.[113] The influx of students and masters from all parts of the kingdom is likened to a "semence vertueuse deriviee de tout le corps de la chose publique" [a virtuous semen derived from the entire body of the public entity] which gestates "ou ventre de l'Universite pour naistre gens de toute perfection" [in the womb of the University to bear people of every perfection] (7.2.1146).[114] These "gens de toute perfection," derived from the kingdom and born of the University, are responsible for the generation and transmission of knowledge over time, thereby preserving the mystical body of the University and also ensuring that the kings of France will always be equipped with royal servants who combine learning with devotion to the *chose publique*. The powerful fecundity of the University therefore guarantees the reproduction of a set of hierarchically ordered mystical bodies, those of the kingdom, its king, and of course the University herself. Gerson thus inscribes within the cultural and political imaginary a body at once metaphorical and allegorical, capable of supplying what is wanting when the kingdom's head is absent, assuring the continued existence of the kingdom of France in this life, and providing the conditions for attaining salvation in the next.

4
Envisioning the Body Politic before and after the Treaty of Troyes

... un moyen dangereux, un secours menaçant,
la réponse critique à une situation de détresse.

Jacques Derrida, *De la grammatologie*

The accession of Henry V to the English throne in 1413, and his interest in pressing – both militarily and ideologically – the English claims to the kingdom of France, gave renewed urgency to the French responses to these combined challenges. In this chapter I shall examine how the conflicts that arose from the contested exercise of power came to be articulated through discourses that focused on gender. This is in part because the dynastic crises of the fourteenth century, and the English challenges to Valois legitimacy, raised questions concerning the rights of women to rule or to transmit such a right to their male offspring. But in addition, gender provided a ready-made and apparently natural hierarchy that allowed French writers to draw boundaries, found or proclaim legitimacy, and conceptualize the relationship between self and society.

In the first part of this chapter we shall observe the fabrication of a myth of national identity. The sixth-century legal code of the Salian Franks, or *Lex Salica*, on the one hand, and on the other hand the principles concerning female exclusion from royal rule that were developed over the course of the fourteenth century,[1] were brought together in the fifteenth century by the humanist writer Jean de Montreuil under the rubric of Salic Law.[2] Although Salic Law was – and still is – often discussed in relation to the fitness of women to occupy certain social and political roles, it was not resurrected and refashioned in the fifteenth century exclusively for the purpose of condemning women, but rather as a post-facto justification for a series of contested royal successions.[3] The royal secretary Jean de Montreuil was the first explicitly to employ Salic Law[4] to argue that women could neither succeed to the throne of France nor serve as "pont et planche" on behalf of their male issue, thereby demonstrating that the claims of the English kings to the kingdom of France – claims based upon Edward III of England's descent from Isabelle of France – were unfounded.[5] Jean's primary aim was the defence of the kingdom, and Salic Law was an important instrument in his pursuit of this larger goal. As Jean presents it, Salic Law does not articulate any new principles concerning hereditary succession, but it does function as a kind of shorthand or conceptual container for a complex set of ideas about French collective identity that were then deployed by subsequent writers with great regularity. By examining the works of Jean de Montreuil I will show how Salic Law was used to define, proclaim, and diffuse a nationalistic agenda.

In the second part of the chapter we shall see how the Treaty of Troyes (21 May 1420) between Charles VI of France and Henry V of England fundamentally transformed the issues to which the French were forced to respond. Excluding the dauphin Charles from royal succession, and proclaiming the English king Henry V, who was to wed Charles VI's daughter Catherine, to be the French king's son and heir, the Treaty of Troyes attempted to divert the line of French royal succession by legal means. The extent and nature of English territorial possessions on the continent, including the long and bitterly contested rights of sovereignty and ressort (that is to say, judicial appeal) were no longer the bone of contention between England and France. Instead, Henry V laid claim to the entire kingdom by substituting himself for the dauphin as the rightful heir of Charles VI. By virtue of Henry's marriage to Catherine, the treaty affirmed, "il est devenu nostre filz" [he has become our son], and Charles VI designated this adopted son the "héritier de France" [heir of France].[6] Moreover, the treaty required virtually all the French subjects and institutions to swear elaborate oaths to uphold the treaty and to remain loyal to Henry V and his heirs.[7] Even the allies of the two kingdoms were asked to respect the terms of the treaty. These events forced a generation of royal administrators, diplomats, and legal experts to re-examine the principles that governed royal succession, as well as the nature and limits of the king's authority, especially with regard to rights understood or said to belong not to the king but to the crown or kingdom.

Supporters of the dauphin, later Charles VII, countered the Treaty of Troyes with Nature, arguing in a variety of texts for the inviolability of biological succession. The idea that the dauphin possessed rights to the throne even during his father's lifetime was already current in French political thought. We saw in chapter 3 that Jean Gerson defined the dauphin as "une mesme personne avecquez le roy" [the same person with the king] (7.2.1147). Similarly, in the royal ordinances promulgated by Charles VI, the king affirms that "sitost qu'il plaist à Dieu envoier sur terre au Roy qui est pour le temps, hoir masle premier nez, droit de nature le baille héritier dudit Royaume" [as soon as it pleases God to send to earth to the current king a male heir, first-born, the law of nature makes him heir of the aforesaid kingdom].[8] The jurist Jean de Terre Rouge (sometimes called Terrevermeille), in a series of Latin legal treatises composed after the dauphin was deprived of the regency (December 1418) but before the Treaty of Troyes, extended the rights of the dauphin by demonstrating that by virtue of his birth, by the "nature of things," he possessed rights to the kingdom of France that the king did not have the authority to alienate.[9] In this chapter we shall see such ideas developed in texts intended for a more expansive audience than the Latinate and learned public envisioned by Jean de Terre Rouge.[10]

The royal secretary and diplomat Alain Chartier, in a vernacular dream vision, used the allegory of France to show how political structures and action were grounded in Nature. Chartier's *Quadrilogue invectif* was composed in the wake of the Treaty of Troyes, but prior to the deaths of Henry V and Charles VI, which occurred on 31 August and 21 October 1422, respectively. In this prose dialogue, the narrator describes the lamentations of a crowned lady, identified in the rubric as France, and her forceful denunciation of her three children, Peuple, Chevalier, and Clergé, followed by the responses and self-justifications of the latter. Chartier's France, as both a maternal and a political body, epitomizes the convergence of the natural and the political that characterizes much of late medieval French political thought. In her discourse she employs terms such as *nature*, *naturelle*, *desnaturez*, *naissance*, *nez* – all derived from the Latin root *nascor* (*nascere*, *natus*, *naturus*), to be born – in order to describe and prescribe the appropriate relationships between people, lands, and leaders. Chartier's France both incarnates and employs nature as a paradigm for political feeling and action, for within her opening discourse the facts of one's birth – themselves manifestations of God's will – are indissociable from a set of political loyalties and commitments. Those who fail to show the appropriate zeal in the defence of their country are *desnaturez*, inferior to the birds and beasts who defend their homes with tooth and claw. By defining the natural world as both a source and a model for political sentiment and action, Chartier is able to forge a feeling of national unity based on loyalty to the place of one's birth and shared fidelity to the king of France.

The royal lawyer and bishop Jean Juvénal des Ursins composed his own allegorical dream vision, *Audite celi*, in the months preceding the peace conference held in Arras in 1435, which did not succeed in ending the Hundred Years' War, but which did result in a separate peace between Charles VII and Philip the Good of Burgundy. Jean Juvénal's dream vision features a conversation between France, Angleterre, and Sainte Église, with shorter appearances by other allegorical figures such as Sedition, Prudence, and Good Counsel (Bon Conseil). Unlike Christine de Pizan and Alain Chartier, Jean Juvénal does not focus on the allegory of France as a maternal figure. Not the *materfamilias* caught up in a family drama of the *Quadrilogue*, the France of *Audite celi*, still insistently female, is a knowledgeable and articulate historian, legal expert, and diplomat. In a lengthy response to the English claims, France reviews the principles and history of Salic Law, explains why it would not be appropriate or acceptable for women to rule the kingdom of France, recounts the history of Normandy and Guyenne, and finally shows that the English kings do not possess legitimate rights to their own kingdom, much less to the kingdom of France. The allegory of France affirms national boundaries and serves to establish and proclaim the unity and coherence of the kingdom of France, which includes her errant prince, Philip the Good, and his duchy of Burgundy.

Jean de Montreuil and the Forging of Myth

The study of Salic Law has largely been undertaken by historians, and has tended to focus on actual women, and the circumstances in which they wielded – or were excluded from – political power and authority.[11] In what follows I propose to reorient the discussion about Salic Law in order to illuminate the ways in which ideas about women and discourses of gender provided a language and a conceptual framework with which to think through other sorts of issues, in particular the profound anxiety on the part of the French about domination of the kingdom by foreign kings, specifically by the English. As we shall see, the threat of foreign invasion is articulated in gendered terms, and queens are imagined as the means by which foreign elements insinuate themselves into the kingdom. At the same time, the vulnerability of the kingdom is conveyed using the language of sexual violence in which the English attempt to force their king, their laws, and their rule, upon the unwilling French. The kingdom of France is feminized in this scenario, and it is this fragility – coded as feminine – that

Salic Law seeks to overcome by erasing women from royal rule, imagining a transmission of authority in which men succeed to one another in a fantasy of generation from which women are entirely absent.[12] Salic Law thus provided for a manly kingdom, one able to resist and oppose the violence of the English and to ensure that "France seroit tousjours aux Françoiz, et aux Angloiz Angleterre" [France would belong always to the French, and to the English, England] (179).[13]

The royal secretary and diplomat Jean de Montreuil has been credited with "inventing" Salic Law, but both the *Lex Salica* and the idea that women ought be excluded from royal rule existed long before he began composing his treatises in the early fifteenth century.[14] The *Lex Salica*, in its earliest redaction, dates from the sixth century, while the principle of female exclusion from royal rule was first articulated in the context of the crises of succession that marked the final years of Capetian rule.[15] First, in 1316, Louis X's brother served as regent for the pregnant queen and, upon the death of her infant son, succeeded as king.[16] Second, in 1328, Charles IV's first cousin, Philippe de Valois, similarly served as regent for the pregnant queen, and then, when she gave birth to a daughter, succeeded as king.[17]

At the time of Philippe de Valois's succession, there was another claimant, Edward III of England (r. 1327–77), the son of Philippe IV's daughter Isabelle and nephew of the last three Capetian kings. Edward was the closest male heir to Charles IV, but his claim passed through a cognate line. Could a woman transmit a right that she could not herself exercise or possess? Given the overlapping and sometimes conflicting legal authorities that might be invoked, and the lack of any royal ordinance or directive on this subject, both sides were able to marshal plausible arguments in favour of their candidate. In the end, an assembly of barons decided in favour of Philippe de Valois on the basis that just as women could not rule in France, neither could they transmit the right to rule to their male issue.[18]

Over a century later Jean Juvénal des Ursins affirmed that at the time of Louis X's death in 1316, "il fut dit, jugié, sentencié et prononcié par maniere d'arrest que fille ne devoit point succeder ne ne succederoit ou royaulme" [it was said, judged, concluded, and proclaimed in the form of a decree that a maiden ought not succeed nor would succeed to the kingdom] (46). If only this were true the events of the fourteenth century might have unfolded quite differently than they did. Unfortunately for the Valois, the various assemblies of notables and of the University masters who approved first the regency, and later the succession, of Louis's brother Philippe – and later of Philippe de Valois – produced no proclamations or ordinances governing royal succession. Indeed, it is precisely this documentary void that the Valois supporters found themselves still seeking to overcome a century later, and in the context of which Salic Law proved so useful.[19]

All of this legal to and fro-ing obscures one of the most important questions at issue in the Valois succession, which, for Paul Viollet, could be summed up in clear and simple terms: "La France devait rester aux Valois parce que les Valois étaient français" (149). While one might argue that Viollet overstated the role played by identity politics with respect to the Valois succession of 1328, I contend that nationalistic concerns were very much at the heart of the fifteenth-century refashioning of Salic Law. In 1413, the central issue was not whether women were fit to rule, but how to ensure that only French might rule the kingdom of France.[20] As we shall see, the perception of fundamental difference from the English, and the anxiety about the vulnerability of France to foreign elements – both far more pronounced in Jean de Montreuil's time than in the decisions of 1316 and 1328 – are conceptualized through discourses that focus on gender, and in particular through discussions of the Salic Law.

Though initially he accepted the kingship of Philippe VI, Edward III soon pressed his rights of sovereignty and ressort in Aquitaine, and eventually asserted his claim to the French throne, resulting in the ongoing series of conflicts that we know as the Hundred Years' War (1337–1453).[21] In the treaty of Brétigny (1360) Edward renounced his claims to the throne in exchange for greatly expanded continental possessions which he was to hold in full sovereignty, that is, not as a fief from the king of France. These are more or less the claims that the English would continue to press until Henry V once again asserted – though on an entirely new basis – his right to the kingdom of France.

Jean de Montreuil is known for his supposed creation of Salic Law, but in fact Salic Law occupies only a small part of his political thought. Jean's textual production needs to be considered in light of nascent French humanism, and Jean's purposeful promotion of textual production as a means to combat the English.[22] One of the most striking aspects of his two principal treatises, *Regali ex progenie* (1406–13), often referred to by its French title, *À toute la chevalerie*, and the *Traité contre les anglais* (1413–16), is the fact that both exist in a number of versions, in both Latin and the vernacular, in expanded forms and as précis.[23] Jean was clearly trying to reach as many readers as he possibly could, by repeating the same central arguments in forms designed for use and consultation by disparate publics.[24] The objects of Jean's efforts, I would argue, are not only diplomats and royal administrators, but also the groups Bernard Guenée identified as the "people of authority" and the "wise."[25] Jean insists upon the practical utility of his works, explaining for instance in *À toute la chevalerie*, a text explicitly directed to the French nobility, that he has provided a "somme" or summa of the most illustrious French deeds of chivalry that will be inspiring to his contemporary public. Similarly, in the third redaction of the *Traité contre les anglais* Jean observes that he has summarized the legal and theoretical bases for French legitimacy "par maniere d'abregié, pour relever le liseur de tant d'escriptures veoir et chercher" [in the form of an abridgement, to relieve the reader of the burden of consulting and looking for so many documents] (269). In his vernacular texts he is particularly aware that he is addressing a public with neither the technical background, nor perhaps even the attention span, to follow complex legal arguments. With respect to the ways in which the English failed to adhere to the terms of the treaty of Brétigny, therefore, he says that "[m]aintes loiz et decretalles pourroient estre aleguees en ceste partie et par tout ce present traictié, se la besongne n'en fust trop prolixe et obscure a gens laiz non lectréz, pour lesquelz principalement informer du commancement et procés de ceste matiere cecy a esté fait grossement et plainement, par maniere de somme et d'abregié" [many laws and decretals could be cited in this part and throughout this treatise, if the work were not too wordy and obscure for unlettered laypeople, for whom principally to inform of the origins and development of this subject the present text has been made, clearly and plainly, in the manner of a summa and an abridgement] (296). Unlettered, here, means not Latinate. Jean recognizes the presence in society of a group for whom the historical and political knowledge he provides is useful, even essential, but which is not capable of consulting sources such as those Jean employs in the redaction of his texts. Accordingly, his treatise repeats the key components of the French position, without citing all the authorities from which these points are derived.

In Jean's treatises written sources provide information, and serve as evidence of legal and historical truth. In *À toute la chevalerie* Jean defends himself from the imagined accusation that clerics ought not opine upon military matters of which they have no experience with the assertion that since clerics are the ones who write the histories of chivalric encounters and events, they are well informed on such topics and able to speak about them knowledgeably.[26] In the third version of his *Traité contre les anglais* he names the sources for his discussion of the history of English holdings in Guyenne, and his combination of historical and documentary sources is presented as proof of the accuracy of Jean's own redaction of these events.

In the case of Edward III's liege homage to Philippe VI, one of Jean's key points in his refutation of the English king's claims to the French throne, he reproduces the text of the letter in which Edward acknowledges his homage for Guyenne, rendered in 1329, to have been liege. Jean reproduces not only the contents of the letter, but also describes the physical details of the document itself, in order to produce a literary artefact that testifies to the truth of his own writing.[27]

Just as Jean deploys written sources to support his arguments, so too his treatises constitute authentic and truthful testimonies to the events that he describes. His *Traité contre les anglais* is a "tesmoingnage de verité" [testimony of truth] (162, also 268) that will make clear to participants and observers on both sides of the conflict the ill-founded and unjust nature of the English claims. The written word provides a way to fix meaning such that it cannot, in principle, be manipulated or misunderstood. In the conclusion to his *Traité contre les anglais* Jean de Montreuil addresses his potential readers, including the English. If they believe they have better evidence of right on their side Jean invites them to produce it, and he will consider it with care. "Mais qu'ilz baillent, ainsi que nous faisons, par escript; car on ne doit pas ne n'appartient mie a parler de voulenté en si haulte matiere comme celle qui est cy devant ouverte et aucunement traictié [But may they provide it, as we do, in writing, for one should not, nor is it appropriate to speak at will on so lofty a subject as that which is disclosed, and in a certain manner treated, above] (216)."[28] In this passage Jean insists that documentary evidence supports all the claims in his treatise. He also affirms that diplomatic matters should be handled in writing so that the other side may carefully weigh and examine the arguments of their opponents, and so that the words cannot later be changed.[29] Oral promises and agreements can be forgotten, modified, or denied; only the written word has legal and evidentiary value. With respect to the offers allegedly made by Charles V, for instance, Jean challenges the English to provide written evidence of them.[30] For Jean it is as though only that which appears in writing truly exists. The spoken word is ephemeral, mutable, vulnerable.[31]

If, on one hand, written documents substantiate both historical events and recent political negotiations, they also play an important role in the contested realm of public opinion. Jean understands the power of texts to shape perceptions, and the importance of attempting to do so.[32] In *À toute la chevalerie* Jean provides a historical account of English holdings on the continent in which he emphasizes the perfidiousness of the English vassals and the sovereignty of the French king throughout his kingdom. He concludes with a chapter on recent history entitled *Les journeez et rencontres en brief que lez François ont eu sur les Angloiz puis XL ans ou environ.* The opening paragraph of this chapter describes "une grande rencontre" [a great encounter] (110) between French and English forces, and the subsequent paragraphs – almost one hundred of them – begin with "une autre" or "item," and each provides a brief summary of a French victory. Jean's use of anaphora and the list-like structure of the chapter – a characteristic of administrative documents that bespeaks Jean's professional status – suggest that his account of the French victories could go on forever. It is not so much the details of any given skirmish that are important, but rather the rhetorical effects of repetition and accumulation. If any reader should suggest that some of the encounters Jean includes were of little importance or involved few people, Jean retorts that "les Anglois ... ne prengnent mie ... une povre maison plate tant soit petitement garnie ou foible, ou font a peine escarmuches dont ilz aient l'avantaige, qu'i ne mettent tout en cronique et par escript" [the English do not take even a poor unfortified house, be it ever so weak or modestly garrisoned, or have the slightest skirmish in which they have the upper hand, without putting all of it in a chronicle and in writing] (121). On one hand, Jean mocks the English for making much of their smallest victories, but on the other hand he recognizes that the English have been beating France not only on the battlefield, but also in the realm of public opinion. The French must engage in this war of words "au bien et au prouffit de che royaume" [for the good and profit of this kingdom] (121). Since the major French losses at Crécy, Poitiers, and Agincourt were commonly interpreted as signs of God's disfavour, it was imperative to represent the French as victors, and therefore worthy of success, and an important way to achieve this aim, as Jean well understood, was by documenting and publicizing French chivalric achievements.

In the third version of the *Traité contre les anglais* Jean again refers to the documentary skills of the English. Thanks to the texts they have compiled and that they carry and consult, the English are far more knowledgeable about the legal and historical details of their conflict than are the French, and this places them at a diplomatic advantage.[33] Their superiority in this regard is not only evident among England's professional jurists and administrators, but among the "grand seigneurs" [great lords] as well.[34] In order to compete effectively with such opponents, the French must become better acquainted with the scope and basis of their own claims, and Jean's many treatises are intended to serve this purpose. Unlike the previous versions of this treatise, the third redaction of the *Traité contre les anglais* has a dedicatee, the dauphin, who is held accountable, in particular, for mastering its contents.[35] As Jean says in his dedication, "semble que, veue la grandeur de ceste matiere, qui est celle du monde qui plus touche le roy, vous et tout le royaume de France, vous la devez savoir pour en parler en lieu et en temps et avoir a cueur pour y pourvoir sur toutes choses" [it seems that, given the magnitude of this subject, which is that which in all the world most touches the king, you, and all the kingdom of France, you ought to know about it in order to speak of it in the appropriate times and places, and be resolved to prepare for all eventualities] (266). Jean's treatise provides what are essentially talking points for use by the dauphin, nobles, diplomats, and administrators. As we shall see, they are relatively few in number and are endlessly repeated within each of Jean's treatises, which themselves, as we have observed, are rewritten, expanded, and abridged time and again.

The "invention" of Salic Law, then, must be understood in relation to Jean de Montreuil's humanist spirit of philological inquiry, reliance upon documentary evidence, and faith in the capacity of the written word to effect cultural and political change. Salic Law provides yet another example of how Jean deploys historical documents as proof of French rights. Yet, Salic Law is not the unique foundation for Jean's defence of Valois legitimacy and sovereignty, but is an important component of a broad counterattack. What I have referred to as Jean's talking points fall into three main categories: the history of the English presence on the continent; the conduct of the English following the succession of Philippe VI in 1328; and the theoretical and legal justifications for Valois legitimacy, including Salic Law.

As Jean depicts it, over the relatively recent and brief history of their presence in France, the English have distinguished themselves by their systematic feudal misconduct. Jean reviews the battles and treaties in which the English acquired and lost various territories in Aquitaine and Normandy concluding, in his *Résumé du traité contre les anglais*, that the English "n'en eulrent onc ung pié en France, fust par mariage ou aultrement, que [finablement] ilz n'en feissent au roy [et au royaume] de France guerre et moleste" [never had even a foot in France, be it by marriage or otherwise, but that in the end they did not make war and cause injury to the king and the kingdom of France] (329). Jean's account demonstrates the antiquity of French control of the contested territories, and the sovereignty that they have never relinquished over the said lands, as well as the perfidy of the English from the time of their earliest interactions with the French to the present day. As Peter Lewis and Nicole Pons have pointed out, the significance of this historicizing impulse should not be underestimated.[36]

Jean fashions a version of French history that endeavours to shape and even to impose a consciousness of a collective identity, one that embraces a disparate and potentially resistant public that includes Gascons, Bretons, Normans, and others with little sympathy for the notion of France. Moreover, Jean seeks to project his vision of a shared identity backward in time such that questions that were part of contemporary debates – like the sovereignty of the French king over the totality of his territory – appear to have been resolved long ago in a manner than rendered them constitutive, even, of French national identity.[37]

With regard to more recent history, Jean shows that the conduct of the English invalidated any claims to the French throne that they might, in principle, have had. First, Edward himself swore homage to Philippe VI de Valois. In a subsequent letter which, as we have seen, is both materially described and textually reproduced in a number of Jean's treatises, Edward acknowledges that homage to have been liege. Moreover, Edward waited many years to make his claim, and in the interim he sent his procurer to Philippe's Parlement in tacit and reiterated acknowledgment of the latter's sovereignty.[38] Jean often refutes multiple alternatives arising from the same point. With respect to the Treaty of Brétigny, for instance – which ended the first phase of the Hundred Years' War after the French defeat at Poitiers and capture of their king, Jean II – he says that Edward III renounced his claims to the throne, an argument that supposes the validity of the treaty, and also that Edward rendered the treaty null by failing to adhere to its terms. After denying Edward's claim in every possible way, Jean then affirms that even if one were to concede that Edward did have a right to the throne, the Lancastrians Henry IV and Henry V, who ruled England during the years of Jean's literary production, did not. Henry IV deposed and killed his liege lord Richard II, Edward's grandson, and is therefore himself a usurper.

Jean's final set of points are legal and theoretical, and in his multiple iterations of these points, he will consistently present three related ideas: the French adhere to a law that is unique to them; it is a reasonable and a just law; it enjoys the support and consent of the French people. In the first redaction of the *Traité contre les anglais*, and again in the third, Jean affirms that "selon la diversité des pays sont diverses constitutions et loys" [according to the diversity of countries there are different constitutions and laws] (166, also 272).[39] In conformity with this principle, the French possess a unique law that governs royal succession, stipulating that women may neither inherit nor transmit the right to rule. Since, as Jean observes, French history offers no example of a queen ruling the kingdom in her own right, the principle of female exclusion must be very old, as old as the kingdom itself. With respect to English claims to the throne, Jean explains that since Edward III's pretensions are based on his descent from Isabelle of France, the daughter of Philippe le Bel, they are entirely unfounded, for "par constitucion et ordonnance bien fondee et approuvee par tout le royaume, femme ne masle qui ne vient que de par femme ne succedent point au royaume ne a la couronne de France" [by a law and ordinance well founded and approved throughout the kingdom, a woman, or a man who is descended only from a woman, does not succeed to the kingdom or to the crown of France] (131). This is essentially what the assemblies of 1328 had indeed said, though their deliberations pertained specifically to the Valois succession, and they did not frame their conclusions more broadly in the guise of an ordinance, or legal precedent. As Jean's use of the passive voice makes clear, he is not able to say precisely who "founded and approved" what, nor in what context. Yet since, according to Jean, the custom of female exclusion is a reasonable one ("bien fondee") so "il appert que ladite ordonnance pouoit et devoit estre faicte en tous temps" [it is clear that the aforesaid ordinance could and should have been made for all times] (132). However reasonable this ordinance may have been, Jean was nevertheless faced with a troubling documentary lacuna.[40] In response, I contend that Jean did not so much invent Salic Law, as go looking for something that he believed from the outset *must* exist somewhere among the French archives and histories: a written legal basis for the exclusion of women from royal power. What he found, of course, was the *Lex Salica*.

What comes to be referred to simply as the Salic Law in France is in fact but one clause of one article from the law code of the Salian Franks. This code was first compiled c. 507–11, and consisted originally of 65 articles, most of which specify the price to be paid for various injuries and harms inflicted upon others. It was updated during the reign of Pepin the short, c. 763–4, and expanded to some 100 articles. During the reign of Charlemagne a new version of the code was promulgated, with 70 articles. The article that so interested Jean de Montreuil and others is called *De alode* or *De alodis*, that is to say, immovable goods, or *alleux*[41] in Old French. This article lists, in order of preference, who should inherit the goods of individuals who die without leaving living children, and the final clause states, in one of the most ancient versions: *De terra vero nulla in muliere hereditas non pertinebit, sed ad virilem sexum qui fratres fuerint tota terra perteneunt* [As for the land, none of the inheritance will belong to the woman, but to the virile sex who were brothers all of the land belongs].[42]

In its original context, the article says nothing about transmission of the crown, nor does it identify the *terra* as the kingdom of France.[43]

In *À toute la chevalerie* Jean describes how "j'ay oy dire au chantre et croniqueur de Saint Denis, personne de grant religion et reverence, qu'il a trouvé par tres anciens livres que ladicte coustume et ordonnance, qu'il appelle la loy Salica, fu faicte et constituee devant qu'il eust oncques roy chrestien en France. Et je mesmes l'ay veu, et leu ycelle loy en un ancient livre, renouvelee et confermee par Charlemaingne" [I heard it said by the chanter and chronicler of Saint Denis, a person of great devotion and piety, that he had found in a very ancient book that the aforesaid custom and ordinance, which he called the Salic Law, was made and constituted before there ever was a Christian king in France. And I myself saw it, and read this law in an ancient book, updated and confirmed by Charlemagne] (132). This passage contains many elements intended to demonstrate the authenticity and inviolability of the law in question, as well as its applicability to the kingdom and the crown of France: Jean's information comes from a reliable individual; the text is associated with the abbey of Saint Denis, the source and repository of the official history of the kingdom; the manuscript in question is very ancient, which Jean had supposed it must be, given the timeless quality he attributes to the principle of female exclusion; the law code was crafted by the original founders of the kingdom of France and predates even the conversion of the kingdom to Christianity; finally, the code was revised and reaffirmed by none other than the emperor Charlemagne.[44] Jean then quotes the relevant passage.[45] This genealogy of Salic Law, always with the repetition of the most important elements – pre-Christian establishment of the law, reaffirmation by Charlemagne – is included in Jean's subsequent treatises; indeed, it often appears more than once in a given text. In this manner Jean counters the English assertion that the law of female exclusion was unearthed or formulated specifically in order to oppose the claims of Edward III. More importantly, his history of Salic Law endows the French with a law that is particular to them, and that defines France as a kingdom distinct from all others. *France* and *French* are emergent categories that are produced precisely as an effect of law, for the Salic Law of the French helps to forge a consciousness of community and shared identity.[46]

Thus the interest of Jean's Salic Law is not the exclusion of women from rule per se, or its place within misogynistic discourses.[47] Indeed, there would have been little point in searching for and promoting a law that affirmed the inferiority of women, since authorities from the Church fathers to Aristotle had already furnished a range of frameworks within which to discuss women's many physical, moral, and intellectual failings. Rather, the force of Salic Law, which Jean clearly understood and exploited, resides in the law's capacity to shape and define the French as a people.

In addition to the authority and inviolability that history confers upon Salic Law, Jean further legitimizes this law by demonstrating that it is based upon reason, and upon the consent of the people. In order to support his claim that the law of female exclusion is "tres raisonnablement fondee" [very reasonably founded] (131), Jean invites us to imagine that a king of France died, leaving but a single daughter, married to the king of Constantinople. "Ne seroit ce pas mieulx raison ... que un autre masle du sang royal – et fust encores tres loingtain de la couronne – fust roy de France, que tel empereur estrangier venist a tout ses Grez gouverner un tel royaume comme cely de France, qui est le plus noble des chrestiens?" [Would it not be more reasonable ... that another male of royal blood – be he even far removed from the crown – become king of France, than that such a foreign emperor come with all his Greeks to govern a kingdom like France, which is the most noble among all Christians?] (131).[48] It is important to note that the justification alleged first and foremost for female exclusion has nothing to do with the aptitude of women to rule, but rather with anxiety about the penetration of the French body politic by foreign elements, specifically foreign men. Royal women, who marry foreign men and bear their children, are the means by which France is rendered vulnerable to domination, contamination, and miscegenation, and it is their marital and sexual associations with non-French partners that make possible this transgressive crossing or blurring of boundaries. In order to render the body politic impermeable, to preclude the disturbing potential for foreign control, royal women – and their offspring – must be completely foreclosed from rule.

This – very reasonable – exclusion of women and their offspring from rule also enjoys the unanimous support and consent of the French people. In *À toute la chevalerie* Jean stages an allegory of the crown of France, who rhetorically asks the English king, "ne sces tu pas que femmes, par qui cause le roy Edouart prenoit le tiltre, ne succedent point en ce royaume? et – la merci Dieu – oncques n'ot en ce royaume ne ja n'aura – se Dieu plaist – creature du plus grant au plus petit qui voulsist souffrir ou consentist jusques a la mort que Angloiz en chief ou comme roy seignorist en France" [do you not know that women, by whom king Edward took the title, do not succeed in this kingdom? and – thank God – there never has been in this kingdom, nor will there ever be – may it please God – a creature from the most important to the most humble who would suffer or consent, under pain of death, that an Englishman rule as head or as king in France] (108). In this passage the mere thought of female rule and English rule are both categorically rejected by the French people. What Jean depicts as the collective French refusal of the English king Edward III may be understood as an expression of virility and self-determination, coded as masculine. This is not the only passage in which gender is employed to explore ideas of consent, legitimacy, political autonomy, and the integrity of the French body politic.

In the first redaction of the *Traité contre les anglais* Jean repeats nearly verbatim his previous affirmation that no one in France would consent to be ruled by an English king, and adds that "n'est il nulle droite ne permanent seignorie que celle qui est de juste tiltre approuvee et de bonne voulenté obeye, car le contraire est tirannie" [there is no legitimate or lasting lordship than that which is rightfully approved and in good will obeyed, for the contrary is tyranny] (178), thereby emphasizing the importance of consent to legitimate rule. He goes on to affirm that the English "facent que folz de se efforcier d'avoir terres ne seigneuries en ce royaume contre la voulenté du souverain et des subgiéz" [behave quite outrageously in striving by force to possess lands or lordship in this kingdom against the will of the sovereign and the subjects] (178). The word *efforcier*, unlike the closely related term *forçoier*, can be used to denote rape.[49] This linguistic choice, together with the precision that the English are acting "contre la voulenté" of the French, suggests a sexualized violence perpetrated against the French by the (feminized, sodomite) English, the rape of the kingdom by the English king. We find a similar formulation in the third *Traité contre les anglais*. Here, Jean denounces the English disregard of the French law of female exclusion and their efforts to impose other laws upon the French monarchy: "estoit grant oultrage et temerité aux Anglois d'entreprendre et eulx efforcer de mectre sus telles nouveletéz, et que si noble et puissant royaume comme celluy de France, contre ses loiz et ses coustumes, se gouvernast et feust limitéz et rieugléz a l'ordonnance de gens d'estranges païs et diverse langue" [it was a great outrage and imprudence on the part of the English to undertake and to impose such novelties, and that so noble and powerful a kingdom as is that of France, against its laws and customs, be governed and delimited and ruled according to the disposition of people of a foreign land and a different tongue] (276). The effort to impose foreign laws is conveyed using the word *efforcer*, once again imagining the imposition of foreign rule as gendered, sexual violence perpetrated against a body politic whose integrity and masculinity is thereby threatened.[50]

In attempting to violently force himself and his customs upon the French, Edward infringes upon not only French law, but also natural law: "Et comme il ne soit droicte ne seure seigneurie ... que celle qui vient de bonne amour et vraie obeissance des subgectz, ainsi qu'il a esté de *tous les natiz du royaume de France*, qui tousjours ont exposé corps et chevance jusques a la mort pour le droit du roy Phelipe ... et pour ses successeurs roys de France, s'ensuit ... que Edoart, qui contre la voulenté des François et par violence vouloit regner sur eulx, faisoit incivilement et contre droit naturel" [and since there is no legitimate or sure lordship ... but that which comes from good love and true obedience of the subjects, as has been the case with *those born of the kingdom of France*, who always have exposed their persons and their goods unto death for the rights of king Philip ... and for his successors, kings of France, it follows ... that Edward, who, against the will of the French and by violence wanted to reign over them, acted uncivilly and against natural law] (emphasis added, 279). The word *natiz* distinguishes between native and foreign, and aligns political loyalty with the facts of one's birth. It is on the basis of their birth that the French exhibit the "good love and true obedience" that is the foundation for legitimate rule. Positive or enacted law aside, natural law says that the French could never consent to English rule. As we have seen, moreover, Edward's unnatural efforts to impose himself upon the French are conveyed using the language of sexualized violence, language that suggests Edward's sodomization of the French body politic. This "unnatural" sexual act further reinforces the illegitimacy of the English king's pretentions to the kingdom of France.

Jean de Montreuil's fabrication and repetition of the content, history, and significance of Salic Law allows us to observe the construction of a legend of French collective identity. His works were employed and diffused by later authors, and in spite of the subsequent recognition that Salic Law did not hold up from a juridical standpoint, nevertheless it remained meaningful because, I would argue, it had become one of the constitutive elements of French national identity.[51] Just as the French monarchs had thaumaturgic powers, a holy balm, and arms sent by God, so too they had a special law that governed the succession of their kings. As Jean and his followers would have it, Salic Law was ancient, unique to the kingdom of France, confirmed by Charlemagne, and it ensured that the "most christian king" would never be a queen.[52]

It is perhaps a happy thing that Jean de Montreuil did not witness the English occupation of France, or the crowning of an English king in Paris. Jean was one of the many victims of the massacres that accompanied and followed the Burgundian takeover of Paris in May 1418. In December 1415 and April 1417, respectively, the king's sons Louis de Guyenne and Jean de Touraine had died, unexpectedly making the king's fifth son, Charles, heir to the throne of France. Charles was associated with the Armagnacs, and was therefore a political enemy of the king's powerful and ambitious cousin, Jean sans peur, duke of Burgundy. Charles fled Paris when the Burgundians entered the city – along with Christine de Pizan, the extensive des Ursins clan, and countless others – and he soon established a counter government in opposition to that of Jean sans peur. The dauphin had been named lieutenant general of the kingdom in 1417, and in 1418 he assumed the title of regent, but Charles VI, ill and apathetic, and under the control of Jean sans peur, revoked the dauphin's powers. The dauphin Charles and Jean sans peur signed a peace treaty in July 1419, but neither side adhered to its terms. On 10 September 1419 Jean sans peur, the unrepentant author of the assassination of Louis d'Orléans so many years previously, was himself killed by the dauphin's men on the bridge at Montereau, in the very presence of the dauphin. The infamous murder of Montereau had devastating political consequences for the young Charles. In January 1420 Charles VI sent letters to his "bonnes villes" announcing that because of the dauphin's terrible crimes, "ledit Charles s'est rendu indigne de nostre succession et de toute aultre honneur et dignité, et ne doit avoir aide, secours ne confort, ains doivent estre touz contre luy" [the aforesaid Charles has rendered himself unworthy of our succession and of all other honour and dignity, and he should not have aid, rescue or comfort, instead all should be against him].[53] The king's repudiation of the dauphin, referred to throughout the letter as "our so-called son," and the refusal of his political rights, paved the way for the Treaty of Troyes. In this document, "par l'aliance du mariage fait, pour le bien de ladicte paix, entre nostredit filz, le Roy Henry, et nostre très chière et très amée fille, Katherine, il est devenu nostre filz" [by virtue of the marriage alliance made, for the good of the aforesaid peace, between our aforesaid son, King Henry, and our very dear and very beloved daughter, Katherine, he has become our son].[54] On the basis of this adoption, which establishes a direct relationship between Charles VI and Henry V, the latter became heir to the former, and regent of France.[55] It is difficult to overstate how fundamentally the Treaty of Troyes transformed the political landscape. Henry V was no longer the foreign enemy and invader, but the son of the French king, regent, and heir presumptive. The very survival of France and the

French was at stake. It is within the context of these diplomatic, legal, and political events that Alain Chartier and Jean Juvénal des Ursins composed the texts we shall now examine.

Alain Chartier and the Naturalization of the Political

Alain Chartier was born in Bayeux between 1385 and 1395, the eldest son of a bourgeois family. After obtaining the title of maître ès arts at the University of Paris he entered the service of Yolande of Aragon, the future mother-in-law of the future Charles VII.[56] In 1417 Chartier became the new dauphin's secretary, and he remained loyal to Charles following his exile from Paris in 1418 and during his years of peregrinations across France, when much of his kingdom was occupied by English and Burgundian forces. When Charles VI and Henry V both died in 1422, Charles VII and the infant Henry VI were each proclaimed king of France by their respective supporters. However, Charles VII, the so-called *roi de Bourges*, was unable to inhabit his capital or to have himself crowned in the English-held city of Rheims, as required by French royal tradition. It was not until July of 1429, with the help of Joan of Arc, that Charles was crowned in Rheims, and many years would pass before he was able to reclaim Paris. Chartier himself would not live to see the peace within France that he so longed for and strove to create through his writings, for he died in Avignon in 1430.[57]

Alain Chartier travelled extensively on behalf of Charles, and like Eustache Deschamps, he found time to compose literary works in between his professional duties.[58] The *Quadrilogue invectif* was composed during the summer of 1422 in the wake of the Treaty of Troyes, following a string of English victories, and before the death of Henry V.[59] In contrast to Jean de Montreuil's treatises, which confronted the problem of the war with England and which imagined an English as well as a French public, the *Quadrilogue* is inscribed within the context of the French civil war, addressed to Chartier's fellow subjects who were, however, divided in their political loyalties. The *Quadrilogue* seeks to reinvigorate the French,[60] inciting them to abandon sloth and despair and to dedicate themselves to the common good of the kingdom.

With its dream-vision structure and its staging of the allegorical figure of France, the *Quadrilogue* owes a clear debt to the works of both Eustache Deschamps and Christine de Pizan, examined in chapter 2.[61] However, the time for sorrow and gentle remonstrance has passed; the post–Treaty of Troyes era demands an honest recognition of past faults, but more importantly, the energetic support of the dauphin's efforts to reclaim his rights. Accordingly, Chartier's France, in marked distinction to that of his predecessors, is an angry one.[62] With righteous indignation she denounces the inaction of her "children," thereby provoking the debate which ensues. Moreover, Chartier's France does not lament her widowhood. Indeed, after the narrator's affirmation of loyalty to Charles VI in the prologue, the king is notably absent from the text. As we shall see, this unnatural father, who by his own admission has rejected "tout amour filiale, toute inclination charnelle" [all filial love, all carnal inclinations],[63] is displaced by the mother figure, France.

The *Quadrilogue*'s dream vision is introduced by a prologue composed by "Alain Charretier, humble secretaire du roy nostre sire et de mon tresredoubté seigneur monseigneur le regent" [Alain Chartier, humble secretary of the king our lord and of my very feared lord, my lord the regent] (3) which sets up the terms of the debate to follow. The narrator identifies himself legally, socially, and professionally in a manner that demonstrates his loyalty to both king and dauphin, while his use of "nostre" serves to inscribe him within a collective that presumes similar allegiance on the part of his readership. The narrator addresses his text to the "majesté des princes," the "magnificence des nobles," the "circonspection des clers," and the "bonne industrie du peuple françois," thereby identifying both his public and the four voices of his *Quadrilogue*, as well as the qualities that should characterize each group.[64]

In his prologue, the narrator explains that the "drois de nature qui ont leur commencement en la divine providence" [laws of Nature, which have their origins in divine providence] tell us that written in the "livre des cieulx" [book of the heavens] is information about the course and duration of earthly lordships and cities which, like men, "ont leurs maladies et leur mort" [have their illnesses and their deaths] (4).[65] In this manner Chartier connects the cosmos to human history, and political bodies to human bodies, thereby inscribing the polity as a third term to be placed in dialogue with the micro- and the macrocosm, the individual and the cosmos.[66] The polity is likened to a human organism which possesses a natural lifespan, and the laws of Nature, which themselves are instituted by Divine Providence, do not refer only to the elements of the natural world, but equally to the cultural and political world of humankind.[67] The narrator then invokes a series of historical examples of political transformation and the fall of cities and empires to demonstrate that his own historical moment, to which he is an eyewitness,[68] likewise reflects the actions of "la main de Dieu" [the hand of God] (7). Moved by compassion, the narrator decides to compose the work we are reading, the title of which he explains, as well as the reading approach his public should adopt. The debate which the narrator composes is prefigured, indeed provoked, by one which takes place within his own heart concerning how to interpret the signs he reads in the book of the world.[69] Are the French being chastised by God so that they might reform, or are vengeance and destruction upon them? Thus, the narrator's prologue constitutes a microcosm of the text which follows, in which representatives of all orders of French society debate the origins of and solutions to the troubles facing the kingdom.

The dream narrative which follows is a highly self-conscious one. Though it is introduced in strict accordance with the conventions of the form – the narrator lies awake in bed at dawn preoccupied by the troubles of the kingdom, he falls back into a light sleep and introduces his vision with the familiar formula, "Or me fut advis en sommeillant ..." [Now, it seemed to me in dozing] (10) – the dream is characterized as a "petit traictié" [little treatise] (8), is introduced by an *incipit*, and the dreamer, within the confines of his dream, refers to the literary undertaking of the narrator.[70] The dreamer's demonstrated awareness of the constructed nature of his text and the existence of the *Quadrilogue* as a literary artefact allow the narrator to occupy two places at once.[71] On the one hand, the narrator-as-dreamer plays the role of privileged witness. Once France and her children begin their dialogue the presence of the dreamer is almost completely effaced. He speaks only to note the passage from one speaker to the next, and it is not even clear that he is visible to the other characters until the end of the text when France turns to the dreaming narrator and enjoins him to write down the words he has heard "afin qu'elles demeurent a memoire et a fruit" [so that they might remain in memory and bear fruit] (83). Like other dream visions, the text of the *Quadrilogue* is legitimized by this request, for it appears to consist of a revelation to a chosen figure who obediently registers what he has heard. The harsh words spoken over the course of the *Quadrilogue* are distanced from the narrator-dreamer, who recorded but did not invent them, and their good intent is affirmed by France herself, who commanded them to be written and disseminated for the benefit of all those who might read the text. On the other hand, if the voice of France frames those of her children, that of the narrator in turn frames the entire text. The narrator remains outside of the dispute, able to witness and judge the speeches of the figures, but is himself above the fray. He is thus firmly in control of his text, and partakes of the authority both of the author and of the divinely chosen witness and scribe.[72]

At the start of the dreamer's vision a noble lady, whose mantle *fleurdelisé* allows the reader to identify as France, reprimands her three children, *Chevalier*, *Peuple*, and *Clergé*, for the sorry condition in which she finds herself. She opens the text with a scathing rebuke of her children, who respond to their mother's charges, and subsequently to those of one another, in a kind of round robin of blame.[73] Although Chartier's Dame France never actually acknowledges her interlocutors as her children – it is the dreamer-narrator who tells us that France "apperceut trois de ses enfans" [perceived three of her children] (14) and Peuple who begins his response with the apostrophe "Haa, mere" [Ah, Mother] (26) – the fact of her motherhood is essential to her discourse. In the diatribe which opens the *Quadrilogue* France elaborates a theory of the natural that focuses very much on birth and generation and which links these concepts to political duties and loyalties. Her repetition of words such as *nature*, *naturelle*, *desnaturez*, *naissance*, *nez* creates a network of meaning that links the place of one's birth, construed in a broad sense, to a series of obligations.[74] France nourishes her children in three main senses: as the biological mother who gave birth to them, as a Mother Earth figure whose soil sustains them throughout their lives and receives their remains in death, and as their motherland, the country of their birth in a political sense.[75] It is therefore highly significant that Chartier places his discourse on the natural in the mouth of the mother. The use made by Chartier of the natural goes beyond comparing the body politic to a human body. Instead, the natural is part of a broader reflection on medieval legal philosophy. In the *Quadrilogue* the maternalized figure of France employs the natural world as a framework within which to describe and prescribe the moral, social, and political relationships among people, lands, and leaders within the fraught context of the late stages of the Hundred Years' War and the French civil war.[76]

In the *Quadrilogue* the beautiful exterior of Christine's Libera has fallen into tatters. The lady observed by the dreamer is beautiful and clearly highly-born, but "dolente et esplouree" [afflicted and tearful] (10). She wears a remarkable garment which he describes in considerable detail. The upper portion of her "mantel ou paille" [mantle or pallium] (10) is embroidered with precious stones, and depicts *fleurs de lis*, banners, and insignia of princes and kings. The middle portion is covered with letters and figures which represent the various arts and sciences. The lower portion, which touches the ground, is decorated with animals, plants, fruits, tall trees, and grains of all sorts.[77] Despite the beauty of its design and execution, the whole of it is so ragged and dirty that it would be unrecognizable even to those who had made it.

Dame France's mantle, whose design evokes the three orders of French society and the three children to whom she will presently speak, recalls that of another female allegorical authority figure: Alain de Lille's Nature, whose clothing bore images of the entire created world.[78] Like de Lille's Nature, France will complain bitterly of the misconduct of humans who – alone in the created world – fail to conform to the precepts of nature. This parallel between the allegorical figures of France and Nature effectively reframes the sexual deviance of which Nature complained as political deviance. Indeed, in France's first words to her children she calls them "hommes forvoiez" [deviant men] (14), and accuses them of being "feminins de couraiges et de meurs" [womanly in courage and habits] (14). Thus, as in the writings of Jean de Montreuil, Chartier defines and condemns certain political conduct as unnatural by using the languge of gender and (non-normative) sexuality.

In addition to France's connection to the figure of Nature, Florence Bouchet has noted that the word "paille" used to designate France's garment has distinctly priestly and liturgical overtones which suggest that France has been invested with a sacred office.[79] The figure of France therefore possesses political, natural, and theological dimensions, which reinforce the relationship between the political realm, the individual life, and the cosmos and creation that the narrator had evoked in his prologue.

When the dreamer first sees France she is struggling to hold up a palace which, like her garment, is splendid and beautifully made but broken and in disrepair, and listing so much to one side that it seems about to fall, a second allegory then, or perhaps a metonym, for the kingdom of France. Casting her eyes about in search of possible help, France spies her own children and is disgusted by their inaction when confronted with her plight. She then elaborates a theory of political duty and loyalty which conjoins these values to birth, generation, and the natural world.

At the heart of France's denunciation of her children is the naturalization of love for one's *pays*. France proclaims that "aprés le lien de foy catholique, Nature vous a devant toute autre chose obligiez au commun salut du pays de vostre nativité et a la defense de ceste seigneurie soubz laquelle Dieu vous a fait naistre et avoir vie" [after the bond of the Catholic faith, Nature has, before all other things, dedicated you to the common good of the country of your birth and the defence of that lordship under which God made you be born and have life] (15). Love of *pays* trumps self-advancement or even self-preservation. Indeed, France has clearly read her Aristotle,[80] for her speech is punctuated by expressions such as "commune utilité" [shared use] (15), "commun besoing" [shared need], and "chose publique" [public good] (16) which are used to define the duties of her children.[81] From the instant of their birth, arguably the most solitary moment of a person's life, France's children are part of a collective, and it is to this collective that they owe their primary allegiance and whose good they should pursue before all other.[82] "[C]eulx sont desnaturez qui au commun besoing et pour le salut de leur païz et seigneurie n'efforcent leur pouoir" [they are denatured, those who for the common good and for the well-being of their country and lordship do not strive with all their power] (16) says France, again following Aristotle in her affirmation that political community is natural, and even suggesting that loyalty to lord and land is a natural virtue, not a civic or political one. Moreover, the link between individual and country is divinely ordained, for God determines where each person is born. Thus, the "amour naturelle du païz" [natural love of country] (15) is as natural as the cycle of birth and death, which France repeatedly evokes. Indeed, the idea of "pays" is itself maternalized, for it "repaist et nourrit" [feeds and nourishes] (15) its children.

The obligations that France's children have towards her are based very much upon the natural world in a literal and physical sense. The structure that France is supporting is her children's "naturel heberge et retrait" [natural lodging and refuge] (14), which renders their inaction inexplicable to her. In former times "amour naturelle du païz" [natural love of country] (15) was so deeply rooted in people that – to paraphrase France – their bodies sought to return to their birthplace as to their proper place, their hearts were happiest there, life and health flourished there, people sought security, peace, refuge there, rest in old age and their final sepulture.[83] Chartier's France presents the natural love that governs the relationship between mother and child as the basis for political feeling and action. Chartier radically expands and redefines the concept of natural love so that it not only unites literal families, but also binds men to their symbolic mother, the soil of their motherland. The "loy de Nature" [law of Nature] (16), France tells her children, has decreed that nothing should be too difficult or arduous to undertake for that country[84] which from your birth until your death has provided you with all sustenance, feeding and nourishing you in life, and in death receiving your remains. France's insistence on death as well as birth maps love of country onto a natural order, the cyclical pattern of life whose events recall, and are as ineluctable, as the rising and setting of the sun. As in the metaphor of the body politic, nature provides a model for human conduct, though here nature is understood in much broader terms, as the inhabitants and systems of the entire created world. Though deprived of reason, the bird defends its nest with beak and nails, the bear and the lion their lairs with tooth and claw (16). Thus, the law of Nature is more perfectly upheld by dumb beasts than by France's three children, who are "desnaturez" [denatured] (16, lines 1 and 9).

France's allusions to the law of Nature may be interpreted simply with regard to the natural world, as illustrated by her references to birds and beasts, birth and death. However, natural law also belongs in legal contexts. The phrase "droit de nature" [law of nature] is used in the ordinances of Charles VI with respect to the right of the first-born son of the king to succeed to his father immediately upon the death of the latter. Likewise, the jurist Jean de Terre Rouge uses the principles of filiation and of primogeniture, both grounded in nature, to demonstrate that the king does not have the authority to alienate the rights of the first-born son and heir.[85] Similar ideas are found in shorter and less technical documents that circulated in the wake of the Treaty of Troyes and to which Chartier may have had access, such as *Super omnia vincit veritas*, or the *Réponse d'un bon et loyal françois*.[86] Alain's predecessor, Philippe de Mézières, in his *Songe du vieil pélerin* presents natural law as something that is common to all people, even those without the benefit of revelation. The pagan Grand Khan, for instance, is exemplary for the administration of justice among his people; "toutesfois ilz sont ydolatres, sans science divine ou civile, et par la loy naturelle et moralle ilz se gouvernent" [nevertheless they are idolaters, without divine or civil knowledge, and they govern themselves by natural and moral law].[87] Philippe characterizes Nature as the "ancelle" [servent] of Divine Providence, thus subservient to and in accordance with God's will, while natural law forms the basis upon which civil and divine law are constructed. Similarly Jean Gerson, in the sermon *Diligite justiciam* (8 May 1408), reflects on the various types of law, their aims and relationship to one another. Gerson claims that natural law, including what we would call the natural sciences, is no more or less than the will of God ("prima lex nature est voluntas Dei").[88] Similarly, the narrator of the *Quadrilogue* affirms in the prologue that "les drois de nature ... ont leur commencement en la divine providence" [the laws of nature find their origin in divine providence] (4). We see that natural law precedes reason, and constitutes a sort of substratum of conduct that applies equally to men and animals. The fact that animals protect their homes seems to be a matter of what we might call instinct, for they behave thus even though they "n'ont pas entendement de raison" [do not have the mental faculty of reason] (16). Consequently, the unconcern manifested by France's children renders them "desnaturez" [denatured] (16). In all cases natural law, irrespective of its relationship to divine law or to man's reason, constitutes the most basic level of human action and interaction. The failure of France's children to adhere to and respect natural law, whether understood as a legal construct or as a natural science, is one that occurs on the most fundamental level possible.

Lest her children imagine that the laws governing the natural world do not apply to them, France makes this connection explicit by turning from the paradigm of nature to the affairs of men and to historical examples of love of birthplace. The Trojans, believed to be the ancestors of the French, withstood the siege of Troy for ten years. The Scythes retreated before King Darius of Persia until they reached the burial grounds of their forefathers and predecessors, and there they fought to the death, for "pitié naturelle" [natural pity] obliged them to defend "le lieu de la naissance et sepulture de leurs lignees" [the place of the birth and burial of their ancestors] (16). France's repeated conjoining of birth and death inscribes the historical and political events she describes within the cycles of life processes and the natural world. Moreover, the historical examples she has chosen are both pre-Christian, demonstrating that even without the benefit of divine revelation, these populations behaved more *naturally* than the French. How much more perfectly, then, should the children of France love and protect their mother, since they enjoy the advantages of reason and knowledge of God?

France exploits the related concepts of natural love and natural law in order to shape the conduct of her children in a social and political framework. She repeatedly affirms the idea that natural love binds one to one's birthplace as well as to one's family. However, in how large a sense is one's birthplace to be understood? In the case of the animals she invokes it is obviously to be interpreted in a narrow sense, but does the birthplace of humans refer to their home, their parish, their region? France provides the answer for us; it is one's *pays*. The word *pays* has a certain ambiguity in terms of referent. Bernard Guenée has discussed the origin of the term *pays* from the Latin *pagus*, which in the early Middle Ages was a synonym for diocese. The word *patria* also came to mean *pays*, but in a sense sometimes large and sometimes small. Therefore France, Guenée argues, is a kingdom comprised of *pays*.[89] The idea that *pays* operates within a more limited framework is supported by Chartier's "Epistola de puella" (1429), in which he defines Joan's *patriam* as Vaucouleurs, in opposition to her *nacionem*, which is France.[90] In the *Quadrilogue* Chartier does not employ the term *nation*; however, he conveys an understanding of *pays* that surpasses the purely local by systematically conjoining it with the term *seigneurie*.[91] As we saw in the passage cited previously, France reminds her children that

"Nature vous a devant toute autre chose obligiez au commun salut du pays de vostre nativité et a la defense de celle seigneurie soubz laquelle Dieu vous a fait naistre et avoir vie" [Nature has, before all other things, obliged you to the common well-being of the country of your birth and the defence of that lordship under which God made you be born and have life] (15). If *pays* refers to a physical space, *seigneurie* refers to a political-institutional one, a lordship or rule.[92] Florence Bouchet, in her modern French translation of the *Quadrilogue*, employs here the term "état." So, birds and beasts may be born in nests or holes in the ground, but men are born into geo-political spaces which are both literal and conceptual, and which they are obliged to defend just as vigorously as the lion guards his den. The same natural love that binds a person to his kin regardless of their qualities or conduct also binds a person to his "pays et seigeurie" [country and lordship] (11). It is France's very conjoining of these terms, of the territorial and the political, here and throughout her long discourse that enables her to construct birthplace in a geo-political sense, as, I propose, what one might call one's *nation*.[93] Ardis Butterfield, in her thoughtful corrective to our modern scholarly preoccupation with *nation*, suggests that nation might more fruitfully be thought of less as a "category of analysis" than as an "act of imagination" (29), one that, in the present instance, might help us discern how Chartier and his contemporaries understood and negotiated "that obscure boundary between individual and collective desires" (35).[94] Setting aside the limitations of the term nation, it is neverthess clear that Chartier's allegorical text is an "act of imagination" that seeks to mobilize its readers into a collective force capable and willing to act on behalf of the kingdom of France, and the dauphin Charles.

France further develops the relationship between the natural and the political over the course of her speech, as love of country is extended to embrace also love and loyalty for the lord of that country. France asks her children what has become of their constancy towards their "seigneur naturel" [natural lord] (19) and reminds them of their "natural devoir" [natural duty] (20). The co-mingling of natural law and natural love, with all of their respective connotations and attendant duties, can be observed in the expression "seigneur naturel," which had long been employed to characterize the legitimate bond, based on heredity, that united a man to his lord.[95] Thus, one's *seigneur natural* is one's rightful lord in a political sense, and also the lord whom one is bound to honour and serve as a son does his father. One can no more ally oneself with a different king, one who is not *naturel*, than one can elect a new father – or a new son. The author of the *Réponse d'un bon et loyal françois*, writing in reaction to the Treaty of Troyes, highlights the absurdity of such an idea when he exclaims, "est icy une merveilleuse et reverse adopcion; car le pere doit adopter le filz, et non le filz le pere" [here is a marvellous and backward adoption, for the father should adopt the son, and not the son the father] (126). Chartier's France condemns the people of Paris, who embraced the Burgundian takeover of 1418, and who did not rise up against the Treaty of Troyes, which renounced the dauphin and proclaimed the English king successor in his place.[96]

If love of king and country are natural and linked to birth, so too is enmity, and the English are the "ennemis anciens and naturelz" [ancient and natural enemies] of the French (24). France relies upon the idea of lineage to explain the inherent and constant treachery of the English people.[97] They are of the lineage of Forgestus and Hangestus, the Saxons who, under the pretext of helping the king of Great Britain, then usurped the throne and killed the nobles loyal to him. More recently, they are "la lignee de cellui qui debouta et occist son souverain seigneur, roy d'Angleterre, pour usurper tiranniquement sa seigneurie" [the lineage of he who eliminated and killed his sovereign lord, king of England, in order to tyrannically usurp his lordship] (23).[98] In short, France explains to her children that the English are "ceulx qui voz peres et voz predecesseurs ont souvent guerroiez, ars et degastez voz champs et voz villes et qui de tele ligne sont issuz que naturelment couvoitent anyentir du tout vostre generacion" [those who have often made war against your fathers and predecessors, who have burned and ruined your fields and your cities and who have issued from such a lineage that they naturally desire to completely destroy your descendents] (24). In this way Anglo-French enmity is neither contingent nor temporally limited, but is grounded in the immutable facts of heredity and birthplace and is as inevitable as one's birth and death.

This initial naturalization of the political allows France to push her analogy even further. In the conclusion to her discourse she places in parallel a series of loves and obligations which mirror and reinforce one another. France reminds her children that "nature" obliges them to defend themselves and their homes, and that the English are trying to kill the wives and children "que Nature vous contraint a doulcement nourir et tendrement amer" [that nature obliges you to gently nourish and tenderly love] (24). The urge to defend oneself from harm, and the love one feels for one's own family are sentiments which few would contest.[99] To these two indisputable objects of one's natural affection France then adds the essential third term, love of "vostre prince droiturier et seigneur naturel" [your rightful prince and natural lord] (24), thereby reaffirming the legitimacy of Charles VII, the *roi de Bourges.*

Chartier's France falls silent after her initial speech, while the self-justifications and mutual accusations of her three children form the bulk of the *Quadrilogue*. Finally weary of her children's arguing, France puts an end to their dispute in terms that again recall Aristotelian notions about the common good. In her conclusion France opposes the "bien publique" [public good], the "commun salut" [shared well-being], and the "commune salvation, utilité et defense" [shared salvation, use, and defence] to her offspring's "desordonnances singulieres" [individual quarrels] and the "divers remedes" [conflicting remedies] (82) they seek to their collective troubles. To the very end, the examples and images provided by the natural world structure France's discourse. She asks her children to be like honey bees, united in the defence of hive and king, and she also asks the dreamer-narrator to record what he has heard so that the words of the debate might "demeurent a memoire et a fruit" [remain in memory and bear fruit] (83).[100] Thus, the very text of the *Quadrilogue*, like France herself, has the capacity to provide nourishment and to sustain life.

It is not surprising to observe that the discourse of the natural is almost entirely confined to France's speeches. The term *natural* is employed a handful of times in the remainder of the *Quadrilogue*, but not as part of a sustained reflection. The ideas put forth in the opening of the *Quadrilogue*, constructed around the concepts of birth, birthplace, and lineage, take on added resonance when placed in the mouth of the mother figure, France. France's discourse combines examples drawn from nature with important philosophical, legal, and ideological reflections on the relationship of human society to the natural world. The presence of the allegorical figure of France concretizes the very ideas she puts forth. France is a collective, indeed she is a single body, and subjects naturally love and are loyal to the place of their birth – their mother in what is here presented in a literal and a bodily sense – and their lord. Chartier employs the allegory of France and the discourse of the natural in order to redefine the instincts of self-preservation and protection of one's young, and of one's habitat, in collective terms, as the efforts to be carried out on behalf of France and her *seigneur naturel*.

Jean Juvénal des Ursins and the Dismantling of the Treaty of Troyes

Jean Juvénal des Ursins was the second of the sixteen children of Jean Jouvenel and Michelle de Victry. They were a family deeply involved in royal politics and administration, loyal to the so-called Armagnacs, and later to

Charles VII. Following the Burgundian takeover of Paris in 1418 the family fled to Poitiers, where they became integral to the counter government of the dauphin. Jean Juvénal was a lawyer in the household of the duke of Orléans, and later of the king. In 1432 he became bishop of Beauvais, newly reconquered from the English, and it was there that he composed the allegorical dream vision *Audite celi*.[101]

In terms of surviving manuscripts, *Audite celi* is Jean Juvénal des Ursins's best preserved work, which suggests that it was the most widely circulated during the later Middle Ages.[102] Jean Juvénal's political thought as expressed in *Audite celi* and elsewhere, and the relationship of his ideas to those of Jean de Montreuil, Jean de Terre Rouge, and others, have been studied by historians in terms of sources and influence.[103] In addition, *Audite celi*'s similarities to Alain Chartier's *Quadrilogue invectif* have been duly noted.[104] Both are dream visions framed by the situation of a narrator figure, and both texts are comprised of a dialogue in which the allegorical figure of France is a key participant. I propose to examine Jean Juvénal's radical reinscription of the conventional dream-vision narrative within the framework of late medieval visionary culture, on the one hand, as well as his original use of allegory, on the other. In *Audite celi* Jean Juvénal presents himself as a political visionary whose text both heralds and makes possible the peace of Arras, and the eventual victory of a united France over her English foes.

At the start of the text the narrator finds himself at Beauvais, although unlike Chartier, Jean Juvénal does not identify the narrator as himself, or refer to the narrator's social or professional position. The narrator does, however, specify the date: 1 May 1435. In the lyric tradition May 1 was associated with renewal and with poetic creation and exchange, and thus this date, which functions both literarily and historically, prefigures the ways in which Jean Juvénal will combine the generic with the particular, and the poetic with the political. Two or three hours after midnight the narrator finds himself seated at the window of a small, rather secluded room, reflecting on the troubles of France and the uncertain prospect of peace. In this liminal space between indoors and out, between waking and sleep, the narrator is visited – not by a dream, as the reader might expect – but by "une creature de bonne, honneste et saincte conversacion" [a creature of good, honest, and holy conversation] (146). The narrator's expectation that this figure might "aucunement consoler" [somewhat console] (146) him suggests an allegorical interlocutor, like Philosophy or Hope;[105] however, the creature is never identified. It is this creature's vision, rather than his own, that the narrator will recount in the text.

By displacing the dream from the narrator to a "creature," Jean Juvénal departs from the conventions of the amorous or political dream vision, and exploits the authority of a different textual and spiritual tradition – that of visions experienced by holy women, and recorded by male clerics. Many scholars have noted that the later Middle Ages saw a proliferation of such visions, as well as mounting anxiety surrounding their authenticity. Renate Blumenfeld-Kosinski identifies the Great Schism of the West as the moment that marks the rise of a new kind of holy woman, "the layperson whose visionary and prophetic gifts allowed her to try to intervene in the political events of her time."[106] However, the distinction between demonic possession and holiness was a fine one, and visions were subjected to careful scrutiny by the proper authorities, typically defined as male clerics. Raymond de Sabanac, Alfonso of Jaén, and Jean Gerson all wrote on the subject that came to be called the discernment of spirits, a process that attempted to define the criteria which would allow the clerical authority to pronounce upon the authenticity of the vision, and the visionary, in question.[107]

Gerson advises one evaluating a vision, "Tu, quis, quid, quare, cui, qualiter, unde, require?" [you ask, who, what, how, to whom, in what manner, whence?][108] These questions focus not only on the substance of the vision – what does it mean or refer to? where does it come from? – but also on the person of the visionary: who is this person? what sort of life does she lead? In *Audite celi*, the narrator guides the reader through his own version of the discernment of spirits. Having affirmed that his "creature" is of good, honest, and saintly conversation, he then says that the creature is initially reluctant to describe the vision, which she dismisses as nothing but a "songe" [dream] and as such, "on ne si devoit arrester" [one should not pause over it] (146).[109] This reluctance in and of itself constitutes a preliminary indication that the creature's vision is authentic, for the humility of the visionary is one of the measures by which the authority is able to evaluate the authenticity of the vision. A true visionary is humble and reticent about her visions, while one who presumes to publicize her visions is likely to be the victim of demonic possession.

Here the narrator redefines the creature's experience as a visionary one, for "quant une personne devote, qui a acoustumé de orer et prier Dieu de grant desir ou devocion, a en dormant aucune avision qui touche le bien de la chose publique, on ne doit mie dire que se soit songe, mez vision, et se doit dire et desclairer, voire executer" [when a devout person, one in the habit of praying to and entreating God with great desire or devotion, has, in sleeping, a vision that touches upon the public good, one should not call this a dream, but a vision, and it should be told and declared, even carried out] (147). The narrator identifies objective criteria, touching upon both the visionary and the vision, that allow an observer to judge the authenticity of the latter. Playing the role of spiritual authority à la Gerson, the narrator judges his creature's dream a vision, and as such it is not only to be credited, but acted upon. Previous holy women had experienced visions related to religious or political topics.[110] However Jean Juvénal innovates with respect to such models by citing the political good imagined in his creature's vision among the proofs of its authenticity. The narrator supports his assertions with citations from Scripture and from classical sources on dreams, and the creature agrees, finally, to recount the vision, provided that the narrator ensures her anonymity. This final proof of the creature's humility reaffirms the authenticity of the vision, and the narrative of the vision, duly vetted by the proper authorities, follows.

The devout creature's vision opens with the sight of three ladies hastening along various roads, and meeting at a crossroads in the city of Arras, "ou on disoit estre une sente qui aloit en ung chastel…ou Paix estoit logee" [where it was said there was a path that led to a castle … where Peace was housed] (150). The mention of Arras and the castle of peace would have signalled to Jean Juvénal's readers that his text was to be read within the framework of the peace talks between France, England, and Burgundy that were to begin in that city in July 1435. Unlike the *Quadrilogue*, which focused on conditions and relationships within France, the subject of *Audite celi* is the relationship between France, England, and Burgundy.

Over the course of the vision the creature manifests a simplicity, indeed an ignorance, that serves as additional confirmation of her status as a true visionary.[111] In the passage where the allegory of France discusses the Treaty of Troyes, for instance, the narrator remarks that "en ces matieres sembloyt a ladicte devote creature que ladicte dame nommee France alleguet plusieurs auctorités, tant de droyt civil que canon, mais elle ne pot retenir que seullement l'effect et substance desdis droys" [regarding these matters it seemed to the aforesaid devout creature that the aforesaid lady named France cited several authorities, both from civil law and from canon, but she {the dreamer} could retain only the effects and essence of the aforesaid laws] (182–3). The creature's ignorance confirms the genuineness of her vision, while also rendering the account of her vision more readable to a public of nobles and powerful bourgeois by glossing over legal details, and emphasizing the broad contours and important implications of France's arguments.[112]

Jean Juvénal's original combination of a traditional dream-vision narrative with the conventions associated with the female visionary/male author also allow him to incorporate into his text the passage of time, and hence the intervention of history. While the experience of a dream, by definition, can only take place during the space of one period of sleep, the narration of that dream, or of a series of dreams, might unfold over a longer time.[113] Such is apparently the case here. The narrator had told us that his encounter with the creature, and thus her retelling of the dream or vision, took place on 1 May, but at the moment in the dream when the allegory of France is discussing the many signs of God's favour for Charles VII, the narrator interrupts his redaction of the dream to advise his readers that "moy qui ay escript ceste vision ne le fitz pas tout en ung jour" [I who have written down this vision did not do so all in one day] (198), but that he wrote some each day, according to his availability and that of the creature, both of whom were quite busy. On Monday 9 May, the narrator specifies, the creature had just finished retelling the contents of the preceding paragraph (on signs of God's favour) when that evening "vindrent nouvelles certaines et vrayes que le conte d'Arondel ... avoit esté desconfit ... qui fut une chose merveilleuse. Et lors il me souvint de ladicte parolle que France dist a Angleterre, que il luy mescherroit brief se elle ne se advisoit, car ladicte victoire estoit grant commencement" [there came sure and true news that the count of Arundel ... had been defeated ... which was a marvellous thing. And then I remembered the aforesaid word that France spoke to England, that it would soon turn out ill for her {i.e., England} if she did not watch out, and the aforesaid victory was a great beginning] (198).[114] In this way contemporary events confirm the truth of the creature's dream; indeed, they seem to contribute to or prolong the dream, as the actions of 9 May are the most recent in a series of events that demonstrate God's will that the French should be victorious. In the return to the narrative of the dream, the "devote creature" describes the intervention of Saincte Esglise, who expresses her conviction that Charles VII is the rightful king of France, a judgment that is substantiated both by the preceding parts of the dream and by the victory of 9 May.[115]

At the end of the vision, which concludes with Bon Conseil's speech, "lors sembla a laditte devote creature que lesdittes trois dames Saincte Esglise, France et Angleterre furent consolees, et qu'elles se disposaient a entrer en la matiere; mais quelle conclusion elles prindrent, riens ne luy vint en advision" [then it seemed to the aforesaid devout creature that the aforesaid three ladies, Holy Church, France, and England, were consoled, and that they were preparing to enter into the subject {of peace}, but of what conclusion they reached, nothing appeared to her in the vision] (277). In this way the narrator reminds his public of the peace talks that were soon to begin between France, England, and Burgundy, and he conveys the creature's optimism about the results of the negotiations. Moreover, just as the victory over Arundel was presented as the fulfilment of the creature's vision, so too the upcoming peace talks are depicted as capable of fulfilling the aims of the vision as a whole: the re-establishment of peace. The prophetic nature of the text is confirmed by its relationship to history, and the text helps to make possible the outcome that it foretells by providing a truthful account of past events, as well as divinely sanctioned advice to the parties involved in the talks.

At the conclusion of the text the creature again protests that her "songe" is not worthy of being recorded, but the narrator, "pour ma plaisance et me donner aucune occupacion en ceste place e Beauvez ou la guerre est forte et merveilleuse" [for my pleasure and to provide myself with some occupation in this place of Beauvais where the war is furious and marvellous] (277), has written it down nonetheless. He issues disclaimers concerning the contents of the text, which were not of his own invention but merely the record of another's experience. The narrator's statement that he recorded the text for personal reasons and the reminder that he did not compose it serve to deflect possible criticisms of what he has written.[116] However, at the same time, the narrator also claims ownership over the whole of the text by reminding his public of its title or theme, which he appended to the vision because it was "propice" [suitable] (277): *Audite celi que loquor, audiat terra verba oris mei* [Hear, o heavens, the things that I say, may the earth hear the words of my mouth] (Deut. 32:1). *Audite celi* are the first words of Deuteronomy 32, the canticle taught by God to Moses to announce the fall of the children of Israel and God's subsequent anger and vengeance. Thus, in the opening of his work the narrator had exploited the authority of the male cleric who judges, records, and appropriates a woman's privileged access to the divine, while in the epilogue the narrator distances himself from the creature whose vision he has recorded, and substitutes himself for her as the prophetic figure. In pronouncing the words *audite celi*, the narrator speaks as Moses addressing God's chosen people, the French, while the vision that he records occupies the place of God's canticle, and the creature is excluded from this economy of divine revelation and warning. Citing additional scriptural passages, the narrator affirms that truth (which his text provides) and peace (which he hopes will be forthcoming) are inseparable. His text is destined for a universal public of "bons crestiens" [good Christians] (145), but is particularly directed to the three estates of France and of England, who are expected to heed its advice.[117]

I would like to turn now from this examination of the narrative situation of *Audite celi*, and the ways in which Jean Juvénal authorizes his text, to a consideration of the text itself, and in particular the presence and praxis of Jean's allegorical figures. Like the narrator of the *Quadrilogue invectif*, the creature of *Audite celi* appears only to observe, not to interact with, the figures portrayed in the vision, who are themselves representationally and ontologically distinct from one another. Some of the allegories stand for political bodies, like France or England, others represent institutions, like the Church, while many of the less prominent allegories are of virtues or vices, including Ambicion and Convoitise, who accompany England, and Tribulacion, Affliccion, Murmuracion, and Dissimulacion, who accompany France.[118] The end of the text features interventions from Sedicion, Paix, Prudence, and Bon conseil. Many of these allegories are mentioned but do not act. Rather, like the qualities that accompany France and England, they serve to characterize other allegories. The vision also evokes historical figures, such as the kings of France and England, and it describes the actions and prayers of saints Clovis, Louis, Charlemagne, Denis, Edward, and Thomas of Canterbury. Among this vast collection of characters of widely disparate ontological and semiotic types, it is quite striking that an allegorical figure one would expect to see is completely absent from the text: that of Burgundy. Philippe le bon of Burgundy was not only a participant in the peace talks of Arras, according to Joycelyne Dickinson, "Duke Philip was, indeed, the dominant figure at the Congress" (177).[119] Given the failure of France and England to conclude a general peace, the separate peace between France and Burgundy, outlined and confirmed in the Treaty of Arras, might be considered the principal, even the only, successful outcome of the Congress.[120]

In light of Philippe's considerable historical prominence, the extraordinary allegorical absence of Burgundy requires commentary. I contend that the excision of Burgundy from the text allows Jean Juvénal to depict what he does or cannot state openly in his text. That is to say, the duchy's erasure allows him to deny the existence, or even the possibility, of Burgundy as a coherent, bounded, and autonomous political body, and this, at a time when the duke of Burgundy's ambitions clearly lay in the direction of the establishment of his duchy as an independent political power.[121] We have seen that at the start of the vision the creature observes "troys dames estans en troys divers chemins tandans toutes a une fin, c'est assavoir a trouver paix" [three ladies in three different paths all headed to one end, that is to say, to find peace] (149). England and France are described first, and the reader might well imagine that the third lady is Burgundy, only to discover that she is in fact Saincte Esglise.

In France's first words to England she proclaims that she would not be in such difficult circumstances "se se n'eust esté la separacion *d'aucuns de ma langue*" [if it had not been for the secession[122] *of certain {people} of my language*, emphasis added] (153), that is, the defection of those who also spoke French.[123] The Burgundians are thus identified periphrastically and in absentia, and are connected to the French by virtue of their shared language. This evocation of a common language serves as a reminder that the Burgundians and the French belong to one nation, in the sense of possessing common origins.[124] They are born, as it were, of one mother (tongue).[125]

The notion that a shared language constitutes a key component of national identity is not newly introduced in this text. In his translation of Aristotle's *Politics*, executed for Charles V more than fifty years before the composition of *Audite celi*, Nicole Oresme defines language as an element of identity.[126] We saw also that in Jean de Montreuil's third redaction of his *Traité contre les anglais* the English are identified, negatively, as those of "diverse langue" [different language] (276).[127] One of the most poignant clauses of the Treaty of Troyes itself specifies that "toutes personnes, tant nobles comme autres, qui seront entour nous [i.e., Charles VI] pour nostre personnel et domestique service ... seront telz qu'ilz auront esté nez ou royaume de France, ou des lieux de langage françois" [all persons, be they noble or otherwise, who will be in our company for our personal and domestic service ... will be such that they will have been born in the kingdom of France, or in places of the French language].[128] On behalf of the poor king of France, whose mental faculties had never really recovered after the French defeat at Agincourt (25 October 1415), Philippe ensures that at the very least Charles is accompanied and cared for by people he can understand. These various passages all show that language is increasingly perceived as a factor that unites some speakers and divides others, thereby furnishing a basis for collective identity formation.[129]

Although language had long been a distinguishing feature among people of different kingdoms, language much more clearly divided France and England after the ascension of the Lancastrians to the throne of England.[130] Richard II had arguably been the last king for whom French was a native language, while Henry V, in contrast, energetically promoted the use of English.[131] The idea that language serves both as a basis and as a sign of political loyalty is reintroduced at the end of *Audite celi*, when France commands "que ceulx de ma langue qui sont avecques toy boutent hors Vengence, Erreur, Avuglement de vraye cognoissance, Hainne, Honte et Obstinacion, et se reduisent a moy dont ilz sont partis" [that those of my language who are with you kick out Vengeance, Error, Blindness of true understanding, Hatred, Shame, and Obstinacy, and submit themselves to me from whom they have departed] (216), and the dreamer remarks that "lors aucunement ses aliés de la langue de France" [then to some degree her allies of the language of France] (217) began to think better of their past actions, and to desire peace.

In addition to serving as an indication of where political loyalties (ought to) lie, expressions such as "those of my language" function as a periphrase that allow Jean Juvénal to make reference to Burgundy without actually naming it. This denial of the proper name constitutes yet another refusal to acknowledge the independent existence of Burgundy, which has neither form nor name. Indeed, France affirms that England would have no power in the kingdom of France, if only the aforementioned people of her language "vouloient me recongnoistre qui les ay faiz tielx que ilz sont, et par moy et non par aultre et a cause de moy sont tieulx et ont les seignouries que ilz ont" [wanted to recognize me, who made them such as they are, and by me and not by another, and because of me, they are such, and have the lordships that they have] (154). Thus, Burgundy – and, implicitly, other large and important duchies and counties – do not exist separately from France. Indeed, they owe their political existence, territorial form, and lord to France, their creator.

Significantly, Burgundy is not cast as the enemy of France in *Audite celi*, but rather as a kind of lost sheep, one who has wandered from the fold and who must return to her shepherd and her fellows. This is not to say that Burgundy has not acted poorly. Philippe le bon was not simply allied with the English; he delivered Charles VI into the hands of his enemies.[132] However, these actions are ascribed to an individual, one who, moreover, France hopes will "se reduira a sa souche et a celuy qui est son vray chef et le mien" [submit to his stock and to he who is his true leader and mine] (186). This relationship is quite unlike that between France and England, in which the enmity between the allegorical figures of the two kingdoms suggests that their subjects, their kings, the very land of which they are comprised exist in historical and permanent opposition to one another. As Bon conseil says at the conclusion to the vision, "a la fin France sera France et Angleterre Angleterre separeement, et est impossible qu'elles soient compatibles ensemble" [in the end France will be France, and England England, separately, and it is impossible that they be compatible together] (270).

Jean Juvénal's allegorical figure of France is markedly different from the one depicted in Christine de Pizan's *Livre de l'advision Cristine* (discussed in chapter 2), Chartier's *Quadrilogue*, or the anonymous *Débats et appointements*, known also by its incipit, *Après la destruction de Troye*.[133] In these texts France's primary rhetorical mode is affective. The France of the *Advison* and the *Débats et appointements* laments her mistreatment and the loss of her glorious past, and expresses fear and anxiety about the future that awaits her. Chartier's France employs righteous anger to spur her interlocutors to action. In all these cases, France's speech and presence are designed to move her public. Jean Juvénal's France, in contrast, is a learned figure who reads Latin, displays her familiarity with the two laws, and is well versed in the genealogical, military, and diplomatic histories of France and England. Indeed, we have seen that her erudition surpasses the competence of her observer, the devout creature. Following England's initial accusation that France has refused to recognize and obey her "espoux, maistre et seigneur le roy Henry" [spouse, master, and lord the king Henry] (151), France speaks for over sixty pages, first affirming the right of Philippe VI de Valois to the throne, then discussing the conduct of Edward III, and finally demonstrating that the Treaty of Troyes was "une chose illusoire et non allegable ne soustenable" [an illusory thing, not defensible or sustainable] (184). In the second half of her discourse, following the news of Arundel's defeat, France reviews the history of the English presence in Normandy – and that of English holdings on the continent generally – in order to refute the English claims to the contested regions.

One might almost imagine that it were Jean Juvénal himself speaking, except that France reminds the reader of her presence and of her status as a woman. For example, the physical portrait of France traced at the start of the vision, in which she is described as "deschevelee, dessiree, dissipee, gastee et desrompue" [dishevelled, broken, destroyed, ravaged, torn apart] (149), corresponds to conventional descriptions of female distress. Later, in discussing the Treaty of Troyes, France has a rare moment of lamentation. "Hélas," she cries, "a quoy penssoient ceulx qui se firent, sy non tout mal?" [Alas, what were they thinking, those who accomplished it, if not entirely of evil?] (190). She inserts phrases such as "moy qui suis France" [I who am France] (163) and "moy qui suis terre France nommee" [I who am named the land of France] (186) both to remind her public of her presence and to authorize her discourse. Who better than the kingdom herself might denounce the actions that were said to be perpetrated with her well-being in mind, but which in reality seek to destroy her? The allegorical figure of France is thus insistently female, but at the same time capable of speech that would be more fitting in the mouth of a jurist than a medieval noblewoman. One might imagine that the prominence of such a learned female figure would suggest the acceptability of female rule, but in fact it is France herself, in a long and heated passage, who rejects this possibility.

France's lengthy and virulent denunciation of female rule is remarkable. In the opening of this section she says to England, "Comme il se pourroit faire que une femme fut roy de France, car elle ne peut ester homme, et toutevoie ce mot roy si est masculin?" [How could it be that a woman be king of France, for she cannot be a man, and nonetheless this word "king" is masculine] (160). This grammatical argument is presented as incontrovertible, and France then launches into her other justifications for female exclusion from rule: women cannot be anointed or bear arms, being king is a virile office, the king of France is a "personne ecclesiastique" [ecclesiastical person], the throne is a *dignitas*, not a *hereditas*, and as such cannot be transmitted to or exercised by a woman.[134]

A considerable amount of narrative space is dedicated to reviewing these familiar arguments, especially since France herself acknowledges that whether women can or ought to rule is not the contested issue, but rather whether they can serve as "pont et planche" [bridge and plank] (161) for their male issue.[135] Even the latter debate was moot by 1435, since in the Treaty of Troyes Henry V was obliged to acknowledge – however implicitly – the legitimacy of the Valois king Philippe VI in order to base his claims to the French throne upon his own marriage to Catherine of France and his adoption by Charles VI.[136] Nevertheless, France continues to develop at considerable length her arguments for female exclusion. In response to the imagined objection that other kingdoms allow for female rule, France replies that "c'est alleguer ung inconvenient; et font folie les pais de le souffrir, et est comme *ung monstre en nature*" [it is to allege an absurdity, and it is folly of kingdoms to suffer it, and it is like *a monster in nature*] (163, emphasis added).[137] France's allegation of monstrosity based upon the idea that nature furnishes the appropriate model for legitimate (i.e., male) political rule signals the true interest of this passage.

I contend that what France is condemning is not (or not only) female rule, but political actions that contravene nature, and the true target of her speech is the Treaty of Troyes. Philippe le bon and countless others had sworn to uphold the treaty, and its legal foundations had to be dismantled in order for the peace of Arras to be possible.[138] Removing the obstacle posed by the Treaty of Troyes is precisely the object of France's discourse, and of the treatise *Audite celi* as a whole. The gender hierarchy that is naturalized by France, a hierarchy dramatized by the monstrosity of female rule, provides a paradigm according to which only rule by the natural son is legitimate, while governance by one who is of another blood or another language is, like female rule, a monster in nature.

In her discussion of the Treaty of Troyes, France declares that "en moy qui suis terre France nommee, au regard de la couronne et des ascendens les *heritiers du sanc* sont neccessaires" [in I who am named the land of France, with regard to the crown and to successors, *blood heirs* are necessary] (186, emphasis added). Ralph Giesey has shown how Jean Juvénal des Ursins grounds political legitimacy and the right to rule in the biological relationship of father to son.[139] According to this logic Charles VI did not have the right to disinherit his biological son or to name Henry V as his heir, because "ceulx du sanc royal et mesmement le plus prochain du vivant du roy ont droyt au royaulme, et approprement parler le roy n'y a que une maniere de administracion et usage durant sa vye seullement" [those of royal blood and even the closest during the lifetime of the king have a right to the kingdom, and properly speaking the king has but a kind of administration and use of the kingdom during his lifetime only] (187).

France extends the idea that blood provides the foundation for political legitimacy, loyalties, and rights to include figurative kinship as well. With respect to those of her language who have allied themselves with England, France affirms with confidence that "ilz congnoistront verité, et revendront a leur nature et a moy qui suis leur mere" [they will know truth, and will return to their nature and to I who am their mother] (195). In this passage France posits a connection between correct political conduct, nature, and kinship.[140] Here the kinship is not literal, as between Charles VI and his son, but figurative. As in the allegorical texts of Alain Chartier and Christine de Pizan, France is depicted as the mother of the French subjects, and this genealogical bond constitutes the basis for the latter's political loyalties. Real blood thus guarantees the rights of the son, Charles VII, while figurative blood places certain obligations upon the subjects-children. In both cases, structures of power are legitimized by nature, who furnishes the measure of appropriate, or monstrous, political conduct. The incontestable hierarchy between men and women, inscribed in and justified by nature, thus provides a way to articulate and affirm another – possibly more contentious – set of ideas about nature and political rights and duties, in which the rights of the son supercede those of the father, and in which the loyalty of the subjects is determined by their mother country and their mother tongue.

At the conclusion of the creature's vision Bon conseil offers final pieces of advice to the participants in the conflict. To those allied with the English but "yssus de la maison de France, ravisés vous et vous retournés a la maison dont vous avés tout l'onneur et bien que vous avés. C'est une chose bien aisee, *quia res de facili revertitur ad suam naturam*. Vous estes tous denaturés et hors a proprement parler de vostre tabernacle; retournés y" [issued from the house of France, take counsel, and return to the house from which you have all the honour and the good that you possess. It is a very easy thing, for a thing easily returns to its nature. You are all denatured and, properly speaking, outside of your tabernacle. Return there] (261).[141] A return to political order is thus the equivalent of a return to one's nature. The peace talks to be held at Arras present an opportunity to reverse the monstrous Treaty of Troyes, and to restore the natural order between fathers and sons, men and women, lords and subjects.

The Treaty of Troyes transformed the terms according to which royal succession, and the relationship of the king to crown and kingdom, might be discussed and understood. This dynastic and political crisis provoked a number of legal, intellectual, and literary reactions. In this chapter we have focused on the ways in which key interventions in this conversation employed discourses of nature – natural law, natural love, natural rights – in order to articulate and justify opposition to the treaty. As these writers would have it, the Treaty of Troyes failed; indeed, it could not do otherwise, because fundamentally it was unnatural.[142]

In attempting to divert the line of French royal succession, the treaty contested the principles of Salic Law as well as the ordinances concerning succession that had been promulgated during the reign of Charles V and reinforced throughout that of Charles VI.[143] In a number of ordinances, Charles VI sought to ensure the political rights of the dauphin, rights that these documents persistently characterize as "droit naturel" [natural law] and "droit de nature" [law of nature], and that exist from the moment of the child's birth.[144] This perception of, and belief in, the political legitimacy and power of the king's son was not confined to the king alone, as is clearly evidenced by the efforts of the rival dukes of Orléans and Burgundy in 1404, for instance, or 1413, to assure their control over the physical body of the dauphin.[145]

From our vantage point, with our knowledge of who the eventual victors in this political struggle would be, it may appear that the failure of the Treaty of Troyes was inscribed in it from the outset. Henry V was certainly aware of its potential for failure. The numerous and elaborate oaths that he required of the signatories to the treaty, as well as the University of Paris, the "bonnes villes" [good towns], and all who held administrative offices,[146] attest to his concern to make the terms of the treaty "*look* right."[147] Given the long history between the kingdoms of France and England of peace agreements made and broken, Henry was not wrong to be cautious.[148] And in fact, the oaths did give pause to the duke of Burgundy and others, who feared to perjure themselves. Inducing Philippe le bon to abandon the Treaty of Troyes and the English alliance required considerable diplomatic, spiritual, and ideological efforts, efforts in which the texts we have examined had an important role to play.

The Treaty of Troyes galvanized French jurists and intellectuals into theorizing and articulating the foundations for French royal succession, thus demonstrating not only the illegality, but the unnaturalness, of the treaty. The ever-useful Salic Law was mobilized in this cause, as "the French jurists opposed to the Treaty [of Troyes] invoked the law in a new and expanded interpretation as a fundamental constitutional principle prohibiting the alienation of the French crown to a foreigner."[149] It was simply not possible to adopt an heir, because "fust encores tres loingtain de la couronne" [be he even very distant from the crown] a male heir of French royal blood could always be found.[150]

Already in the writings of Jean de Montreuil, we observed that Salic Law was not only placed at the service of nationalistic needs, it helped to trace and define the nation itself. Jean de Montreuil's extensive writing about the collective history of the kingdom of France, the military exploits of French chivalry, his concerns about the infiltration of France by foreign elements, and his refashioning of an ancient Frankish law that was able to serve as the unique and venerable law regulating the succession of the kings of France – all of these were components of Jean's efforts to build a kingdom not just in territorial or legal terms, but in conceptual and in emotional ones.

Alain Chartier's *Quadrilogue invectif* responds to the Treaty of Troyes by staging an allegorical figure of the kingdom who displaces the unnatural king and father, Charles VI, and who uses the language and images of birth and generation to define political identity and loyalty. The kingdom is not (only) a social or a political construction; it is naturalized, because founded on birth. Within the conceptual framework of the *Quadrilogue* it is no more possible to have a new king than to have a new father or mother. France is the mother of the French, the king of France their natural lord, and these allegiances, determined by birth, cannot be altered or ignored. The allegory of France is a textual representation of the ideas of coherence, boundedness, and integrity that Chartier sought to establish and to broadcast in his text.

Finally, Jean Juvénal des Ursins's *Audite celi*, written over a decade after the *Quadrilogue*, attempts to dismantle the Treaty of Troyes in order to make possible the peace of Arras. Here too allegory defines and stages political spaces that are likewise presented as natural, while the allegorical absence of certain entities, notably of Burgundy, constitutes a refusal to acknowledge their political, territorial, or cultural autonomy. Indeed, as France repeatedly says, Burgundy and others are bound to France by their common language, which is the sign of their shared culture and history, and evidence of where their political loyalties ought to lie. Here again, as in the works of Jean de Montreuil, discourses and hierarchies of gender are employed to define and impose natural (and therefore appropriate) structures of power, and to exclude the foreign, thereby preserving France for the French.

The texts we have examined inscribe their ideological positions within a nature that is itself carefully constructed. Had it suited the political ambitions of the Valois and their supporters, we can imagine discourses of the natural being exploited to justify an entirely different position. It is plausible to envision the elaboration of a rhetorical position according to which the allegorical representation of France as mother might be assimilated to royal daughters in order to justify the succession of a male through the female line, or even the succession of a queen. However, it is in the nature, as it were, of what we might call *doxa* to mask the processes of its own fabrication, to make an alternative position or course of action appear not only wrong, but impossible, unthinkable, *unnatural*. It is the working of these processes with respect to a specific set of circumstances that I have sought to lay bare in this chapter. In the coda, I shall address in broader terms the question of why gender is such a useful ideological instrument.

Coda: What to Say about Joan of Arc?

> puis fut le feu tiré arrière, et fut vue de tout le peuple toute nue et tous les secrets qui peuvent être ou doivent [être] en femme, pour ôter les doutes du peuple.
>
> *Journal d'un bourgeois de Paris*

Given the present volume's concerns with the mechanisms by which structures of power, political authority, and legitimacy are naturalized and promulgated, and the processes by which myths of national identity are fashioned, it seems impossible not to talk about the improbable life, and rather more predictable death, of Joan of Arc.[1] Joan was born c. 6 January 1412 into a prosperous peasant family in the village of Domrémy, situated at the eastern border of the kingdom of France, near the duchies of Bar and Lorraine. She claimed to have heard, from a young age, voices from God calling upon her to go to the assistance of Charles VII, the rightful king of France,[2] and to help him drive the English from his kingdom. With the help of Robert de Baudricourt, the captain of the nearby town of Vaucouleurs, Joan was eventually escorted to the royal palace at Chinon, where she arrived 4 March 1429, and was admitted into the presence of the king.[3] Joan was subjected to lengthy and careful investigations – both physical and theological – at Chinon and then at Poitiers.[4] As a result of these it was determined that, at the very least, Joan's visions ought not to be discounted out of hand, and she was entrusted with the leadership of the French army at the siege of Orléans, where she arrived in late April 1429. Within a week, the city was in French hands. Joan then led Charles's armies towards Rheims, the town of the royal coronation and consecration, and the contested king there received his crown on 17 July 1429. Joan's next military goal was Paris,[5] but the attack of September 1429 proved unsuccessful. The following spring Joan was taken prisoner by Burgundian forces outside of Compiègne (23 May 1430), and was ransomed to the English in November 1430. The English brought Joan to Rouen on 23 December 1430 to be tried by the Church for heresy. Joan's judges were Pierre Cauchon, the bishop of Beauvais, and Jean Le Maistre, a Dominican friar from Rouen. Found guilty on 19 May 1431, she famously abjured on 24 May, then returned to her so-called heresy on 28 May. She was burned at the stake on 30 May 1431. Some twenty-five years later Charles VII oversaw Joan's nullification trial, in which the "evidence" against her was revisited, and the former charges and verdict declared to be null. She was canonized in 1920.

The scholarship on Joan of Arc is vast, and I intend neither to revisit it nor to address the importance of Joan's astonishing life, death, and afterlife *en tant que tel*. Joan's interest, in the present context, resides in the important cultural, political, and ideological work that she performed for the authors I have studied in this volume. I will offer some reflections on why this might be so, and also what ideas she may illuminate for us. I will be interrogating a hermeneutical Joan, then, one who will allow us perhaps to draw some conclusions about the extraordinary flexibility and utility of both allegorical and metaphorical figures, and of discourses of gender, to elucidate relationships of power, authority, and identity.

Among the authors whose works I have discussed in this book, Eustache Deschamps and Jean de Montreuil both predeceased Joan. For each of the others, however, she occupies an important intellectual space. Christine de Pizan and Alain Chartier celebrated and wondered at the accomplishments of Joan in texts that postdate her spectacular victories at Orléans and Rheims, but that predate her capture, trial, and execution. Jean Gerson was a recognized expert on the discernment of spirits whose writings were instrumental in addressing the all-important question of whether the Pucelle's visions were in conformity with, or contrary to, the faith. Gerson was also the author of a short tract in support of Joan written after the victory at Orléans and prior to his own death on 12 July 1429. Perhaps the most puzzling textual response among the authors in this volume is that of Jean Juvénal des Ursins, who maintains a firm silence on the topic of Joan, even when it seems that her presence is perceptible, even palpable, within the confines of his work.

The years just preceding and following Christine de Pizan's redaction of the *Livre de l'advision Cristine*, discussed in chapter 2, were extraordinarily productive ones.[6] Christine remained in Paris and continued to write until 1418, when the Burgundian faction took over the city. At this time she took refuge at the Abbey of Poissy, where her daughter had lived for some years. The opening verses of her *Ditié de Jehanne d'Arc*, "ay plouré / XI ans en abbaye close" [For 11 years I have wept in a walled abbey], refer to this period of exile and relative silence, from which the *Ditié*, the final text of her career, emerged like a cry of joy and triumph.[7] The *Ditié* is dated 31 July 1429, after the Pucelle's victory at Orléans and the coronation of Charles VII at Rheims, but prior to her capture, trial, and death.[8]

Christine's text conveys all of the triumph and optimism of those loyal to Charles VII, as well as their anxiety concerning the eventual outcome of the unfolding military and ideological campaign against the combined English and Burgundian forces. As scholars have noted, Christine presents herself in the *Ditié* as a Christian, a French loyalist, and a woman, and these identities are mutually reinforcing.[9] The French are God's chosen people, and Joan his chosen instrument. The fact that he selected a figure of apparently overdetermined inappropriateness as his instrument serves to highlight this fact.[10] God and Joan are very much the agents in this text, rather than Charles, who has been "hault eslevé par la Pucelle" [raised by the Maid] (v. 102).[11] Further, Christine asks rhetorically, "N'a el le roy mené au sacre, / Que tousjours tenoit par la main?" [Did she not lead the king to the sacre, holding him always by the hand?] (vv. 378–9). Christine compares Joan to the Old Testament figures Moses, Joshua, and Gideon, as well as to Esther, Deborah, and Judith. In military force she surpasses Hector and Achilles. At the same time, she serves as a Marian figure who, though a "jeune pucelle" [young virgin] (v. 186), gave to France "la mamelle / De paix et doulce norriture" [the breast of peace and sweet nourishment] (189–90).[12] Joan thus both nurtures and protects, evidence of her divine origin and mission, for "ce fait Dieu, qui la conseille, / En qui cuer plus que d'omme a mis" [God did this, who advises her, in whom he has placed more than a man's heart/courage] (207–8). Joan is living evidence of God's favour of the French, and of the "feminin / Sexe" [womanly sex] (265–6).

Alain Chartier wrote his *Epistola de puella* to an anonymous foreign prince in late July 1429. The introduction to his letter provides evidence of the interest and curiosity that Joan provoked far from the arena of her actions, since Chartier's recipient sent an ambassador to France specifically in order to provide a report on "que de Puella dicerentur" [what is said about the Pucelle] (326).[13] Chartier first discusses Joan's pastoral origins and the circumstances in which she left her native Vaucouleurs[14] and sought out Charles VII, at the urgent command of "voce ex nube" [a voice coming from the clouds] (326). Beyond referring to her as "puella," Chartier does not discuss Joan's virginity per se, or her physical evaluation. Instead, he describes the interrogations of Joan, conflating those of Chinon and Poitiers into a single "spectaculum profecto" [wonderful spectacle] (327) in which she responded to questions on topics "humanis ac divinis" [both human and divine] (327). In a manner that suggests comparison with St Catherine,[15] and that, like the *Ditié*, emphasizes Joan's apparent weakness, Chartier vividly evokes the unlikely presence of "[mulier] cum viris, indocta cum doctis, sola cum multis, infima de summis disputat" [the woman with the men, the unlearned one with the learned ones; one against many; the most junior person discussing the highest matters] (327). In Chartier's letter Joan assumes a superlative clerical identity, one that is all the more remarkable because the accidents of Joan's person should normally preclude such a performance of scholarly exchange and discourse.[16]

Not only her conduct before her learned interrogators, but also Joan's chivalric accomplishments, from riding a horse, to capturing the English fortifications at Orléans, to traversing enemy territory to reach Rheims for the king's coronation, are cause for wonder. Chartier highlights their difficulty – Joan had never ridden a horse, the fortifications "nullo pacto expugnare posse videbantur" [appeared impossible to subdue by any means] (328), her voyage to Rheims seemed "non tantum difficile sed impossibile" [not only difficult but impossible] (328) – in order to highlight the value of her achievement. There is no one, even if he does not admire Joan (an allusion to those who maintained that her visions were not of divine origin) who "stupeat, factis eciam" [would not wonder at ... these facts] (328).

While affirming that her visions are from heaven, and consequently that she is an instrument of God, Chartier also highlights Joan's personal qualities and agency. She possesses the characteristics and skills required of renowned military leaders like Hector, Alexander, and Caesar: tactical skill, strong spirit, attentiveness, justice, strength, good fortune. In the final paragraph of Chartier's letter Joan is the grammatical subject of a series of phrases of which the objects are France, the king, and the English, respectively. Rather than highlighting God's miracle and mystery in making use of so fragile a creature, Chartier depicts Joan as a strong and worthy instrument of divine intent, thereby implicitly condemning the French knights and leaders who presumably shared her qualities, and yet were unable or unwilling to prosecute the French cause to good effect.

It is quite remarkable to observe to what degree Joan is already, during her lifetime, a discursive construct, or a sign whose semantic content is subject to debate.[17] Christine and Chartier both demonstrate a desire to exercise hermeneutic control of Joan, shaping her meaning for their own purposes.[18] For these authors the advent of Joan of Arc appears to be a miraculous confirmation of their own long-held beliefs – in the legitimacy of the kingship of Charles VII, the justice of the French position in the Hundred Years' War, the status of France and the French as God's chosen people with a divine mission to fulfil on behalf of all of Christendom, and, for Christine at least, the possibility (indeed necessity) for women to take their place in the political realm.

For Jean Gerson, the chancellor of the University of Paris from 1395 to 1415 and a leading authority on the discernment of spirits, Joan's claims to have heard divine voices would have presented a particularly compelling case of an issue that had interested him from the earliest years of his career. Gerson is the author of numerous treatises on the discernment of spirits, including *De distinctione verarum visionum a falsis* (1401–2), *De probatione spirituum* (1415), and *De examinatione doctrinarum* (1423), as well as a letter to Jean Morel written in connection with the visionary Ermine de Reims (the *Judicium de vita sanctae Erminae*, possibly before 1401). Despite Gerson's conviction that only the Holy Spirit could provide certain knowledge of the truth of a vision or prophecy, his writings on discernment were nonetheless employed to evaluate the visions of Ermine de Reims, Birgitta of Sweden, and others.[19] Over the course of his long career Gerson affirmed that spiritual knowledge and access to the divine were not the exclusive purview of men, or of the learned, but that the simple at heart often had a more pure faith, based upon love of God and not compromised by pride. With respect to visionaries and visions, Gerson's byword was caution. On the one hand, one ought never dismiss or reject visions out of hand, because this would be an affront to the Holy Spirit. Indeed, condemning visions accepted by many as true could cause "scandal."[20] On the other hand, one must be careful not to lend credence too readily, for this can lead to heresy. Gerson developed criteria which might permit an evaluation of the probable truth of a vision, many of which focus upon the person of the visionary: who is this person? what are their background, character, habits, and actions? As for the vision, its purpose and its outcome – if known – were the most important factors to consider.[21]

Over the course of the Chinon and Poitiers investigations and the military and ideological campaigns that followed, numerous documents were generated both in favour of and in opposition to Joan. Two of these – *De quadam puella* (DQP) and *Super facto puellae et credulitate sibi praestanda*, the latter often referred to as the *De mirabili victoria* (DMV) – have been of disputed authorship, with Gerson cited as the author of one or the other, both, or neither. It is my view that Daniel Hobbins effectively resolved this debate in his 2005 article "Jean Gerson's Authentic Tract on Joan of Arc: *Super facto puellae et credulitate sibi praestanda* (14 May 1429)." Hobbins reviews the scholarship on Gerson (including editions of his works) in order to situate the origins of the misattribution of these texts, and he argues based on scrupulously examined manuscript evidence that the DQP, a kind of university *determinatio* that weighs the evidence both for and against the authenticity of Joan's visions, is the work of Henry of Gorkum, while the *Super facto*, "an opinion piece strongly in support of Joan" (113) was certainly written by Gerson in the weeks before his death.[22]

In *Super facto* Gerson considers Joan's case (though without naming her directly) in light of his own beliefs about visions and prophecies. Gerson explains that certain matters are necessary to the faith, and it is not permitted to doubt them. However, other beliefs may be held out of piety or devotion, but "Qui ne le croit, il n'est pas dampné" [Whomsoever does not believe it, he is not damned].[23] Joan's visions fall into the latter category. When evaluating such matters Gerson proposes three criteria for assessing probable truth. First, they should excite piety and devotion to God; second, they should partake of more or less general credence, founded either upon shared belief ("ex communi relatione") or upon the testimony of the faithful who claim to have seen or heard them ("ex fidelium attestatione qui dicunt se vidisse vel audisse," 148); and finally, they should introduce no falsity or error that might undermine faith or good morals. Based upon these general premises, Gerson concludes that it could be pious and salutary ("pie et salubriter potest") to believe in the "factum illius puellae" [deeds of this girl] (149). Another important element of assessing visions for Gerson was their purpose or result. In the case of Joan, her objectives and outcome were both clearly praiseworthy: the restitution of his kingdom to the king of France, and the expulsion of his enemies (149). It is quite remarkable to observe that in Joan's case the good intention and outcome is not connected (at least in explicit terms) to salvation, but to the political circumstances in which Gerson and his public found themselves. In this respect we can observe once again the connection between the individual, temporal, and spiritual realms that we examined throughout this study and that are foundational to the political thought of Gerson, as well as of Christine de Pizan and Alain Chartier. Gerson concludes his short treatise with a defence of Joan's male attire. As Hobbins has shown, this passage (lines 110–42) was not part of the text as it initially circulated, though it was added very shortly thereafter.[24] In what seems retrospectively to have been a prescient move, Gerson seeks to silence Joan's detractors on the subject of what would form one of their principal accusations against her – her refusal to conform to conventions of femininity, illustrated in flagrant terms by her adoption of masculine dress.

Among the contemporaries of Joan whose works are discussed in this volume, the most curious reaction is perhaps that of Jean Juvénal des Ursins, a supporter of Charles VII from his earliest days, and later one of the three judges in charge of the nullification trial. In *Audite celi*,[25] an allegorical dream vision composed in 1435, well after Joan's trial and execution, but still in the context of the ongoing war between Charles VII's France and the combined Anglo-Burgundian forces, Jean Juvénal very pointedly avoids any mention of Joan. This silence is most striking in a passage in which he is enumerating signs of God's favour for Charles VII, and yet he very noticeably does not include Joan.[26] To counter the English argument that their victories were evidence of God's favour, the allegorical figure of France affirms in *Audite celi* that these victories were not signs of God's grace but were intended to punish the sins of the French, for often sinners are punished by people even more wicked than they.[27] France then declares that God clearly favours Charles VII, and in support of her claim she cites the dauphin's miraculous escape from Paris in 1418,[28] the battles of Baugé and La Gravelle,[29] the deaths of the duke of Clarence and other English nobles, including Henry V, the raising of the sieges of Montargis,[30] and of Orléans,[31] and "les choses merveilleuses qui ont esté faictes devant le tres noble, digne et presque miraculeux sacre du roy Charles fait a Reins" [the marvellous things that were done before the noble, worthy, and almost miraculous anointing of King Charles, performed at Rheims] (197),[32] notably the way in which villages and towns spontaneously and voluntarily declared their allegiance to Charles so that he arrived safely and without shedding blood in the town of the royal anointing. Since Joan was directly involved in the siege of Orléans, as well as Charles's anointing at Rheims, it is actually quite shocking that Jean Juvénal would bring up these events without mentioning her. Jules Quicherat, himself puzzled by the silence on the subject of Joan that dominated texts produced in the wake of her trial, suggested that perhaps a kind of gag order had been issued in the entourage of Charles VII following Joan's condemnation and execution.[33] And yet, Jean Juvénal's text cannot be said to be exactly silent. By raising the question of God's favour, by recalling the specific events with which Joan was most closely associated, by qualifying these events as "choses merveilleuses" [marvellous things] and "miraculeux" [miraculous], Jean Juvénal is quite definitely conjuring the spectre of Joan, inviting his readers to supply for themselves her name, generating her presence in their minds even as he inscribes her absence in his text. To name is to summon or bring into being, rather than suppress or repress what one fears to bring into the light. As we saw in chapter 4, absence weighs as heavily as presence in *Audite celi*, so what does Joan's spectacular absence tell us? What dangers does Joan pose, such that she cannot be named?

I suggest that for her detractors, Joan represents a kind of return of the repressed. By 1429 France and the Valois had spent over a century affirming the exclusion of women from royal rule, both as the basis for Valois legitimacy, and eventually as one of the constitutive elements of a painstakingly elaborated ideological structure comprised of a shared historical past, laws and legends, and collective beliefs that over time shaped and promulgated a sense of national identity. Joan threatened not only the institutions of political and spiritual authority, but masculinity itself, and this in multiple ways.[34]

By identifying herself as the "Pucelle," a term with connotations of both youth and sexual purity, Joan made her virginity a constitutive element of her identity.[35] And yet Joan did not conform to the usual reglementation of female sexuality. She was not a virgin consecrated to Christ and safely enclosed in a religious community, nor yet was she precisely a maiden guarding her virginity for an eventual husband.[36] The term "pucelle," in contradistinction to "vierge," promises sexual availability and inscription into a heteronormative marital and reproductive economy, and yet Joan refused to relinquish control over her virginity, instead preserving it for God, for so long as it would please him.[37] Joan thus situated herself "perpetually on the brink," as it were, her epithet both promising and withholding acquiescence to masculine desire.[38]

Joan similarly disrupted class norms by refusing to adhere to the expectations associated with her social order. As we have seen, she intervened in political and military affairs, assuming a role normally reserved for knights. Indeed, Christine de Pizan asserts that God gave Joan "cuer plus que d'omme" [a heart/courage greater than that of a man] (v. 208).[39] At the same time, Joan usurped or put into question male prerogative in the clerical and religious sphere as well. Chartier depicts Joan silencing and confounding her clerical interrogators at Poitiers, while her consistent refusal to bend to the Church militant's authority was arguably a significant reason for her condemnation as a heretic.

Joan's actions, outside of and beyond the norms and limits of female conduct, reveal – or perhaps create the perception of – a certain weakness and inadequacy on the part of the dauphin. As the visible agent of God's intervention on behalf of France, Joan's active presence casts Charles in the role of feminized beneficiary of protection and support. However, the king's political weakness is not, in and of itself, the origin of his potential feminization. Charles VII's grandfather, Charles V, was himself politically vulnerable at the start of his reign, and, moreover, was physically frail and decidedly unknightly in appearance. Charles V was championed by his constable Bertrand DuGuesclin, who led Charles's armies and achieved many victories against the English. DuGuesclin was a kind of uber medieval male, often named the tenth worthy, the subject of chivalric biography and a model of French knighthood, and yet DuGuesclin does not challenge either Charles's royal authority or his masculinity. In her *Livre des fais et bonnes meurs du sage roy Charles V* Christine de Pizan compared DuGuesclin to Bucephalus, the famous warhorse of Alexander the Great, an analogy that served to highlight the king's cooperation with, but ultimately mastery of, his famous constable. In contrast, Joan's destabilization of the male-female binary and her non-conformity to her culturally assigned role threatened the king's masculinity, and masculinity in general. DuGuesclin may have been great among men, but Joan was more, or other, than a man, and herein lay her danger for Charles VII, and for French kingship.

Joan's cross-dressing furnished a visible focal point for the problematic nature of her gender performance. Susan Schibanoff has persuasively argued that the threat posed by Joan's refusal of women's clothing was not so much that she cross-dressed, but that she did not cross-dress completely and successfully enough to pass for a man.[40] Joan's "partial male attire did not mask but drew attention to her materiality, her female body, and thus "seduced" its viewers."[41] Schibanoff uses the distinction between the image (understood as a likeness that allows for transcendence to a higher realm on the part of the viewer) and the idol (a simulacrum that counterfeits another thing, while calling attention to its own facture and artificiality) to suggest that Joan violated boundaries, not only that which divided male from female, but more importantly that which divided truth from lies.[42] Judith Butler provides us with another framework within which to think about the threat Joan posed to masculinity, and to conventional gender norms of her time and place, with her example of the transvestite on the stage versus the transvestite next to us on the bus. The former can be safely relegated to the realm of the fictive, the unreal, even the ludic, while the latter not only blurs the distinction between the imaginary and the real, but even suggests that perhaps "there are no conventions that facilitate making this separation."[43] Joan's partial or imperfect conformity to late medieval gender conventions, her simultaneous claims to an authority available only to virgins *and* to the liberty of action accorded to men, the very both/and-ness of her identity, exposed Joan to the wrath of her contemporaries.[44] As Judith Butler further observes, "Performing one's gender wrong initiates a set of punishments both obvious and indirect."[45] This was amply true in Joan's case.

The "both/and-ness" of Joan, her incarnation of semantic multiplicity, invites us to think about her in relation to the praxis of allegory.[46] As we have seen, the foreign or the strange, the alien or Other, the incommensurability of form and meaning, are characteristics of what I discussed in chapter 1 in terms of the structure of allegory, or the allegorical condition. For many of her contemporaries, Joan enacted the most dangerous possibilities inherent in allegory – those of perversion and of violence.

The organological metaphor for the body politic and the allegory of France both performed and projected the unity and coherence of the kingdom at a time when France was literally and symbolically dismembered, as it were, by the claims of the English kings to rule over vast continental territories in full sovereignty, and even to be the rightful rulers of France. As we have seen, the metaphor of the body politic focuses on the relationships of people or groups to one another within a single and unified whole. It can be employed to promote cooperation and unity of purpose within the body politic, and to privilege the collective over the private good. The allegory of France, in contrast, posits a direct and affective relationship between each subject and an exteriorized, conceptual entity – the kingdom. This allegorical imagining of the realm was particularly useful during the reign of Charles VI because the king's minority, and later his psychological "absence," created a void or disquieting non-presence at the centre or summit of the structure of political authority.

This move from metaphor to allegory, from indefinite to definite article, from collective whole to exteriorized other, entails – perhaps even requires – the feminization of the realm. The texts I have examined in this volume show that once the reader is no longer inscribed within the metaphor of the body politic, but is invited to contemplate the allegorical figure of the kingdom from without, France becomes Other, and also feminine.[47] The allegory of France is not (only) represented as a woman because the noun France is feminine, rather, it is represented as a woman because the allegorical figure of France is employed to construct a masculine political subject. We have observed that the allegory of France is cast in a range of highly conventional female roles – courtly beloved, damsel in distress, noble widow, tearful mother. All of these gendered identities call forth the affection and loyalty of the publics interpellated by the allegory, and therefore they reinforce and comfort traditional notions of masculinity. Chivalric ideals required knights to protect ladies, while natural love supposed the affection and loyalty of children for their mothers.

The figure of France compensates for the weakness or "absence" of the king by providing an alternative focal point for the political loyalty and love of the French subjects. In some texts, like Chartier's *Quadrilogue invectif*, the king is in fact displaced by the kingdom. The king is entirely absent from this text, and it is France who serves as the source and guarantor of political authority and legitimacy. It may be that the overdetermined femininity of allegories of France, their perfect conformity to traditional gender binaries in which France is both beautiful, noble, and worthy, and also mistreated, weak, and needy, serve to mask or veil the radical nature of what is actually being suggested: the notion that the French owe their loyalty, indeed their very lives not to the person of the king, but to the kingdom.

As we have seen, late medieval France produced another important allegorical figure with quite a different relationship to the king than the figure of France: the University of Paris. In Jean Gerson's allegorical representation of the University, this institution is analogous to both king and kingdom. The University is the *fille du roy*, the king's good daughter. She is a loyal and effective daughter who provides an avenue for political continuity and coherence even during the absence of the king, but she does not constitute a rival for his political authority. The imaginary kinship that joins king and University is presented as superior to the literal kinship that united the king and his principle advisers, the princes of the blood, because while the latter have their own ambitions and agendas, the University is wholly dedicated to the interests of king and kingdom. It is worth observing that Joan, unlike the University, is not the *fille du roy*, but rather the *fille de Dieu*. Charles is the privileged beneficiary of Joan's military and propagandistic efforts, but Joan's primary concern is to serve God.

Thus, the allegorical figures that I have examined over the course of this book and Joan of Arc both function on some level as supplements to or substitutes for the king, but whereas the overdetermined femininity of the allegory of France serves to construct masculine political subjects, Joan of Arc, with her ambiguous gender and her refusal to dress or behave like a woman while fashioning an identity whose authority is founded on female virginity,[48] has the effect of calling masculinity and the male-female binary into question. In Jean Juvénal's text Joan and the allegorical figure of France appear in their closest, yet unacknowledged, proximity. In *Audite celi* it is France herself who affirms the legitimacy of Charles VII and his selection by God as the leader of God's new chosen people. And yet, in France's discourse the king does not owe his anointing to a woman, and Joan's advent is not included among the miracles that confirmed God's election of Charles and the French. The allegory of France thus silences the subversively allegorical Pucelle.

The anxiety that clearly surrounded Joan's enactment of gender may explain in part the peculiar and creepy gesture, remarked upon by many scholars, of her executioners after her death, who drew her corpse from the fire and displayed it to those present in order to show that she was, in fact, a woman.[49] One wonders if in pointing to Joan's literal body her executioners hoped to arrive at and proclaim the truth of her existence? I would suggest instead that this attachment to the literal serves only to draw attention to the allegorical surplus beyond the body.

When I embarked upon this project, I was struck by the simultaneous emergence of Salic Law, on the one hand, and, on the other, the allegorical representations of France as a woman in many literary texts, and I puzzled over what seemed to constitute the simultaneous exclusion and celebration of women within the cultural and political imaginary. I now find, instead, that these are like two sides of the same coin, that the fabrication of Salic Law and of female allegories of the kingdom both work, though in different ways, to create a national identity founded in part upon the exclusion of women from royal rule, a masculine political subject, and structures of authority, as well as to master, control, and delimit the parameters within which women may function. The hasty repression of Joan, her forcible inscription into the role of heretic, even witch, and the need for ocular confirmation of her female human body, attest to the threat she posed to the structures of authority then being elaborated and deployed. At the dawn of the modern era, France may bear a woman's likeness, but the French have asserted themselves as a kingdom of masculine subjects, ruled by a *roi* très chrétien.

Notes

Introduction

1 On the reign of Charles VI the Mad, or the Beloved, see Autrand, *Charles VI*, Famiglietti, *Royal Intrigue*, Guenée, *Un meurtre, une société* and Guenée, *La folie de Charles VI*.

2 The expression is that of Jean de Montreuil, whose work will be studied in chapter 4, and comes from his first *Traité contre les anglais*. Jean de Montreuil. *Opera. L'œuvre historique et polémique*, vol. 2, at 169. The expression will be picked up by a range of other authors.

3 On the problematic series of successions that marked the end of the Capetian dynasty see Lewis, *Royal Succession in Capetian France* and Wood, "Queens, Queans, and Kingship." For additional references see chapter 4.

4 The fact that Louis's first wife, Marguerite de Bourgogne, was found guilty of adultery did not help the cause of their young daughter. Louis's posthumous son, Jean, was born of the king's second wife, Clemence of Hungary. On the implications of the queen's sexual conduct see McCracken, *The Romance of Adultery* and Wood, "Queens, Queans, and Kingship."

5 For many generations the reigning king had his son crowned during his lifetime in an effort to establish the hereditability of the royal office. The eldest son of the king was the *rex designatus*. It was not until the reign of Philippe Auguste that this practice was sufficiently entrenched as to make such precautions unnecessary. Philippe III was the first Capetian king to date his rule from the day of his father's death, rather than from that of his own coronation and annointing, thereby showing that the king's heir ruled from the moment of the king's own death. On the instantaneity of royal succession see Krynen, "'La mort saisit le vif.'"

6 Viollet, "Comment les femmes ont été exclues, en France," and Giesey, *Le rôle méconnu de la loi salique*.

7 From the text *Tres crestien, tres hault, tres puissant roy*. See *Écrits politiques de Jean Juvénal des Ursins*, vol. 2, 46. Jean Juvénal des Ursins's *Audite celi* will be discussed in chapter 4.

8 As Philippe Contamine so aptly put it, "Quant à la loi salique, son intérêt fut de donner à la très banale et très vague 'coutume de France' un nom, un statut, une ancienneté, bref des titres de noblesse." See his article "'Le royaume de France ne peut tomber en fille," 71.

9 Which he did, becoming Charles IV of France. On the agreement between Charles de la Marche and Philippe of Poitiers see Giesey, *Le rôle méconnu de la loi salique*, chapter 2.

10 Philippe de Valois was the son of Philippe le Bel's brother Charles de Valois, and therefore the first cousin of the last three Capetian kings and a direct descendent of Saint Louis through a cadet line.

11 "[E]n quatorze ans les femmes furent exclues à trois reprises du trône de France. Le droit public était fixé sur ce point. Les prétentions des femmes ne pouvaient renaître." See Viollet, "Comment les femmes ont été exclues, en France,"149.

12 In addition to the question of the transmissability of political rights, Edward's youth and the political prominence of his mother and her lover, Roger Mortimer, surely affected the deliberations of the French.

13 For an overview of the Hundred Years' War see Curry, *The Hundred Years War*, and Favier, *La guerre de cent ans*.

14 This division of authority was intended to ensure that royal power would not be concentrated in the hands of any single person, in the hope that an equilibrium might be maintained until the new king was old enough to rule. In fact, Charles VI was crowned far earlier than provided for by his father's ordinances, in an effort to obviate the tension and rivalry between his paternal uncles that erupted almost immediately. See Autrand, "La succession à la couronne de France."

15 See Guenée, *La folie de Charles VI*.

16 "plus prochains de son sang." Cited in de Miramon, "Aux origines de la noblesse et des princes du sang," 183.

17 On the queen's role in the council see Adams, "Christine de Pizan, Isabeau of Bavaria, and Female Regency" as well as *The Life and Afterlife of Isabeau of Bavaria*.

18 The changes in royal policy with respect to the subtraction of papal obedience provides an excellent example of how the changing political fortunes of the members of the council shaped the official French position on the most important questions of the day. See Kaminsky, "The Politics of France's Subtraction of Obedience from Pope Benedict XIII."

19 "Réponse d'un bon et loyal françois," 124.

20 On the corporeal metaphor see, among others, Briguglia, *Il corpo vivente dello stato* and LeGoff, "Head or Heart?" as well as the additional references in chapter 1, where I will discuss the organological metaphor in greater detail.

21 Indeed, I am not aware of any texts that discuss the sexual organs of the body in relation to any component of medieval society. The same cannot be said of images. The manuscript of the *Avis aus roys* made for Louis d'Anjou and contained in the Pierpont Morgan library (M. 456) features an image of a crowned male nude that is explicitly identified as representing the body politic. See Michael Camille's discussion of this image and this manuscript in "The King's New Bodies." Though the figure's genitals are clearly evident in the image, they are unmentioned in the text.

22 *Les grandes chroniques de France*, 1: 5.

23 The concept of the crown had already been employed to discuss the distinction between the king as an individual person and the institution of kingship or the kingdom of France. See Krynen, *Idéal du prince et pouvoir royal*, on the idea that the crown is representative of a nascent notion of the state. Jean de Montreuil stages the discourse of an allegorized crown.

24 Blumenfeld-Kosinski discusses gendered violence and the "affective power of the female voice" in "Dramatic Troubles of Ecclesia," 184.

25 Spiegel, "The *reditus regni ad stirpem Karoli Magni*," 146.

26 See Post, "Parisian Masters as a Corporation" as well as McKeon, "The Status of the University of Paris as *Parens Scientiarum*."

27 See, among others, Bernstein, *Pierre d'Ailly and the Blanchard Affair*, Lusignan, "'*Vérité garde le roy*,'" McLoughlin, "Gerson as a Preacher in the Conflict between Mendicants and Secular Priests," Rashdall, *The Universities of Europe in the Middle Ages*, esp. 1: 370–97, and Weber, "Suitable for Crown and Gown."

28 See Wei, "The Masters of Theology at the University of Paris."

29 See Denifle and Châtelain eds, *Chartularium Universitatis Parisiensis*, 3: 53. This formulation recalls the prologue of the *Grandes chroniques de France*, in which France is characterized as the favoured daughter of the Church, thereby suggesting a homology between kingdom and University which, as I shall demonstrate in chapter 3, is extensively developed in the works of the theologian and University chancellor Jean Gerson. "Se nule autre nation fait à sainte Eglise force ne grief, en France en vient fere sa complainte, en France vient à refui et à secors; de France vient l'espée et li glaives par quoi ele est vengée, et *France comme loiaus fille secourt sa mere en touz besoinz*; si a touz jors la sele mise pour li aidier et secorre" [If any other nation causes the holy Church difficulty or trouble, she comes to France with her complaint, to

France she comes for refuge and succor, from France comes the sword and the blade by which she is avenged, and *France, like a loyal daughter, comes to the aid of her mother in every need*, for she always has the saddle ready to help and to save her] (emphasis added). *Les grandes chroniques de France*, 1: 5.

30 On the fictive kinship that bound University and king see also Lusignan, "L'université de Paris comme composante de l'identité du royaume de France."

31 Indeed, as Berlant has argued, "the experience of identity might be personal and private, but its forms are always 'collective' and political. The relation of personal experience to public form is not, however, a relation of the 'real' to the 'inauthentic.'" See *The Anatomy of National Fantasy*, 3.

32 On the myths and memories of France and the French see *Les lieux de mémoire*, ed. Nora, and Beaune, *Naissance de la nation France*.

33 Berlant, *The Anatomy of National Fantasy*, 2.

34 See also Ardis Butterfield, who has proposed that the nation be understood as "something creative," the effect of "an act of imagination rather than of political philosophy." See *The Familiar Enemy*, 28–9.

35 Berlant, *The Anatomy of National Fantasy*, 5.

36 Such as that which affirmed the Trojan descent of the Franks. See Wood, "Defining the Franks."

37 Exemplified by the conversion of Clovis, the dove which furnished the sacred oil for his anointment, and the establishment of France as the oldest Christian kingdom. This is a key foundational moment for France, and is one of the earliest episodes recounted in the *Grandes chroniques*.

38 Like that communicated by the notion of *translatio studii et imperii*, which posited France, and in particular Paris, as the successor of Greece and Rome.

39 On the development of these and other myths see Beaune, *Naissance de la nation France*.

40 See Zorach, *Blood, Milk, Ink, Gold* and Bouchet, "L'intertexte oublié."

41 On the relationship of legal to literary fictions see Steiner, *Documentary Culture*, especially chapter 1.

42 It is precisely the anchoring of collective belief in local and individual consciousness that creates what Berlant calls the National Symbolic. "We are bound together because we inhabit the *political* space of the nation, which is not merely juridical, territorial (*jus soli*), genetic (*jus sanguinis*), linguistic, or experiential, but some tangled cluster of these. I call this space the 'National Symbolic.'" See *The Anatomy of National Fantasy*, 5.

43 The bibliography on this subject is vast. While I do not subscribe to the modernist position articulated by Anthony Smith, Benedict Anderson,

and others, I do not pretend to weigh in on the nuances of this scholarly debate.

44 See Butterfield, *The Familiar Enemy*, especially her introduction.

45 See, for instance, *The Cambridge Companion to Allegory*, ed. Copeland and Struck, *Thinking Allegory Otherwise*, ed. Machosky, and *Interpretation and Allegory*, ed. Whitman.

46 See, for example, Kamath, *Authorship and First-Person Allegory in Late Medieval France and England*, Guynn, *Allegory and Sexual Ethics in the High Middle Ages*, Johnson, *The Vitality of Allegory*, Raskolnikov, *Body against Soul*, and Teskey, *Allegory and Violence*.

47 For instance, those of Astell, *Political Allegory in Late Medieval England*, Lassabatère, *La cité des hommes*, and Minet-Mahy, *Esthétique et pouvoir de l'œuvre allégorique*.

48 See the bibliography for full references.

49 See Paxson, "Personification's Gender," 152.

50 Because the nouns of Latin and the Romance languages are masculine or feminine, allegorical representations of places, institutions, or virtues are aligned with the grammatical gender of the word they embody.

51 Pitkin shows that the female figure of Fortune embodies all the varied threats to masculine honour posed by women, and is often represented as an exacting and implacable courtly *domna*. See *Fortune Is a Woman*.

52 Newman, *God and the Goddesses*.

53 Francomano, *Wisdom and Her Lovers*.

54 Quilligan, "Allegory and Female Agency," 166. See also Quilligan, *The Allegory of Female Authority*.

55 Scott, "Gender: A Useful Category of Historical Analysis," 1069.

56 See, for instance, Adams, *The Life and Afterlife of Isabeau of Bavaria*, Allirot, *Filles de roy de France*, Cosandey, *La reine de France*, Cheyette, *Ermengarde of Narbonne and the World of the Troubadours*, and Weissberger, *Isabel Rules*. See also the essays contained in the edited volumes *Women and Sovereignty*, ed. Fradenburg, *Medieval Queenship*, ed. Carmi Parsons, and *Power of the Weak*, ed. Carpenter and MacLean.

57 See, for instance, Crawford, *Perilous Performances* and Earenfight, *The King's Other Body*. Earenfight shows that "medieval monarchy admitted a plurality of power arrangements that permitted a range of power-sharing options situated in dispersed and localized sites clustered around the king" (13).

58 See, for example, the works of Bynum, Richard and Mary Rouse, or Blumenfeld-Kosinski, as well as the wide range of scholarship included in edited volumes such as *Gendering the Master Narrative*, ed. Erler and

Kowaleski, *Gender in Debate from the Early Middle Ages to the Renaissance*, ed. Fenster and Lees, *Gender and Christianity in Medieval Europe*, ed. Bitel and Lifshitz, *Voices in Dialogue*, ed. Olson and Kerby-Fulton, and *Troubled Vision*, ed. Campbell and Mills.

59 As Gordon Teskey has written, allegorical meaning "is an instrument used to exert force on the world as we find it, imposing on the intolerable, chaotic otherness of nature a hierarchical order in which objects will appear to have inherent 'meanings.'" See *Allegory and Violence*, 2.

60 As Michel Winock has written, "Les Français ne s'aiment pas mais ils aiment la France." See "Jeanne d'Arc," 727.

61 Just before the treaty Charles VI had repudiated his son, the dauphin Charles, for "le dampnable et énorme crime de lui et des siens" [the damning and enormous crime of himself and his allies], an allusion to Charles's involvement in the murder of Jean sans peur in 1419. See *Ordonnances des roys de France de la troisième race, recueillies par ordre chronologique*, 12: 273.

1. Allegory Is a Woman

1 Or object. I focus in this study on allegorical texts, but many of my remarks are equally applicable to visual allegory.

2 See, for instance, Macrobius's commentary on the dream of Scipio, in which he affirms that "philosophers ... realize that a frank, open exposition of herself is distasteful to Nature, who, just as she has withheld an understanding of herself from the uncouth senses of men by enveloping herself in variegated garments, has also desired to have her secrets handled by more prudent individuals through fabulous narratives ... Only eminent men of superior intelligence gain a revelation of her truth." *Commentary on the dream of Scipio*, 86–7.

3 Modern discussions of allegory have had to contend with the Romantic predilection for the symbol, distinguished perhaps most famously by Coleridge, in his *Statesman's Manual* of 1816, and reanimated by C.S. Lewis in the twentieth century. See Lewis, *The Allegory of Love* and Hodgson, "Transcendental Tropes." As Stephen Barney quips, "Romantics called good allegory symbolism, and bad allegory, allegory." See *Allegories of History, Allegories of Love*, 25. On the Romantic privileging of the symbol see also de Man, "The Rhetoric of Temporality."

4 See Whitman, *Allegory*.

5 Like Rousseau's "dangerous supplement," discussed by Derrida, allegory can be added to, or displace, an original work. See his *Of Grammatology*.

6 Cicero is the first to employ the term "allegory" in Latin, and he does so in the sense of compositional allegory, defining it as a series of metaphors. In Quintilian too we see the idea of a "sustained rhetorical composition." See Whitman, *Allegory*, 265.

7 Like allegory, personification was demoted, its signifying potential radically circumscribed, by Romantic critics. Morton Bloomfield has argued that the Romantic tradition focused too narrowly on the speeches of personifications, whereas the interest of personifications resides in their predicates, in what they do. See Bloomfield, "A Grammatical Approach to Personification Allegory."

8 Many critics cite the use of personification as a signal that one is in the presence of an allegorical text. See, among others, Barney, *Allegories of History*, Fletcher, *Allegory*, Jung, *Études sur le poème allégorique*, Levin, "Allegorical Language," and Tuve, *Allegorical Imagery*.

9 According to François Rouy personification is quite simply "la représentation, sous la forme d'une personne, humaine en général, d'un être qui, dans la réalité, n'en était pas lui-même une." *L'Esthétique du traité moral d'après les œuvres d'Alain Chartier*, 9.

10 For James Paxson personification occupies a "key, privileged role as a figure always telling something about figuration itself." *The Poetics of Personification*, 21.

11 Similarly, the *Rhetorica ad Herennium* defines personification as "representing an absent person as present, or … making a mute thing or one lacking form articulate, and attributing to it a definite form and a language of certain behavior appropriate to its character." The author of the *Rhetorica ad Herennium* further notes that "personification … is most useful in the divisions under Amplification and in Appeal to Pity." The preceding are cited in Paxson, *The Poetics of Personification*, chapter 1. The classical tradition of civic or otherwise political allegories continues throughout the Middle Ages. See, for instance, Baskins, "Shaping Civic Personification" and Keen, "Sex and the Medieval City."

12 Or between object and viewer. I share with Virginie Minet-Mahy my conviction that the role of the reader is of paramount importance in late medieval allegory. See her *Esthétique et pouvoir de l'œuvre allégorique*.

13 Jung distinguishes between what he calls static allegory, which might be perceived in settings, clothing, accoutrements, and personifications, and dynamic allegory, in which "the *narratio* itself (voyage, battle, siege) contains the *sensus allegoricus*." Allegorical meaning would consequently be produced by action, movement, or change. *Études sur le poème allégorique en France au Moyen Âge*, 20. My translation.

14 Minet-Mahy, *Esthétique et pouvoir de l'œuvre allégorique*, 12, emphasis in original.
15 See Copeland and Melville, "Allegory and Allegoresis."
16 Whitman's term.
17 The word *allēgoria* does not initially appear in such contexts. Instead, we often see the term *hyponoia*, or under-sense, used to distinguish the philosophic meaning from the poetic text.
18 Early Christian writers such as Augustine, Lactantius, and Fulgentius composed allegorical interpretations of Virgil's *Aeneid*, for instance, and such a practice continued throughout the Middle Ages, both in Latin and in the vernacular. See Kaufman, "Virgil's Underworld."
19 From the first century CE the term *allegoria* was used with reference to biblical exegesis. The word *allegoria* appears once in the Bible, in Galatians 4:24, concerning "quae sunt per allegoriam dicta" [things which are expressed by means of an allegory].
20 Mitchell, *Paul, the Corinthians, and the Birth of Christian Hermeneutics.*
21 *On Christian Teaching*, 75.
22 It is important to observe that the "literal sense" of the Bible was equally under construction, changing over the course of the Patristic and medieval periods. I thank Aden Kumler for highlighting this fact. On the richness of literal meaning, see also Minnis, "*Quadruplex Sensus, Multiplex Modus.*"
23 In his *Commentary on the Gospel according to John* Origen observes that an imprudent reader might try to force the literal, in a "way that does violence to the text." *Commentary on the Gospel according to John Books 1–10*, 312.
24 On the importance of the literal and its relationship to the allegorical see also Turner, "Allegory in Christian Late Antiquity."
25 See Cassian, *Conferences*, 160.
26 As Augustine of Dacia tidily summarized in 1260, "Litera gesta docet, quid credas allegoria / Moralis quid agas, quo tendas anagogia" [the literal teaches deeds, the allegorical, what you ought believe, the moral, how you ought behave, the anagogical, whither you are bound]. Cited in de Lubac, *Exégèse médiévale*.
27 Turner, "Allegory in Christian Late Antiquity."
28 Albert Ascoli argues that "the famous paragraph 7 of the *Epistle to Cangrande* claims not, as is usually argued, to describe the 'mode of signifying' of the *Commedia*, but rather to exemplify the meaning of the word 'polysemous.' The *Epistle*'s gloss on *Paradiso* then makes no attempt at all to apply the model of biblical exegesis: rather, it is resolutely, explicitly, literal." See "Dante and Allegory," 135.

29 The literal meaning of the psalm, Dante tell us, refers to the departure of the children of Israel from Egypt in the time of Moses, the allegorical meaning is our redemption in Christ, the moral sense refers to the conversion of the soul from the misery of sin to a state of grace, and the anagogical points to the passing of the sanctified soul from the corruption of this world to everlasting glory. See the introductory essay and extracts from the letter to Can Grande in *Medieval Literary Theory and Criticism*, ed. Minnas and Scott.
30 "generaliter omnes dici possunt allegorici, quum sint a literali sive historiali diversi." Dante Alighieri, *Dantis Alagherii Epistolae*, 174.
31 *Didascalicon*, book 6, chapter 8 and following.
32 See book 3, chapter 8.
33 A lie, its detractors will affirm. See Aquinas, *Metaphysicorum Aristotelis Expositio*, in which Aquinas details the metaphysical errors promulgated by poets, concluding that "poetae non solum in hoc, sed in multis aliis mentiuntur" [poets not only in this, but in many others things lie], 1, 3, 61–2.
34 *The Song of Songs: Commentary and Homilies*, book 3, 218.
35 "[T]he thing," Hugh tells us, "is a resemblance of the divine Idea," thereby allowing God's divine wisdom, which is invisible, to be recognized through his creatures and in them. *Didascalicon*, 122.
36 "The Rhetoric of Temporality," 207.
37 See Boyarin, "Origen as Theorist of Allegory."
38 On modern and post-modern understandings of allegory, see also Copeland and Struck's introductory essay in the *Cambridge Companion to Allegory*.
39 See Owens, "The Allegorical Impulse," part 1, 68. Owens writes with modern visual-art practices in mind, but we see a similar impulse at work in the Christianizing rewritings of classical texts. Paul de Man affirms, in contrast, that allegory renounces nostalgia and the desire to coincide.
40 As David Nirenberg has observed, these two modes of recuperation differ fundamentally, however, in that Auerbach's typology respects and preserves the prefigural moment, while Owens's (and others') allegorical impulse erases, supplements, or supplants, the original. (Oral communication, symposium, "Allegory, Allegoresis, and the Allegorical before Modernity," 10 March 2012.)
41 For Auerbach, allegory can represent a virtue, a passion, or an institution, but "never a definite event in its full historicity." "Figura," 54.
42 Ibid., 53.
43 Ibid., 72.
44 Whitman, *Allegory*, 265.
45 In their analysis of allegory and allegoresis, or what one might call compositional and interpretive allegory, Rita Copeland and Steven Melville

depict a struggle for anteriority. Allegoresis, Copeland and Melville explain, substitutes itself for the text, offering itself as the true and overt meaning which the literal level of the text has provided, but in veiled terms. In this manner, the author of the allegoresis "inserts himself into the very *dispositio* of the text, not changing its order, but pronouncing that order to be the result of his own correct, revelatory reading." Copeland and Melville, "Allegory and Allegoresis," 172.

46 *Commentary on the Song of Songs*, 201.

47 Boyarin, "Origen as Theorist of Allegory," 51. For medieval exegetes, careful reading of Scripture has the capacity to elevate the soul and enable the spiritually striving reader to move from word to concept to thing to its idea to Truth. See the *Didascalicon*, book 5, chapter 3. Friedrich Ohly explains that for the Victorines Scripture possessed a twofold meaning; a first one that moves from the *vox* to the *res*, the sound of the word to the thing, and a higher one, that moves from the thing (*res*) to something higher. See Ohly, "On the Spiritual Sense of the Word in the Middle Ages," 4–5.

48 Ohly at 29, emphasis added.

49 Owens, "The Allegorical Impulse," part 2, 64. Owens concludes that "the allegorical impulse that characterizes postmodernism is a direct consequence of its preoccupation with reading" (64). One might quibble with Owens's assertion that a preoccupation with reading is somehow a postmodern condition, but his larger point about the importance of reading to the production of allegorical meaning is well taken.

50 I paraphrase W.B. Yeats's poem "Among School Children." Paul de Man used this poem to explore the functioning of allegory in *Allegories of Reading*, chapter 1, "Semiology and Rhetoric."

51 As Owens writes, "Still, the allegorical supplement is not only an addition, but also a replacement. It takes the place of an earlier meaning, which is thereby either effaced or obscured. Because allegory usurps its object it comports within itself a danger, the possibility of perversion: that what is 'merely appended' to the work of art may be mistaken for its 'essence.'" See "The Allegorical Impulse," part 1, 84.

52 See Copeland and Melville's discussion of the ways in which allegoresis competes with the original text.

53 See Adams, *The Life and Afterlife of Isabeau of Bavaria*, especially chapter 3, "Isabeau Mediatrix: Defining the Mediator Queen."

54 This is the term preferred by Fradenburg, who observes that the term "liminal" may "inhibit consideration of alliance-formation as a queenly practice" and consequently terms like 'interstitiality' or 'in-betweenness' are sometimes used in order to suggest that the condition of many forms of

queenship may be found not so much in the glamorized, special, suspended states associated with *communitas* as in the fact of queens' being so often at the nodal points of cultural work, of their working to enable the crossing-over of difference into identity, the unfamiliar into the familiar." See her "Introduction: Rethinking Queenship," 5.

55 A notable exception is studied by Theresa Earenfight in *The King's Other Body*. Earenfight examines the office of the lieutenant general and the queens that occupied it. As she suggests, greater attention to "the relational and dialectical character of kingship and queenship" (13) would yield a more complex, and probably more capacious, vision of queenly power.

56 Carmi Parsons, "The Queen's Intercession in Thirteenth-Century England." See also Strohm, *Hochon's Arrow: the social imagination of fourteenth-century texts*.

57 Stafford, *Queen Emma and Queen Edith. Queenship and Women's Power in Eleventh-Century England*, 150.

58 Earenfight, *The King's Other Body*, 13.

59 See Rachel Gibbons's seminal article, "Isabeau of Bavaria, Queen of France (1385-1422): The Creation of an Historical Villainess" as well as Adams, *The Life and Afterlife of Isabeau of Bavaria*.

60 For a chronology of the ordinances and an interpretation of their import, see Guenée, *Un meurtre, une société*, as well as the works by Gibbons and Adams cited above.

61 See Miriam Shadis's insightful "Blanche of Castile and Facinger's 'Medieval Queenship' Reassessing the Argument." On female regency in a slightly later period of French history see Crawford, *Perilous Performances. Gender and Regency in Early Modern France*.

62 See also my article "*Advocate et moyenne*: Christine de Pizan's Elaboration of Female Authority."

63 *Le Livre des trois vertus*, 31.

64 Ibid., 32.

65 Ibid.

66 As Parsons notes, the intermediary "helps to secure that 'difficult alchemy' of consent that bound his subjects to him [i.e., the king]." "The Queen's Intercession in Thirteenth-Century England," 160.

67 On kings' daughters in historical terms see Allirot, *Filles de roy de France*.

68 See "... That Dangerous Supplement ..." in *Of Grammatology*, 145.

69 Not so in the case of the University, which is defined precisely in relation to the king.

70 See Seiferth, *Synagogue and Church in the Middle Ages*.

71 See examples in *Synagogue and Church*.

72 See, for instance, M. Warner, *Alone of All Her Sex.*
73 Toubert, "Les représentations de l'Ecclesia dans l'art des Xe–XIIe siècles."
74 See Blumenfeld-Kosinski, "Dramatic Troubles of Ecclesia."
75 See Blumenfeld-Kosinski, *Poets, Saints, and Visionaries of the Great Schism.*
76 Origen, *The Song of Songs Commentary and Homilies*, 188.
77 On the later development and use of this fable see Harf-Lancner, "*Les membres et l'estomac.*"
78 Today scholars generally agree that the letter is a fabrication of John's, attributed to Plutarch. See Nederman, "Introduction," *Policraticus.*
79 Bernstein, *Pierre d'Ailly and the Blanchard Affair*, 9. On the history of the University of Paris see Rashdall, *The Universities of Europe in the Middle Ages.*
80 Post, "Parisian Masters as a Corporation, 1200–1246."
81 Ibid. Hastings Rashdall identifies four rights or powers as constituting the existence of a corporation: by-laws, the right to sue and be sued as a corporation, the appointment of common officers, and the use of a common seal. See his *Universities of Europe in the Middle Ages.* See also McKeon, "The Status of the University of Paris as *Parens Scientiarum*: An Episode in the Development of its Autonomy," Lusignan, "*Vérité garde le roy*" *La Construction d'une identité universitaire en France (XIIIe-XVe siècle)*, and Verger, *Les Universités au Moyen Âge.*
82 According to the *Chartularium Universitatis Parisiensis* the University is first referred to as the daughter of the king in 1354. See Riché and Verger, *Des nains sur des épaules de géants.*
83 *Poetics*, chapters 9.3 and 9.4.
84 *The Etymologies of Isidore of Seville.* Bede is discussed in Paxson, *The Poetics of Personification*, 21. Augustine's definition of metaphor in *De doctrina christiana* is actually quite different. He says that signs are metaphorical "when the actual things which we signify by the particular words are used to signify something else: when, for example, we say *bovem* and not only interpret these two syllables to mean the animal normally referred to by that name but also understand, *by that animal*, 'worker in the gospel,'" 37, emphasis added. See Todorov's discussion of Augustinian semiotics in "On Linguistic Symbolism."
85 See Black's discussion of the shortcomings of what he refers to as the substitution and comparison views of metaphor. *Models and Metaphors*, 134–44.
86 Ricœur, "The Metaphorical Process as Cognition, Imagination, and Feeling," 152.
87 Black, *Models and Metaphors*, 40 and Beardsley, *Aesthetics.*

88 Or, it may simply be dismissed as an example of bad metaphor.

89 Gabrielle Spiegel's term. See her "Genealogy." Black also uses the metaphors of filter or screen to explain how metaphors organize thought.

90 See Lakoff and Johnson, *Metaphors We Live By*.

91 *The Etymologies of Isidore of Seville*, trans. Stephen Barney. "Metaphora est verbi alicuius usurpata translatio, sicut cum dicimus … [exampla] in quibus haec verba aliunde transferuntur. Sed hac atque aliae tropicae locutiones ad ea, quae intellegenda sunt, propterea figuratis amictibus obteguntur, ut sensus legentis exerceant, et ne nuda atque in promptu vilescant." *Etimologie o Origini di Isidoro di Siviglia*, 1: 150. It is interesting to note that Barney, in his translation, adds the word "veiled," thereby moving metaphor towards allegory.

92 On the capacity of late medieval allegorical texts to engage with contemporary reality see also Minet-Mahy, *Esthétique et pouvoir de l'œuvre allégorique*.

93 *The Psychomachia of Prudentius*. Prudentius lingers over the vice's "counterfeited character" and "lying," showing how she "conceals her snaky locks with the soft covering of piety … and keeping secret her dreadful fury," 28.

94 See, among others, Akbari, *Seeing through the Veil*, Fleming, *The Roman de la Rose* and *Reason and the Lover*, Gunn, *The Mirror of Love*, Guynn, *Allegory and Sexual Ethics in the High Middle Ages*, Roazen, *Fortune's Faces*, Minnis, *Magister Amoris*, and Poirion, *Le Roman de la rose*.

95 See, for instance, Jauss, "La transformation de la forme allégorique."

96 Origen explains that when attempting to understand the non-literal meaning of Scripture, readers need to know the properties and nature of, for instance, the amoyr tree "so that we may suitably adjust the spiritual explanation to the natural." *The Song of Songs*, 196. See also Augustine's *De doctrina christiana*, 43–7, and book 6 of Hugh of St Victor's *Didascalicon*, in which he emphasizes the importance and utility of broad knowledge of both texts and the world.

97 Suzanne Akbari argues that for Isidore and his readers, "the actual derivation of the word's source was relatively unimportant; instead, the purpose of etymology was both to demonstrate a link between the word's form and its meaning and to serve as an aid to memory." *Seeing through the Veil*, 61.

98 In his translation Charles Dahlberg renders "coilles" by the more neutral and anodyne term "testicles," thereby stripping Reason's discourse of much of its piquancy.

99 See Minnis's rich discussion of the speech of Reason in *Magister Amoris*, chapters 2 and 3.

100 Minnis argues that at the time Jean de Meun was writing, the conventional nature of language was commonly accepted. See his *Magister Amoris*, in particular chapter 3, "Parler proprement."

101 Dante is also writing in the context of an on-going debate about the value and potential of poetry. See Curtius, *European Literature and the Latin Middle Ages*, chapter 12, "Poetry and Theology," as well as "The Transformation of Critical Tradition: Dante, Petrarch, and Boccaccio" in *Medieval Literary Theory and Criticism.*

102 See Hollander, "Dante *Theologus-Poeta.*" Ronald Martinez has pointed out that Hollander's interpretation has not gone uncontested, arguing that what Dante's works in fact reveal is the poet's understanding of "the difficulty the reader faces in distinguishing what is allegorical from what is untrue." See his "Allegory," 34. Similarly, Albert Ascoli has argued that Dante does not make this claim in direct terms, and indeed focuses extensively on the literal meaning of his texts. See his "Dante and Allegory."

103 On Christine's relationship to Dante see Brownlee, "Literary Genealogy and the Problem of the Father," Huot, "Seduction and Sublimation," and Richards, "Christine de Pizan and Dante."

104 On the so-called quarrel of the *Rose* see, Christine de Pizan, Jean Gerson, Jean de Montreuil, and Gontier and Pierre Col, *Le débat sur le Roman de la rose.*

105 See Blumenfeld-Kosinski, "Jean Gerson and the Debate on the *Romance of the Rose.*"

106 See the introduction to this volume for a historical overview.

107 In their introductory essay to the *Convivio*, Wallace, Minnis, and Scott write that "the whole of Dante's career as poet and literary theorist is, then, inclusive of a process of 'auto-exegesis.'" *Medieval Literary Theory and Criticism*, 443. I do not believe, as they seem to suggest, that this phenomenon is limited to Dante.

108 Philippe de Mézières, *Le songe du vieil pelerin*, 270. Since my focus is on allegorical representations of kingdom and University, I do not examine Philippe's works in any detail in this volume. However, he is an important practitioner of allegorical literature in the late fourteenth century.

109 Armand Strubel argues that the two allegorical representations of the author correspond to a historical and an allegorical mode, respectively. See "*Le songe du viel pelerin.*"

110 On the preface see Reno, "The Preface to the *Avision-Christine.*" Note that only one extant manuscript of the text contains the prologue, ex-Phillipps 128.

111 I shall explore in the next chapter the ways in which Christine both adopts and adapts Dante's suggestion that his poetry requires the allegorical interpretive methods of Scripture.

112 Dante Alighieri, *Il convivio*, 30. Translation from Wallace, *Medieval Literary Theory and Criticism*, 395.

113 My thanks to Martin Schwarz for calling this contrast to my attention.

114 Reno interprets these phrases not so much as directives but as a series of suggestions. See "The Preface."

115 Black discusses the ways in which authors can prepare their readers for certain associations or connotations, thereby shaping the interpretation of their metaphors. See *Models and Metaphors*, 41–6.

116 Jauss cites the advent of a subjective first-person presence in allegorical texts as one of the innovations of thirteenth-century allegory. See "La transformation de la forme allégorique." For Strubel, the advent of a subjective first-person narrative presence signals the dislocation of allegory that he situates in the work of, for example, Philippe de Mézières. See "*Le songe du viel pelerin.*"

117 On late medieval first-person allegorical narratives see also Kamath, *Authorship and First-Person Allegory in Late Medieval France and England.*

118 See Piehler, *The Visionary Landscape.* The allegorical dream vision was already a well-established form, but not one with an auto-exegetical focus.

119 Mitchell, *Paul, the Corinthians, and the Birth of Christian Hermeneutics*, chapter 5.

120 In the early ninth century ambassadors from the Byzantine emperor, aware that the French believed their patron Saint Denis, the beheaded martyr, to be the same individual as the Athenian Areopagite and author, brought Louis the Pious a Greek manuscript of the Dionysian corpus. This treasure was placed in the Abbey of Saint Denis in the care of Hilduin, who had the manuscript translated. John Scot Eriugena, not long after, carried out another translation of the Dionysian corpus. In the twelfth century Hugh of St Victor wrote a commentary on Dionysius's *The Celestial Hierarchy*, renewing intellectual interest in the Areopagite's work. See Rorem, "The Early Latin Dionysius." Turner affirms that the works of Pseudo-Dionysius were like the air breathed by late medieval theologians. See "Dionysius and Some Late Medieval Mystical Theologians."

121 Rorem, "The Early Latin Dionysius," 603. In Eriugena history is understood "as procession from God (creation) and return to God (salvation)."

122 Strubel has argued that in the late Middle Ages allegorical narrative, having explored the worlds of morality and psychology, takes on history, and in so doing, "la forme allégorique se disloque." See "*Le songe du viel pelerin*," 70.

2. From *douce France* to the *dame renommée*

1 *Les grandes chroniques de France*, 1: 4. Guenée has explained that this was not the work's original title, though it has become the generally accepted one. See "Les grandes chroniques de France."

2 Many writers, such as the anonymous authors of the *Antequam essent clerici* and the *Avis aus roys*, Giles of Rome, and Nicole Oresme, employed organological metaphors to conceptualize the kingdom of France.

3 See Paxson, *The Poetics of Personification*.

4 See, respectively, Pick, "Gender in the Early Spanish Chronicles," 232, Post, "'Blessed Lady Spain,'" and Bäuml, *Medieval Civilization in Germany*. Plate 26 from the Aachen Otto Codex shows the nations of the empire, Sclavinia, Germania, Gallia, and Roma, all represented as female figures paying tribute to the emperor. See also Brühl, *Naissance de deux peuples*, plates 5, 6, and 8 for other representations of Francia.

5 See Brose, "Petrarch's Beloved Body."

6 On the Trojan origins of the French see Wood, "Defining the Franks."

7 This is a key foundational moment for France, and is one of the earliest episodes recounted in the *Grandes chroniques*. See Beaune, *Naissance de la nation France*.

8 See laisse 176. "Li quens Rollant se jut desuz un pin; / Envers Espaigne en ad turnet sun vis. / De plusurs choses a remembrer li prist, / De tantes teres cum li bers cunquist, / De dulce France, des humes de sun lign, / De Carlemagne, sun seignor, kil nurrit; / Ne poet muer n'en plurt e ne suspirt" [The count Roland lay beneath a pine. Towards Spain he turned his face. He began to remember many things: the many lands that, like a brave man, he conquered, sweet France, the men of his lineage, Charlemagne, his lord, who nurtured him. He cannot keep from crying and sighing.] (vv. 2375–81). The adjective *dulce* is repeatedly used in the *Song of Roland* to qualify France, for instance, in laisses 8, 83, and 84. Similarly, in the *Carolinus* of Gilles de Paris, the author addresses "tu Francia pollens, tu bona, tu dulcus" [O mighty France, you good, you sweet]. Cited in Duchet-Suchaux, "Émergence d'un sentiment national chez Eustache Deschamps," 77.

9 "Et dit Guillelmes: 'Ce vos sai ge bien dire: / En douce France l'ai ge auques conquise'" [And Guillaume said, This I can well tell you: In sweet France I conquered it] (vv. 1189–90). *Le charroi de Nîmes*.

10 Libera's story operates on the paradigm of Erich Auerbach's *figura*, or like biblical allegory or typology.

11 Here, Dante's mode of allegorical writing is a key model that Christine both invokes and transforms.

12 Deschamps studied law at Orléans, but did not earn a degree. He first entered the service of the counts of Vertus, and later became the bailiff of the Valois in the service of Philippe d'Orléans and his wife. Between 1375 and 1378 Deschamps became royal sergeant-at-arms (huissier d'armes), a post which he appears to have retained until his death. After 1392 Deschamps served Louis d'Orléans as an adviser and maître d'hôtel, and later as maître des eaux et forêts in Champagne and in Brie. He attained the most important position of his career, that of bailiff of Senlis, in 1389, and held this post until shortly before his death. For Deschamps's biography see Laurie, "Eustache Deschamps" and the introduction to *Eustache Deschamps et son temps*.

13 This manuscript, BnF fr. 840, was edited in the nineteenth century by the marquis de Queux de Saint-Hilaire and Gaston Raynaud. See their *Œuvres complètes d'Eustache Deschamps*. All citations from Deschamps come from this edition. Modern editions of selections of Deschamps's works include *Eustache Deschamps: Selected poems*, *L'art de dictier*, and *Eustache Deschamps en son temps*. Deschamps's lack of interest in establishing and preserving his works as a unified corpus stands in stark contrast to the practices of his predecessor and mentor, Guillaume de Machaut, and his successor, Christine de Pizan, both of whom were very closely involved with the assembling, ordering, copying, and illumination of their literary works.

14 Philippe de Mézières, *Le songe du vieil pelerin*, 2: 223.

15 On Deschamps's relationships with some of his contemporaries see Lacassagne, "L'échange épistolaire de Christine de Pizan et Eustache Deschamps" and Richards, "The Lady Wants to Talk."

16 See the historical overview of this period provided in the introduction.

17 The Schism began in 1378 when Clement VII and Urban VI were both elected to the Holy See, and was not resolved in Deschamps's lifetime. On the history of the Schism see Favier, ed., *Genèse et débuts du Grand Schisme d'Occident* and on literary representations of the Schism see Blumenfeld-Kosinski, *Poets, Saints, and Visionaries of the Great Schism*.

18 Lassabatère has produced an excellent monograph on Deschamps, *La cité des hommes*. Of particular interest with respect to metaphorical and allegorical representations of the kingdom is chapter 4, "Approche rhétorique du concept de nation." While Lassabatère's analysis and my own have points of convergence, Lassabatère does not focus on the figure of allegory as such, nor does he evince especial interest in the relationship of gender to rhetoric.

19 Absent from the very important works of Laccassagne, Lassabatère, and Dulac is a sustained reflection on how considerations of gender shape Deschamps's use of metaphor and allegory in his representations of the kingdom of France. See Dulac, "La représentation de la France chez Eustache

Deschamps et Christine de Pizan," Laccassagne, "Poétique et politique du corps dans l'œuvre d'Eustache Deschamps,' Lassabatère, "Sentiment national et messianisme politique en France pendant la guerre de cent ans" and "La personnification de la France dans la littérature de la fin du Moyen Âge."

20 See Bliggenstorfer, "Les ballades dialoguées d'Eustache Deschamps." On Deschamps's staging of female voices see Sinnreich-Levi, "The Feminist Voice of the Misogynist Poet" and "The Female Voice of the Male Poet."

21 The *envoi* is a shortened stanza that concludes the poem and that consists of a dedication – usually to a lady or a patron – or a farewell. See Bliggenstorfer, "Les ballades dialoguées d'Eustache Deschamps."

22 On the relationship of the micro- to the macrocosm see Camille, "The Image and the Self" and Fritz, "Figures et métaphores du corps dans le discours de l'histoire."

23 On Deschamps's attitude towards social mobility see Dudash, "Eustache Deschamps: Poète et commentateur politique." On the political dangers of hybridity see Mühlethaler, "Entre amour et politique."

24 See vv. 34–8. Certain fashions were seen as particularly representative of moral degradation: the shoes with extremely long and upward curling toes, and the men's tunics that were so short and fitted that they allowed the outlines of the buttucks to be visible. Philippe de Mézières expresses similar concerns in the *Songe du vieil pelerin*, 2: 209 and 211. Carnes notes that after 1340 men's tunics, which had been long and similar to those of women, grew shorter. See her "Cutting a Fine Figure." Newton further remarks that during the reign of Charles V men's tunics had become extremely short and form-fitting. See *Fashion in the Age of the Black Prince*. See also M. Scott, *Medieval Dress and Fashion*, which includes many full colour plates.

25 Minet-Mahy, "Eustache Deschamps," 231.

26 Camille has described how medieval manuscripts of physiology sometimes depicted the soul as a little humunculus entering or leaving the body at the moment of birth or death. "This also alerts us to the power of the mouth in medieval culture as a dangerous liminal zone, a hole in the crucial barrier between inside and outside." See "The Image and the Self," 70.

27 On the political connotations of gluttony see Laccassagne, "Poétique et politique du corps."

28 Deschamps's contemporary Nicole Oresme likewise affirms that it is "chose denaturele ou hors nature que un homme soit roy d'un royalme et qu'il soit de estrange païs et principalment d'autre gent, d'autre nation et d'autre lignage" [unnatural, or outside of nature, that a man be king of a kingdom and that he be of a foreign land and principally of other people, of another nation and another lineage]. *Commentaire de Nicole Oresme sur le livre de Politiques*

d'Aristote, 72. Lassabatère reads the "estranges" as the Marmousets, and the rightful limbs as the princes of the blood. See *La cité des hommes*, 243–8.

29 The metaphor of the body politic was extremely flexible, and lent itself to a variety of uses. One could focus on the relationship between body and soul, between head and heart, between head or heart and members, or one could focus on physiological systems – muscular, skeletal, or nervous. In this way authors were able to examine an array of sociopolitical configurations and relationships. See Nederman, "Body Politics."

30 Blamires problematizes the head-body hierarchy in "Paradox in the Medieval Gender Doctrine of Head and Body."

31 See "*Les membres et l'estomac.*"

32 Nederman's work supports the idea that the metaphor of the body can be used to convey concern for communal, rather than hierarchical, values. See "The Living Body Politic." Lassabatère identifies a hierarchical organization, and a centre-periphery model, in Deschamps's organological metaphors. See *La cité des hommes*, 248–52.

33 See Briggs, *Giles of Rome's "De regimine principum."* Perret observes that while for Giles of Rome, author of the famously influential *De regimine principum*, the family is the basic unit of human society, he adds another element that is absent in both Aristotle and Aquinas: the village and castle as intermediary units that constitute the kingdom which, for Giles, is the ultimate expression of the natural evolution of human community. See *Les traductions françaises du De regimine principum de Gilles de Rome*, chapter 7.

34 See Oresme's translation/adaptation of Aristotle, the *Livre de Politiques*, 70.

35 See "Head or Heart?"

36 As Origen writes, even though we ought to love all of our neighbours "not as alien bodies, but as our own limbs," nevertheless, "there are in the body some members that are more honourable and comely, and others that are more uncomely and more feeble." *The Song of Songs Commentary and Homilies*, 188–9.

37 Indeed, Giles of Rome affirms that in the event that an heir is not himself capable of good rule, his wise counsellors will supplement his abilities. See *Li Livres du Gouvernement des rois*, 309.

38 "De toutes pars est mon chief assailli, / Qui cause estoit a mon corps de sa vie; / A mes bras sont vaines et nerfs failli, / Les mains, les doiz gardans ma seignourie; / Fievre m'assault et mes cuers se varie" [From all sides my head – which is the reason that my body has life – is assailed. The nerves and veins of my arms have failed, my hands, my fingers, guarding my lordship. Fever assaults me, and my heart beats irregularly] (vv. 1–5). The litany of woe continues in the second half of the stanza.

39 On visual and textual representations of the Church during the Schism see Blumenfeld-Kosinski, "Dramatic Troubles of Ecclesia."
40 See Martinez, "Dante between Hope and Despair."
41 Whitman, *Allegory*.
42 On the semantic potential of the literal sense, see Minnis, "*Quadruplex Sensus, Multiplex Modus*."
43 See the examples in Godefroy, *Dictionnaire de l'ancienne langue française*.
44 The rubric "Acte de contrition de Paris" was added by Deschamps's nineteenth-century editors, and is not found in the manuscript.
45 It is not until verse 15, with the phrase "serve sui" [I am a slave], that the first-person voice is identified as a female one.
46 Struck affirms that for Plotinus "allegorical reading itself might offer a kind of pathway for this ascent, and that hermeneutic activity might lift one up through ontological layers, anagogically, toward the One." See "Allegory and Ascent in Neoplatonism," 59. See also Hugh of St Victor, *Didascalicon*.
47 A third poem, Ballade 942, in which the city of Babylon confesses her sin of pride, might fruitfully be considered in conjunction with the two Paris prosopopeia ballades, but space does not allow us to do so here. Strohm has discussed the ways in which queenly intercessors made possible courses of conduct that were politically desirable, but difficult to achieve without a loss of face. See *Hochon's Arrow*, especially chapter 5, "Queens as Intercessors."
48 *Le livre des trois vertus*, 35. On mediating figures in Christine de Pizan see my articles "*Advocate et moyenne*" and "En quoi la ville est-elle un espace féminin/féministe?"
49 See, for instance, Ballades 112, 141, 159, 164, 255, 263, 388, 1142, 1317, and 1430, and Chanson royal 387.
50 In addition to the poems discussed below, see also Ballades 263, 1430, and 1463 and the *Lay de plour*, for poems which feature a speaking voice that may be understood to represent the kingdom. Ballade 1426, the plaint of the world, is also interesting in this framework. Space does not permit me to analyse these poems in detail.
51 See v. 2. The nine worthies were conventionally grouped as follows: three classical heroes, often including Alexander, Caesar, and Hector; three biblical figures, often Judas Maccabeus, David, and Joshua; and three "contemporary" figures, which were more variable but usually included Charlemagne.
52 According to many medieval histories of France the name "franc" was given to the ancestors of the French because they were free, or *franc*, of the obligation of tribute to the Romans. See Wood, "Defining the Franks." See also Lassabatère, *La cité des hommes*, 270–2.
53 See Kantorowicz, *The King's Two Bodies*.

54 On Mary as the centre of the holy family see Newman, "Intimate Pieties." On the rise of the cult of Mary see Warner, *Alone of All Her Sex*.

55 On political dream works in the late Middle Ages see Badel, *Le Roman de la rose au XIVe siècle*, especially 379–409, Kruger, *Dreaming in the Middle Ages*, Lynch, *The High Medieval Dream Vision*, Marchello-Nizia, "Entre l'histoire et la poétique," and Quillet, "Songes et songeries dans l'art politique au XIVe siècle."

56 For instance, in the opening lines of the *Roman de la Rose*, one of the Middle Ages' most important and influential allegorical, dream-vision narratives.

57 Macrobius, *Commentary on the Dream of Scipio*, 90.

58 Struck, "Allegory and Ascent in Neoplatonism," 64.

59 Kruger discusses the varying significance accorded to external causes of dreams in the writings of different medieval theorists of dreams and visions.

60 See Köhler, *L'aventure chevaleresque*.

61 See Marchello-Nizia, "Entre l'histoire et la poétique," 51.

62 On the prophetic vision see also Jauss, "La transformation de la forme allégorique," especially 123–5.

63 The verb "figurer" suggests both the representation of France and the transformation of the kingdom into an allegorical figure.

64 The narrator says of the figure in Chanson royale 387, "sa biauté descripre ne pourroye / Ne sa grandeur" [I could not describe his beauty, nor his size] (vv. 13–14), while the figure in Chanson royale 388 "corps avoit bel et grant" [had a large and fair body] (v. 8).

65 On Deschamps's critique of the failings of the French as a whole, see Bonnafoux, *L'animal miroir de l'homme dans la "Fiction du lyon" d'Eustache Deschamps*. See also Bliggenstorfer's analysis of these two chansons in *Eustache Deschamps*, 151–62.

66 On this fusion of metaphor and personification see also Lassabatère, "La personnification de la France" as well as his monograph *La cité des hommes*.

67 "Ce fu un corps, comme de creature" [It was a body, as of a creature] (Chanson royale 387, v. 5); "une creature / qui corps avoit bel et grant" [a creature which had a large and fair body] (Chanson royale 388, vv. 7–8). Also in Chanson royale 388 Nature notes, "Je t'ay bien fait et fourmé chascun membre, / Piez, jambes, mains, ventre, cuisses et pis, / Bras et genouls, col et chief" [I made you well and formed each member: feet, legs, hands, stomach, thighs and chest, arms and knees, neck and head] (vv. 12–14).

68 In Chanson royale 387 several masculine pronouns have for referent "le corps," thereby leaving the sex of the body in doubt. Elsewhere we see masculine pronouns and adjectives such as "il brait et crie" [he brays and cries] (v. 19) and "te fault estre vaillant et brief. / Et il respont" [you must be

courageous, and promptly so. And he replied] (vv. 49–50). In Chanson royale 388 the figure in question is "desconfis" [discouraged] (v. 21) "grans et gros" [tall and large] (v. 22), "de gens et de terre garnis" [well endowed with people and land] (v. 31), and "esbahis" [stunned] (41), to cite but a selection.

69 The standard reference work on Christine de Pizan remains Willard, *Christine de Pizan: Her Life and Works*. The bibliography on Christine is vast. Of great value are the bibliographical guides produced by Angus Kennedy: *Christine de Pizan. A Bibliographical Guide*, *Christine de Pizan. A Bibliographical Guide. Supplement 1*, and *Christine de Pizan. A Bibliographical Guide. Supplement 2*.

70 See Christine de Pisan, Jean Gerson, Jean de Montreuil, and Gontier and Pierre Col. *Le débat sur Le Roman de la Rose*.

71 See Brownlee, "Discourses of the Self."

72 All references are to Christine de Pizan, *Le livre de l'advision Cristine*, ed. Reno and Dulac. Translations are my own.

73 See my discussion of auto-exegesis in chapter 1.

74 This is the base manuscript of Reno and Dulac's edition. The other manuscripts are Paris, BnF fr. 1176 and Brussels, B.R. 10309. On the preface see Reno, "The Preface to the *Avision-Christine* in ex-Phillipps 128."

75 Walters discusses a very similar passage from the *Livre des fais et bonnes meurs du sage roy Charles V*, composed shortly before the *Advision*. There too Christine defines poetry in terms of multiplicity of meaning. As Walters observes, "rather than restricting the sense of poetry to works in verse, Christine adopts a broader definition, making the term 'poetry' equivalent to 'allegorical fiction,' whether that fiction is rendered in prose or in verse." See her "Gerson and Christine, Poets," 73.

76 *The Etymologies of Isidore of Seville*.

77 *Knowing Poetry*, 9.

78 See my discussion of the *Convivio* in chapter 1.

79 *The Divine Comedy of Dante Alighieri*, ed. and trans. Durling.

80 See Strubel, *La Rose, Renart, et le Graal*, especially chapter 1, "La lettre et le sens."

81 Augustine, *The Literal Meaning of Genesis*, 2: 196. As Minnis has pointed out, Augustine's *Literal Commentary on Genesis* later became one of the standard sets of prologues in the "Paris Bible." "Because of its privileged position in the 'Paris Bible,' this version of the *triplex genus visionum* received the attention of successive generations of exegetes." See his "Langland's Ymaginatif," 93.

82 The name Libera recalls the fiscal freedom or *franchise* of the French, which Christine had used to explain the etymology of France at the start of the

Livre des fais et bonnes meurs du sage roy Charles V, while the second Athens alludes to the principle of *translatio studii*, according to which learning and culture spread from Greece, to Rome, to Paris.

83 On the parallels between the narrator and Libera see, among others, Blumenfeld-Kosinski, "'Enemies within/enemies without," D'Arcens, "Petit estat vesval," Dulac, "À propos des représentations du corps souffrant," Dulac and Reno, "The *Livre de l'advision Cristine*," and Walters, "Christine's Symbolic Self."

84 Libera recognizes the narrator's affection, as well as her intellect and dedication to study. See page 16 of the *Advision*. Birk and Walters both observe that the term *antigraphe* connects the narrator to the figure of Sapience. See, respectively, *Christine de Pizan and Biblical Wisdom*, 96–7 and "The Royal Vernacular," 154.

85 See Kruger's discussion of dream hierarchies.

86 What seems certain, in any case, is that she knew her older contemporary's poems. Christine wrote an epistolary poem to Deschamps, the "Epistre a Eustace Morel," and he responded with Ballade 1242 to the "muse eloquent."

87 Considerations of maternity in Christine's works largely relate to literal motherhood. See Arden, "Her Mother's Daughter," Dziedzic, "À la recherche d'une figure maternelle," Ribémont, "Christine de Pizan et la figure de la mère," and Tarnowski, "Maternity and Paternity."

88 On Christine's use of gardens see Dulac, "De l'arbre au jardin."

89 See the historical overview provided in the introduction.

90 The exceptional nature of Libera's sorrow associates the kingdom, as in Deschamps, with the Jerusalem of Lamentations, especially 1:12.

91 See chapter 1.

92 See Blamires, *The Case for Women in Medieval Culture*.

93 Kantorowicz, "*Pro patria mori* in Medieval Political Thought." See also Contamine, "Mourir pour la patrie."

94 On representations of the suffering female body in Christine's works see Blumenfeld-Kosinski, "'Enemies within/enemies without'" and Dulac, "À propos des représentations du corps souffrant."

95 In this respect the *Advision* is unlike Alain Chartier's *Quadrilogue invectif*, discussed in chapter 4, which consists of a conversation between France and her three children.

96 Camille, "The King's New Bodies," 2: 397.

97 In chapter 3 we shall see that a similar three-part system is at work throughout the sermons of Jean Gerson.

98 On the allegory of the poets and of the theologians see Badel, *Le Roman de la rose au XIVe siècle*, chapter 1, Freccero, "Allegory and autobiography," Jung,

Études sur le poème allégorique, especially 9–17, Martinez, "Allegory," and Strubel, "Allégorie médiévale."

99 See chapter 1.

100 "qui tant estoit hault, grant et eslevé que jusques au ciel attaingnoit; si branchu estoit que ses branches s'estendoient de tous lez du monde" [which was so tall, great, and lofty that it reached the heavens; its branches were so full that they extended over all the parts of the world] (32). This tree reminds the reader of the golden tree which the ancient gods, according to the poets, had reserved for their use and from whose transplanted offshoots, as Libera had explained in chapter 6, sprang the kings of France. See 1: 6, lines 19ff.

101 See for instance part 1, chapter 20, line 10 and chapter 21, lines 31–2, chapter 22, and chapter 26, lines 17–30.

102 On Libera's prophetic visions see also Brown-Grant, "*L'Avision Christine*" and Laennec, "Prophétie, interprétation et écriture dans *L'Avision-Christine*."

103 On Dante as a source for the *Advision* see Reno and Dulac, "Introduction," xxvii–xxviii, Richards, "Christine de Pizan and Dante," and Huot "Seduction and Sublimation."

104 Singleton, "The Irreducible Dove." Hollander affirms, similarly, that Dante's "poem is divinely inspired and theologically true." See "Dante *Theologus-Poeta*," 117.

105 On the other side of this question, see Martinez, "Allegory," Ascoli, "Dante and Allegory," and Freccero, "Allegory and Autobiography."

106 Auerbach, "Figura," 53.

107 On this point I disagree with Reix who, though she acknowledges the sophistication of Christine's use of allegory, concludes nevertheless that "il serait sûrement abusif de voir en Christine de Pizan un *poeta theologus* comme le fut Dante." See "Christine de Pizan et l'écriture de l'allégorisation," 66.

108 See Kelly, *Christine de Pizan's Changing Opinion*.

109 See Reno and Dulac, notes, pp. 165–70.

110 Dame Opinion discusses the reception of Christine's works in 2: 22, including the observation that "les aucuns dient que clercs ou religieux les te forgent et que de sentement de femme venir ne puissent" [some say that clerics or monks forge them for you, and that they cannot come from the sensibility of a woman] (88). Christine's Latinity has likewise been placed in doubt in modern times. For an intervention into this debate see Dulac and Reno, "L'humanisme vers 1400."

111 The whole passage reads "comme la matiere soit obscure, de ce atant souffise. Et ainsi comme en une riche marcerie ou tresor sont avec perles

diverses pierres precieuses de plusieurs vertus, couleurs et pris, lesquelles au goust et plaisirs de divers bargigneurs sont requises, soient ycestes choses ou tresor de ton volume reservees aux hommes scienceux de soubtil entendement, et passent oultre les moins expers aux choses plus legieres et communes" [as the subject is difficult, let this suffice. And just as in a wealthy marketplace or treasure house there are, along with pearls, various precious stones of several virtues, colours, and worth, which are suited to the tastes and pleasures of different merchants, may these things be reserved in the treasure house of your volume for knowledgeable men of subtle understanding, and may those who are less expert pass them by in favour of things that are lighter and more common] (74–5). Opinion's comparison of Christine's work to a marketplace of various jewels is to be placed in parallel with the concluding image of the *Advision*, which compares the three parts of the text to a diamond, a cameo, and a ruby, respectively (see 1: 27, lines 72–81).

112 The passages that Christine adapts are from book 1, lectio 4, paragraphs 77ff., but they are preceded in Aquinas by other important reflections on the relationship of poetry to philosophy. See Aquinas, *S. Thomae Aquinatis in Metaphysicam Aristotelis Commentaria.*

113 Curtius, *European Literature and the Latin Middle Ages*, 221.

114 In Aquinas, those who "de principiis rerum tractaverunt, dicti sunt poetae theologizantes, sicut fuit Perseus, et quidam alii, qui fuerunt septem sapientes" [treated the origins of things were called theologizing poets, such as Perseus, and certain others, who were the seven sages]. 1, 3, 55.

115 See Paupert, "Philosophie 'en fourme de sainte Théologie,'" 48.

116 Cited in Curtius, *European Literature and the Latin Middle Ages*, 221.

117 See Curtius, chapter 12, as well as Minnis, Scott, and Wallace, *Medieval Literary Theory and Criticism*, in particular chapter 9, "The Transformation of Critical Tradition." Christine's awareness of this debate demonstrates her ties to Italian humanism.

118 On the relationship of philosophy to theology in Christine's works see Cropp, "Philosophy, the Liberal Arts, and Theology" and Paupert, "Philosophie 'en fourme de sainte Théologie.'" For the broader terms of this debate see the edited volume *La servante et la consolatrice*.

119 See Semple's insightful analysis of the category of the "simples" in "The Critique of Knowledge as Power."

120 Augustine, *The Literal Meaning of Genesis*, 216, 217.

121 See also Jean Gerson's assimilation of the individual, the kingdom, and the heavenly realm, as discussed in chapter 3.

3. Jean Gerson and the University of Paris

1 The bibliography on the medieval university and on the University of Paris is considerable. Among other works, on the history of the medieval university see Rashdall, *The Universities of Europe in the Middle Ages* and Verger, *Les universités au Moyen Âge*. On the development of the University of Paris see McKeon, "The Status of the University of Paris as *Parens Scientiarum*," Post, "Parisian Masters as a Corporation," Weber, "Suitable for Crown and Gown," and Wei, "The Masters of Theology at the University of Paris in the Late Thirteenth and Early Fourteenth Centuries." On the late medieval University of Paris see Bellitto, "The Early Development of Pierre d'Ailly's Conciliarism," Bernstein, *Pierre d'Ailly and the Blanchard Affair*, Kaminsky, "The Politics of France's Subtraction of Obedience from Pope Benedict XIII," and Lusignan, "*Vérité garde le roy.*"

2 See *Chartularium Universitatis Parisiensis*, ed. Denifle and Châtelain, 53.

3 See *Diligite justiciam*, 7.2.599 for the first two expressions, *Pax hominibus*, 7.2.763 for second two. Unless otherwise noted all citations from Gerson come from the *Œuvres complètes*. Volume and page numbers will be provided for all references. Translations are my own.

4 On the context and chronology of Gerson's French sermons see Mourin, *Jean Gerson, prédicateur français*. On Gerson as a preacher see C.D. Brown, *Pastor and Laity in the Theology of Jean Gerson* and Burger, "Preaching for Members of the University in Latin, for Parishioners in French."

5 Gerson's allegories do not exhibit the dangerous indeterminacy of the allegories of the *Roman de la Rose*, but contribute instead to a recuperation of allegory for moral purposes. See Gerson's *Contre le Roman de la rose*, in Christine de Pisan, Jean Gerson, Jean de Montreuil, and Gontier and Pierre Col, *Le débat sur Le Roman de la Rose* as well as Blumenfeld-Kosinski, "Jean Gerson and the Debate on the *Romance of the Rose*," Bose, "Jean Gerson, Poet," and Walters, "Gerson and Christine, Poets."

6 Which was no stranger to quarrels and debates, such as those that opposed the mendicant and the secular masters, or those that addressed what works and ideas were permissible to teach.

7 See the excellent account of the University's attempts to cope with the Schism in Meyjes, *Jean Gerson, Apostle of Unity*. In 1381 it was effectively Louis d'Anjou, Charles VI's uncle, who determined royal policy on the Schism.

8 Gerson's advocacy of moderation was often perceived as favouritism of the Avignonese pope, then Benedict XIII. See again Meyjes, *Jean Gerson, Apostle of Unity*, as well as McGuire, *Jean Gerson and the Last Medieval Reformation*.

9 See McLoughlin's study of a specific instance in which Gerson "manufactured consensus" among the University masters: "Personal Narrative and the Systematization of Knowledge in the Thought of Jean Gerson," 83.
10 See Hobbins, "The Schoolman as Public Intellectual" and the related monograph, *Authorship and Publicity before Print*.
11 On Gerson as a champion of University rights see McLoughlin, "Gerson as a Preacher in the Conflict Between Mendicants and Secular Priests."
12 For a short biography of Gerson see McGuire, "In Search of Jean Gerson."
13 For an overview of this period see Famiglietti, *Royal Intrigue* and Guenée, *Un meurtre, une société* and *La folie de Charles VI*.
14 Ferruolo observes that given the diverse origins of those connected to the University in the early 13th century, the students and masters did not conceive of themselves as *the* University *of* Paris, but as *a* university *in* Paris. See "Parisius-Paradisus." Lusignan has shown that over the course of the later Middle Ages the University became distinctly more French, and even more northern French, than it previously had been. See "*Vérité garde le roy.*"
15 Lieberman has argued that Gerson's letter, *Brevis instructio ad senem quomodo se ad mortem preparet*, was not addressed to his biological father, as Glorieux believed, but to Philippe de Mézières. See "Jean Gerson et Philippe de Mézières." On Philippe de Mézières see Jorga, *Philippe de Mézières*.
16 Philippe de Mézières, *Le songe du vieil pelerin*. See also Blanchard's excellent modern French translation, *Songe du vieux pèlerin*.
17 Spiegel, "Genealogy: Form and Function in Medieval Historiography."
18 On medieval kinship structures see Guerreau-Jalabert, "Sur les structures de parenté dans l'Europe médiévale" and Klapisch-Zuber, *L'ombre des ancêtres*.
19 Bouchard, "*Those of My Blood.*"
20 See ibid.
21 Hélary, "La place des questions de succession," 127.
22 On spiritual kinship see Guerreau-Jalabert, "*Spiritus et caritas.*"
23 Stahuljak, *Bloodless Genealogies of the French Middle Ages*, especially the introduction.
24 Post-Aristotelian writers such as Giles of Rome, Engelbert of Admont, and William of Ockham used the paradigm of the family to discuss, and sometimes to promote, various forms of government. See Blythe, "Family, Government, and the Medieval Aristotelians."
25 Hyams, *Rancor and Reconciliation in Medieval England*, 23.
26 Indeed, the language of kinship is nearly ubiquitous in Gerson, employed to communicate ideas about proximity, filiation, and descent. Thus, for instance, avarice can manifest itself in four ways, like four sons or daughters (7.2.872),

the virtues temperance, patience, justice, and truth are the daughters of grace (7.2.564), and ambition is the mother of cruel treason (7.2.1148).

27 The sermon is found at 7.2.862–8, the questions to which I refer at 7.2.864.

28 In fact, there is also a third kind of birth, which occurs if/when a soul is born into glory and permitted to sit with God in heaven, but we will not focus on this third birth here.

29 Gauvard, *Violence et ordre public au Moyen Age*, 235.

30 On natural love in literary contexts see Zink, "L'amour naturel."

31 See E.A.R. Brown, "Ritual Brotherhood in Western Medieval Europe."

32 On spiritual kinship see Bynum, *Jesus as Mother*.

33 On baptism see again Guerreau-Jalabert, "*Spiritus et caritas*."

34 For instance, in *Ave Maria, gratia plena*. Gerson emphasizes the spiritual kinship that unites nobles and non-nobles.

35 On the Virgin Mary see the sermon *Tota pulchra es* (8 Dec. 1401).

36 On the priest, Adam, and Christ as mothers see Guerreau-Jalabert, "*Spiritus et caritas*" and Bynum, "Jesus as Mother and Abbot as Mother: Some Themes in Twelfth-Century Cistercian Writing," in *Jesus as Mother*.

37 See *Un meurtre, une société*, 161–75.

38 Guenée discusses these royal ordinances in *Un meurtre*, 161–75. See also Adams, "Christine de Pizan, Isabeau of Bavaria, and Female Regency."

39 Or between France and England for that matter. The Hundred Years' War may be said to have originated as a family conflict, born of a contested succession or inheritance, and fought between cousins.

40 I would nuance this idea slightly by proposing instead that the queen's agenda, i.e., the protection of the kingdom and her children's rights, was substantially identical to that of the king. Louis d'Orléans, in contrast, may have harboured ambitions to place his own children on the French throne in the place of Charles VI's. See Adams, "Christine de Pizan, Isabeau of Bavaria, and Female Regency" as well as *The Life and Afterlife of Isabeau of Bavaria*.

41 As will be discussed in chapter 4, the so-called Salic Law stated that royal daughters could neither inherit nor transmit the throne.

42 Nelson, "Women at the Court of Charlemagne," 59.

43 See also my article "The King's Two Daughters."

44 Oresme, *Commentaire de Nicole Oresme sur le livre de Politiques d'Aristote*, 71. In *Vivat rex* Gerson cites Aristotle to the effect that in a monarchy the king is "comme le pere aux enfans" [like a father to his children] (7.2.1164).

45 In the later Middle Ages even the king's close family members constituted themselves as subjects. See Guenée, *Un meurtre*, 43–5.

46 See her "Joseph as Mother," 102.

47 On Gerson's efforts at Constance see Sheingorn, "'Illustris patriarcha Joseph.'"

48 On Gerson's dedication to Joseph see McGuire, "Patterns of Male Affectivity in the Late Middle Ages" as well as Roccati, "La 'Josephina' di Jean Gerson" and "Humanisme et préoccupations religieuses au début du XVe siècle."

49 Hobbins, "The Schoolman as Public Intellectual," 1310.

50 On the ways in which Gerson placed early French humanism and scholasticism at the service of pastoral care and preaching, see respectively Mazour-Matusevich, "Gerson et Pétrarque" and McGuire, "Jean Gerson and the Renewal of Scholastic Discourse."

51 In this respect Gerson's thought may be shaped by Hugh of St Victor, for whom study is but the first stage of ascent of the soul towards God, followed by performance, and surpassed only by contemplation (*Didascalicon*, book 5). See also Pascoe, "Jean Gerson: The 'Ecclesia Primitiva' and Reform." The importance of applied knowledge emerges also from an Aristotelian tradition. In the *De regimine principum* Giles of Rome writes that "[N]os n'aprenon pas la science de bones meurs principaument por savoir, ainz l'aprenon principaument pour ce que nos soion boens" [We do not acquire knowledge of good morals principally to know them, on the contrary, we acquire such knowledge so that we might be good]. *Li Livres du gouvernement des rois*, 5.

52 Cited in McGuire, *Jean Gerson and the Last Medieval Reformation*, 186. McGuire provides the original, cited from the *Chronique du règne de Charles VI*, in his footnote to this passage: livre 26, ch. 16, tome 3, vol. 2, p. 314: "Recedentes igitur, studendo ministerium vestrum debite compleatis, quoniam, et si filia regis Universitas vocetur, tamen de regimine regni ipsam intromittere non decet." On Louis's remarks to the University see also Mourin, *Jean Gerson, prédicateur français*, 171 n. 10 and Guenée, *Un meurtre*, 166–71.

53 The text of the sermon was diffused in written form as well. See Mourin, *Jean Gerson, prédicateur français*, 169ff.

54 On Gerson's remarkable ventriloquism with respect to his sermon on St Bernard, see McGuire, "Gerson and Bernard." In this sermon Gerson uses the same phrase, "Turn then for a little while your minds from me and think that it is Bernard himself speaking and not I" (cited in McGuire, 135).

55 Early in Gerson's career he enjoyed the patronage of Philippe de Bourgogne; however, he had less affinity for the new duke of Burgundy. Gerson seems to have tried very hard to steer a course between the rival princes, but his efforts at neutrality and moderation, as in the case of the Schism, often resulted in accusations of partisanship on the part of his opponents. In any case, his efforts to have Jean Petit's defence of the murder of Louis d'Orléans condemned placed him definitively in the Armagnac camp. Even so, it is

worth observing that upon his return from Constance he did not rejoin the court of Charles VII, but settled instead in Lyon.

56 See 7.2.1151, 1165, and 1182.

57 See Guenée, *Un meurtre*, 87–8, also 104–6.

58 On the University's relationship to Parlement during the later Middle Ages, and in particular the occasions on which theologians preached sermons before Parlement, see Lusignan, "*Vérité garde le roy*," especially chapter 4.

59 As in the poems of Deschamps and in Alain Chartier's *Quadrilogue invectif*, we see that the natural world provides a model for human conduct.

60 On the relationship of reputation to honour see the essays contained in the volume *Fama: The Politics of Talk and Reputation in Medieval Europe*, and with regard to women in particular, and the role of male relatives in preserving female honour, see Gauvard, "Honneur de femme et femme d'honneur en France à la fin du Moyen Âge."

61 On the notion of *simplesse* see Semple, "The Critique of Knowledge as Power," 116–20. On Gerson's concern for the "simple" see Walters, "Gerson and Christine, Poets."

62 Since women were excluded on the basis of their sex from the ranks of the clerical hierarchy and from the University, mystical theology provided a framework within which they could nevertheless achieve intimacy with God. The privileged addressees of this treatise, written in the vernacular, were Gerson's own sisters. The speculative theology taught at the University would have been both linguistically and intellectually beyond his sisters' reach, but in the *Montaigne de comtemplation* he has no intention "de dire chose qu'elles ne puissent bien comprendre" [to say anything that they might not understand well] (7.1.16). Instead, he affirms that "clergie" [learning/culture] is not necessary for contemplation. Indeed, "aucune fois telle science y donne empechment, non mie de soy mais pour l'orgueil et l'enfleure que la personne lettrée en prent" [sometimes such learning is a hindrance, not in and of itself, but because of the pride and self-satisfaction that the lettered person takes in it] (7.1.16). See 1 Corinthians 8:1, "Scientia inflat, caritas vero aeædificat" [Knowledge puffs up, while love edifies]. On spiritual roles open to (or carved out by) women see Matter, "The Undebated Debate."

63 See Fisher, "Gerson's Mystical Theology." On Gerson's privileging of affect see Turner, "Dionysius and Some Late Medieval Mystical Theologians of Northern Europe."

64 On depictions of gendered violence to elicit action see Blumenfeld-Kosinski, "Dramatic Troubles of Ecclesia."

65 Cited in McInerney, "In the Meydens Womb," 168. Bynum provides many similar examples in *Jesus as Mother*.

66 This is true not only in medieval France. For a broader anthropological discussion of the question see Ortner, "The Virgin and the State."

67 See Guenée, *Un meurtre*, 25–7.

68 Gauvard discusses the case of Charles de Savoisy in "La violence commanditée."

69 See Gauvard, *Violence et ordre public au Moyen Âge*, especially chapter 9, "L'honneur du roi."

70 Claude Gauvard has worked extensively in these areas. In addition to the works already cited, see her "Les clercs de la Chancellerie royale française" and of course "*De grace especial.*"

71 Or *doxa*. See Bourdieu, "Structures, Habitus, Power."

72 See my discussion of metaphor in chapter 1.

73 See Pascoe, *Jean Gerson: Principles of Church Reform*, 211.

74 On both the thought and the medieval reception of Dionysius, see the articles contained in the special issue of *Modern Theology* 24.4 (2008). On Gerson's engagement with the thought of Pseudo-Dionysius, see Combes, *Jean Gerson, commentateur dionysien*.

75 See *Jean Gerson: Principles of Church Reform*, especially chapter 1, "The Church: Order, Hierarchy, and Reform."

76 See *Jean Gerson, Apostle of Unity*, especially chapter 10, "Church, Hierarchy and General Council."

77 Ibid., 291.

78 See *L'ordonnance cabochienne 1413* as well as Coville, *Les Cabochiens et l'ordonnance de 1413*.

79 See Ross, "Anger and the City." In "*Vérité garde le roy*" Lusignan discusses the awkward position in which the University found itself when it had to condemn the ordinance that it had previously supported. See chapter 4, "L'Université de Paris et le Parlement."

80 The party that constituted itself around the sons of Louis d'Orléans was called Armagnac in reference to Charles d'Orléans's father in law, Bernard d'Armagnac, who was one of the centres of resistance to Jean sans peur. See Guenée, *Un meurtre*, 225.

81 These two letters are analysed both by Mazour-Matusevich and Bejczy, "Jean Gerson on Virtues and Princely Education" and by Verger, "*Ad prefulgidum sapiencie culmen prolem regis inclitam provehere*." The former date the letter *Claro eruditori* to 1408–10 and the letter *Erunt omnes docibilis* to c. 1417. Verger, following Max Lieberman, dates the first letter to 1417 and the second to 1429.

82 See Verger, "*Ad prefulgidum*," 437.

83 See chapter 2.

84 See McLoughlin's analysis of this sermon and the events that prompted it in her "Gerson as a Preacher."

85 On Scripture as the source or foundation for all knowledge see de Lubac, *Exégèse médiévale*, 74ff.

86 A similar version of the University's origins is contained in *Vivat rex*. See 7.2.1138.

87 On this tradition see Fritz, "*Translatio studii* et déluge," Jongkees, "*Translatio studii*," and Lusignan, "L'université de Paris comme composante de l'identité du royaume de France." On Gerson's version of *translatio studii* see also Lusignan, "*Vérité garde le roy*," especially chapter 5, "L'Université de Paris dans l'ordre politique de la France."

88 As Meyjes observes, "Gerson developed his ecclesiological ideas on the basis of the 'mystical body.' This idea was as central to his ecclesiology as it was characteristic of it." Gerson applies the idea of the mystical body to entities apart from the Church, but always relying on Paul, thereby suggesting that he believed that Paul had in mind "other ontological entities and structures which could be distinguished in the cosmic order." *Jean Gerson, Apostle of Unity*, 298.

89 See Pascoe, *Jean Gerson: Principles of Church Reform*, especially chapter 6, "Personal Reform." See also Hamburger, *St John the Divine*.

90 Kantorowicz, *The King's Two Bodies*, chapter 6.

91 See for instance the articles of Harf-Lancner, "*Les membres et l'estomac*" and LeGoff, "Head or Heart?" I cite by way of exception the article of Nederman, "Body Politics," in which the author shows the disparate and even subversive uses of the organological metaphor.

92 Blamires, "Paradox in the Medieval Gender Doctrine of Head and Body."

93 In "Body Politics" Nederman discusses the importance of equilibrium in relation to the metaphor of the body politic.

94 On the virtues and vices in Gerson, and the role of the University in regulating political life, see McLoughlin, "The Deadly Sins and Contemplative Politics."

95 Blamires notes that the most common ways to envision the relationship between head and body were the top-down model, and the lead-and-follow model. See his "Paradox in the Medieval Gender Doctrine of Head and Body."

96 Although it is true that the Great Schism precipitated the departure of many Urbanist masters and students in the years following the beginning of the Schism. See Bernstein, *Pierre d'Ailly and the Blanchard Affair*, chapter 2, "The University of Paris and the Great Schism." Lusignan shows that the population of the University became increasingly French over the course of the fourteenth century, and even more particularly northern French (i.e., langue d'oïl), and this,

even before the Schism. See "*Vérité garde le roy,*" especially chapter 3, "Les universitaires dans la société française."

97 *Traictie de la première invention des monnoies de Nicole Oresme*. Oresme also cites Plutarch's letter to Trajan, a reference to the *Policraticus*, as his inspiration for his remarks in this chapter.

98 On the relationship of the king to the tyrant see my article "How to Become the 'roy des frans.'"

99 See Pascoe, *Jean Gerson: Principles of Church Reform*, chapter 6.

100 Here Gerson inscribes himself in a long tradition of scriptural interpretation and commentary, which both recognizes that sometimes Scripture employs figurative language, and grapples with the problem of how a reader is to know when to interpret literally, and when figuratively. See chapter 1 for a longer discussion of this problem.

101 See Nederman, "Property and Protest," 324. As Nederman is careful to point out, however, it would be imprudent to assume that Gerson is a direct precursor or link to modern constitutionalist thought, as some scholars have affirmed. See his "Conciliarism and Constitutionalism."

102 According to Gerson, the ruler's concern for his progeny explains why legitimate succession is superior to election.

103 John of Salisbury attributed to Plutarch the letter to Trajan in which he outlines how the polity may fruitfully be compared to a human body.

104 See Nederman, "Property and Protest."

105 Gerson also envisioned limits to papal authority. See for instance Meyjes, *Jean Gerson, Apostle of Unity*, on Gerson's increasing conciliarism.

106 See Giles of Rome, 352–5.

107 Nederman, "Conciliarism and Constitutionalism."

108 See, for instance, Nederman, ibid.

109 This argument is reminiscent of Gerson's affirmation that Jesus's obedience to Joseph does not constitute subjection.

110 See, for instance, Mazour-Matusevich and Bejczy, "Jean Gerson on Virtues and Princely Education."

111 Denis Foulechat, *Le Policratique de Jean de Salisbury (Livre V).*

112 In "*Vérité garde le roy*" Lusignan shows that Gerson's promotion of the University may be understood within the context of a rivalry between University and Parlement, or theologians and jurists. See also Krynen, "Les légistes 'tyrans de la France'?"

113 In this respect we can observe a substitution of the University for the king, the traditional spouse of the (conventionally female) kingdom.

114 As Meyjes has observed, Gerson also uses the notion of semen in connection to the Church. "The essence of the Church, created by God and therefore

perfect ... is described in more detail as a potential, a *semen*, which over time had developed and achieved its full realisation," and this semen is a spiritual force "which was operative in the mystical body of the Church and which would preserve it in its unalterable hierarchical form until the end of time." *Jean Gerson, Apostle of Unity*, 305.

4. Envisioning the Body Politic before and after the Treaty of Troyes

1 On fourteenth-century references to female exclusion from royal rule see, among others, Beaune, *Naissance de la nation France*, the chapter entitled "La loi salique," Contamine, "'Le Royaume de France ne peut tomber en fille,'" Giesey, *Le rôle méconnu de la loi salique*, Krynen, *L'empire du roi*, and Taylor, "The Salic Law and the Valois Succession to the French Crown." Taylor notes that actually the English were the first to cite Salic Law in connection to the Valois succession, in 1389.

2 I shall employ the term *Lex Salica* to speak of the original code of the Salian Franks, and Salic Law when referring to the fifteenth-century formulation of this code.

3 On the contested successions of 1316 and 1328 see Contamine, "'Le Royaume de France ne peut tomber en fille,'" Taylor, "Edward III and the Plantagenet Claim to the French Throne," and Viollet, "Comment les femmes ont été exclues, en France, de la succession à la couronne."

4 Actually, as Nichols has shown in his very illuminating article, "The Narrative of Nation. Political Allegory in 14th-Century France," Richard Lescot referred to the "Legem vero salicam" [true Salic Law] (178) in 1358 in his *Genealogia Aliquorum Regum Francie per quam apparet quantum attinere potest regi francie rex navarre* in order to counter the claims of Charles of Navarre to the French throne. Lescot does not provide the text of the law, but its genealogy, in support of the notion that "mulier in regno Francie non succedat" [a woman may not succeed in the kingdom of France] (176). To the best of my knowledge, no one took note of or developed Lescot's association between the principle of female exclusion and the Salic Law prior to Jean de Montreuil who, as we shall see, vastly develops the potential of this connection.

5 The expression "pont et planche" [bridge and plank], which will be picked up by a number of subsequent authors, is Jean's. See Jean de Montreuil, *Opera*, *L'œuvre historique et polémique*, for instance at 2: 169, 211, 276. All references are to this edition. Translations are my own. Jean de Montreuil's role in the so-called Quarrel of the *Rose* has caused him to be cast, in the eyes of many modern scholars, in the unsavoury role of misogynist. It is not my

intent to discuss the Quarrel here, except to suggest that considerations of Jean's textual production ought not to be limited by this perspective. On the quarrel of the *Rose* see Christine de Pisan, Jean Gerson, Jean de Montreuil, and Gontier and Pierre Col, *Le débat sur Le Roman de la Rose*.

6 The Treaty of Troyes is contained in Cosneat, ed., *Les grands traités de la guerre de cent ans*. The entire first clause reads as follows: "Premierement, que, pour ce que, par l'aliance du mariage fait, pour le bien de ladicte paix, entre nostredit filz, le Roy Henry, et nostre très chière et très amée fille, Katherine, il est devenu nostre filz et de nostre très chière et très amée compaigne, la Royne, ycellui nostre filz nous aura et honnourera et nostre dicte compaigne comme père et mère, et ainsi comme il appartient honnourer telz et si grans prince et princesse et devant toutes personnes temporelles du monde" [First that, on account of the marriage alliance established for the good of the aforesaid peace, between our aforesaid son, King Henry, and our very dear and very beloved daughter, Katherine, he has become our son and {the son} of our very dear and very beloved companion, the queen, this one, our son, will keep and honour us and our aforesaid companion as father and mother, and in a manner befitting to such ones, and so great a prince and princess, and {will do so} before all temporal persons of the world]. Clause 6 of the treaty identified Henry V as the heir to the kingdom of France: "Item, est accordé que, tantost après nostre trespas et dèslors en avant, la couronne et royaume de France, avecques tous leurs droiz et appartenances, demourront et seront perpetuelement de nostre filz le Roy Henry et de ses hoirs" [Likewise, it is agreed that immediately following our death and from that moment forward, the crown and kingdom of France, with all of its rights and appurtenances, will belong and will be perpetually to our son King Henry and his heirs].

7 Oaths were a routine component of peace agreements, but the Treaty of Troyes required oaths of an unusually large and disparate population.

8 *Ordonnances des roys de France de la troisième race*, 8: 581. This ordinance will be confirmed, in near identical terms, in December 1407.

9 See Giesey, "The Juristic Basis of Dynastic Right to the French Throne," Giesey, *Le rôle méconnu de la loi salique* and Krynen, "'La mort saisit le vif.'"

10 The so-called Dual Monarchy also had its proponents and theorists, and though these are not the focus of the present work, it is important to recognize that the texts I examine, and others not discussed in detail here, were produced and inscribed in an atmosphere of debate.

11 See, for instance, the seminal study of Viollet, "Comment les femmes ont été exclues, en France, de la succession à la couronne."

12 Giesey observes that Aristotelian theories of generation, in which the nature of the father was imparted to the son through his semen, were sometimes more useful than those based upon blood, which accorded a greater role to the woman. See "The Juristic Basis of Dynastic Right to the French Throne," 16.

13 This passage is from Jean de Montreuil's first redaction of his *Traité contre les anglais* .

14 The most comprehensive study of Salic Law, from its sixth-century origins to its late medieval development and its applications during the Renaissance and beyond, is that of Viennot, *La France, les femmes, et le pouvoir.* Viennot takes a perspective that emphasizes continuity and that situates female exclusion from rule and the emergence of the late medieval and Renaissance version of Salic Law within a long-standing tradition of misogyny.

15 In addition to the works cited in the historical background provided in the introduction, see also A.W. Lewis, *Royal Succession in Capetian France*.

16 Following the death of Philippe V in 1322, the succession of his brother instead of his daughter provoked no comment or objections.

17 See my introduction for a more comprehensive account of these events.

18 In addition to the question of the transmissability of political rights, Edward's youth and the political prominence of his mother and her lover, Roger Mortimer, surely affected the deliberations of the French.

19 As Contamine so aptly put it, "Quant à la loi salique, son intérêt fut de donner à la très banale et très vague 'coutume de France' un nom, un statut, une ancienneté, bref des titres de noblesse." See "'Le royaume de France ne peut tomber en fille,'" 71.

20 Cosandey similarly emphasizes the pre-eminence of the question of political integrity over that of the capacity of women to govern. See *La reine de France*, especially chapter 1.

21 For an overview of the Hundred Years' War see Favier, *La guerre de cent ans.* Sumption provides a detailed account of the early phases of the war in *The Hundred Years War.*

22 On Jean de Montreuil as a humanist scholar see Ornato, "Les humanistes français et la redécouverte des classiques."

23 See the introduction to the edition of Jean's political works, 3–64 of vol. 2. On pages 5–6 the editors list the eighteen known manuscripts that contain one or more of Jean's political treatises. This relatively high number of surviving manuscripts attests to the successful diffusion of Jean's work.

24 On the use of Jean de Montreuil's writings by subsequent authors see the articles of Pons, "Propagande et sentiment national pendant le règne de Charles VI," "Jean de Montreuil et Guillebert de Mets," and "Un exemple

de l'utilisation des écrits politiques de Jean de Montreuil." On fifteenth-century propagandistic writing generally see P.S. Lewis, "War Propaganda and Historiography in Fifteenth-Century France and England," Pons, "La propagande de guerre française avant l'apparition de Jeanne d'Arc," and Taylor, "War, Propaganda and Diplomacy in Fifteenth-Century France and England."

25 Guenée, *L'opinion publique à la fin du Moyen Âge.*

26 "me semble que clers peuent tres bien parler d'armes, car, par les grans faiz des vaillans hommes du temps passé et lacheté des autres, qui tous par iceulx clers s'escrisent, ilz peuent tres bien donner generaulx consaulx en armes" [it seems to me that clerics can perfectly well speak of arms because, based upon the great deeds of courageous men of the past, as well as the cowardice of others, all of which was written about by such clerics, they can very well give general advice about arms] (130).

27 "fy ycellui hommage envoié par solennelz messages audit roy Philippe [a Paris] soubz chartre en laz de soye et cire verte et autres lettres patentes en cire blanche d'icelui Edouart, qui sont au tresor des chartres royaulx a Paris, ausquelles collation a été faite mot a mot du transcript dont la teneur s'ensuit" [and this homage was sent by official messengers to the aforesaid King Philip {in Paris} under covers in straps of silk and with green wax, and other letters patent with white wax of this Edward, which are in the royal charterhouse in Paris, of which a copy was made word for word of the content, which is as follows] (174–5).

28 See also version 3, page 309.

29 Jean's insistance on writing is remarkable given the fact that it was the English who, for instance, at the peace talks at Leulinghem in the 1390s and in a departure from former diplomatic practice, insisted that the French make their proposals for the peace in writing. See Lusignan, "Parler français."

30 "quant aux offres que lesdis Anglois aleguent estre faictes par le roy Charles derrenierement trespassé, il faudroit qu'ilz les monstrassent par lectres ou autres souffisans enseignemens, pour veoir et savoir par quelle condicion ledit roy Charles faisoit icelles offres qu'on seult appeller ouvertures" [as for the offers which the aforesaid English claim to have been made by King Charles, recently deceased, it is necessary that they show them by letters or other adequate authenticating signs, in order to see and to know under what condition the aforesaid King Charles made these offers which they used to call proposals] (305).

31 It is interesting to contemplate Jean's privileging of the written word in light of Derrida's analysis of speech and writing in Rousseau, for whom, according

to Derrida, speech was natural and immediate, while writing signalled the "destruction of presence." *Of Grammatology*, 142.

32 On the growing awareness of the importance and the impact of public opinion during the early fifteenth century, see Guenée, *L'opinion publique à la fin du Moyen Âge*.

33 The dossier discussed by Taylor in his article "Edward III and the Plantagenet Claim to the French Throne" is one such example, though Taylor argues elsewhere that in fact the English produced fewer legal-political works of propaganda and diplomatic preparation than their French counterparts. See his "War, Propaganda and Diplomacy in Fifteenth-Century France and England."

34 "Et comme les Anglois aient livres les plus beaulx et plus notables qu'ilz puent faire de ce qu'ilz demandent en France, lesquelz ils portent communement avec eulx quant ilz doyvent assembler avec les François pour traictier, et scevent par espicial les grans seigneurs tout ce qu'ilz cuident qui face pour eulx" [and since the English have books, the most beautiful and remarkable that they can make them, about that which they claim in France, which they usually bring with them when they have to meet with the French to negotiate, and the great lords know in particular all that which they believe to work in their favour] (266).

35 It is not entirely clear which dauphin Jean addressed. Louis de Guyenne died 18 December 1415, and at least part of the third version of the treatise is dated 24 September 1416. Jean de Touraine was dauphin from the time of his brother's death to 5 April 1517.

36 Similarly, Guenée observes that "en un sens, ce sont les historiens qui créent les nations." *L'Occident aux XIVe et XVe siècles*, 123.

37 See Lewis, "War Propaganda and Historiography in Fifteenth-Century France and England" and Pons, "Propagande et sentiment national pendant le règne de Charles VI."

38 As Jean says, by claiming the throne after several years instead of immediately, it is as though Edward "apparçut le jour a midy" [perceived daybreak at noon] (133).

39 In his translation/adaptation of Aristotle's *Politics*, Nicole Oresme similarly observes that "selon la diversité des regions, des complexions, des inclinations et des meurs des gens, il convient que leur droiz positifs et leur gouvernemens soient differens" [according to the diversity of regions, and of the physical characteristics, preferences, and mores of people, it is appropriate that their positive laws and their governments be different]. See *Le livre de politiques d'Aristote*, 291.

40 This documentary absence must have been disturbing to one who expended considerable energy searching for the most complete and correct classical

texts available. On Jean's efforts to locate and acquire the best versions possible of classical texts see Ornato, "Les humanistes français et la redécouverte des classiques."

41 The Dictionnaire du Moyen Français defines *alleu* as lands held in full ownership, exempt from feudal rights. See http://www.atilf.fr/dmf/.

42 Cited in Viennot, *La France, les femmes, et le pouvoir*, 34. Later versions of the clause add the word *salica* after *terra*.

43 Viennot shows how this article was modifed over time to gradually privilege inheritance by men and paternal relatives.

44 Richard Lescot, in his genealogy of Salic Law, likewise affirms that it predates the conversion of the Franks, and he too mentions both Clovis and Charlemagne in connection to the law's development.

45 In fact, as numerous scholars have noted, he misquotes it – whether intentionally or in error we shall never know with certainty – by adding the phrase *in regno*, a mistake that he corrects in subsequent citations of the law. See chapter 5 of Giesey, *Le rôle méconnu*. Jean's interpolation has been called a "forgery" (see Hanley, "The Politics of Identity," 295), but I find that such strong and negative terms overstate the case. What were called translations in the Middle Ages were in fact works of linguistic and cultural adaptation which were often unfaithful, in a literal sense, to their originals. I contend that Jean provided what he believed to be the intent of the clause. Indeed, in his later citations of the Salic Law Jean omits the words *in regno*, and simply explains the meaning of the passage as he understood it (or wanted it to be understood), that is, "absolument que femme n'ait quelconque portion ou royaume, c'est a entendre a la couronne de France" [absolutely that a woman might not have any part in the kingdom, that is to say, in the crown of France] (168).

46 Indeed, as Cosandey has argued, in subsequent centuries Salic Law becomes constitutive of French monarchy, the law "dont découlent toutes les autres." See *La reine de France*, 42.

47 On this point I disagree with Hanley, who has argued in a series of articles that Jean de Montreuil invented Salic Law as a direct response to what she perceives as Christine de Pizan's humiliating defeat of Jean in the quarrel of the *Roman de la Rose*. See Hanley, "Introduction," "Mapping Rulership in the French Body Politic," "Identity Politics and Rulership in France," and "The Politics of Identity and Monarchic Government in France." Given the historical scholarship which traces the development of the principle of female exclusion from rule over the course of the fourteenth century (see note 1 of this chapter), I find this argument unconvincing. See also Taylor's refutation of Hanley's argument in "The Salic Law, French Queenship, and the Defense of Women in the Late Middle Ages."

48 The Greek emperor in fact visited Paris in the early fifteenth century.

49 See Godefroy, *Dictionnaire de l'ancienne langue française*. Among the many meanings and connotations of *forçoier*, rape is not included, whereas the terms *esforcement*, *esforceor*, and *esforcier* all include rape or sexual violence among their meanings. Indeed, it is one of the principal meanings of *esforcier*, as Godefroy lists it third of over a dozen possible meanings. The DMF provides similar results. See http://www.atilf.fr/dmf.

50 Moreover, linguistic difference is introduced as the element that signals the fundamental foreignness of the English, and therefore their unsuitability to rule over the French. Loomis discusses the importance of linguistic difference to nascent ideas about nations in her fascinating article "Nationality at the Council of Constance." I will examine the question of language further in part three of this chapter, "Jean Juvénal des Ursins and the Dismantling of the Treaty of Troyes."

51 Jean's original misquotation of Salic Law was soon discovered, as well as the ways in which he had framed the text to suggest an application not present in the original document. On the later influence and applications of Salic Law see the second half of Giesey, *Le rôle méconnu de la loi salique*, Taylor, "Introduction," in *Debating the Hundred Years War* and "Sir John Fortescue and the French Polemical Treatises," and volume 1 of Viennot, *La France, les femmes, et le pouvoir*. As Viennot observes, even after the discovery of Jean de Montreuil's philological sleight of hand, his successors could not bear to abandon Salic Law, for this would mean saying goodbye to "une trouvaille dont on commençait à comprendre l'immense utilité" (16).

52 On the French appropriation and exploitation of this epithet see Krynen, "*Rex christianissimus*."

53 *Ordonnances*, 12: 273.

54 Cosneau, *Les grands traités de la guerre de cent ans*.

55 On these historical events see Autrand, *Charles VI: La folie du roi* and Favier, *La guerre de cent ans*.

56 Charles of France was betrothed to Marie d'Anjou in 1413, at the age of ten. According to custom, he lived with his future bride's family. The couple was married in 1422.

57 For a short biography of Chartier see Laidlaw, "Alain Chartier."

58 Chartier's *œuvre* is considerable and disparate, including both prose and verse works, in French and in Latin. See *The Poetical Works of Alain Chartier*, ed. Laidlaw, and *Les œuvres latines d'Alain Chartier*, ed. Bourgain-Hemeryck.

59 The *Quadrilogue* survives in over 50 manuscripts, a testament to its considerable success. Here I have used the edition by Bouchet, which takes

as its base manuscript BnF f. 126. Other texts contained in this manuscript include *Le regime des princes*, *De senectute*, *De amicitia*, *Le dialogus familiaris amici et sodalis*, and *Le traité de l'espérance*. A list of manuscripts that contain the *Quadrilogue invectif* is included in Cayley, *Debate and Dialogue*, appendix B. Translations are my own.

60 Understood and depicted as those loyal to the Valois.

61 On Chartier's use of allegory see Altmann, "Alain Chartier's *Livre des Quatre Dames*" and Brown, "Allegorical Design and Image-Making in Fifteenth-Century France."

62 On expressions of emotion in Chartier's works see my forthcoming article, "Performance and Polemic."

63 This language is from the ordinance of 17 January 1420 (12: 273).

64 On depictions of Chartier's narrator, especially in prologues and prefaces, see Kinch, "'De l'ombre de mort en clarté de vie.'"

65 On the use of organological metaphors to conceptualize human history see Fritz, "Figures et métaphores du corps dans le discours de l'histoire."

66 Similarly, we saw in chapter 2 that Eustache Deschamps inscribed the temporal realm between micro- and macrocosm, and that Christine de Pizan invited her readers to interpret her allegorical text in connection to the individual, the kingdom, and the cosmos. Jean Gerson's three lives or modes of existence, discussed in chapter 3, also invite his public to imagine the salvific potential of the political realm. Here Chartier's focus is less on how proper political conduct can guide the individual soul to salvation, and more on the desperate plight of the kingdom, to which the subjects, as natural and divine law show, should dedicate their efforts.

67 "comme les enfans naiscent et croiscent en hommes parfaiz et puis declinent a viellesce et a mort, ainsi ont seigneuries leur commencement, leur accroissement et leur declin" [just as children are born and grow into perfect men, and then decline in old age and until death, so too lordships have their beginning, their rise, and their decline] (5). France will make a similar connection in her discourse to her children.

68 Or is he? As Bouchet has noted, the use of the subjunctive, "je veisse" (10), rather than the indicative puts into question the status of the dream vision as lived experience. See Bouchet, "Introduction," 16.

69 The narrator "en grant craincte debatu en ma pensee" [in great fear debated in my thoughts] (7), "Aprés lesquelz partis ainsi debatuz a par moy" [after these positions {on the reasons for France's troubles} had been thus debated within me] (9), "Tandiz que en ce debat entre espoir et desesperance mon entendement traveilloit" [while in this debate between hope and despair my understanding was tormented] (10). On medieval debate literature and

the place of Alain Chartier within this tradition see Cayley, *Debate and Dialogue*.

70 Following his description of France's cloak, the dreamer-narrator says, "Du mantel me deporteray a tant de present pource que trop longuement ne vueil sur descripcion demourer, ne ce n'est la fin de ce present quadrilogue" [About the mantle I will leave off now, for I do not wish to linger over description, nor is this the objective of the present quadrilogue] (12). The text is here named the *Quadrilogium invectivum et comicum ad morum Gallicorum correctionem* [Four-part invective and comedy aimed at the correction of the mores of the French]. The word *comicum* recalls Dante's *Divine Comedy* which, he explained, was a comedy because although it depicted suffering it ended in joy. Such a title applied to Chartier's text suggests his faith in the ultimate redemption of the French.

71 See Minet-Mahy's analysis of the functioning of the dream and the fragmentation of the narrative *I* in the *Roman de la Rose*, and in late medieval dream visions more generally. As she points out, allegorical texts and dream visions "impliquent ambiguïté, polyphonie et lecture," thereby inviting the interpretation and the reformation of the reader. See her "Le songe," 202.

72 On the relationship of these two narratorial figures see the insightful analysis of Haidu, *The Subject Medieval/Modern*, especially 324–7.

73 France's condemnation of her contemporary society prefigures the critiques of Chartier's *Belle Dame*. See Cayley, *Debate and Dialogue*, chapter 3, Corbellari, "À la place du mort," Jennequin, "La *Belle dame sans mercy* d'Alain Chartier et sa dimension politique," and Solterer, "The Freedoms of Fiction for Gender in Premodern France."

74 On the vocabulary and category of the natural see Nichols, "The Narrative of Nation," 155.

75 On the perceived abundance of France and her relationship to Nature in the sixteenth century see Zorach, *Blood, Milk, Ink, Gold*, especially the chapter "Milk."

76 On the use of nature and the natural in political thought see Krynen, "Naturel."

77 On the portrait of France and her mantle see Rouy, *L'esthétique du traité moral d'après les œuvres d'Alain Chartier*, 40–5.

78 Alain de Lille, *Plaint of Nature*.

79 See Bouchet, "Introduction," 57 n. 21, as well as Bouchet, "'Vox Dei, vox poetae.'" Bouchet suggests that mistreated lady France functions as the political equivalent of the dishonoured Christ, and that "patriotism is her political version of faith," "'Vox Dei,'" 35.

80 Perhaps in the French translation/commentary completed by Nicole Oresme during the reign of Charles V. See Nicole Oresme, *Commentaire de Nicole Oresme sur le livre de politiques d'Aristote*. On the rise of the vernacular as a language of philosophical and intellectual works, see Lusignan, *Parler vulgairement*.

81 See Kempshall, *The Common Good in Late Medieval Political Thought*.

82 "peu doit priser sa naissance et mains desirer la continuation de sa vie qui passe ses jours ainsi que fait homme nez pour soy seulement, sans fructifier a la commune utilité, et comme cellui qui estaint sa memoire avecques sa vie" [little should he esteem his birth, and even less desire the continuation of his life, he who spends his days in the manner of a man born for himself only, without producing anything for collective use, and like one who extinguishes with his life all memory of him.] (15).

83 "Helas, tant est es anciens couraiges prouchaine et si inseparablement enracinee l'amour naturelle du païz que le corps tent a y retourner de toutes pars comme en son propre lieu, le cuer y est donné come a celle habitacion qui plus lui est aggreable, la vie et la sancté y croissent et amendent, l'omme y quiert sa sceurté, sa paix, son refuge, le repos de sa vieillesce et sa derreniere sepulture" [Alas, in ancient hearts natural love of country was so intimately and so inseparably rooted that from all places the body tended to return there, as to its proper place, the heart was dedicated there as to that habitation which is most agreeable to it, life and health grow and flourish there, man seeks there his safety, his peace, his refuge, rest in his old age and his final burial place] (15).

84 "celui pays et seigneurie sauver" [to save that country and lordship] (15) is what France actually says. We shall discuss the conjoining of these terms presently.

85 Though Jean de Terre Rouge's works were unknown at this time. See Giesey, "Juristic Basis," 12–17 and Krynen, "'La mort saisit le vif.'"

86 The texts of both are contained in *Quatre libelles contre les Anglais (vers 1418–1429)*.

87 Philippe de Mézières, *Le songe du vieil pelerin*, 1: 485.

88 *Œuvres complètes*.

89 See Guenée, "Un royaume et des pays."

90 "si nacionem queritis, de regno est; si patriam, de Valle Colorum oppido, quod est prope flumen Meuse" [if you ask about her nation, she is of the kingdom; if of her fatherland, of the town of Vaucouleurs, which is next to the river Meuse] . See *Les œuvres latines d'Alain Chartier*, 326. See also Craig Taylor's English translation in *Joan of Arc. La Pucelle*, selected sources.

91 France conjoins *pays* and *seigneurie* at 15, lines 6–7, page 15, line 24, and page 16, lines 2–3.
92 See Haidu's discussion of *seigneurie* in *The Subject Medieval/Modern*, 319ff.
93 Guenée discusses the gradual conjoining of a territory, a people united by birth and blood, and a political order in *L'Occident aux XIVe et XVe siècles*, especially book one, chapter 3, "État et nation." Moreover, since God determines where a person is born, the natural obligations towards one's country are also divine obligations.
94 See Butterfield, *The Familiar Enemy*. I cite from the introduction to her work.
95 As observed by Krynen, "Naturel," 184. See also Guenée, *L'Occident aux XIVe et XVe siècles.*
96 "Qu'est devenue," France asks rhetorically, "la constance et loyauté du peuple françois ... vers son naturel seigneur sans querir nouvelles mutacions?" [What has become of the constancy and the loyalty of the French people ... towards its natural lord, without seeking new changes?] (19).
97 Indeed, as we saw in Jean de Montreuil's history of the English presence on the continent, the treachery and violence of the English became a topos in French propaganda.
98 Here France is referring to the deposition and murder of Richard II in 1399. It is remarkable to observe that in this passage France unites the ideas of tyranny and of usurpation. Any rule that is not based upon heredity, that does not pass from one *seigneur naturel* to the next, constitutes tyranny. The opposition between natural lordship and tyranny may be observed in the works of Philippe de Mézières and Christine de Pizan as well.
99 On literary representations of natural love see Zink, "L'amour naturel."
100 Similarly, she desires the *Quadrilogue*'s readers to see in it a debate that is not "haineuse, mais fructueuse" [hateful, but fruitful] (83).
101 On the life of Jean Juvénal des Ursins see volume 3 of *Écrits politiques de Jean Juvénal des Ursins*, 25–102.
102 *Audite celi* is preserved in over a dozen manuscripts. The works of Jean Juvénal des Ursins are contained in *Écrits politiques de Jean Juvénal des Ursins*. Lewis's insightful presentation of Jean Juvénal's works is in volume 3. *Audite celi* is found in volume 1: 145–277, with a introduction on pages 93–142. The surviving manuscripts are discussed in pages 211–32.
103 On the legal arguments made by Jean Juvénal, as well as his predecessors and contemporaries, see Lewis's introduction, as well as Giesey, "The Juristic Basis of Dynastic Right to the French Throne," Giesey, *Le rôle méconnu de la loi salique*, Taylor, "Introduction," in *Debating the Hundred Years War*, and Taylor, "The Salic Law and the Valois Succession to the French Crown."

104 The *Quadrilogue invectif*, and other texts by Chartier, appear with *Audite celi* in BNF f. ms 1128.

105 As featured, for instance, in the works of Boethius, Guillaume de Machaut, and Alain Chartier.

106 Blumenfeld-Kosinski, "The Strange Case of Ermine de Reims," 324. See also her *Poets, Saints, and Visionaries of the Great Schism*.

107 Raymond de Sabanac was the confessor of the visionary Constance de Rabastans and author of her life and visions; Alfonso of Jaén was the confessor of Birgitta of Sweden and author of her life and visions; Gerson was asked to judge the visions of Ermine of Reims, was involved in the confirmation of the canonization of Birgitta of Sweden that was undertaken at the Council of Constance, and also wrote about the visions of Joan of Arc. Thus, those who wrote about the discernment of spirits were also attempting to advance specific, though various, theological and political agendas. See Blumenfeld-Kosinski, "Raymond de Sabanac, Preface to Constance de Rabastens, *The Revelations*" as well as Anderson, *Free Spirits, Presumptuous Women, and False Prophets*, Coakley, *Women, Men, and Spiritual Power*, Elliott, "Seeing Double," and Voaden, *God's Words, Women's Voices*. Elliott notes that while early treatises on the discernment of spirits focus on self-evaluation, later visionaries, so often women, who were easily deceived, required the imprimatur of male clerical authority.

108 Cited in Blumenfeld-Kosinski, "Raymond de Sabanac."

109 The narrator never identifies his creature as a woman, but based upon the feminine gender of the word "creature" and the tradition of female visionary and male confidant/author, I have chosen to designate the dreamer with feminine pronouns.

110 Political visions are one of Coakley's three categories of visionary experience. See *Women, Men, and Spiritual Power*, 13–15.

111 Newman notes that illiterate people were more obviously divinely inspired, since they presumably lacked the intellect to invent a vision. See "What Did It Mean to Say 'I Saw'?" Similarly, Voaden observes with respect to unlearned visionaries that "God's choice of a seemingly inappropriate instrument – a fool, a madman, or a woman – is evidence of his absolute power, and a reminder of the inscrutable ways of the Divine." See *God's Words, Women's Voices*, 71.

112 On the omission of potentially boring legal citations see P.S. Lewis, "War Propaganda and Historiography in Fifteenth-Century France and England."

113 Indeed, visionary experiences often consisted of a series of dreams or waking visions.

114 John Fitzalan, earl of Arundel, was an English military commander in Normandy. His defeat and subsequent death were a significant blow for the English. See Curry, "Fitzalan, John," *Dictionary of National Biography*, online ed., http://www.oxforddnb.com/index/101009532.

115 This remark of Saincte Esglise recalls the affirmation of the papal legate, the cardinal Albergati, that Charles VII was the rightful king of France, and that Henry VI ought to be content with one crown and one kingdom. However, Albergati's remarks were not made in May 1435, but shortly before the departure of the English from the peace talks on 6 September. See Dickinson, *The Congress of Arras,* especially chapter 6, "The Anglo-French Discussions." On the Church's position on the Treaty of Troyes see also Izbicki, "The Canonists and the Treaty of Troyes." According to Izbicki, the Church's view that the Treaty of Troyes constituted an impediment to peace was clear well before the Congress of Arras.

116 "Si me tiennent pour excusé ceulx qui verront ceste presente espitre, se il y a chose qui leur desplaise, car je n'y ay mis que ce que m'a esté dit" [May they excuse me, those who will see the present epistle, if there is anything in it which may displease them, for I included only that which was told to me] (277), he writes. The narrator's ambivalence towards the text he has recorded recalls Gerson's hesitant support of Joan of Arc. See Elliott, "Seeing Double." It is important to note, in this context, that Jean Juvénal very pointedly avoids all mention of Joan of Arc, a question that I shall discuss in the coda to this book.

117 The three estates of the two kingdoms are precisely the populations who had been asked to uphold the Treaty of Troyes. Article 13 of the treaty contains the oath to be sworn by the "grans seigneurs, barons et nobles et les estas dudit royaume, tant spirituelz que temporelz, et aussi les citez et notables communitez, les citoiens et bourgeois des villes" [great lords, barons and nobles, and the estates of the aforesaid kingdom, both spiritual and temporal, and also the cities and communities of note, the citizens and bourgeois of the towns] (107). See Cosneau, ed., *Les grands traités de la guerre de cent ans.*

118 The names of these *poursuivants* of France and England recall some of the appellations of the real-life *poursuivants* present at the Congress of Arras, including Vray Desir, Bonne Querelle, and Il dit vrai. See Dickinson, *The Congress of Arras*, chapter 5.

119 The authoritative text on the peace talks of Arras remains Dickinson, *The Congress of Arras.* I cite here from page 177. On contemporary accounts of the Congress see Contamine, "France et Bourgogne." On the various events that paved the way for the dissolution of the Anglo-Burgundian alliance

see Armstrong, "La double monarchie France-Angleterre et la maison de Bourgogne" and Warner, "The Anglo-French Dual Monarchy and the House of Burgundy."

120 The English delegation pulled out of the talks on 6 September 1435, and France and Burgundy quickly arrived at the terms of a separate peace, which they signed on 21 September.

121 On the duke of Burgundy's ambitions see the edited volume *The Ideology of Burgundy: The Promotion of National Consciousness 1364–1565*.

122 The Dictionnaire du Moyen Français cites "dislocation (d'une communauté)" among the meanings of "separation." See http://www.atilf.fr/dmf.

123 On the question of language as a component of identity see Butterfield, *The Familiar Enemy* as well as my article "'Aucuns de ma langue.'"

124 Guenée observes that for Cicero and Isidore de Seville, a nation is defined by birth. "C'est un ensemble d'hommes qui ont une origine commune et sont liés par le sang." One of the factors that permits the identification of common origins is language. See his *L'Occident aux XIVe et XVe siècles*, 117.

125 Armstrong has discussed language use in the multilingual duchy of Burgundy. He argues that the Valois dukes employed French in their central government of the duchy, and also that they were important literary patrons. Thus, the dukes contributed, both politically and culturally, to the diffusion of French. See his "The Language Question in the Low Countries." On language use in Burgundy under the Valois dukes see also Boone, "Langue, pouvoirs et dialogue." and Wrisley, "Burgundian Ideologies and Jehan Wauquelin's Prose Translations."

126 Oresme writes: "Item, il semble que Dieu et nature ne veulent pas tele monarchie [ie, of one over all]; mes semble que il aient ordoné terre que pluseurs soient souverains princes parce que pluseurs regions sunt divisees ou separees par mers ou par grans fleuves ou palus, par forests, par desers, par montaignes, par lieuz inaccessibles ou inhabitables pourquoi les uns ne pevent converser avec les autres de tele conversation comme requise est entre gens d'un royalme ou d'une policie. Item … nature a donné a homme parole pour entendre l'un l'autre afin de communication civile. Et donques la division et diversité des langages repugne a conversation civile et a vivre de policie. Et a cest propos dit Saint Augustin ou xix livre de la Cité de Dieu que ii bestes mues de diverses especes s'acompaignent plus legierement ensemble que ne funt ii hommes dont l'un ne congnoist le langage de l'autre. Et di assés tost apres que un homme est plus volentiers ovec son chien qu'ovecques un homme de estrange langue" [Likewise, it seems that God and nature do not want such a rule {i.e., of one over

all}; it seems rather that they have ordered the land such that many might be sovereign princes, for many regions are divided or separated by seas or by great rivers or swamps, by forests, by deserts, by mountains, by inaccessible or uninhabitable places such that the ones cannot communicate with the others in the manner that is required of people of one kingdom or one polity. Likewise ... nature has given man language to understand one another and in order to carry on civic communication. And therefore the division and the diversity of languages repels civic conversation and living in a polity. And on this subject Saint Augustin says in Book 19 of the City of God that two dumb beasts of different species keep company more readily than do two men of whom one does not know the language of the other. And he says just after that a man remains more willingly with his dog than with another man of a foreign tongue], 291. Moreover, according to Oresme, "Et pour ce est ce une chose aussi comme hors nature que un homme regne sus gent qui ne entendent son maternel langage. Et est contre l'ordenance de Dieu en Deuteronomie" [And for this reason it is a thing, as it were, outside of nature that a man might reign over people who do not understand his maternal language. And it is against the commandment of God in Deuteronomy] (292). See also Krynen, "'La mort saisit le vif.'"

127 Interestingly, Latin is also depicted as a foreign, and potentially suspect, language in contrast to the truth and transparency provided by French. The first reproach of the author of the "Réponse d'un bon et loyal françois" is that the letters of the duke of Burgundy which contained what would become the clauses of the Treaty of Troyes were not promulgated in French, but in Latin. This choice, the author affirms, was intended to deceive those who do not speak Latin, including the king and queen of France and the other nobles. One of the main aims of the *Réponse* is to provide a rough translation of each of the clauses in the letter so that the French people might better understand what is at stake in the proposed agreement between Charles VI and Henry V, brokered by Philippe le bon. See "Réponse d'un bon et loyal François."

128 See E. Cosneau, *Les grands traités de la guerre de cent ans*, clause 27.

129 On the rise of the French and English vernaculars and the political implications thereof, see Lusignan, *La langue des rois au Moyen Âge*. See also Crane, "French and Anglo-Norman during the Hundred Years War" and Russell, "Language: A Barrier or a Gateway?"

130 Dickinson notes that Henry V, whether in good faith or as a strategic ploy, refused to use French in negotiations with France, but insisted upon the

use of Latin. See *The Congress of Arras*, chapter 5. On the language of diplomacy see also Lusignan, "Parler français."

131 On language use in late medieval England see Fisher, "A Language Policy for Lancastrian England" and Ormrod, "The Use of English."

132 "il bailla et delivra ledit roy Charles en la main de ses ennemis; et n'est point de si maulvaix ennemy que le familier" [he abandoned and delivered the aforesaid King Charles into the hands of his enemies, and there is no enemy so wicked as that which is intimate] (185–6).

133 Included in *L'honneur de la couronne de France: Quatre libelles contre les Anglais*.

134 This final allegation is quite remarkable, for it runs counter to the original *Lex Salica*, which referred to *hereditas*. Taylor provides an overview of the standard misogynistic arguments that appeared in connection to Salic Law in "The Salic Law, French Queenship, and the Defense of Women."

135 "ne fault ja tant me arrester sur ce point, car ladicte dame Yzabel ne vouloit pas maintenir aultrement se que dit est, mais elle vouloit maintenir que son filz Edouart par le moyen d'elle avoit droit en moy" [nor is it necessary that I linger over this point {i.e., the claim that women cannot rule}, for the aforesaid lady Isabel did not wish to maintain anything contrary to what is said, but she wished to affirm that her son Edward, by means of her, had a right to me] (160–1).

136 On this point I disagree with Curry, who argues that the Treaty of Troyes ended Salic Law in France at the time of the treaty, and retrospectively. See her article "Two Kingdoms, One King."

137 Jean Juvénal also employs the expression "monstre en nature" to refer to the murder of Richard II (2: 152).

138 The powers accorded to the papal and conciliar legates present at the Congress of Arras included the power to release people (e.g., Philippe le bon) from oaths that were deemed detrimental to peace and thus to salvation. Philippe's numerous counsellors provided the moral, economic, chivalric, and political arguments for and against peace with France. See Dickinson, *The Congress of Arras* as well as Izbicki, "The Canonists and the Treaty of Troyes."

139 See Giesey, "The Juristic Basis" and *Le rôle méconnu*. On the importance of blood see also de Miramon, "Aux origines de la noblesse et des princes du sang."

140 It is noteworthy that even modern scholars such as Keen subscribe to the notion that political loyalties are somehow natural. In the article "Diplomacy" in *Henry V: The Practice of Kingship* Keen opines that even if

Henry V had lived, his chances of long-term success were slim because the Anglo-Burgundian alliance was itself unnatural.

141 Bon conseil refers to Job 18, in which Job is said to be turned out of his tabernacle.

142 The "Réponse d'un bon et loyal françois" expresses the repugnance of many to the terms of the Treaty of Troyes, characterized as "un tel desraisonnable, tres deshonneste et desnaturel traictié" [so unreasonable, so dishonest, and so unnatural a treaty] (124) because it sunders the bonds of parents and children, in opposition to the most fundamental principles of natural love, and of reason. See also Oresme with regard to natural love.

143 On the ordinances of Charles V see Autrand, "La succession à la couronne de France."

144 The ordinance of April 1403 (8: 581) states that "La disposicion et introduccion *de droit divin et naturel* démontre que les Peres doivent labourer et traveiller à ce que leurs enfans, après leur décès, usent paisiblement de leur succession" [the organization and introduction *of divine and natural law* shows that fathers should labour and work so that their children, after their death, might peacefully enjoy their succession] and that "sitost qu'il plaist à Dieu envoier sur terre au Roy qui est pour le temps, hoir masle premier nez, *droit de nature* le baille héritier dudit Royaume" [as soon as it pleases God to send to earth to he who is king at that time, a first-born male heir, the *law of nature* makes him the heir of the aforesaid kingdom] (emphasis added). As soon as the king dies his eldest son is to be crowned and called king "sanz ce qu'il puist estre donné à nostre dit ainsné Filz en son droit qui lui est deu par *droit de nature*, aucun empeschement soubz umbre de Régence ou Gouvernement de nostredit Royaume." [without it being necessary that our aforesaid eldest son be established in his right, which is due to him by the *law of nature*, without any opposition in the guise of a regency or government of our aforesaid kingdom]. The ordinance of 26 December 1407 repeats in similar terms the provisions of the previous ordinance, but broadens its scope by regulating the principles of succession for all future kings. The language includes references to the kings Charles's successors, and their sons the dauphin's successors. Charles VI sought to ensure that the documentation that was so wanting in 1328 would not pose a problem for his successors, for he has "ordonné et decerné, ordonnons, decernons et declairons, et par maniere de Loy, Edict, Constitucion et Ordonnance perpetueles et irrevocables" [ordered and decreed, we order and we decree and we declare, and in the form of a law, edict, constitution, and perpetual and irrevocable ordinance] (12: 267).

145 See chapter 3.

146 The "Réponse d'un bon et loyal françois" remarks, "quelles obligacions de juremens et de feauté lige ledit Henry d'Angleterre veult et requiert des maintenant de tous ceulx du royaume, trop plus que le roy n'a accoustumé de recevoir ou requerir" [what demands for oaths and for liege fidelity the aforesaid Henry of England wants and requires immediately from all those of the kingdom, many more than the king is accustomed to receive or to require] (130).
147 Keen has astutely observed, using the very apt medieval metaphor of the game of chess, that in diplomatic negotiations "the moves, and especially the taking of pieces, must follow the rules: they must be made to *look* right, and whether justifiable or not must be made to look justifiable to reasonably independent onlookers." See "Diplomacy," 182.
148 The Flemish circumvented their oath to the French king in 1340. See also Dickinson's discussion of the papal and conciliar legates.
149 See Meron, "The Authority to Make Treaties in the Late Middle Ages," 12.
150 Jean de Montreuil, *À toute la chevalerie*, in *Opera*, 2: 131.

Coda: What to Say about Joan of Arc?

1 There are countless biographies of Joan of Arc. For a helpful short overview of her life, trial, and re-trial see Taylor, "Introduction," in *Joan of Arc, La Pucelle*. On her afterlife, see Winock, "Jeanne d'Arc."
2 Some modern scholarship has latched onto later rumours that Isabeau de Bavière had had an adulterous affair and that Charles VII may have been illegitimate. Taylor notes that the "first suggestion of such an affair had appeared in *Le Pastoralet*, a Burgundian pamphlet that was probably written between 1422 and 1425, but this claim does not appear to have been taken seriously at this time by either the French or the English. It was never referred to during the drafting of the Treaty of Troyes or in any of the pamphlets and tracts written either for or against it." See his "Introduction," 12.
3 I shall not address the many stories that circulate concerning Joan's (miraculous?) recognition of the king at Chinon.
4 See Fraioli, *Joan of Arc, the Early Debate*.
5 Some in Charles's entourage wished to pursue a diplomatic solution rather than a military one at this juncture. The delay and internal discord may have contributed to Joan's failure to take Paris. See Lutkus and Walker, "The Political Poetics of the *Ditié de Jehanne d'Arc*."
6 In close succession she composed an autobiographical dream vision, the *Chemin de long estude* (1402) and a vast historical and autobiographical

poem, the *Mutacion de Fortune* (1403). The latter earned her a commission from Philippe, duke of Burgundy, for the *Livre des fais et bonnes meurs du sage roy Charles V*, completed in 1404. The year 1405 witnessed the composition of the *Livre de l'advision Cristine*, as well as the *Livre des trois vertus*, a moral guide for women, and Christine's now-famous defence of women, the *Livre de la cité des dames*.

7 All citations are from *Ditié de Jehanne d'Arc*, ed. Kennedy and Varty. Translations are my own.

8 One can only hope that Christine's own death spared her such a demoralizing spectacle. The exact date of Christine's decease is not known, but may be situated before 1434, in which year the Burgundian courtier Guillebert de Mets referred to her in the past tense. See Willard, *Christine de Pizan*, 207. Lutkus and Walker have argued that the *Ditié* was in fact composed later than 31 July, more likely mid- to late August or even September of 1429, and was predated in order to give greater prophetic force to Christine's text. See "The Political Poetics of the *Ditié de Jehanne d'Arc*." Cornford also subscribes to this argument. See "Christine de Pizan's *Ditié de Jehanne d'Arc*."

9 See Kennedy and Varty, "Introduction," *Ditié de Jehanne d'Arc*.

10 Christine refers to the prophecies of "Merlin et Sebile et Bede" [Merlin and the sybil and Bede] (v. 241), which supposedly predicted Joan's coming. See Arden, "Christine de Pizan's *Ditié de Jehanne d'Arc*."

11 Indeed, Lutkus and Walker argue that Christine's purpose in writing this text was to convince Charles to embrace Joan's goal of retaking Paris by force, and that Christine is subtly critical of him here.

12 Crane discusses Christine's positive representation of Joan's adoption of both masculine and feminine practices and traits. See her "Clothing and Gender Definition: Joan of Arc."

13 Chartier's letter is reproduced in Alain Chartier, *Les œuvres latines*, ed. Bourgain-Hemeryck. The translations are those of Taylor, from *Joan of Arc, La Pucelle*.

14 Chartier cites Vaucouleurs as Joan's "patriam"; he does not mention Domrémy.

15 Joan will later identify one of her voices as that of St Catherine.

16 We can observe a similar wonder at Joan's speech in the *Chronique de la Pucelle, ou Chronique de Cousinot*, ed. M. Vallet de Viriville. The theologians assembled at Poitiers "estoient grandement esbahis, comme une si simple bergère, jeune fille, pouvoit ainsi prudemment respondre" [were greatly stupefied, when so simple a shepherdess, a young girl, could respond so prudently] (275). Joan surpasses the expectations for both her class and her sex.

17 On the ways in which Joan's own voice is silenced, translated, and transformed see Meltzer, *For Fear of the Fire*, in particular the introduction and chapter 4, "*Responsio Mortifera*: The Voice of the Maid." Butterfield similarly explores "how a life emerges from written sources that seek to suppress or distort that life. Moreover it is in that process of suppression or distortion that the life becomes a means, for those writers, of expressing other kinds of individual and political allegiance." See "Converting Jeanne d'Arc," 68.

18 They are hardly alone in this endeavour, as the dozens of surviving documents surrounding Joan's life and trials make amply clear. See Taylor's source book for a sampling of this material.

19 On Gerson's views on discernment see Anderson, *Free Spirits, Presumptuous Women, and False Prophets*, Blumenfeld-Kosinski, "The Strange Case of Ermine de Reims," Elliott, "Seeing Double," Fogleman, "The Remedies of Hippocrates or Divine Counsel?" Fraioli, *Joan of Arc, the Early Debate* and "Gerson Judging Women of Spirit," and Hobbins, "Jean Gerson's Authentic Tract on Joan of Arc."

20 See Anderson, *Free Spirits, Presumptuous Women, and False Prophets*, 274.

21 On late medieval visionary culture more generally, see chapter 4.

22 See Hobbins, "Jean Gerson's Authentic Tract on Joan of Arc." The article also includes an edition of *Super facto*. On the connections between the views articulated in *Super facto* and Gerson's other works, see also Mazour-Matusevich, "A Reconsideration of Jean Gerson's Attitude toward Joan of Arc" and McGuire, "Jean Gerson, the Shulammite, and the Maid."

23 I cite from Hobbins's edition, 147.

24 Hobbins, "Jean Gerson's Authentic Tract on Joan of Arc, " 118–19.

25 See chapter 4 for my anaylsis of this work.

26 As Taylor notes, Jean Juvénal also avoids mentioning Joan in a letter composed in 1433 to the Estates General, and in a treatise written in 1446. See *Joan of Arc*, 242 n. 24.

27 "souvent Dieu punist les gens pecheurs par pires pecheurs que eulx, et les bons mesmes sont affligés par les maulvaix" [often God punishes sinners by even worse sinners than they, and even good ones are afflicted by the wicked] (196).

28 An allusion to the Burgundian takeover of Paris, which was followed by massacres of the so-called Armagnacs. The family of Jean Juvénal was also fortunate to escape the city at this time.

29 Which occurred 22 March 1421 and 26 September 1423, respectively.

30 5 September 1427.

31 The English withdrew from Orléans on 8 May 1429.

32 Charles was crowned at Rheims on 17 July 1429.

33 Quicherat writes, "Il semble qu'alors, pour accorder ceux qui la réputaient sainte et ceux qui ne voulaient pas quelle fût telle, on imposa silence sur sa mémoire. L'absence de son nom dans des écrits où elle ne s'explique pas, me conduit à cette conjecture." One of the two texts cited by Quicherat as an example of a textual setting in which Joan's absence is inexplicable is a letter by none other than Jean Juvénal des Ursins to the three Estates when they met at Blois in 1433. *Aperçus nouveaux sur l'histoire de Jeanne d'Arc*, 156.

34 Indeed, Joan seems to have emasculated those who beheld her. In the *Chronique de la Pucelle* we read that initially Robert de Baudricourt thought that Joan "seroit bonne pour ses gens, à esbattre en pesché; et y eu aucuns qui avoient volonté d'y essayer; mais aussi tost qu'ils la voyoient, ils estoient refroidis et ne leur en prenoit volonté" [would be good for his men, to amuse themselves in sin, and there were some who wished to try, but as soon as they saw her, they were chilled and they had no desire] (272). One can find many similar such remarks, especially in the documents of the nullification trial. McInerney has remarked that Joan "posed, in her very person, a threat to all the hierarchies of gender, of class, of religion which upheld the political systems of the late Middle Ages." See *Eloquent Virgins*, 211.

35 On the power and connotations of virginity generally see Brown, "The Notion of Virginity in the Early Church," Bugge, *Virginitas*, Beard, "The Sexual Status of Vestal Virgins," and Bynum, *Fragmentation and Redemption*. On the significance of Joan's virginity see McInerney, *Eloquent Virgins from Thecla to Joan of Arc*, Meltzer, *For Fear of the Fire*, and Warner, *Joan of Arc*.

36 Joan testified during her trial that she had defied her parents by refusing marriage. Thus, while Joan did not preclude the possibility that she might marry and bear children, her assumption of these roles was deferred to an undefined point in the future.

37 See Warner's discussion of the term "pucelle" in chapter 1 of *Joan of Arc*. McInerney further notes that the term "pucelle" had distinct hagiographic connotations, and also that the saints Joan eventually identified with her voices – Margaret of Antioch and Catherine of Alexandria – were both virgin martyrs. See *Eloquent Virgins*, 199.

38 Beard locates the sacredness of vestal virgins in their capacity to inhabit multiple and mutually exclusive categories, such as virgin and matron. She asserts that interstitial creatures or things are "particularly powerful, sacred or dangerous." See "The Sexual Status of Vestal Virgins," 20.

39 Crane has suggested that Joan embraced the role of knight only partially or imperfectly, thereby highlighting her own combined masculinity and femininity. See "Clothing and Gender Definition: Joan of Arc."

40 In this respect Joan departs from the tradition of medieval cross-dressing saints, who "passed" effectively for men. See Castelli, "'I Will Make Mary Male.'"

41 Schibanoff, "True Lies: Transvestism and Idolatry in the Trial of Joan of Arc," 47.

42 On the idol see Camille, *The Gothic Idol.*

43 Butler, "Performative Acts and Gender Constitution," 527.

44 See chapter 1 on the both/and-ness of metaphor.

45 Butler, "Performative Acts and Gender Constitution," 528.

46 Cynthia Brown argues that Joan was allegorized by her contemporaries. See "Allegorical Design and Image-Making in Fifteenth-Century France." This may be the case, but Brown does not account for the profound ambiguity of Joan as an allegorical figure. If, as Brown suggests, Joan's trial was a kind of morality play or psychomachia, who occupied the roles of the virtues, and who the vices?

47 As Meltzer has observed, "For patriarchy to mark its sovereignty as subject … it must posit an other that has just as consistently been feminine." See *For Fear of the Fire*, 6.

48 While the term "vierge" might be applied to either sex, "pucelle" was specifically feminine.

49 This gesture echoes the repeated examinations of Joan's body at Chinon and Poitiers to determine not only whether she was a virgin, but also whether she was a woman. See the testimony of Jean Pasquerel in the *Procès en nullité de la condamnation de Jeanne d'Arc*, 1: 389.

Bibliography

Primary Sources

Alain Chartier. "Epistola de puella." In *Joan of Arc. La Pucelle, Selected Sources.* Trans. Craig Taylor. Manchester and New York: Manchester University Press, 2006. 108–12.

– *Les œuvres latines d'Alain Chartier*. Ed. Pascale Bourgain-Hemeryck. Paris: Éditions du centre national de la recherche scientifique, 1977.

– *The Poetical Works of Alain Chartier*. Ed. James Laidlaw. Cambridge: Cambridge University Press, 1974.

– *Le quadrilogue invectif*. Trans. Florence Bouchet. Paris: Champion, 2002.

– *Le quadrilogue invectif*. Ed. Florence Bouchet. Paris: Champion, 2011.

Alain de Lille. *Plaint of Nature*. Trans. James Sheridan. Toronto: Pontifical Institute of Mediaeval Studies, 1980.

Aquinas, Thomas. *S. Thomae Aquinatis in Metaphysicam Aristotelis Commentaria.* Ed. M.-R. Cathala. Turin: Libraria Marietti, 1926.

Aristotle. *Poetics*. Trans. Malcolm Heath. New York: Penguin, 1996.

Augustine. *The Literal Meaning of Genesis*. Trans. John Hammond Taylor. New York: Newman Press, 1982.

– *On Christian Teaching*. Trans. R.P.H. Green. Oxford and New York: Oxford University Press, 2008.

Cassian, John. *Conferences*. Trans. Colm Luibheid. New York: Paulist Press, 1985.

Le Charroi de Nîmes. Chanson de geste du XIIe siècle. Ed. Duncan McMillan. Paris: Éditions Klincksieck, 1978.

Chartularium Universitatis Parisiensis. Ed. Heinrich Denifle and Émile Châtelain. Vol. 3. Paris, 1894.

Christine de Pizan. *Ditié de Jehanne d'Arc.* Ed. Angus Kennedy and Kenneth Varty. Oxford: Society for the Study of Medieval Languages and Literature, 1977.

– *Le livre de l'advision Cristine*. Ed. Christine Reno and Liliane Dulac. Paris: Champion, 2001.
– *Le livre des trois vertus*. Ed. Charity Cannon Willard. Paris: Champion, 1989.
Christine de Pizan, Jean Gerson, Jean de Montreuil, and Gontier and Pierre Col. *Le débat sur Le Roman de la Rose*. Ed. and trans. Eric Hicks. Paris: Champion, 1977.
Dante Alighieri. *Il convivio*. Ed. Maria Simonelli. Bologna: Casa Editrice Prof. Riccardo Patron, 1966.
– *Dantis Alagherii Epistolae. The Letters of Dante*. Ed. Paget Toynbee. Oxford: Clarendon Press, 1966.
– *The Divine Comedy of Dante Alighieri*. Ed. and trans. Robert Durling. Vol. 1, *Inferno*. New York and Oxford: Oxford University Press, 1996.
Debating the Hundred Years War: Pour ce que plusieurs (La loy salicque) and A Declaracion of the trew and dewe title of Henry VIII. Ed. Craig Taylor. Cambridge: Cambridge University Press, 2006.
Denis Foulechat. *Le Policratique de Jean de Salisbury (Livre V). Édition critique et commentée des textes français et latin*. Ed. Charles Brucker. Geneva: Droz, 2006.
Eustache Deschamps. *L'art de dictier*. Ed. and trans. Deborah Sinnreich-Levi. Michigan: Colleagues Press, 1994.
– *Eustache Deschamps: Selected Poems*. Ed. Ian S. Laurie and Deborah Sinnreich-Levi. Trans. David Curzon and Jeffrey Fiskin. New York: Routledge, 2003.
– *Eustache Deschamps et son temps*. Ed. Jean-Patrice Boudet and Hélène Millet. Paris: Publications de la Sorbonne, 1997.
– *Œuvres complètes d'Eustache Deschamps*. Ed. A.H.E. Marquis de Queux de Saint Hilaire and Gaston Raynaud. 11 vols. Paris: Société des Anciens Textes Français, 1878–1903.
Giles of Rome. *"Li Livres du gouvernement des rois": A XIIIth Century French Version of Egidio Colonna's Treatise De Regimine Principum Now First Published from the Kerr ms*. Ed. Samuel Paul Molenar. New York: AMS Press, 1966.
Grandes chroniques de France. Ed. Jules Viard. 10 vols. Paris: Société de l'Histoire de France, 1920–53.
Guillaume Cousinot. *Chronique de la Pucelle, ou Chronique de Cousinot*. Ed. M. Vallet de Viriville. Paris: Delahays, 1859.
Guillaume de Lorris and Jean de Meun. *The Romance of the Rose, by Guillaume de Lorris and Jean de Meun*. Trans. Charles Dahlberg. Hanover, NH: University Press of New England, 1983.
– *Le Roman de la Rose*. Ed. Armand Strubel. Paris: Lettres gothiques, 1992.
L'honneur de la couronne de France: Quatre libelles contre les Anglais (vers 1418–vers 1429). Ed. Nicole Pons. Paris: Klincksieck, 1990.

Hugh of Saint Victor. *Didascalicon. A Medieval Guide to the Arts*. Trans. Jerome Taylor. New York: Columbia University Press, 1961.

Isidore of Seville. *Etimologie o Origini di Isidoro di Siviglia*. Ed. Angelo Valastro Canale. Vol. 1, books 1–11. Turin: Unione Tipografico, 2004.

– *The Etymologies of Isidore of Seville*. Trans. Stephen Barney. Cambridge: Cambridge University Press, 2006.

Jean Gerson. *Œuvres complètes*. Ed. M. Glorieux. 10 vols. Paris: Desclée et Cie, 1960–73.

Jean Juvénal des Ursins. *Écrits politiques de Jean Juvénal des Ursins*. Ed. P.S. Lewis. 3 vols. Paris: Klincksieck, 1992.

Jean de Montreuil. *Opera*. Vol. 2: *L'œuvre historique et polémique*. Ed. Nicole Grévy, Ezio Ornato, and Gilbert Ouy. Turin: Giappichelli, 1975.

Les grands traités de la guerre de cent ans. Ed. E. Cosneau. Paris: Picard, 1889.

Macrobius. *Commentary on the Dream of Scipio*. Trans. William Harris Stahl. New York: Columbia University Press, 1990.

Nicole Oresme. Commentaire de Nicole Oresme sur *Le livre de politiques d'Aristote. By Maistre Nicole Oresme*. Ed. Albert Menut. Transactions of the American Philosophical Society, n.s. vol. 60, part 6. Philadelphia, 1970.

– *Traictie de la première invention des monnoies de Nicole Oresme*. Ed. M.L. Wolowski. Paris: Librairie de Guillaumin et Cie, 1864.

L'ordonnance cabochienne 1413. Ed. Nathalie Desgrugillers-Billard. Clermont-Ferrand: Paleo, 2008.

Ordonnances des roys de France de la troisième race, recueillies par ordre chronologique. Paris: Imprimerie royale, 1723–1849.

Origen. *Commentary on the Gospel according to John Books 1–10*. Trans. Ronald Heine. Washington, DC, 1989.

– *The Song of Songs Commentary and Homilies*. Trans. and annotated by R.P. Lawson. London: Longmans, Green, and Co., 1957.

Philippe de Mézières. *Le songe du vieil pelerin*. Ed. G.W. Coopland. 2 vols. Cambridge: Cambridge University Press, 1969.

– *Songe du vieux pèlerin*. Trans. Joël Blanchard. Paris: Pocket, 2008.

Procès en nullité de la condamnation de Jeanne d'Arc. Ed. Pierre Duparc. 5 vols. Paris: Klincksieck, 1977–88.

Prudentius. *The Psychomachia of Prudentius*. Trans. Mary Louise Porter. Raleigh, NC: Meredith College, 1929.

Quatre libelles contre les Anglais (vers 1418–1429). Ed. Nicole Pons. Paris: Klincksieck, 1990.

"Réponse d'un bon et loyal françois." in *Quatre libelles contre les Anglais (vers 1418–vers 1429)*. Ed. Nicole Pons. Paris: Klincksieck, 1990.

Secondary Sources

Adams, Tracy. "Christine de Pizan, Isabeau of Bavaria, and Female Regency." *French Historical Studies* 32.1 (2009): 1–32.

– *The Life and Afterlife of Isabeau of Bavaria*. Baltimore: Johns Hopkins University Press, 2010.

Akbari, Suzanne Conklin. *Seeing through the Veil. Optical Theory and Medieval Allegory*. Toronto: University of Toronto Press, 2004.

Allirot, Anne-Hélène. *Filles de roy de France: Princesses royales, mémoire de saint Louis et conscience dynastique (de 1270 à la fin du XIVe siècle)*. Turnhout: Brepols, 2010.

Altmann, Barbara. "Alain Chartier's *Livre des Quatre Dames* and the Mechanics of Allegory." *Chartier in Europe*. Ed. Emma Cayley and Ashby Kinch. Woodbridge: Brewer, 2008. 61–72.

Anderson, Wendy Love. *Free Spirits, Presumptuous Women, and False Prophets: The Discernment of Spirits in the Late Middle Ages*. Unpublished doctoral dissertation, University of Chicago Divinity School, 2002.

Arden, Heather. "Christine de Pizan's *Ditié de Jehanne d'Arc*: History, Feminism, and God's Grace." In *Joan of Arc and Spirituality*. Ed. Ann W. Astell and Bonnie Wheeler. New York: Palgrave, 2003. 195–208.

– "Her Mother's Daughter: Empowerment and Maternity in the Works of Christine de Pizan." In *Contexts and Continuities: Proceedings of the IVth International Colloquium on Christine de Pizan, published in honour of Liliane Dulac*. Ed. Angus Kennedy, Rosalind Brown-Grant, James Laidlaw, and Catherine Müller. Vol. 1. Glasgow: University of Glasgow Press, 2002. 31–42.

Armstrong, C.A.J. "La double monarchie France-Angleterre et la maison de Bourgogne (1420–1435). Le déclin d'une alliance." In *England, France and Burgundy in the Fifteenth Century*. London: The Hambledon Press, 1983. 343–74.

– "The Language Question in the Low Countries: The Use of French and Dutch by the Dukes of Burgundy and Their Administration." In *England, France and Burgundy in the Fifteenth Century*. London: The Hambledon Press, 1983. 189–212.

Ascoli, Albert. "Dante and Allegory." In *The Cambridge Companion to Allegory*. Ed. Rita Copeland and Peter Struck. Cambridge: Cambridge University Press, 2010. 128–35.

Astell, Ann. *Political Allegory in Late Medieval England*. Ithaca and London: Cornell University Press, 1999.

Auerbach, Erich. "Figura." In *Scenes from the Drama of European Literature* (Theory and History of Literature, 9; Minneapolis: University of Minnesota Press, 1984): 11–76.

Autrand, Françoise. *Charles VI: La folie du roi*. Paris: Fayard, 1986.

– "La succession à la couronne de France et les ordonnances de 1374." In *Représentation, pouvoir et royauté à la fin du Moyen Âge*. Ed. Joël Blanchard. Paris: Picard, 1995. 25–32.

Badel, Pierre-Yves. *Le Roman de la rose au XIVe siècle: Étude de la réception de l'œuvre*. Genève: Droz, 1980.

Barney, Stephen. *Allegories of History, Allegories of Love*. Hamden, CT: Archon Books, 1979.

Baskins, Cristelle. "Shaping Civic Personification: *Pisa Sforzata, Pisa Salvata*." In *Early Modern Visual Allegory: Embodying Meaning*. Ed. Cristelle Baskins and Lisa Rosenthal. Aldershot: Ashgate, 2007. 91–108.

Bäuml, Franz. *Medieval Civilization in Germany, 800–1273*. New York: Frederic Praeger, 1969.

Beard, Mary. "The Sexual Status of Vestal Virgins." *Journal of Roman Studies* 70 (1980): 12–27.

Beardsley, Monroe. *Aesthetics: Problems in the Philosophy of Criticism*. New York: Harcourt, 1958.

Beaune, Colette. *Naissance de la nation France*. Paris: Gallimard, 1985.

Bellitto, Christopher. "The Early Development of Pierre d'Ailly's Conciliarism." *Catholic Historical Review* 83.2 (1997): 217–32.

Benjamin, Walter. *The Origin of German Tragic Drama*. Trans. John Osborne. London: NLB, 1977.

Berlant, Lauren. *The Anatomy of National Fantasy: Hawthorne, Utopia, and Everyday Life*. Chicago and London: University of Chicago Press, 1991.

Birk, Bonnie. *Christine de Pizan and Biblical Wisdom: A Feminist-Theological Point of View*. Milwaukee, WI: Marquette University Press, 2005.

Bernstein, Alan. *Pierre d'Ailly and the Blanchard Affair: University and Chancellor of Paris at the Beginning of the Great Schism*. Leiden: Brill, 1978.

Black, Max. *Models and Metaphors: Studies in Language and Philosophy*. Ithaca: Cornell University Press, 1962.

Blamires, Alcuin. *The Case for Women in Medieval Culture*. Oxford: Clarendon Press, 1997.

– "Paradox in the Medieval Gender Doctrine of Head and Body." In *Medieval Theology and the Natural Body*. Ed. Peter Biller. York: York Medieval Press, 1997. 13–29.

Bliggenstorfer, Susanna. "Les ballades dialoguées d'Eustache Deschamps." In *Autour d'Eustache Deschamps*. Ed. Danielle Buschinger. Amiens: Presses du Centre d'Études Médiévales, 1999. 15–26.

– *Eustache Deschamps: Aspects poétiques et satiriques*. Tübingen: Verlag, 2005.

Bloomfield, Morton. "Allegory as Interpretation." *New Literary History* 3.2 (1972): 301–17.

– "A Grammatical Approach to Personification Allegory." *Modern Philology* 60.3 (1963): 161–71.

Blumenfeld-Kosinski, Renate. "Dramatic Troubles of Ecclesia: Gendered Performances of the Divided Church." In *Cultural Performances in Medieval France*. Ed. Eglal Doss-Quinby, Roberta Krueger, and E. Jane Burns. Cambridge: Brewer, 2007. 181–93.

– "'Enemies Within/Enemies Without': Threats to the Body Politic in Christine de Pizan." *Medievalia et Humanistica* 26 (1999): 1–15.

– "Jean Gerson and the Debate on the *Romance of the Rose*." In *A Companion to Jean Gerson*. Ed. Brian Patrick McGuire. Leiden and Boston: Brill, 2006. 317–56.

– *Poets, Saints, and Visionaries of the Great Schism, 1378–1417*. University Park: Pennsylvania State Press, 2006.

– "Raymond de Sabanac, Preface to Constance de Rabastens, *The Revelations*." In *Medieval Christianity in Practice*. Ed. Miri Rubin. Princeton: Princeton University Press, 2009. 290–5.

– "The Strange Case of Ermine de Reims (c. 1347–1396): A Medieval Woman between Demons and Saints." *Speculum* 85.2 (April 2010): 321–56.

Blythe, James. "Family, Government, and the Medieval Aristotelians." *History of Political Thought* 10 (1989): 1–16.

Bonnafoux, Emmanuelle. "L'animal miroir de l'homme dans la 'Fiction du lyon' d'Eustache Deschamps." Unpublished doctoral dissertation, University of Chicago, 2012.

Boone, Marc. "Langue, pouvoirs et dialogue: Aspects linguistiques de la communication entre les ducs de Bourgogne et leurs sujets flamands (1385–1505)." *Revue du Nord* 91 (2009): 9–32.

Bose, Mishtooni. "Jean Gerson, Poet." In *Poetry, Knowledge and Community in Late Medieval France*. Ed. Rebecca Dixon and Finn Sinclair, with Adrian Armstrong, Sylvia Huot, and Sarah Kay. Cambridge: Brewer, 2008. 56–68.

Bouchard, Constance Brittain. *"Those of My Blood." Constructing Noble Families in Medieval Francia*. Philadelphia: University of Pennsylvania Press, 2001.

Bouchet, Florence. "L'écrivain et son lecteur dans le prologue et l'épilogue du *Quadrilogue invectif* d'Alain Chartier." *Bien dire et bien aprandre: Bulletin du Centre d'études médiévales et dialectales de l'Université de Lille* III 19 (2001): 19–29.

– "L'intertexte oublié: Ronsard et Chartier." *Nouvelle Revue du XVIe siècle* 17.2 (1999): 205–17.

– "Introduction." *Le Quadrilogue invectif*. Trans. Florence Bouchet. Paris: Champion, 2002. 7–40.

– "'Vox Dei, vox poetae': The Bible in the *Quadrilogue invectif.*" In *Chartier in Europe*. Ed. Emma Cayley and Ashby Kinch. Woodbridge: Brewer, 2008. 31–44.

Bourdieu, Pierre. "Structures, Habitus, Power: Basis for a Theory of Symbolic Power." In *Culture/Power/History: A Reader in Contemporary Social Theory*. Ed. Nicholas Dirks, Geoff Eley, and Sherry Ortner. Princeton, NJ: Princeton University Press, 1994. 155–99.

Boyarin, Daniel. "Origen as Theorist of Allegory: Alexandrian Contexts." In *The Cambridge Companion to Allegory*. Ed. Rita Copeland and Peter Struck. Cambridge: Cambridge University Press, 2010. 39–56.

Briggs, Charles. *Giles of Rome's "De regimine principum": Reading and Writing Politics at Court and University, c. 1275–1525.* Cambridge: Cambridge University Press, 1999.

Briguglia, Gianluca. *Il corpo vivente dello stato: Una metafora politica.* Milan: Bruno Mondadori, 2006.

Brose, Margaret. "Petrarch's Beloved Body: 'Italia mia.'" In *Feminist Approaches to the Body in Medieval Literature*. Ed. Linda Lomperis and Sarah Stanbury. Philadelphia: University of Pennsylvania Press, 1993. 1–20.

Brown, Catherine D. *Pastor and Laity in the Theology of Jean Gerson.* Cambridge: Cambridge University Press, 1987.

Brown, Cynthia. "Allegorical Design and Image-Making in Fifteenth-Century France: Alain Chartier's Joan of Arc." *French Studies: A Quarterly Review* 53. 4 (1999): 385–404.

Brown, Elizabeth A.R. "Ritual Brotherhood in Western Medieval Europe." *Traditio, special issue, Ritual Brotherhood in Ancient and Medieval Europe: A Symposium* 52 (1997): 357–81.

Brown, Peter. "The Notion of Virginity in the Early Church." In *Christian Spirituality: Origins to the Twelfth Century*. Ed. Bernard McGinn, John Meyendorff, and Jean Leclercq. New York: Crossroad, 1985. 427–43.

Brown-Grant, Rosalind. "*L'Avision Christine*: Autobiographical Narrative or Mirror for the Prince?" *Politics, Gender, and Genre. The Political Thought of Christine de Pizan*. Ed. Margaret Brabant. Boulder, CO: Westview Press, 1992. 95–112.

Brownlee, Kevin. "Discourses of the Self: Christine de Pizan and the *Romance of the Rose*." *Rethinking the Romance of the Rose: Text, Image, Reception*. Ed. Kevin Brownlee and Sylvia Huot. Philadelphia: University of Pennsylvania Press, 1992. 234–61.

– "Literary Genealogy and the Problem of the Father: Christine de Pizan and Dante." *Journal of Medieval and Renaissance Studies* 23.3 (1993): 365–87.

Brühl, Carlrichard. *Naissance de deux peuples: "Français" et "Allmands" IXe–XIe siècle*. Trans. Gaston Duchet-Suchaux. Paris: Fayard, 1994.

Bugge, John. *Virginitas: An Essay in the History of a Medieval Ideal*. The Hague: Martinus Nijhoff, 1975.

Burger, Christoph. "Preaching for Members of the University in Latin, for Parishioners in French: Jean Gerson (1363–1429) on 'Blessed are they that mourn.'" In *Constructing the Medieval Sermon*. Ed. Roger Andersson. Turnhout: Brepols, 2007. 207–20.

Butler, Judith. "Performative Acts and Gender Constitution: An Essay in Phenomenology and Feminist Theory." *Theatre Journal* 40.4 (1988): 519–31.

Butterfield, Ardis. "Converting Jeanne d'Arc: Trahison and Nation in the Hundred Years' War." *New Medieval Literatures* 8 (2006): 67–97.

– *The Familiar Enemy: Chaucer, Language and Nation in the Hundred Years War*. Oxford: Oxford University Press, 2009.

Bynum, Caroline Walker. *Fragmentation and Redemption: Essays in Gender and the Human Body in Medieval Religion*. New York: Zone Books, 1991.

– *Jesus as Mother: Studies in the Spirituality of the High Middle Ages*. Berkeley: University of California Press, 1982.

The Cambridge Companion to Allegory. Ed. Rita Copeland and Peter Struck. Cambridge: Cambridge University Press, 2010.

Camille, Michael. *The Gothic Idol: Ideology and Image-Making in Medieval Art*. Cambridge: Cambridge University Press, 1989.

– "The Image and the Self: Unwriting Late Medieval Bodies." In *Framing Medieval Bodies*. Ed. Sarah Kay and Miri Rubin. Manchester and New York: Manchester University Press, 1994. 62–99.

– "The King's New Bodies: An Illustrated Mirror for Princes in the Morgan Library." In *Künstlerischer Austausch. Artistic Exchange*. Ed. Thomas W. Gaehtgens. 3 vols. Berlin: Akademie Verlag, 1993. 393–405.

Carnes, Paula Mae. "Cutting a Fine Figure: Costume on French Gothic Ivories." In *Medieval Clothing and Textiles*. Ed. Robin Netherton and Gale Owen Crocker. Woodbridge: Boydell Press, 2009. Vol. 5: 55–92.

Castelli, Elizabeth. "'I Will Make Mary Male': Pieties of the Body and Gender Transformation of Christian Women in Late Antiquity." In *Body Guards: The Cultural Politics of Gender Ambiguity*. Ed. Julia Epstein and Kristina Straub. New York: Routledge, 1991.

Cayley, Emma. *Debate and Dialogue: Alain Chartier in His Cultural Context*. Oxford: Clarendon Press, 2006.

Cheyette, Fredric. *Ermengarde of Narbonne and the World of the Troubadours*. Ithaca: Cornell University Press, 2001.

Coakley, John. *Women, Men, and Spiritual Power: Female Saints and Their Male Collaborators*. New York: Columbia University Press, 2006.

Combes, A. *Jean Gerson, commentateur dionysien: Pour l'histoire des courants doctrinaux à l'Université de Paris à la fin du XIVe siècle*. Paris, 1973.

Contamine, Philippe. "France et Bourgogne, l'historiographie du XVe et la paix d'Arras (1435)." In *Arras et la diplomatie européenne, XVe–XVIe siècles*. Ed. Denis Clauzel, Charles Giry-Deloison, and Christophe Leduc. Artois: Artois Presses Universitaires, 1999. 81–100.

– "Mourir pour la patrie. Xe–XXe siècle." In *Les lieux de mémoire*. 3 vols. Ed. Pierre Nora. Vol. 2, "La Nation," book 3. Paris: Gallimard, 1986. 11–43.

– "'Le Royaume de France ne peut tomber en fille': Fondement, formulation et implication d'une théorie politique à la fin du Moyen-Âge." *Perspectives Médiévales* (June 1987): 67–81.

Copeland, Rita, and Stephen Melville. "Allegory and Allegoresis." *Exemplaria* 3.1 (1991): 159–87.

Copeland, Rita, and Peter Struck. "Introduction." In *The Cambridge Companion to Allegory*. Cambridge: Cambridge University Press, 2010. 1–11.

Corbellari, Alain. "À la place du mort: Une lecture politique de *La Belle Dame sans mercy*." *Le Moyen Français* 64 (2009): 55–66.

Cornford, Benjamin. "Christine de Pizan's *Ditié de Jehanne d'Arc*: Poetry and Propaganda at the Court of Charles VII." *Parergon* 17.2 (Jan 2000): 75–106.

Cosandey, Fanny. *La reine de France: Symbole et pouvoir*. Paris: Gallimard, 2000.

Coville, A. *Les Cabochiens et l'ordonnance de 1413*. Paris, 1888.

Crane, Susan. "Clothing and Gender Definition: Joan of Arc." In *Inscribing the Hundred Years' War in French and English Cultures*. Ed. Denise Baker. Albany: State University of New York Press, 2000. 195–219.

– "French and Anglo-Norman during the Hundred Years War." In *The Cambridge History of Medieval English Literature*. Ed. David Wallace. Cambridge: Cambridge University Press, 1999. 52–60.

Crawford, Katherine. *Perilous Performances: Gender and Regency in Early Modern France*. Cambridge, MA: Harvard University Press, 2004.

Cropp, Glynnis. "Philosophy, the Liberal Arts, and Theology in *Le Livre de la mutacion de Fortune* and *Le Livre de l'advision Cristine*." In *Healing the Body Politic: The Political Thought of Christine de Pizan*. Ed. Karen Green and Constant Mews. Turnhout: Brepols, 2005. 139–59.

Curry, Anne. "Fitzalan, John (VI), Seventh Earl of Arundel (1408–1435)." In *Oxford Dictionary of National Biography*. Oxford: Oxford University Press, 2004.

– *The Hundred Years War*. 2nd ed. New York: Palgrave, 2003.

– "Two Kingdoms, One King: The Treaty of Troyes (1420) and the Creation of a Double Monarchy of England and France." In *"The Contending Kingdoms": France and England 1420–1700*. Ed. Glenn Richardson. Aldershot: Ashgate, 2008. 23–41.

Curtius, Ernst Robert. *European Literature and the Latin Middle Ages*. Trans. Willard Trask. Princeton: Princeton University Press, 1990.

D'Arcens, Louise. "Petit estat vesval: Christine de Pizan's Grieving Body Politic." In *Healing the Body Politic: The Political Thought of Christine de Pizan*. Ed. Karen Green and Constant Mews. Turnhout: Brepols, 2005. 201–26.

Delogu, Daisy. "*Advocate et moyenne*: Christine de Pizan's Elaboration of Female Authority." In *Desireuse de plus avant enquerre ... Actes du VIe colloque international sur Christine de Pizan* (Paris, 20–24 juillet 2006). Ed. Liliane Dulac, Anne Paupert, Christine Reno, and Bernard Ribémont. Paris: Champion, 2008. 57–67.

– "'Aucuns de ma langue': Language and Political Identity in Late Medieval France." *Explorations in Renaissance Culture* 39.2 (2013): 97–112.

– "En quoi la ville est-elle un espace féminin/féministe ? Les corps politiques de Christine de Pizan." In *Cités humanistes, cités politiques (1400–1600)*. Ed. Elisabeth Crouzet-Pavan, Denis Crouzet, and Philippe Desan. Paris: Presses de l'Université Paris-Sorbonne, 2014. 89–107.

– "'How to Become the 'roy des frans.' The Performance of Kingship in Philippe de Mézières's *Le songe du vieil pelerin*." In *Philippe de Mézières and His Age: Piety and Politics in the Fourteenth Century*. Ed. Renate Blumenfeld-Kosinski and Kiril Petkov. Leiden: Brill, 2012. 147–64.

– "The King's Two Daughters: Isabelle of France, and the University of Paris, *fille du roy*." *Republics of Letters: A Journal for the Study of Knowledge, Politics, and the Arts* 3.2 (2013): 1–21.

– "Performance and Polemic: Gender in the Works of Alain Chartier." *Alain Chartier c.1385–1430: Père de l'éloquence française*. Ed. Daisy Delogu, Emma Cayley, and Joan McRae. Leiden: Brill, forthcoming.

de Lubac, Henri. *Exégèse medieval: Les quatre sens de l'écriture*. Paris: Aubier, 1959.

de Man, Paul. *Allegories of Reading: Figural Language in Rousseau, Nietzsche, Rilke, and Proust*. New Haven and London: Yale University Press, 1979.

– "The Rhetoric of Temporality." In *Blindness and Insight. Essays in the Rhetoric of Contemporary Criticism*. 2nd ed. Minneapolis: University of Minnesota Press, 1983. 187–228.

de Miramon, Charles. "Aux origines de la noblesse et des princes du sang: France et Angleterre au XIVe siècle." In *L'hérédité entre Moyen Âge et Époque moderne. Perspectives historiques*. Ed. Maaike van der Lugt and Charles de Miramon. Florence: Edizioni del Galluzzo, 2008. 157–210.

Derrida, Jacques. *Of Grammatology*. Trans. Gayatri Spivak. Baltimore and London: Johns Hopkins University Press, 1997 (1974).

Dickinson, Joycelyne Gledhill. *The Congress of Arras, 1435: A Study in Medieval Diplomacy*. Oxford: Clarendon Press, 1955.

Duchet-Suchaux, Gaston. "Émergence d'un sentiment national chez Eustache Deschamps." In *Autour d'Eustache Deschamps*. Ed. Danielle Buschinger. Amiens: Presses du Centre d'Études Médiévales, 1999. 73–7.

Dudash, Susan. "Eustache Deschamps: Poète et commentateur politique." In *Les "dictez vertueulx" d'Eustache Deschamps, forme poétique et discours engagé à la fin du Moyen Âge*. Ed. Miren Lacassagne and Thierry Lassabatère. Paris: Presses de l'Université Paris-Sorbonne, 2005. 147–62.

Dulac, Liliane. "À propos des représentations du corps souffrant chez Christine de Pizan." In *Mélanges de langue et de littérature françaises du Moyan Âge offerts à Pierre Demarolle*. Ed. Charles Bruckner. Paris: Champion, 1998. 313–24.

– "De l'arbre au jardin, de la pastorale à la politique: Quelques transpositions métaphoriques et allégoriques chez Christine de Pizan." In *Desireuse de plus avant enquerre ... Actes du VIe Colloque international sur Christine de Pizan* (Paris, 20–24 juillet 2006). Ed. Liliane Dulac, Anne Paupert, Christine Reno, and Bernard Ribémont. Paris: Champion, 2008. 191–208.

– "La représentation de la France chez Eustache Deschamps et Christine de Pizan." In *Autour d'Eustache Deschamps*. Ed. Danielle Buschinger. Amiens: Presses du Centre d'Études Médiévales, 1999. 79–92.

Dulac, Liliane, and Christine Reno. "L'humanisme vers 1400, essai d'exploration à partir d'un cas marginal: Christine de Pizan, traductrice de Thomas d'Aquin." In *Pratiques de la culture écrite en France au XVe siècle*. Ed. Monique Ornato and Nicole Pons. Louvain-la-neuve: Fédération Internationale des Instituts d'Études Médiévales, 1995. 161–78.

– "The *Livre de l'advision Cristine*." In *Christine de Pizan: A Casebook*. Ed. Barbara Altmann and Deborah McGrady. New York and London: Routledge, 2003. 199–214.

Dziedzic, Andrzej. "À la recherche d'une figure maternelle: L'image de la mère dans l'œuvre de Christine de Pizan." *Neophilologus* 86.4 (October 2002): 493–506.

Earenfight, Theresa. *The King's Other Body: Maria of Castile and the Crown of Aragon*. Philadelphia: University of Pennsylvania Press, 2010.

Elliott, Dyan. "Seeing Double: John Gerson, the Discernment of Spirits, and Joan of Arc." *American Historical Review* 107.1 (2002): 26–54.

Fama: The Politics of Talk and Reputation in Medieval Europe. Ed. Thelma Fenster and Daniel Lord Smail. Ithaca: Cornell University Press, 2003.

Famiglietti, R.C. *Royal Intrigue: Crisis at the Court of Charles VI (1392–1420)*. New York: AMS Press, 1986.

Favier, Jean. *La guerre de cent ans*. Paris: Fayard, 1980.

Ferrante, Joan. *Woman as Image in the Middle Ages*. New York: Columbia University Press, 1975.

Ferruolo, Stephen. "Parisius-Paradisus: The City, Its Schools, and the Origins of the University of Paris." In *The University and the City: From Medieval Origins to the Present*: Ed. Thomas Bender. Oxford: Oxford University Press, 1988. 22–43.

Fisher, Jeffrey. "Gerson's Mystical Theology: A New Profile of Its Evolution." In *A Companion to Jean Gerson*. Ed. Brian Patrick McGuire. Leiden and Boston: Brill, 2006. 205–48.

Fisher, John. "A Language Policy for Lancastrian England." *Publications of Modern Language Association* 107.5 (1992): 1168–80.

Fleming, John. *Reason and the Lover*. Princeton: Princeton University Press, 1984.

– *The Roman de la Rose: A Study in Iconography and Allegory*. Princeton: Princeton University Press, 1969.

Fletcher, Angus. *Allegory: The Theory of a Symbolic Mode*. Ithaca: Cornell University Press, 1964.

Fogleman, Andrew. "The Remedies of Hippocrates or Divine Counsel? Jean Gerson and Religious Visionaries during the Great Western Schism." *Comitatus: A Journal of Medieval and Renaissance Studies* 39 (2008): 101–11.

Fradenberg, Louise Olga. "Introduction: Rethinking Queenship." In *Women and Sovereignty*. Ed. Louise Olga Fradenburg. Edinburgh: Edinburgh University Press, 1992. 1–13.

Fraioli, Deborah. "Gerson Judging Women of Spirit: From Female Mystics to Joan of Arc." In *Joan of Arc and Spirituality*. Ed. Ann W. Astell and Bonnie Wheeler. New York: Palgrave, 2003. 147–65.

– *Joan of Arc, the Early Debate*. Woodbridge: The Boydell Press, 2000.

Francomano, Emily. *Wisdom and Her Lovers in Medieval and Early Modern Hispanic Literature*. New York: Palgrave, 2008.

Freccero, John. "Allegory and Autobiography." In *The Cambridge Companion to Dante*. 2nd ed. Cambridge: Cambridge University Press, 2007. 161–80.

Fritz, Jean-Marie. "Figures et métaphores du corps dans le discours de l'histoire: Du 'mundus senescens' au monde malade." In *Apogée et déclin*. Ed. Claude Thomasset and Michel Zink. Paris: Presses de l'Université de Paris-Sorbonne, 1993. 69–86.

– "*Translatio studii* et deluge: La légende des colonnes de marbre et de brique." *Cahiers de civilisation médiévale, Xe–XIIe siècles* 47.2 (2004): 127–46.

Gauvard, Claude. "Les clercs de la Chancellerie royale française et l'écriture des lettres de rémission aux XIVe et XVe siècles." In *Écrit et pouvoir dans les chancelleries médiévales: Espace français, espace anglais*. Ed. Kouky Fianu and DeLloyd Guth. Louvain la neuve, 1997. 281–91.

– *"De grace especial": Crime, état, et société en France à la fin du Moyen Âge*. Paris: Publications de la Sorbonne, 1991.
– "Honneur de femme et femme d'honneur en France à la fin du Moyen Age." *Francia* 28.1 (2001): 159–91.
– "La violence commanditée: La criminalisation des 'tueurs à gages' aux derniers siècles du Moyen Âge." *Annales. Histoire, Sciences Sociales* 62.5 (2007): 1005–29.
– *Violence et ordre public au Moyen Âge*. Paris: Picard, 2005.
Gender and Christianity in Medieval Europe. Ed. Lisa Bitel and Felice Lifshitz. Philadelphia: University of Pennsylvania Press, 2008.
Gender in Debate from the Early Middle Ages to the Renaissance. Ed. Thelma Fenster and Clare Lees. New York: Palgrave, 2002.
Gendering the Master Narrative. Women and Power in the Middle Ages. Ed. Mary Erler and Maryanne Kowaleski. Ithaca and London: Cornell University Press, 2003.
Genèse et débuts du Grand Schisme d'Occident (1362–1394). Ed. Jean Favier. Paris: Éditions du Centre national de la recherche scientifique, 1980.
Gibbons, Rachel. "Isabeau of Bavaria, Queen of France (1385–1422): The Creation of an Historical Villainess." *Transactions of the Royal Historical Society*, 6th series, vol. 6.
Giesey, Ralph. "The Juristic Basis of Dynastic Right to the French Throne." *Transactions of the American Philosophical Society*, new series, vol. 51, no. 5 (1961): 3–47.
– *Le Rôle méconnu de la loi salique: La succession royale XIVe–XVIe siècles*. Paris: Les Belles Lettres, 2007 (1996). 51–73.
Godefroy, Frédéric. *Dictionnaire de l'ancienne langue française et de tous ses dialectes du IXe au XVe siècles*. Paris, 1885.
Guenée, Bernard. *La folie de Charles VI. Roi Bien-Aimé*. Paris: Perrin, 2004.
– "Les grandes chroniques de France." In *Les lieux de mémoire*. 3 vols. Ed. Pierre Nora. Vol. 1, part 1. Paris: Gallimard, 1986. 189–214.
– *Un meurtre, une société: L'assassinat du duc d'Orléans 23 novembre 1407*. Paris: Gallimard, 1992.
– *L'Occident aux XIVe et XVe siècles. Les États*. Paris: Presses Universitaires de France, 1998.
– *L'opinion publique à la fin du Moyen Âge d'après la "Chronique de Charles VI" du Religieux de Saint-Denis*. Paris: Perrin, 2002.
– "Un royaume et des pays: La France et Michel Pintoin." In *Identité régionale et conscience nationale en France et en Allemagne au Moyen Âge*. Ed. Ranier Babel and Jean-Marie Moeglin. Sigmaringen: Jan Thorbecke Verlag, 1997. 403–12.
Guerreau-Jalabert, Anita. "*Spiritus et caritas*: Le baptême dans la société médiévale." In *La Parenté spirituelle. Textes rassemblés et présentés*. Ed.

Françoise Héritier-Augé and Elisabeth Copet-Rougier. Paris: Ed. des archives contemporaines, 1995. 133–203.

– "Sur les structures de parenté dans l'Europe médiévale." *Annales ESC* 36 (1981): 1028–49.

Gunn, Alan. *The Mirror of Love: A Reinterpretation of "The Romance of the Rose."* Lubbock: Texas Tech Press, 1952.

Guynn, Noah. *Allegory and Sexual Ethics in the High Middle Ages*. New York: Palgrave, 2007.

Haidu, Peter. *The Subject Medieval/Modern: Text and Governance in the Middle Ages*. Stanford, CA: Stanford University Press, 2004.

Hale, Rosemary Drage. "Joseph as Mother: Adaptation and Appropriation in the Construction of Male Virtue." In *Medieval Mothering*. Ed. John Carmi Parsons and Bonnie Wheeler. New York: Garland Publishing, 1996. 101–16.

Hamburger, Jeffrey F. *St John the Divine: The Deified Evangelist in Medieval Art and Theology*. Berkeley: University of California Press, 2002.

Hanley, Sarah. "Identity Politics and Rulership in France: Female Political Place and the Fraudulent Salic Law in Christine de Pizan and Jean de Montreuil." In *Changing Identities in Early Modern France*. Ed. M. Wolfe. Durham: Duke University Press, 1997. 78–94.

– "Introduction." In *Les droits des femmes et la loi salique*. Paris: Indigo & Côté-femmes éditions, 1994. 7–20.

– "Mapping Rulership in the French Body Politic: Political Identity, Public Law, and the King's One Body." *Historical Reflections* 23 (1997): 1–21.

– "The Politics of Identity and Monarchic Government in France: The debate over Female Exclusion." In *Women Writers and the Early Modern British Political Tradition*. Ed. Hilda Smith. Cambridge: Cambridge University Press, 1998. 289–304.

Harf-Lancner, Laurence. "*Les Membres et l'Estomac*: La fable et son interprétation politique au Moyen Âge." In *Penser le pouvoir au Moyen Âge (VIIIe–XVe siècle)*. Ed. Dominique Boutet and Jacques Verger. Paris: Presses de l'École normale supérieure, 2000. 111–26.

Hélary, Xavier. "La place des questions de succession dans la politique extérieure de Philippe III le Hardi." In *Making and Breaking the Rules: Succession in Medieval Europe, c. 1000–1600*. Ed. Frédérique Lachaud and Michael Penman. Turnhout: Brepols, 2008. 111–28.

Hobbins, Daniel. *Authorship and Publicity before Print: Jean Gerson and the Transformation of Late Medieval Learning*. Philadelphia: University of Pennsylvania Press, 2009.

– "Gerson on Lay Devotion." In *A Companion to Jean Gerson*. Ed. Brian Patrick McGuire. Leiden and Boston: Brill, 2006. 41–78.

– "Jean Gerson's Authentic Tract on Joan of Arc: *Super facto puellae et credulitate sibi praestanda* (14 May 1429)." *Medieval Studies* 67 (2005): 99–155.
– "The Schoolman as Public Intellectual: Jean Gerson and the Late Medieval Tract." *American Historical Review* 108.5 (2003): 1308–37.
Hodgson, John. "Transcendental Tropes: Coleridge's Rhetoric of Allegory and Symbol." In *Allegory, Myth, and Symbol*. Ed. Morton W. Bloomfield. Cambridge and London: Harvard University Press, 1981. 273–92.
Hollander, Robert. "Dante *Theologus-Poeta*." *Dante Studies* 94 (1976): 91–136.
Honig, Edwin. *Dark Conceit: The Making of Allegory*. Evanston, IL: Northwestern University Press, 1959.
Huot, Sylvia. "Seduction and Sublimation: Christine de Pizan, Jean de Meung, and Dante." *Romance Notes* 25.3 (1985): 361–73.
Hyams, Paul. *Rancor and Reconciliation in Medieval England*. Ithaca and London: Cornell University Press, 2003.
The Ideology of Burgundy: The Promotion of National Consciousness 1364–1565. Ed. D'Arcy Jonathan Dacre Boulton and Jan R. Veenstra. Leiden and Boston: Brill, 2006.
Interpretation and Allegory: Antiquity to the Modern Period. Ed. Jon Whitman. Leiden: Brill, 2000.
Izbicki, Thomas. "The Canonists and the Treaty of Troyes." In *Proceedings of the Fifth International Congress of Medieval Canon Law, held in 1976*. Ed. Stephen Kuttner and Kenneth Pennington. Vatican City: Biblioteca ApostolicaVaticana, 1980. 425–34.
Jauss, Hans-Robert. "La transformation de la forme allégorique entre 1180 et 1240: D'Alain de Lille à Guillaume de Lorris." In *L'humanisme médiéval dans les littératures romanes du XIIe au XIVe siècle*. Paris: Klincksieck, 1964. 107–46.
Jennequin, Marie. "La *Belle dame sans mercy* d'Alain Chartier et sa dimension politique." *Le Moyen Français* 59 (2006): 55–68.
Johnson, Gary. *The Vitality of Allegory: Figural Narrative in Modern and Contemporary Fiction*. Columbus: Ohio State University Press, 2012.
Jongkees, A.G. "*Translatio Studii*: Les avatars d'un theme médiéval." In *Miscellanea Mediaevalia in memoriam Jan Frederik Niermeyer*. Groningen: J.B. Wolters, 1967. 41–51.
Jorga, Nicolas. *Philippe de Mézières (1327–1405) et la croisade au XIVe siècle*. Paris: Librairie Émile Bouillon, 1896.
Jung, Marc-René. *Études sur le poème allégorique en France au Moyen Âge*. Berne: Editions Francke Berne, 1971.
Kamath, Stephanie Viereck Gibbs. *Authorship and First-Person Allegory in Late Medieval France and England*. Woodbridge: Boydell and Brewer, 2012.

Kaminsky, Howard. "The Politics of France's Subtraction of Obedience from Pope Benedict XIII, 27 July 1398." *Proceedings of the American Philosophical Society* 115.5 (1971): 366–97.

Kantorowicz, Ernst. *The King's Two Bodies. A Study in Mediaeval Political Theology*. Princeton: Princeton University Press, 1957.

– "*Pro patria mori* in Medieval Political Thought." *American Historical Review* 56.3 (1951): 472–92.

Kaufman, Helen. "Virgil's Underworld in the Mind of Late Roman Antiquity." *Latomus* 69 (2010): 150–60.

Kay, Sarah, and Adrian Armstrong. *Knowing Poetry: Verse in Medieval France from the Rose to the Rhétoriqueurs*. Ithaca and London: Cornell University Press, 2011.

Keen, Catherine. "Sex and the Medieval City: Viewing the Body Politic from Exile in Early Italian Verse." In *Troubled Vision: Gender, Sexuality, and Sight in Medieval Text and Image*. Ed. Emma Campbell and Robert Mills. New York: Palgrave, 2004. 155–71.

Keen, Maurice. "Diplomacy." *Henry V: The Practice of Kingship*. Ed. G.L. Harriss. Oxford: Oxford University Press, 1985. 181–99.

Kelly, Douglas. *Christine de Pizan's Changing Opinion: A Quest for Certainty in the Midst of Chaos*. Cambridge, UK: Brewer, 2007.

Kempshall, M.S. *The Common Good in Late Medieval Political Thought*. Oxford: Clarendon Press, 1999.

Kendrick, Laura. "Rhetoric and the Rise of Public Poetry: The Career of Eustache Deschamps" *Studies in Philology* 80.1 (1983): 1–13.

Kennedy, Angus. *Christine de Pizan. A Bibliographical Guide*. London: Grant and Cutler, 1984.

– *Christine de Pizan. A Bibliographical Guide. Supplement 1*. London: Grant and Cutler, 1994.

– *Christine de Pizan. A Bibliographical Guide. Supplement* 2. Woodbridge: Tamesis, 2004.

Kinch, Ashby. "'De l'ombre de mort en clarté de vie': The Evolution of Alain Chartier's Public Voice." *Fifteenth-Century Studies* 33 (2008): 151–70.

Klapisch-Zuber, Christiane. *L'ombre des ancêtres: Essai sur l'imaginaire médiéval de la parenté*. Paris: Fayard, 2000.

Köhler, Erich. *L'aventure chevaleresque: Idéal et réalité dans le roman courtois, études sur la forme des plus anciens poèmes d'Arthur et du Graal*. Trans. Eliane Kaufholz. Paris: Gallimard, 1974.

Kruger, Steven. *Dreaming in the Middle Ages*. Cambridge: Cambridge University Press, 1992.

Krynen, Jacques. *L'empire du roi, idées et croyances politiques en France: XIIIe–XVe siècle.* Paris: Gallimard, 1993.

– *Idéal du prince et pouvoir royal en France à la fin du Moyen Age.* Paris: Picard, 1981.

– "Les légistes 'tyrans de la France'? Le témoignage de Jean Juvénal des Ursins, docteur *in utroque.*" In *Droits savants et pratiques françaises du pouvoir (XIe–XVe siècles).* Ed. Jacques Krynen and Albert Rigaudière. Bordeaux: Presses Universitaires de Bordeaux, 1992. 279–99.

– "'La mort saisit le vif.' Genèse médiévale du principe d'instantanéité de la succession royale française." *Journal des Savants,* July–Dec. 1984: 187–221.

– "Naturel: Essai sur l'argument de la Nature dans la pensée politique à la fin du Moyen Âge." *Journal des Savants,* April–June 1982: 169–90.

– "*Rex christianissimus*: A Medieval Theme at the Roots of French Absolutism." *History and Anthropology* 4 (1989): 79–96.

Lacassagne, Miren, "L'échange épistolaire de Christine de Pizan et Eustache Deschamps." In *Contexts and Continuities.* Ed. Angus Kennedy. 3 vols. Glasgow: University of Glasgow Press, 2002. Vol. 2: 453–65.

– "Poétique et politique du corps dans l'œuvre d'Eustache Deschamps." *Sénéfiance* 41 (1998): 319–37.

Laennec, Christine Moneera. "Prophétie, interprétation et écriture dans *L'Avision-Christine.*" In *Une femme de lettres au Moyen Âge: Études autour de Christine de Pizan.* Ed. Liliane Dulac and Bernard Ribémont. Orléans: Paradigme, 1995. 131–8.

Laidlaw, James. "Alain Chartier." In *Literature of the French and Occitan Middle Ages: Eleventh to Fifteenth Centuries.* Ed. Deborah Sinnreich-Levi and Ian Laurie. Detroit: The Gale Group, 1999. 60–71.

Lakoff, George, and Mark Johnson. *Metaphors We Live By.* Chicago and London: University of Chicago Press, 1980.

Lassabatère, Thierry. *La cité des homes: Eustache Deschamps, expression poétique et vision politique.* Paris: Champion, 2011.

– "Diffusion et postérité de l'œuvre politique d'Eustache Deschamps, le témoignage des manuscrits." In *Les "dictez vertueulx" d'Eustache Deschamps: Forme poétique et discours engagé à la fin du Moyen Âge.* Ed. Thierry Lassabatère and Miren Lacassagne. Paris: Presses de l'Université Paris-Sorbonne, 2005. 107–20.

– "La personnification de la France dans la littérature de la fin du Moyen Âge: Autour d'Eustache Deschamps et Christine de Pizan." In *Contexts and Continuities.* Ed. Angus Kennedy. 3 vols. Glasgow: University of Glasgow Press, 2002. 2: 483–504.

– "Sentiment national et messianisme politique en France pendant la guerre de cent ans: Le thème de la fin du monde chez Eustache Deschamps." *Bulletin Jeanne d'Arc*, 1993: 27–56.

Laurie, I.S. "Eustache Deschamps: 1340(?)–1404." In *Eustache Deschamps, French Courtier-Poet: His Work and His World*. Ed. Deborah Sinnreich-Levi. New York: AMS Press, 1998. 1–72.

Le Goff, Jacques. "Head or Heart? The Political Use of Body Metaphors in the Middle Ages." In *Fragments for a History of the Human Body*. Ed. Michel Feher. 3 vols. New York: Zone, 1989. 3: 12–27.

Levin, Samuel R. "Allegorical Language." In *Allegory, Myth, and Symbol*. Ed. Morton W. Bloomfield. Cambridge, MA, and London: Harvard University Press, 1981. 23–38.

Lewis, A.W. *Royal Succession in Capetian France: Studies on Familial Order and the State*. Cambridge, MA, and London: Harvard University Press, 1981.

Lewis, C.S. *The Allegory of Love: A Study in Medieval Tradition*. Oxford: Oxford University Press, 1936.

Lewis, P.S. "War Propaganda and Historiography in Fifteenth-Century France and England." *Transactions of the Royal Historical Society*, 5th series, vol. 15 (1965): 1–21.

Lieberman, Max. "Jean Gerson et Philippe de Mézières." *Romania* 81 (1960): 338–79.

Les lieux de mémoire. Ed. Pierre Nora. 3 vols. Paris: Gallimard, 1984–92.

Loomis, Louise. "Nationality at the Council of Constance: An Anglo-French Dispute." *American Historical Review* 44.3 (1939): 508–27.

Lusignan, Serge. *La langue des rois au Moyen Âge: Le français en France et en Angleterre*. Paris: Presses Universitaires de France, 2004.

– "Parler français: Les enjeux linguistiques des négociations entre Français et Anglais à la fin du Moyen Âge." In *Zwischen Babel und Pfingsten. Sprachdifferenzen und gesprächsverständigung in der vormoderne (8.–16.Jh). Entre Babel et Pentecôte. Différences linguistiques et communication orale avant la modernité (VIIIe–XVIe siècle)*. Ed. Peter von Moos. Berlin and Zurich: Lit, 2008. 409–29.

– *Parler Vulgairement. Les intellectuels et la langue française aux XIIIe et XIVe siècles*. Montreal: Presses de l'Université de Montréal, 1986.

– "L'université de Paris comme composante de l'identité du royaume de France: Étude sur le thème de la *translatio studii*." In *Identité régionale et conscience nationale en France et en Allemagne du Moyen Âge à l'époque moderne*. Ed. Rainer Babel and Jean-Marie Moeglin. Sigmaringen: Thorbecke, 1997.

– *"Vérité garde le roy." La construction d'une identité universitaire en France (XIIIe–XVe siècle)*. Paris: Publications de la Sorbonne, 1999.

Lutkus, Anne D., and Julia Walker. "The Political Poetics of the *Ditié de Jehanne d'Arc*." In *Inscribing the Hundred Years' War in French and English Cultures*. Ed. Denise Baker. Albany: State University of New York Press, 2000. 177–94.

Lynch, Kathryn. *The High Medieval Dream Vision: Poetry, Philosophy, and Literary Form*. Stanford, CA: Stanford University Press, 1988.

Marchello-Nizia, Christiane. "Entre l'histoire et la poétique: Le 'songe politique.'" *Revue des Sciences Humaines* 183 (1981): 39–53.

Martinez, Ronald. "Allegory." In *The Dante Encyclopedia*. Ed. Richard Lansing. New York and London: Garland Publishing, 2000.

– "Dante between Hope and Despair: The Tradition of Lamentations in the *Divine Comedy*." *Logos: A Journal of Catholic Thought and Culture* 5.3 (2002): 45–76.

Matter, E. Ann. "The Undebated Debate: Gender and the Image of God in Medieval Theology." In *Gender in Debate from the Early Middle Ages to the Renaissance*. Ed. Thelma Fenster and Clare Lees. New York: Palgrave, 2002. 41–55.

Mazour-Matusevich, Yelena. "Gerson et Pétrarque: Humanisme et l'idée nationale." *Renaissance and Reformation* 25.1 (2001): 45–80.

– "A Reconsideration of Jean Gerson's Attitude toward Joan of Arc in Light of His Views on Popular Devotion." In *Joan of Arc and Spirituality*. Ed. Ann W. Astell and Bonnie Wheeler. New York: Palgrave, 2003. 167–82.

Mazour-Matusevich, Yelena, and Istvan Bejczy. "Jean Gerson on Virtues and Princely Education." In *Princely Virtues in the Middle Ages 1200–1500*. Ed. Istvan Bejczy and Cary Nederman. Turnhout: Brepols, 2007. 219–36.

McCracken, Peggy. *The Romance of Adultery: Queenship and Sexual Transgression in Old French Literature*. Philadelphia: University of Pennsylvania Press, 1998.

McGuire, Brian Patrick. "In Search of Jean Gerson: Chronology of His Life and Works." In *A Companion to Jean Gerson*. Ed. Brian Patrick McGuire. Leiden: Brill, 2006. 1 39.

– "Gerson and Bernard: Languishing with Love." *Citeaux Commentarii Cistercienses* 46 (1995): 127–56.

– *Jean Gerson and the Last Medieval Reformation*. University Park: Pennsylvania State University Press, 2005.

– "Jean Gerson and the Renewal of Scholastic Discourse." In *Knowledge, Discipline and Power in the Middle Ages: Essays in Honour of David Luscombe*. Ed. Joseph Canning, Edmund King, and Martial Staub. Leiden and Boston: Brill, 2011. 129–44.

– "Jean Gerson, the Shulammite, and the Maid." In *Joan of Arc and Spirituality*. Ed. Ann W. Astell and Bonnie Wheeler. New York: Palgrave, 2003. 183–92.
– "Jean Gerson and Traumas of Masculine Affectivity and Sexuality." In *Conflicted Identities and Multiple Masculinities: Men in the Medieval West*. Ed. Jacqueline Murray. New York and London: Garland, 1999. 45–72.
– "Patterns of Male Affectivity in the Late Middle Ages." In *Varieties of Devotion in the Middle Ages and Renaissance*. Ed. Susan Karant-Nunn. Turnhout: Brepols, 2003. 163–78.
McInerney, Maud Burnett. *Eloquent Virgins from Thecla to Joan of Arc*. New York: Palgrave, 2003.
– "In the Meydens Womb: Julian of Norwich and the Poetics of Enclosure." In *Medieval Mothering*. Ed. John Carmi Parsons and Bonnie Wheeler. New York: Garland Publishing, 1996. 157–82.
McKeon, Peter. "The Status of the University of Paris as *Parens Scientiarum*: An Episode in the Development of Its Autonomy." *Speculum* 39.4 (1964): 651–75.
McLoughlin, Nancy. "The Deadly Sins and Contemplative Politics: Gerson's Ordering of the Personal and Political Realms." In *Sin in Medieval and Early Modern Culture: The Tradition of the Seven Deadly Sins*. Ed. Richard Newhauser and Susan Ridyard. York: York Medieval Press, 2012. 132–56.
– "Gerson as a Preacher in the Conflict between Mendicants and Secular Priests." In *A Companion to Jean Gerson*. Ed. Brian Patrick McGuire. Leiden and Boston: Brill, 2006. 248–91.
– "Personal Narrative and the Systematization of Knowledge in the Thought of Jean Gerson." *Mediaevalia* 29 (2008): 83–108.
Medieval Literary Theory and Criticism c. 1100–c. 1375. The Commentary Tradition. Ed. A.J. Minnas and A.B. Scott with David Wallace. Oxford: Clarendon Press, 1988.
Medieval Queenship. Ed. John Carmi Parsons. Stroud: Sutton Publishing, 1994.
Meltzer, Françoise. *For Fear of the Fire: Joan of Arc and the Limits of Subjectivity*. Chicago: University of Chicago Press, 2001.
Meron, Theodor. "The Authority to Make Treaties in the Late Middle Ages." *American Journal of International Law* 89.1 (1995): 1–20.
Meyjes, G.H.M. Posthumus. *Jean Gerson, Apostle of Unity: His Church Politics and Ecclesiology*. Trans. J.C. Grayson. Leiden: Brill, 1999.
Minet-Mahy, Virginie. *Esthétique et pouvoir de l'œuvre allégorique à l'époque de Charles VI. Imaginaires et discours*. Paris: Champion, 2005.
– "Eustache Deschamps: Images de lecteurs, autoportraits et toile de fond." *Studi Francesi* 49.2 (2005): 225–39.
– "Le songe: De la mort de l'auteur à la naissance du lecteur." In *Le rêve médiéval*. Ed. Alain Corbellari and Jean-Yves Tilliette. Geneva: Droz, 2007. 193–220.

Minnis, Alastair. *Magister Amoris: The Roman de la Rose and Vernacular Hermeneutics*. Oxford: Oxford University Press, 2001.

– "Langland's Ymaginatif and Late-Medieval Theories of Imagination." *Comparative Criticism* 3 (1981): 71–103.

– "*Quadruplex Sensus, Multiplex Modus*: Scriptural Sense and Mode in Medieval Scholastic Exegesis." In *Interpretation and Allegory: Antiquity to the Modern Period*. Ed. Jon Whitman. Leiden: Brill, 2000. 231–56.

Minnis, A.J., A.B. Scott, and David Wallace. "The Transformation of Critical Tradition: Dante, Petrarch, and Boccaccio." In *Medieval Literary Theory and Criticism c. 1100–c. 1375. The Commentary Tradition*. Ed. A.J. Minnis and A.B. Scott, with David Wallace. Oxford: Clarendon Press, 1988. 373–94.

Miramon, Charles de. "Aux origines de la noblesse et des princes du sang: France et Angleterre au XIVe siècle." In *L'hérédité entre Moyen Âge et Époque modern: Perspectives historiques*. Ed. Maaike van der Lugt and Charles de Miramon. Florence: Edizioni del Galluzzo, 2008. 157–210.

Mitchell, Margaret. *Paul, the Corinthians, and the Birth of Christian Hermeneutics*. Cambridge: Cambridge University Press, 2010.

Mourin, Louis. *Jean Gerson, prédicateur français*. Bruges: Rijksuniversiteit te Gent, 1952.

Mühlethaler, Jean-Claude. "Entre amour et politique: La fable d'Hermaphrodite à la fin du Moyen Âge. Pour une relecture du *Lay amoureux* d'Eustache Deschamps." In *Eustache Deschamps, témoin et modèle: Littérature et société politique (XIVe–XVIe siècles)*. Ed. Thierry Lassabatère and Miren Lacassagne. Paris: Presses de l'Université Paris-Sorbonne, 2008. 11–29.

Muscatine, Charles. "The Emergence of Psychological Allegory in Old French Romance." *PMLA* 68 (1953): 1160–82.

Nederman, Cary. "Body Politics: The Diversification of Organic Metaphors in the Later Middle Ages." *Pensiero Politico Medievale* 2 (2004): 59–87.

– "Conciliarism and Constitutionalism: Jean Gerson and Medieval Political Thought." *History of European Ideas* 12.2 (1990): 189–209.

– "Introduction." In *Policraticus. Of the Frivolities of Courtiers and the Footprints of Philosophers*. By Jean of Salisbury. Cambridge: Cambridge University Press, 1990. xv–xxvi.

– "The Living Body Politic: The Diversification of Organic Metaphors in Nicole Oresme and Christine de Pizan." In *Healing the Body Politic: The Political Thought of Christine de Pizan*. Ed. Karen Green and Constant Mews. Turnhout: Brepols, 2005. 19–33.

– "Property and Protest: Political Theory and Subjective Rights in Fourteenth-Century England." *Review of Politics* 58.2 (1996): 323–44.

Nelson, Janet. "Women at the Court of Charlemagne: A Case of Monstrous Regiment?" In *Medieval Queenship*. Ed. John Carmi Parsons. Stroud: Sutton Publishing, 1994. 43–61.

Newman, Barbara. *God and the Goddesses: Vision, Poetry, and Belief in the Middle Ages*. Philadelphia: University of Pennsylvania Press, 2003.

– "Intimate Pieties: Holy Trinity and Holy Family in the Late Middle Ages." *Religion and Literature* 31.1 (1999): 77–101.

– "What Did It Mean to Say 'I Saw'? The Clash between Theory and Practice in Medieval Visionary Culture." *Speculum* 80.1 (2005): 1–43.

Newton, Stella May. *Fashion in the Age of the Black Prince: A Study of the Years 1340–1365*. Woodbridge: Boydell Press, 1980.

Nichols, Stephen. "The Narrative of Nation: Political Allegory in 14th-Century France." *Romanistisches Jahrbuch* 51 (2000): 153–78.

Ohly, Friedrich. "On the Spiritual Sense of the Word in the Middle Ages." In *Sensus spiritualis: Studies in Medieval Significs and the Philosophy of Culture*. Trans. Kenneth Northcott. Ed. Samuel Jaffe. Chicago: University of Chicago Press, 2005. 1–30.

Ormrod, W.M. "The Use of English: Language, Law, and Political Culture in Fourteenth-Century England." *Speculum* 78.3 (July 2003): 750–87.

Ornato, Ezio. "Les humanistes français et la redécouverte des classiques." In *Préludes à la Renaissance*. Paris: Éditions du CNRS, 1992. 1–45.

Ortner, Sherry. "The Virgin and the State." In *Making Gender: The Politics and Erotics of Culture*. Boston: Beacon Press, 1996. 43–58.

Owens, Craig. "The Allegorical Impulse: Toward a Theory of Postmodernism Part 1." *October* 12 (1980): 67–86.

– "The Allegorical Impulse: Toward a Theory of Postmodernism Part 2." *October* 13 (1980): 58–80.

Parsons, John Carmi. "The Queen's Intercession in Thirteenth-Century England." In *The Power of the Weak, Studies on Medieval Women*. Ed. Jennifer Carpenter and Sally-Beth MacLean. Urbana: University of Illinois Press, 1995. 147–77.

Pascoe, Louis. "Jean Gerson: The 'Ecclesia Primitiva' and Reform." *Traditio* 30 (1974): 379–409.

– *Jean Gerson: Principles of Church Reform*. Leiden: Brill, 1973.

Paupert, Anne. "Philosophie 'en fourme de sainte Théologie': L'accès au savoir dans l'œuvre de Christine de Pizan." In *Christine de Pizan: Une femme de science, une femme de lettres*. Ed. Juliette Dor and Marie-Elisabeth Henneau. Paris: Champion, 2008. 39–54.

Paxson, James. "Personification's Gender." *Rhetorica* 16.2 (1998): 149–79.

– *The Poetics of Personification*. Cambridge: Cambridge University Press, 1994.

Perret, Noëlle-Laetitia. *Les traductions françaises du De regimine principum de Gilles de Rome: Parcours matériel, culturel et intellectuel d'un discours sur l'éducation*. Leiden: Brill, 2011.

Pick, Lucy. "Gender in the Early Spanish Chronicles: From John of Biclar to Pelayo of Oviedo." *La Coronica* 32.3 (2004): 227–48.

Piehler, Paul. *The Visionary Landscape: A Study in Medieval Allegory*. London: Edward Arnold, 1971.

Pitkin, Hannah Fenichel. *Fortune Is a Woman: Gender and Politics in the Thought of Niccolo Machiavelli*. Chicago: University of Chicago Press, 1984.

Poirion, Daniel. *Le Roman de la Rose*. Paris: Hatier, 1973.

Pons, Nicole. "Un exemple de l'utilisation des écrits politiques de Jean de Montreuil: Un memorandum diplomatique redigé sous Charles VII." In *Préludes à la Renaissance*. Paris: Éditions du CNRS, 1992. 243–64.

– "Jean de Montreuil et Guillebert de Mets." *Revue Belge de Philologie et d'Histoire* 58 (1980): 565–87.

– "La propagande de guerre française avant l'apparition de Jeanne d'Arc." *Journal des Savants*, February 1982: 191–214.

– "Propagande et sentiment national pendant le regne de Charles VI: L'exemple de Jean de Montreuil." *Francia* 8 (1979): 127–45.

Post, Gaines. "'Blessed Lady Spain' – Vincentius Hispanus and Spanish National Imperialism in the Thirteenth Century." *Speculum* 29.2 (1954): 198–209.

– "Parisian Masters as a Corporation, 1200–1246." *Speculum* 9.4 (1934): 421–45.

Power of the Weak: Studies on Medieval Women. Ed. Jennifer Carpenter and Sally-Beth MacLean. Urbana and Chicago: University of Illinois Press, 1995.

Quicherat, Jules. *Aperçus nouveaux sur l'histoire de Jeanne d'Arc*. Paris: J. Renouard, 1850.

Quillet, Jeannine. "Songes et songeries dans l'art politique au XIVe siècle." *Les Études Philosophiques* 3 (1975): 327–49.

Quilligan, Maureen. "Allegory and Female Agency." In *Thinking Allegory Otherwise*. Ed. Brenda Machosky. Stanford, CA: Stanford University Press, 2010. 163–87.

– *The Allegory of Female Authority. Christine de Pizan's* Cité des dames. Ithaca and London: Cornell University Press, 1991.

– *The Language of Allegory: Defining the Genre*. Ithaca and London: Cornell University Press, 1979.

Rashdall, Hastings. *The Universities of Europe in the Middle Ages*. Ed. F.M. Powicke and A.B. Emden. 3 vols. Oxford: Clarendon Press, 1936.

Raskolnikov, Masha. *Body against Soul: Gender and Sowlehele in Middle English Allegory*. Columbus: Ohio State University Press, 2009.

Reix, Delphine. "Christine de Pizan et l'écriture de l'allégorisation." In *Christine de Pizan: Une femme de science, une femme de lettres*. Ed. Juliette Dor and Marie-Elisabeth Henneau. Paris: Champion, 2008. 55–69.

Reno, Christine. "The Preface to the *Avision-Christine* in ex-Phillipps 128." In *Reinterpreting Christine de Pizan*. Ed. Earl Jeffrey Richards. Athens and London: University of Georgia Press, 1992. 207–27.

Ribémont, Bernard. "Christine de Pizan et la figure de la mère." In *Christine de Pizan 2000: Studies on Christine de Pizan in Honour of Angus J. Kennedy*. Eds. John Campbell and Nadia Margolis. Amsterdam and Atlanta: Rodopi, 2000. 149–61.

Richards, Earl Jeffrey. "Christine de Pizan and Dante: A Reexamination." *Archiv für das Studium der neuren Sprachen und Literaturen* 222 (1985): 100–11.

– "The Lady Wants to Talk: Christine de Pizan's Epistre a Eustace Mourel." In *Eustache Deschamps, French Courtier-Poet: His Work and His World*. Ed. Deborah Sinnreich-Levi. New York: AMS Press, 1998. 109–22.

– "The Uncertainty in Defining France as a Nation in the Works of Eustache Deschamps." In *Inscribing the Hundred Years' War in French and English Cultures*. Ed. Denise Baker. New York: State University of New York Press, 2000. 159–75.

Riché, Pierre, and Jacques Verger. *Des nains sur des épaules de géants: Maîtres et élèves au Moyen Âge*. Paris: Tallandier, 2006.

Ricœur, Paul. "The Metaphorical Process as Cognition, Imagination, and Feeling." In *On Metaphor*. Ed. Sheldon Sacks. Chicago and London: University of Chicago Press, 1979. 141–57.

Roazen, Daniel Heller. *Fortune's Faces: The Roman de la Rose and the Poetics of Contingency*. Baltimore: Johns Hopkins University Press, 2003.

Roccati, Matteo. "Humanisme et préoccupations religieuses au début du XVe siècle: Le Prologue de la Josephina de Jean Gerson." In *Préludes à la Renaissance: Aspects de la vie intellectuelle en France au XVe siècle*. Ed. Carla Bozzolo and Ezio Ornato. Paris 1992. 107–22.

– "La 'Josephina' di Jean Gerson (1418): Un poema virgiliano di contenuto biblico." *Studi Francesi* 121 (1997): 4–15.

Rorem, Paul. "The Early Latin Dionysius: Eriugena and Hugh of St. Victor." *Modern Theology* 24.4 (2008): 601–14.

Ross, Lia. "Anger and the City: Who Was in Charge of the Paris *cabochien* Revolt of 1413?" In *Urban Space in the Middle Ages and the Early Modern Age*. Ed. Albrecht Classen. Berlin: Walter de Gruyter, 2009. 433–62.

Rouse, Richard H. and Mary A. *Manuscripts and Their Makers: Commercial Book Producers in Medieval Paris, 1200–1500*. Turnhout: Harvey Miller, 2000.

Rouy, François. *L'esthétique du traité moral d'après les œuvres d'Alain Chartier*. Geneva: Droz, 1980.

Russell, Joycelyn G. "Language: A Barrier or a Gateway?" In *Diplomats at Work: Three Renaissance Studies*. Gloucester: A. Sutton Pub., 1992.

Schibanoff, Susan. "True Lies: Transvestism and Idolatry in the Trial of Joan of Arc." In *Fresh Verdicts on Joan of Arc*. Ed. Bonnie Wheeler and Charles T. Wood. New York and London: Garland, 1996. 31–60.

Scott, Joan W. "Gender: A Useful Category of Historical Analysis." *American Historical Review* 91.5 (1986): 1053–75.

Scott, Margaret. *Medieval Dress and Fashion*. London: Publication of the British Library, 2007.

Seiferth, Wolfgang. *Synagogue and Church in the Middle Ages: Two Symbols in Art and Literature*. New York: Frederick Ungar Publishing, 1970.

Semple, Benjamin. "The Critique of Knowledge as Power: The Limits of Philosophy and Theology in Christine de Pizan." In *Christine de Pizan and the Categories of Difference*. Ed. Marilynn Desmond. Minneapolis and London: University of Minnesota Press, 1998. 108–27.

La Servante et la Consolatrice: La philosophie et ses rapports avec la théologie au Moyen Âge. Ed. Jean-Luc Solère and Zénon Kaluza. Paris: J. Vrin, 2002.

Shadis, Miriam. "Blanche of Castile and Facinger's 'Medieval Queenship': Reassessing the Argument." In *Capetian Women*. Ed. Kathleen Nolan. New York: Palgrave, 2003. 137–61.

Sheingorn, Pamela. "'Illustris patriarcha Joseph': Jean Gerson, Representations of Saint Joseph, and Imagining Community among Churchmen in the Fifteenth Century." In *Visions of Community in the Pre-Modern World*. Ed. Nicholas Howe. South Bend, IN: University of Notre Dame Press, 2002. 75–108.

Singleton, Charles. "The Irreducible Dove." *Comparative Literature* 9.2 (1957): 129–35.

Sinnreich-Levi, Deborah. "The Female Voice of the Male Poet: Eustache Deschamps' *Voix Feminisée*." In *Voices in Translation: The Authority of "Olde Bookes" in Medieval Literature*. Ed. Deborah Sinnreich-Levi and Gale Sigal. New York: AMS Press, 1992. 207–18.

– "The Feminist Voice of the Misogynist Poet: Deschamps's Poems in Women's Voices." In *Eustache Deschamps, French Courtier-Poet: His Work and His World*. Ed. Deborah Sinnreich-Levi. New York: AMS Press, 1998. 123–30.

Solterer, Helen. "The Freedoms of Fiction for Gender in Premodern France." In *Gender in Debate from the Early Middle Ages to the Renaissance*. Ed. Thelma Fenster and Clare Lees. New York: Palgrave, 2002. 135–63.

Spiegel, Gabrielle. "Genealogy: Form and Function in Medieval Historiography." In *The Past as Text*. Baltimore: Johns Hopkins University Press, 1997. 99–110.

– "The *reditus regni ad stirpem Karoli Magni*: A New Look." *French Historical Studies* 7 (1971): 145–74.

Stafford, Pauline. *Queen Emma and Queen Edith: Queenship and Women's Power in Eleventh-Century England*. Oxford: Blackwell, 1997.

Stahuljak, Zrinka. *Bloodless Genealogies of the French Middle Ages: Translatio, Kinship, and Metaphor*. Gainesville: University Press of Florida, 2005.

Steiner, Emily. *Documentary Culture and the Making of Medieval English Literature*. Cambridge: Cambridge University Press, 2003.

Strohm, Paul. *Hochon's Arrow: The Social Imagination of Fourteenth-Century Texts*. Princeton: Princeton University Press, 1992.

Strubel, Armand. "Allégorie médiévale." In *Dictionnaire des littératures de langue française*. Ed. J.-P. Beaumarchais. Paris: Bordas, 1994. 30–3.

– *"Grant senefiance a": Allégorie et littérature au Moyen Âge*. Paris: Champion, 2002.

– *La Rose, Renart, et le Graal: La littérature allégorique en France au XIIIe siècle*. Geneva and Paris: Éditions Slatkine, 1989.

– "*Le Songe du viel pelerin* et les transformations de l'allégorie au XIVe siècle." *Perspectives* 6 (1980): 54–74.

– "Le style allégorique de Christine." In *Une femme de lettres au Moyen Âge: Études autour de Christine de Pizan*. Ed. Liliane Dulac and Bernard Ribémont. Orléans: Paradigme, 1995. 357–72.

Struck, Peter. "Allegory and Ascent in Neoplatonism." In *The Cambridge Companion to Allegory*. Ed. Rita Copeland and Peter Struck. Cambridge: Cambridge University Press, 2010. 57–70.

Sumption, Jonathan. *The Hundred Years War*. 3 vols. Philadelphia: University of Pennsylvania Press, 1991–2009.

Tarnowski, Andrea. "Maternity and Paternity in 'La Mutacion de Fortune.'" In *The City of Scholars: New Approaches to Christine de Pizan*. Ed. Margarete Zimmermann and Dina de Rentiis. Berlin and New York: Walter de Gruyter, 1994. 116–26.

Taylor, Craig. "Edward III and the Plantagenet Claim to the French Throne." In *The Age of Edward III*. Ed. James Bothwell. Woodbridge: Boydell and Brewer, 2001. 155–69.

– "Introduction." *Debating the Hundred Years War: Pour ce que plusieurs (La loy salicque) and A Declaracion of the trew and dewe title of Henry VIII*. Ed. Craig Taylor. Cambridge: Cambridge University Press, 2006. 1–49.

– "Introduction." *Joan of Arc, La Pucelle*. Manchester and New York: Manchester University Press, 2006.

– "The Salic Law, French Queenship, and the Defense of Women in the Late Middle Ages." *French Historical Studies* 29 (2006): 543–64.

– "The Salic Law and the Valois Succession to the French Crown." *French History* 15.4 (2001): 358–77.

– "Sir John Fortescue and the French Polemical Treatises of the Hundred Years War." *English Historical Review* 114 (1999): 112–29.

– "War, Propaganda and Diplomacy in Fifteenth-Century France and England." In *War, Government and Power in Late Medieval France*. Ed. Christopher Allmand. Liverpool: Liverpool University Press, 2000. 70–91.

Teskey, Gordon. *Allegory and Violence*. Ithaca and London: Cornell University Press, 1996.

Thinking Allegory Otherwise. Ed. Brenda Machosky. Stanford, CA: Stanford University Press, 2005.

Todorov, Tzvetan. "On Linguistic Symbolism." Trans. Richard Klein. *New Literary History* 6 (1974): 111–34.

Toubert, Hélène. "Les représentations de l'Ecclesia dans l'art des Xe–XIIe siècles." In *Un art dirigé: Réforme grégorienne et iconographique*. Paris: Éditions du Cerf, 1990. 37–63.

Troubled Vision: Gender, Sexuality, and Sight in Medieval Text and Image. Ed. Emma Campbell and Robert Mills. New York: Palgrave, 2004.

Turner, Denys. "Allegory in Christian Late Antiquity." In *The Cambridge Companion to Allegory*. Ed. Rita Copeland and Peter Struck. Cambridge: Cambridge University Press, 2010. 71–82.

– "Dionysius and Some Late Medieval Mystical Theologians of Northern Europe." *Modern Theology* 24.4 (2008): 651–65.

Tuve, Rosemond. *Allegorical Imagery. Some Mediaeval Books and Their Posterity*. Princeton: Princeton University Press, 1966.

Verger, Jacques. "*Ad prefulgidum sapiencie culmen prolem regis inclitam provehere*: L'initiation des dauphins de France à la sagesse politique selon Jean Gerson." In *Penser le pouvoir au Moyen Âge*. Ed. Dominique Boutet and Jacques Verger. Paris: Presses de l'École normale supérieure, 2000. 427–40.

– *Les Universités au Moyen Âge*. Paris: Presses Universitaires de France, 1973.

Viennot, Eliane. *La France, les femmes, et le pouvoir: L'invention de la loi salique (Ve–XVIe siècle)*. 2 vols. Paris: Perrin, 2006.

Viollet, Paul. "Comment les femmes ont été exclues, en France, de la succession à la couronne." *Mémoires de l'Institut national de France, Académie des Inscriptions et Belles-Lettres* 34, 2nd part (1895): 125–78.

Voaden, Rosalynn. *God's Words, Women's Voices: The Discernment of Spirits in the Writing of Late-Medieval Women Visionaries*. York: York Medieval Press, 1999.

Voices in Dialogue: Reading Women in the Middle Ages. Ed. Linda Olson and Kathryn Kerby-Fulton. Notre Dame, IN: University of Notre Dame Press, 2005.

Walters, Lori. "Christine's Symbolic Self as the Personification of France." In *Christine de Pizan: Une femme de science, une femme de lettres*. Ed. Juliette Dor and Marie-Élisabeth Henneau. Paris: Champion, 2008. 191–215.

– "Gerson and Christine, Poets." In *Poetry, Knowledge and Community in Late Medieval France*. Ed. Rebecca Dixon and Finn Sinclair, with Adrian Armstrong, Sylvia Huot, and Sarah Kay. Cambridge: Brewer, 2008. 69–81.

– "The Royal Vernacular: Poet and Patron in Christine de Pizan's *Charles V* and the *Sept psaumes allégorisés.*" In *The Vernacular Spirit: Essays on Medieval Religious Literature*. Ed. Renate Blumenfeld-Kosinski, Duncan Robertson, and Nancy Bradley Warren. New York: Palgrave, 2002. 145–82.

Warner, Marina. *Alone of All Her Sex: the myth and cult of the Virgin Mary*. New York: Knopf, 1976.

– *Joan of Arc: The Image of Female Heroism*. New York: Knopf, 1981.

Warner, Mark. "The Anglo-French Dual Monarchy and the House of Burgundy, 1420–1435: The Survival of an Alliance." *French History* 11 (1997): 103–30.

Weber, Christoph Friedrich. "Suitable for Crown and Gown: The Ritual Context of the Royal Privileges for the University of Paris." In *Strategies of Writing: Studies on Text and Trust in the Middle Ages*. Ed. Petra Schulte, Marco Mostert, and Irene van Renswoude. Turnhout: Brepols, 2008. 239–52.

Wei, I.P. "The Masters of Theology at the University of Paris in the Late Thirteenth and Early Fourteenth Centuries: An Authority beyond the Schools." *Bulletin of the John Rylands University Library of Manchester* 71 (1993): 37–63.

Weissberger, Barbara. *Isabel Rules: Constructing Queenship, Wielding Power*. Minneapolis: University of Minnosota Press, 2004.

Whitman, Jon. *Allegory: The Dynamics of an Ancient and Medieval Technique*. Cambridge, MA: Harvard University Press, 1987.

Willard, Charity Cannon. *Christine de Pizan: Her Life and Works*. New York: Persea Books, 1984.

Winock, Michel. "Jeanne d'Arc." In *Les lieux de mémoire*. Ed. Pierre Nora. Vol. 3, "La France," part 3. Paris, Gallimard, 1992. 674–733.

Women and Sovereignty. Ed. Louise Olga Fradenburg. Edinburgh: Edinburgh University Press, 1992.

Wood, Charles. "Queens, Queans, and Kingship: An Inquiry into Theories of Royal Legitimacy in Late Medieval England and France." In *Order and Innovation in the Middle Ages*. Ed. William Jordan. Princeton: Princeton University Press, 1976. 385–400.

Wood, Ian. "Defining the Franks: Frankish Origins in Early Medieval Historiography." In *Concepts of National Identity in the Middle Ages*. Ed. Simon Forde, Lesley Johnson, and Alan Murray. Leeds: University of Leeds, 1995. 47–57.

Wrisley, David. "Burgundian Ideologies and Jehan Wauquelin's Prose Translations." In *The Ideology of Burgundy: The Promotion of National Consciousness 1364–1565*. Ed. D'Arcy Jonathan Dacre Boulton and Jan Veenstra. Leiden: Brill 2006. 131–50.

Zink, Michel. "L'amour naturel: De Guillaume de Saint-Thierry aux Derniers Troubadours." *Journal des Savants*, July–Dec. 2001: 321–49.

Zorach, Rebecca. *Blood, Milk, Ink, Gold: Abundance and Excess in the French Renaissance*. Chicago: University of Chicago Press, 2005.

Zumthor, Paul. *Essai de poétique médiévale*. Paris: Seuil, 1972.

Index

Achilles, 169
Aeneus, 71–2
Agincourt, 133, 159
Alain Chartier: dream vision narratives, 42, 67, 127, 153; and figure of France, 8, 32, 36, 163, 165–6; and Joan of Arc, 168–72; life of, 142
Alain Chartier, works of: *Belle dame sans mercy*, 220n73; *Epistola de puella*, 149, 169; *Quadrilogue invectif*, 17, 43, 127–8, 142–53, 161, 165, 177, 201n95, 208n59
Alain de Lille, 146
Albergati, Cardinal, 224n115
Alexander the Great, 61, 170, 175
Alfonso of Jaén, 154
Alighieri, Dante. *See* Dante Alighieri
Anaxagoras, 21
Antequam essent clerici, 194n2
Aquinas, Thomas, 79–81, 187n33, 197n33
Aquitaine, 134
Aristotle: adaptation of, 54, 116, 118, 120, 146–7, 152, 205n24, 207n51; on metaphor, 33–4; *Metaphysics*, 79–80; *Poetics*, 80, 190n83; *Politics*, 32–3, 94, 104, 159, 197n34, 216n39; theories of generation, 214n12
Armagnac (political faction), 109, 121, 141, 152, 207n55
Arnaud de Corbie, 48
Arras, peace of, 17, 128, 153, 155, 158, 162, 164, 166, 224n115
Athens, 69, 71, 111, 112
Augustine, 113; on allegory, 20; *On Christian Teaching* (also *De doctrina christiana*), 21, 190n84, 191n96; *The Literal Meaning of Genesis*, 22, 71, 82; on metaphor, 190n84
Augustine of Dacia, 186n26
auto-exegesis, 15, 20, 37, 40–2, 56, 69
Avignon, 142
Avis aus roys, 76, 181n21, 194n2

Babylon, 59
Baudricourt, Robert de, 167, 232n34
Bayeux, 142
Beauvais, 153, 157, 168
Bede, 34
Benedict XIII (pope), 204n8
Bernard, Saint, 207n54
Bernard d'Armagnac, 209n80

Bernard Silvestris, 77
Birgitta of Sweden (queen), 171, 223n107
Blanche of Castille (queen of France), 5, 14, 28
Boethius, 69, 223n105
Boniface VIII (pope), 9
Burgundians (political faction), 6, 87, 109, 121, 141–2, 151, 168–9
Burgundy (*also* Bourgogne), duchy of, 17, 128, 155–60, 166

Carolinus, 194n8
Cassian, John, 22
Cassiodorus, 20
Catherine, Saint, 170, 232n37
Catherine of France (queen of England), 126, 141, 162
Cauchon, Pierre, 168
Chanson de Roland, La, 46
Charlemagne, 61, 94, 111, 136–7, 140, 158, 194n8
Charles IV (king of France, *also* Charles de la Marche), 5, 129
Charles V (king of France): and Bertrand DuGuesclin, 175; negotiations with English, 132; ordinances, 164, 180n14; reign, 6, 47–8, 68, 72, 94, 159, 196n24; and University of Paris, 9, 86
Charles VI (king of France): in Alain Chartier, 143; birth of son to, 60–1; death of, 142; and Great Schism of the West, 32; and Treaty of Troyes, 17, 126–7, 141, 159–60, 162–3, 165; and University of Paris, 88–9, 97, 99, 104–5, 108–9, 118
– madness of (*also* absence), 10, 14–15, 30, 36, 44, 46, 48, 64, 76, 83, 85, 87, 109, 159, 176–7; effects of, 3, 6, 105; efforts to cope with, 6, 27–8, 55, 69, 105; onset of, 5
– minority, 4–5, 40, 44, 46, 48, 55, 58, 64, 176; ordinances of, 93, 148, 164
– reign, 3–7, 11–12, 27, 43, 46–7, 176; disorder of, 9, 40, 44, 72–3, 87, 93
See also civil war; council; England; Treaty of Troyes
Charles VII (king of France): and assassination of Jean sans peur, 141; and Joan of Arc, 167–73, 175, 177–8; and Treaty of Troyes, 126, 142–3, 150–1, 163; reign, 128, 153, 156, 208n55
Charles de Navarre, 212n4
Charles d'Orléans, 209n80
Charles de Savoisy, 99, 104
Charles de Valois, 180n10
Charroi de Nîmes, Le, 46
Chartier, Alain. *See* Alain Chartier
Chaucer, Geoffrey, 48
Chinon, 167, 170–1, 233n49
Christine de Pizan, 9, 32, 48; and Aquinas, 79–81; and Dante, 40–1, 68–71, 78–9; dream vision narrative, 67, 70–1, 82; figure of France, 8, 16, 36, 46–7, 72–8, 85, 90, 128, 142, 161, 163, 172; life of, 68, 141, 168–9; and Quarrel of the *Roman de la Rose*, 40, 68, 217n47
Christine de Pizan, works of: *Chemin de long estude*, 229n6; *Ditié de Jehanne d'Arc*, 169–70; *Livre de l'Advision Cristine*, 15–16, 28, 41–3, 47, 63, 69–83, 161, 168; *Livre de la cité des dames*, 230n6; *Livre des fais et bonnes meurs du sage roy Charles V*, 175, 200n75, 202n82, 230n6; *Livre des trois vertus* 28–9, 60, 230n6; *Mutacion de Fortune*, 230n6

Cicero, 7, 71, 185n6, 225n124
civil war, 6, 40, 87, 93, 109, 121, 142, 145
Clemence of Hungary (queen of France), 179n4
Clement VII (pope), 86, 195n17
Clovis (king of the Franks), 45, 119, 158, 182n37, 217n44
Col, Gontier, 68
Col, Pierre, 68
Compiègne, 168
Constance de Rabastans, 223n107
council (governed during absences of Charles VI), 6, 9, 16, 27–8, 93. *See also under* Charles VI; ordinances
Council of Constance, 86, 95, 208–9n55, 223n107. *See also* Great Schism of the West

Dante Alighieri: on allegorical writing and interpretation, 22–3, 39–41, 45, 194n11; *Commedia*, 45, 68–71, 78–9, 186n28, 220n70; connections to the work of Christine de Pizan, 68–71, 78–9, 81, 192n111, 194n11; *Convivio*, 39, 41, 70; *Letter to Cangrande*, 22, 39; *Vita Nuova*, 39
daughter: biological/historical, 5, 29, 94, 100, 126, 129, 136, 138, 141, 166, 189n67; duties of and obligations to, 96–104; France as, 181–2n29; Mary as, 62, 92; University of Paris as, 8–9, 16, 29–30, 33, 36, 86–9, 93–104, 124, 177, 190n82; virtues and vices as, 205–6n26
Demetrius of Phalerum, 12, 20
de Mézières, Philippe. *See* Philippe de Mézières
de Montreuil, Jean. *See* Jean de Montreuil
Denis Foulechat, 123
de Pizan, Christine. *See* Christine de Pizan
de Pizan, Thomas, 68
De regimine principum, 54, 120, 207n51
Deschamps, Eustache. *See* Eustache Deschamps
des Ursins, Jean Juvénal. *See* Jean Juvénal des Ursins
discernment of spirits, 154, 168, 171–2. *See also under* Jean Gerson
Domrémy, 167, 213n14
dream vision narratives, 3, 42; in Alain Chartier, 127, 142–5, 153; in Christine de Pizan, 63, 69, 71–2, 77, 82, 152; in Eustache Deschamps, 47, 63–7; in Jean Gerson, 40; in Jean Juvénal des Ursins, 128, 153–8, 173; in Philippe de Mézières, 48, 63, 89
DuGuesclin, Bertrand, 175

Ecclesia, 31–2, 43
Edward III (king of England), 5, 126, 129–30, 132, 135–40
Edward the Confessor, 158
Engelbert of Admont, 205n24
England: negotiations with, 17, 155–62; war with, 6, 53, 57, 105, 125–6, 142, 165, 206n39; in works of Jean de Montreuil, 128–30, 132–4, 139. *See also* Arras, peace of; Edward III; Hundred Years' War; Treaty of Troyes
envoi, 49–50, 52, 54, 57, 60, 64–5, 67
Eriugena, John Scot, 193nn120, 121
Ermengarde of Narbonne, 14
Ermine de Rheims, 171, 223n107
Eustache Deschamps: dream vision narratives, 63–7, 71; figure of France, 8, 72, 83, 85, 142; life of,

47–8, 75, 168; natural world as model for political realm, 50–1, 208n59; use of allegory, 15–16, 46–9, 55–68; use of metaphor, 15–16, 32, 43, 46–9, 51–5, 62–7, 87, 110

Eustache Deschamps, works of: *Art de dictier*, 47; Ballade **18**, 55; Ballade **68**, 55; Ballade **94**, 55; Ballade **112**, 57–8, 60; Ballade **141**, 61, 198n49; Ballade **159**, 61–2, 66–7, 198n49; Ballade **164**, 61–2, 66–7, 198n49; Ballade **170**, 55; Ballade 171, 55; Ballade **172**, 55; Ballade **193**, 49, 58–9; Ballade **231**, 50; Ballade **243**, 49, 53, 56; Ballade **252**, 53–4; Ballade **255**, 49, 67, 198n49; Ballade **263**, 198n50; Ballade **278**, 66; Ballade **324**, 49; Ballade **358**, 49, 51; Ballade **377**, 50–1; Ballade **385**, 59; Ballade **388**, 198n49; Ballade **398**, 52–4; Ballade **447**, 75; Ballade **834**, 49; Ballade **958**, 52; Ballade **978**, 49, 55–6; Ballade **1011**, 51; Ballade **1056**, 51–5; Ballade **1102**, 51; Ballade **1139**, 55; Ballade **1142**, 60–1; Ballade **1232**, 49; Ballade **1242**, 201n86; Ballade **1317**, 60; Ballade **1426**, 49, 198n50; Ballade **1430**, 67, 198nn49, 50; Ballade **1463**, 198n50; Chant royal **387**, 63–6, 198n49; Chant royal **388**, 63–6; Lay de plour, 198n50; *Miroir de mariage*, 47; Virelai **554**, 49

exegesis, 21–3, 40, 77, 188n47

figura, 24, 47n10, 77

fille du roy, University of Paris as, 3, 9–11, 16, 33, 36, 85–9, 94, 96–8, 100, 105–6, 123–4. *See also under* Jean Gerson

Fitzalan, John, Earl of Arundel, 156–7, 161

Flanders, 55, 93

fortune, allegorical figure of, 13

Franks, 45, 62, 182n36

Fulgentius, 186n18

Gadara, 59

Gerson, Jean. *See* Jean Gerson

Ghent, 55

Giles of Rome, 54, 120, 194n2, 197n37, 205n24, 207n51

grandes chroniques de France, Les, 7, 45, 181–2n29, 182n37

Great Schism of the West, 32, 40, 48, 86, 105, 210–11n96; and Jean Gerson, 87, 112; origins of, 48, 195n17; and visionary culture, 154; in works of Eustache Deschamps, 55–7. *See also* Council of Constance

Guillaume de Machaut, 75, 195n13, 223n105

Guyenne, 128, 131–2

Hector, 169–70

Henry IV (king of England), 135

Henry V (king of England): reign, 125, 127, 135, 142, 159, 173; and Treaty of Troyes, 6, 17, 126, 130, 141–2, 162–3, 165

Henry VI (king of England), 142, 224n115

Henry of Gorkum, 172

Homer, 21

Hugh of Saint Victor, 191n96, 193n120, 207n51; on allegory, 19, 20, 23, 26, 59, 188n47; on metaphor, 35

Hundred Years' War: during reign of Charles VI, 40, 133; and figural representations of France, 34, 53, 145; last phases of, 128, 171; origins and early phases, 4–5, 126, 130, 135, 206n39. *See also* Arras, peace of; Charles VI; civil war; Treaty of Troyes

intercessor, 27, 49, 60, 66, 73, 102, 106, 124. *See also* intermediary; mediation
intermediary, 108; allegory as, 24, 29, 60; queens as, 15, 27–9. *See also* intercessor; mediation
Isabeau de Bavière (*also* Isabeau of Bavaria, queen of France), 5–6, 11, 27–8, 68, 93–4, 97, 118, 229n2. *See also* queens
Isabelle of France (queen of England), 5, 126, 129, 136, 227n135
Isidore of Seville, 38, 225n124; on allegory, 20, 45; on metaphor, 34–5, 70

Jean I (king of France), 179n4
Jean II (king of France), 135
Jean de Berri, 5
Jean Bodin, 11
Jean Gerson: allegory of the *fille du roy*, 9, 16, 33, 36, 85–9, 93–106, 123–4, 177; discernment of spirits, 154–5, 171–2; and Joan of Arc, 168, 171–3, 224n116; life of, 86–7; quarrel of the *Roman de la Rose*, 40, 68; three realms, 43, 107–10, 112–13, 116, 122, 124, 201n97, 203n121, 219n66; use of metaphor, 7, 16, 32–3, 36, 85, 87–8, 93, 105–10, 112–20, 122–4
Jean Gerson, works of: *ABC des simples gens*, 96; *Accipietis virtutem*, 92, 110; *Adorabunt eum*, 88, 107–9, 112; *Ave Maria*, 206n34; *Beati qui lugent*, 91; *Brevis instructio ad senem quomodo se ad mortem preparet*, 205n15; *Claro eduditori*, 209n81; *Considérations sur saint Joseph*, 95; *Contre Charles de Savoisy*, 99–106, 111; *De distinctione verarum visionum a falsis*, 171; *De examinatione doctrinarum*, 171; *De probatione spirituum*, 171; *Diligite justiciam*, 111, 148, 204n3; *Ecce rex tuus*, 88; *École de la conscience*, 122; *École de la raison*, 122; *Erunt omnes docibilis*, 209n81; *Hoc sentite*, 96; *Jacob autem*, 95; *Josephina*, 95; *Judicium de vita sanctae Erminae*, 171; *Montaigne de la contemplation*, 96, 101; *Nimis honorati sunt*, 92; *Omne regnum*, 107, 112, 122; *Pax hominibus*, 110, 112, 117, 204n3; *Poenitemini*, 90; *Puer natus est*, 91; *Rex in sempiternum vive*, 105, 108–9, 112, 118–21; *Super facto puellae et credulitate sibi praestanda*, 171–2; *Tota pulchra es*, 206n35; *Traictie d'une vision faite contre le Romant de la rose par le chancelier de Paris*, 40; *Veniat pax*, 112; *Vivat rex*, 96–9, 101, 105, 108–9, 112–17, 119–21, 124, 206n44, 210n86
Jean Juvénal des Ursins, 153; dream vision narrative, 42, 67, 128, 153–7; and Joan of Arc, 168, 173–4, 178; life of, 141, 152–3; on the succession of 1316, 4, 129; use of

allegorical figures, 8, 36–7, 158–63, 166, 178
Jean Juvénal des Ursins, works of: *Audite celi*, 17, 128, 153–64, 166, 173–4, 178, 180n7; *Tres crestien, tres hault, tres puissant roy*, 180n7
Jean de Meun, 38–40, 68–9. See also *Roman de la Rose*
Jean de Montreuil, 181n23, 222n97; life of, 140–1, 168; natural world as model for the political realm, 140, 146, 166; and quarrel of the *Roman de la Rose*, 40, 68; and Salic Law, 17, 125–6, 129–30, 134, 136–8, 140, 165, 179n2
Jean de Montreuil, works of: *Regali ex progenie*, also called *À toute la chevalerie*, 130–2, 137–8, 225n150; *Traité contre les anglais* (in general), 130, 132; *Traité contre les anglais* (first redaction), 135, 139, 179n2, 214n13; *Traité contre les anglais* (third redaction), 131, 133, 135, 139, 159; *Résumé du traité contre les anglais*, 134
Jean Petit, 207n55
Jean sans peur (duke of Burgundy), 6, 93, 108; assassination of, 9, 87, 141, 184n61; rivalry with Louis d'Orléans, 6, 9, 73, 87, 97, 109, 164, 207n55. *See also* civil war
Jean de Terre Rouge (*also* Terrevermeille), 127, 148, 153
Jean de Touraine (dauphin of France), 141, 216n35
Jerusalem, 22, 55–6, 201n90
Joan of Arc, 17–18, 142, 149, 167–78, 223n107, 224n116
John of Salisbury, 32, 123, 211nn97, 103
Joseph (father of Jesus), 87, 95–6, 103, 211n109
Julius Caesar, 170
Jupiter, 38

language, 40, 139, 183n50; in administration and diplomacy, 159; choice of, 159, 221n80; divine, 25, 117; and figural interpretation, 20, 25–6, 35, 37–9; and identity, 159–60, 163, 166; native, 10, 159
Le Maistre, Jean, 168
Lescot, Richard, 212n4, 217n44. See also *Lex Salica*; Salic Law
Lex Salica, 125, 129, 136, 227n134. *See also* Salic Law
Louis IX (king of France, *also* Saint Louis), 5, 158, 180n10
Louis X (king of France), 4, 129
Louis d'Anjou (duke of Anjou), 5, 181n21, 204n7
Louis de Bourbon, 5, 97
Louis de Guyenne (dauphin of France), 141, 216n35
Louis d'Orléans (duke of Orléans), 195n12, 97; assassination of, 6, 9, 109, 141; and Charles VI, 5–6, 206n40; rivalry with dukes of Bourgogne, 9, 28, 73, 87, 93, 97, 164. *See also* civil war
Louis the Pious (king of France), 193n120
Lucifer, 59
Lyon, 87, 207–8n55

Macrobius, 63, 71–2, 184n2
Marguerite de Bourgogne (queen of France), 179n4
Marianne, 11

Marie d'Anjou (queen of France), 218n56
Marie de France, 32
Martin Le Franc, 10–11
Mary, 27, 31, 62–3, 91–2, 95; as Madonna of Mercy, 76
mediation: allegory, 11, 15, 24, 60; Isabeau de Bavière, 6, 28; women, 11, 15, 27, 46, 60, 73. *See also* intercessor; intermediary
Melun, 93
metaphor, 75, 90, 92; of the body politic, 6–7, 32–4, 43–9, 51–6, 59, 62–6, 72, 83, 110, 112–14, 117–18, 120–1, 123, 147, 176, 219n65; in connection to the University of Paris, 85, 87–8, 93–4, 106–7, 110, 123; as constitutive of poetry, 41, 70, 81–2, 84; relationship to allegory, 7–8, 15–16, 31–7, 43–9, 55–6, 58, 62–3, 65–6, 83, 123–4, 176–7. *See also* Eustache Deschamps: use of metaphor; Jean Gerson: use of metaphor; stomach and members, fable of
miroir du prince (*also* mirrors for princes), 50, 55, 116
Mortimer, Roger, 5n12, 214n18
mother/maternity, 206n36; biological, 5, 16, 27, 77, 90–1, 102–3, 201n87; country, 164; duties of and obligations to, 73–5, 84, 90–1, 93–4, 100–1; earth mother, 75, 145; *Ecclesia* as, 31; France as, 3, 7–8, 10, 14–18, 29–31, 36, 47, 67–8, 72–8, 83–5, 102, 127–8, 143–52, 163, 166, 177; king as, 76; Mary as, 91–2; *mater dolorosa*, 62; Paul as, 92; Spain as, 45; tongue, 164; University as, 17, 87, 97, 100–3, 124
nation, 10–11, 126–8, 130, 135, 140, 149–50, 159, 165, 167, 174, 178, 218n50
nature: allegorical figure of, 30, 46, 51, 64–6, 126, 132, 146, 148, 150–1, 184n, 220n75; divine, 113; monster in/of, 53, 116, 162–4; natural law, 17, 110, 120, 127, 140, 143, 147–50, 164; natural lordship, 53, 150–2, 163, 166; natural love, 17, 47, 73–4, 91, 99–100, 143, 147, 149–52, 164, 177; natural rights, 119, 164; natural world, 17, 19, 23, 33, 46, 50–1, 53, 113, 127, 145–50, 152, 162–6, 184n59, 208n59. *See also under* metaphor
Nebuchadnezzar: statue of, 118; visions of, 71, 77
Nicholas of Lyra, 22
Nicole Oresme. *See* Oresme, Nicole
Ninevah, 59
nine worthies, 61, 198n51
Normandy, 128, 134, 161, 224n114

Ockham, William of, 205n24
ordinances, 4, 6; Cabochien, 108; concerning council of Charles VI, 6, 28; concerning royal succession, 4, 28, 93, 127, 129–30, 136–7, 148, 164, 180n14, 219n63. *See also* succession, royal
Oresme, Nicole: on natural love, 228n142; *Traictie sur les monnoies*, 116; translation/adaptation of Aristotle's *Ethics*, 76; translation/adaptation of Aristotle's *Politics*, 54, 94, 146, 159, 196n28, 216n39, 221n80; on tyranny, 116; use of metaphor, 194n2
Origen, 22–5, 32, 38, 197n36
Orléans, 167–70, 173, 195n12

Paris, 5, 93, 167–8, 215n27, 218n48, 229n11; Burgundian takeover of, 87, 140–2, 151, 153, 173; in Eustache Deschamps, 49, 55, 58–60, 66; popular revolts, 75, 108; as successor to Greece and Rome, 46, 111–12, 182n38, 200–1n82. *See also* civil war; *translatio studii et imperii*
Parlement, 11, 99, 100, 102–5, 135, 211n112
Paul (the apostle), 23, 42, 114, 118, 210n88; as mother, 92, 103; visions of, 64, 71
Pepin the Short (king of France), 136
Petrarch, 45
Philippe III (king of France), 179n5, 89
Philippe IV (king of France), 4–5, 9, 129, 136
Philippe V (king of France), 4–5, 214n16
Philippe VI (king of France, *also* Philippe de Valois), 5, 129–30, 132, 134–5, 140, 161–2. *See also under* succession, royal
Philippe-Auguste (king of France), 86, 179n5
Philippe le bon (*also* Philip the Good, duke of Burgundy), 128, 158–60, 162, 165. *See also* Arras, peace of
Philippe de Bourgogne (duke of Burgundy), 5–6, 28, 93, 207n55, 229–30n6
Philippe de Mézières, 48, 63, 196n24; auto-exegesis, 40–1; natural law/lordship, 148, 222n98; on University as *fille du roy*, 9, 89. See also *Songe du vieil pelerin*
Philippe d'Orléans, 195n12
Philippe de Poitiers, 180n9
philosophy, allegorical figure of, 13, 30, 69, 76, 81–2, 153
Pierre d'Ailly, 86
Plutarch, 32, 118, 211n97
Poissy, Abbey of, 169
Poitiers, 153, 167, 170–1, 174, 233n49
Policraticus. *See* John of Salisbury
Primat, 45–6
princes of the blood, 197n28; and council of Charles VI, 28, 177; discord among, 7; as figurative children of France, 8, 67, 73, 75, 102; as privileged group, 9
Prodicus, 21
prosopopeia, 20, 67, 198n47
Prudentius, 20, 30, 38, 40. *See also* Psychomachia
Pseudo-Dionysius, 25, 42, 59, 107, 111
Psychomachia, The, 20, 30, 37–8; as textual model, 64, 233n46

queens: biological/historical, 14, 27–9, 128, 135, 138, 140, 166, 198n47; *Ecclesia* as, 31; France as, 3, 29; Spain as, 45
Quintilian, 35

Raban Maur, 20
Raoul Tainguy, 48
Raymond de Sabanac, 154
reason, allegorical figure of, 38–9, 64, 66, 78, 122
regent/regency, 4–5, 17, 28, 94, 127, 129, 141
Religieux de Saint Denis, 9
Rheims, 55, 86, 142, 167–70, 173
Rhetorica ad Herennium, 185n11
Richard II (king of England), 222n98, 227n137

Roland, 61
Roman de la Rose, Le: as dream vision narrative, 63, 220n71; quarrel of, 40, 68–9, 204n5, 213n5, 217n47; use of allegory, 30, 37–40, 55, 204n5, 220n71
Rome, 46, 73, 111–12, 182n38
Ronsard, Pierre de, 11
Rouen, 168

Saint Denis: Abbey of, 108, 137, 193n120; person, 158, 193n120
Saint Victor, Hugh of. *See* Hugh of Saint Victor
Salic Law, 4–5, 10, 17, 125–6, 128–30, 134–8, 140, 164–5, 178, 206n41, 227n134. *See also* Jean de Montreuil; *Lex Salica*; succession, royal
Saturn, 38
Senlis, 195n12
Songe du vieil pelerin, Le, 9, 40, 48, 63, 89, 148, 193n116. *See also* Philippe de Mézières
stomach and members, fable of, 7, 32, 53. *See also under* metaphor
subtraction of obediance, 86, 180n18. *See also* Great Schism of the West
succession, royal, 9, 36, 113, 118, 124, 126, 140–1, 148, 163–6; efforts to regulate, 93; exclusion of women from, 4, 5, 126, 129–30; fantasy of continuity, 8; of 1316, 4, 126, 129–30; of 1328 (i.e., Valois), 5, 126, 129–30, 134–6, 162, 212n1. *See also* ordinances; Salic Law; Treaty of Troyes: provisions of
supplement, 8, 16, 36, 56, 76, 84; allegory as, 7, 14, 20, 26, 30, 177, 187n40
Synagoga, 31

Thales, 80
Thomas Aquinas. *See* Aquinas, Thomas
Thomas of Canterbury, 158
Titus Livius, 32
Trajan (emperor), 32, 211n97
translatio studii et imperii, 46, 87, 111–12, 118, 182n38, 201n82
Troy (Trojan origins), 45, 149, 182n36
Troyes, Treaty of: provisions of, 6, 126, 141, 159–60, 162, 224n117, 229n2; responses to, 17, 126–7, 142, 148, 150–1, 155, 161–6. *See also* succession, royal
tyrant/tyranny, 6, 103, 116–17, 120–1, 123, 139, 151

Urban VI (pope), 195n17

Vaucouleurs, 167, 169
Vertus, 47
Virgil, 71, 78, 186n18

wisdom (*and* Sapience), allegorical figure of, 13, 201n84

Yolande of Aragon, 142

www.ingramcontent.com/pod-product-compliance
Lightning Source LLC
LaVergne TN
LVHW090154080826
844660LV00013B/802/J

* 9 7 8 1 4 4 2 6 4 1 8 7 7 *